VISUAL CORTEX: NEW RESEARCH

VISUAL CORTEX: NEW RESEARCH

THOMAS A. PORTOCELLO

AND

RUDOLPH B. VELLOTI

EDITORS

Nova Science Publishers, Inc.
New York

Library of Congress Cataloging-in-Publication Data

Visual cortex : new research / Thomas A. Portocello and Rudolph B. Velloti (editors).
    p. ; cm.
  Includes bibliographical references and index.
  ISBN 978-1-60456-530-0 (hardcover)
  1. Visual cortex. I. Portocello, Thomas A. II. Velloti, Rudolph B.
  [DNLM: 1. Visual Cortex--physiology. 2. Visual Perception--physiology. WL 307 V8342 2008]
  QP383.15.V57   2008
  612.8'255--dc22   2008010234

Published by Nova Science Publishers, Inc. ✤ *New York*

CONTENTS

0213375798

PREFACE

All visual information that the human mind receives is processed by a part of the brain known as visual cortex. The visual cortex is part of the outermost layer of the brain, the cortex, and is located at the dorsal pole of the occipital lobe; more simply put, at the lower rear of the brain. The visual cortex obtains its information via projections that extend all the way through the brain from the eyeballs. The projections first pass through a stopover point in the middle of the brain, an almondlike lump known as the Lateral Geniculate Nucleus, or LGN. From there they are projected to the visual cortex for processing. Visual cortex is broken down into five areas, labelled V1, V2, V3, V4, and MT, which on occasion is referred to as V5. V1, sometimes called striate cortex because of its stripey appearance when dyed and put under a microscope, is by far the largest and most important. It is sometimes called primary visual cortex or area 17. The other visual areas are referred to as extrastriate cortex. V1 is one of the most extensively studied and understood areas of the human brain. Neurons in the visual cortex fire action potentials when visual stimuli appear within their receptive field. By definition, the receptive field is the region within the entire visual field which elicits an action potential. But for any given neuron, it may respond to a subset of stimuli within its receptive field. This property is called tuning. In the earlier visual areas, neurons have simpler tuning. For example, a neuron in V1 may fire to any vertical stimulus in its receptive field. In the higher visual areas, neurons have complex tuning. For example, in the inferior temporal cortex (IT), a neuron may only fire when a certain face appears in its receptive field. The visual cortex receives its blood supply primarily from the calcarine branch of the posterior cerebral artery. This new book presents the latest research in the field from around the globe.

Chapter 1 – This work presents and discusses a series of related mathematical models of the primary visual cortex (V1). The aim is to describe several steps of visual processing in V1, within a unified theoretical framework. The proposed models analyse specific phenomena, both physiological and perceptive, and use different levels of detail in the physiological description, according to the particular cognitive purpose and respecting the modular organization of the visual system. The work starts from the study of visual information processing at a single point of the retina, hypercolumn, (section 2, 3 and 4) and then evolves toward the study of intracortical connectivity in order to process the image in an entire portion of the visual space (section 5, 6, 7 and 8). All models respect the physiological fundamental properties characterizing V1, still providing a good compromise between mathematical/computational simplicity and physiological reliability.

Chapter 2 – This chapter addresses the ventral visual processing stream beyond V1. This part of the visual system is known to be essential for recognition, the most important visual task for humans. In recent years, important progress has been made in regards to two particular areas of the ventral path, namely V2 and LOC (Lateral Occipital Complex), that will be addressed in detail here. There are several reasons for this choice. In the hierarchy of the occipital visual cortex, V2 is the second area and is similar in size to that of V1, and therefore holds a weight in the economy of the visual process that is comparable to V1. The network of areas grouped under the name LOC is human-specific, and is held to be the first area specifically involved in object recognition. While standard neurological research and neuroimaging, in particular, have been essential in advancing the knowledge of the ventral visual system, a thorough understanding of the mechanisms underlying visual object recognition requires assessing the computational functions performed by the cortical maps. In this effort, computational models are extremely helpful and a section of this chapter deals with the achievements obtained in modeling, in the interpretation of the functional role of V2, and in the simulation of object recognition with cortical maps in the ventral stream up to LOC.

Chapter 3 – In the following sections the authors provide brief reviews of the types of structural regularities observed in natural scene imagery with respect to luminance contrast. The authors then consider how such structural regularities have been related to human visual processing of natural scene imagery and how some of the theories drawn by multiple laboratories about those relationships do not hold when tested empirically. They will then present their findings over the past 5 years in support of the horizontal effect perceptual anisotropy obtained when viewing naturalistic images and the variations of this effect as a function of different physical properties of the naturalistic stimuli (e.g., spatial frequency distribution, structural sparseness, spatial frequency and orientation bandwidths). Finally, the authors present a contrast normalization model that can account for the behavioral data as well as the result of recent experiments that directly test this model.

Chapter 4 – A fundamental characteristic of the human visual cortex is its retinotopic organization. Taking advantage of the systematic association between cortical position and visual field position, many important aspects of visual processing have been revealed by functional brain imaging. The authors have investigated, visualized, and characterized retinotopic organization using fMRI, in conjunction with several novel methods of analysis. In this chapter, they describe the methodology used and present findings on the basic functional organization of the visual cortex from two interlocking large- and small-scale perspectives. By larger-scale analyses of retinotopic organization, they have been able to delineate hierarchically organized visual areas (V1, V2, V3, V3A, V3B, V4v, V8, LOc, and MT+) for ten hemispheres and investigated their individual variability in size and location using a probabilistic approach, in which probability maps of the visual areas were created. With smaller-scale analyses of retinotopy, the authors obtained two basic factors of visual field representation within each area (cortical magnification factor and average receptive field size), and with these factors estimated the cortical point spread of fMRI activity. They found that point spread is nearly constant across eccentricities and increases as one ascends the visual cortical hierarchy. Knowledge of retinotopic organization is important not only in itself; it also provides essential information for analysis and interpretation of functional activity in visual cortex. As representative examples, they present their recent findings on visual functions involving contextual effects. The present findings on the large- and small-scale functional organization of the human visual cortex shed new light on the relationship between functional segregation and cortical processing hierarchy in the visual system.

Chapter 5 – The inferotemporal cortex (IT) is a visual integration area. Here, the information arriving from lower visual areas is combined in such a way that the resulting cell activity encodes complex features of the visual stimuli. Furthermore, the output originating in the IT cortex activates many of the cortical and subcortical structures involved in higher brain functions, such as recognition, remembering or emotional and visuomotor associations. For these reasons, the IT cortex has been an appealing area for many investigators during the last decades, who have devoted much of their work to this structure by using a large variety of techniques and approaches. In this review, the authors attempt to summarize the main findings obtained from these studies, outlining the functional characterization of IT neurons. Each section has been illustrated with data obtained in their laboratory after recording the activity of IT cells in behaving monkeys, trained to perform a visual discrimination task.

Chapter 6 – The activation of the human primary visual cortex (V1) is often utilized as a gold standard to test the performances of newly developed methodologies for in vivo functional studies. Recent progresses in magnet technology, gradient system performance, RF coil and pulse sequence design have allowed the implementation of magnetic resonance spectroscopy (MRS) and imaging (MRI) in humans at magnetic fields up to 7T, which resulted in increased sensitivity, reliability and specificity of functional measurements compared to lower fields. Here the authors revise MRS applications which investigated brain metabolism during visual activation. The majority of these studies have used 1H MRS, and few of them implemented 13C and 31P MRS. The experimental findings obtained by these methodologies have provided new insights into the metabolic events occurring during increased neuronal activity, and the interpretation of some of these findings have generated intense scientific debates.

Chapter 7 – As your eyes move across this page, the image on your retina shifts from right to left with each eye movement. Yet you do not perceive the world to be moving, despite the evidence presented to your visual system. It appears that our visual systems are equipped with a mechanism for discounting the portion of the sensory input that is due to our own movements.

Such a mechanism is often called a corollary discharge, because it involves neural pathways that duplicate the commands sent to motor structures. These duplicate pathways lead to sensory areas, which combine the sensory input with the impending motor movement to maintain perceptual stability. Thus the neural commands that activate your eye muscles while you are reading also reach your visual system, which effectively ignores the resulting retinal motion.

This chapter will discuss the anatomical, neurophysiological, and behavioral evidence for corollary discharge signals in the primate visual cortex. In particular, I will focus on oculomotor corollary discharge signals that are thought to reach visual areas responsible for measuring visual motion. There is some controversy as to which cortical areas receive a corollary discharge input, what the corollary discharge conveys, and how it influences individual neuronal responses. I will review the existing literature on these subjects, and suggest future research directions that may shed light on the interaction between corollary discharges and sensory processing.

Chapter 8 – There are many publications dedicated to the studies of the visual cortex and mechanisms of visual information processing. However, it is known that responses of brain visual system sites to adequate stimuli are very different in their properties (including differences in their frequency ranges). It is a matter of fact that some brain electrophysiological phenomena are omitted and sometimes neglected. This happened with infraslow brain potentials (frequencies below 0.5 Hz; periods ranging from several seconds to dozens of minutes). Albeit recently accumulating evidence demonstrated the presence of infraslow activity in the visual cortex, the functional significance and dynamics of this activity remained obscure. The present work is aimed at providing with sufficient evidence their hypothesis that infraslow potentials in the primary visual cortex (V1) are specifically related to some mechanisms of sensory information processing. The experimental subjects were adult rats with chronic stereotaxic electrodes implanted in the V1, lateral geniculate nucleus (LGN), locus coeruleus (LC) and dorsal raphe nucleus (DRN). The recordings of infraslow potentials were performed in these structures during visual stimuli presentation (e.g. darkness, constant illumination and rhythmic flash photostimulation), before and after electrical stimulation of aforementioned subcortical sites of the brain. As a result, specific and significantly different patterns of infraslow potentials appeared in V1 in response to each type of delivered visual stimuli, mainly in the domain of seconds (0.1-0.25 Hz). There were also identified significant spectral changes in the domain of seconds in V1 infraslow activity after LGN electrical stimulation (these alterations were manifested as significant increases in power in the range of 0.1-0.5 Hz). Some responses were detected in V1 multisecond activity (pre- vs. post-stimulus recordings). Finally, it was documented that electrical stimulation of the LC and DRN did not alter significantly V1 activity in the domain of seconds but affected multisecond fluctuation patterns in this structure. The obtained results support the conclusion that different ranges of infraslow activity in the V1 are correlated with different functional mechanisms within this structure: activity in the domain of seconds is related to specific visual information processing, whereas multisecond activity in the V1 is mainly attributed to global transitions and fluctuations of cortical neuronal excitability that are governed both by inputs from visual thalamus and projections from brainstem nuclei (like LC and DRN).

Chapter 9 – Visual cortex exists columns detecting orientations, and can extract the contour of the interesting object by binding orientations detected by orientation columns. The authors proposed a novel orientation and interesting-contour extraction model using Unit-linking Pulse Coupled Neural Network (PCNN). Unit-linking PCNN is the simplified PCNN, which is a kind of spatio-temporal-coding Spiking Neural Network (SNN), and exhibits the phenomena of synchronous pulse bursts in the cat or monkey visual cortex. The orientation and interesting-contour extraction model using Unit-linking PCNN is composed of two layers (the orientation detection layer and the interesting-contour extraction layer). This model mimics orientation detection of the biological visual cortex, and can extract the contour of the interesting object with TOP-DOWN mechanism. The contour of the interesting object periodically oscillates in this model. The authors use periodical oscillation to extract the contour of the interesting object in this model because synchronous oscillation is the important phenomena in the biological visual cortex. In the interesting-contour extraction layer, when introducing TOP-DOWN mechanism, the chain code of the interesting object contour is used to express the prior knowledge. The input of the orientation detection layer is the edge detection result of the input image by using Unit-linking PCNN edge detection algorithm they proposed. The output of the orientation detection layer is the orientation detection result, which inputs to the interesting-contour extraction layer. In the meantime, the chain code of the interesting-contour inputs to the interesting-contour extraction layer as the prior knowledge. The contour of the interesting object periodically oscillates in the interesting-contour extraction layer. Section 1 is the introduction. In Section 2, Unit-linking PCNN is described. In Section 3 and 4, the orientation detection layer and the interesting-contour extraction layer based on Unit-linking PCNN are introduced respectively, followed by the conclusion in the last Section.

Chapter 10 – Age-related macular degeneration (AMD) and Retinitis Pigmentosa (RP) are degenerative diseases that affect the retina and result in a progressive deterioration of vision leading eventually to photoreceptor death and blindness. There are currently a number of therapeutic approaches attempting to rescue vision by trying to stop or replace the loss of photoreceptors. Does the visual system reorganize as a result of loss of visual input? How does this affect the processing of visual information? The success of those therapies will eventually depend on the ability of the neural pathways to transmit and process the signals generated by the photoreceptors.

Chapter 11 – The neural processes that give rise to visual awareness are currently the subject of much debate. One brain region in particular, the primary visual cortex (also known as striate cortex or V1), has been implicated in the neural interactions that give rise to conscious perception. This region, located in and around the calcarine fissure in the occipital lobe, was long regarded merely as a relay station for visual cortical input, with visual awareness believed to arise from the activity of highly specialized visual areas in the parietal and temporal lobes. The perceptual consequences of V1 lesions, however, reveal the indispensable role of this area in conscious perception, and this view is supported by recent neurodisruption and neuroimaging studies carried out in neurologically normal observers. Here the authors review findings from neuropsychology, cognitive neuroscience, and electrophysiology, and discuss what they reveal about the role of V1 in visual awareness.

In: Visual Cortex: New Research
Editors: T. A. Portocello and R. B. Velloti

ISBN 978-1-60456-530-0
© 2008 Nova Science Publishers, Inc.

Chapter 1

MATHEMATICAL MODELING AND COMPUTER SIMULATIONS OF THE VISION EARLY PROCESSING STAGES: A THEORETICAL FRAMEWORK

Giuseppe-Emiliano La Cara and Mauro Ursino

D.E.I.S, Department of Electronic Computer Science and Systems,
University of Bologna, Bologna/Cesena

1. Introduction

This work presents and discusses a series of related mathematical models of the primary visual cortex (V1). The aim is to describe several steps of visual processing in V1, within a unified theoretical framework. The proposed models analyse specific phenomena, both physiological and perceptive, and use different levels of detail in the physiological description, according to the particular cognitive purpose and respecting the modular organization of the visual system. The work starts from the study of visual information processing at a single point of the retina, hypercolumn, (section 2, 3 and 4) and then evolves toward the study of intracortical connectivity in order to process the image in an entire portion of the visual space (section 5, 6, 7 and 8). All models respect the physiological fundamental properties characterizing V1, still providing a good compromise between mathematical/computational simplicity and physiological reliability.

First, a model of orientation selectivity, representing a single hypercolumn is presented to understand the characteristic of simple cells responding preferentially to elongated visual stimuli of a particular orientation. The model is then used to investigate the phenomenon of "Tilt Aftereffect" (TAE): prolonged viewing of an oriented stimulus (adaptation) makes a subsequently viewed stimulus of similar orientation to appear tilted away from the adapting stimulus. Subsequently, the model is temporally characterized in order to explain the direction and velocity selectivity in simple cells, i.e., their preference to respond to stimuli moving to a particular direction with a given velocity.

The next step is to extend the model to scrutinize a region of the visual space by handling more hypercolumns and introducing an original model of cortical circuitry. Synapses among hypercolumns are then included in the model to critically approach the genesis of complex cells as well as to assess the role of intracortical synapses in the discrimination between simple and complex cells.

In the last step, the proposed architecture is further improved assuming synaptic fields, on the basis of some Gestalt perceptual criteria (contiguity and continuity) to investigate the role of the primary visual cortex in contour extraction and perceptual grouping. The model is finally related with activity from higher visual centres, including two fundamental additional aspects, i.e., multi-scale decomposition and attention. Attention from higher hierarchical levels selects the portion of the image to be scrutinized and sets the appropriate scale. This allows an image to be scrutinized at different levels of detail.

2. Orientation Selectivity

2.1. Introduction

Simple cells in the primary visual cortex respond selectively to visual stimuli with particular spatial and temporal characteristics, such as elongated bars or gratings with a specific orientation, velocity and direction of motion (Hubel and Wiesel, 1962;Vidyasagar et al., 1996;Ferster and Miller, 2000;DeAngelis et al., 1993;Reid et al., 1991;Orban et al., 1981b;Orban et al., 1981a;Wörgötter and Eysel, 1991;Wörgötter et al., 1991). The cortical mechanisms at the basis of this property, named selectivity (orientation, direction and velocity selectivity) are still a subject of debate, however both afferents from the lateral geniculate nucleus (LGN) and intracortical connections are thought to participate to this process.

The original hypothesis of Hubel and Wiesel (1962) at the origin of orientation preference assumes that orientation selectivity originates at the particular geometrical organization of the thalamic input to a simple cell, according to a feedforward mechanism. Although a feedforward mechanism receives much consensus in the literature, it alone cannot account for some properties of simple cortical cells.

In the same way, several hypotheses about the direction and velocity selectivity have been proposed, based on alternative and different combinations of mechanisms. In general direction-selective cells are thought to be originated by input signals which are in the spatio-temporal quadrature. In particular, a well-known hypothesis is that direction selectivity in a cat arises from temporal diversity in the response of the LGN. This temporal diversity may be related with the existence of lagged and non-lagged cells (Mastronarde, 1987a;Mastronarde, 1987b; Saul and Humphrey, 1990) which converge in a resulting space-time inseparable receptive field (RF) which may be the basis of direction selectivity (Saul and Humphrey, 1990; Saul and Humphrey, 1992).

The mechanisms which cause orientation selectivity are particularly debated among neurophysiologists and they are centralized in the finding that orientation selectivity is largely independent of the contrast of the visual stimulus. This phenomenon cannot be simply explained on the basis of the excitatory input from LGN only (Sclar and Freeman, 1982; Skottun et al., 1987;Ferster and Miller, 2000). Moreover, the orientation bias of the thalamic input is insufficient to explain the strong orientation tuning exhibited by most simple cells. For these reasons, a classic feedforward mechanism must be integrated with additional mechanisms, in order to achieve contrast invariance and provide the sharp tuning experimentally observed.

These additional mechanisms likely involve the presence of lateral connections among cortical neurons, both excitatory and inhibitory. Although well documented in literature, the arrangement of this intracortical circuitry is still a subject of controversial debate, especially about the disposition of intracortical inhibition (Chung and Ferster, 1998;Ferster and Miller, 2000;Ferster et al., 1996;Ringach et al., 1997).

Several mathematical models have been presented in recent years using different combinations of feedforward (thalamic) and feedback (intracortical) inputs (Wörgötter and Koch, 1991;Somers et al., 1995;Carandini and Ringach, 1997;Troyer et al., 1998;McLaughlin et al., 2000;Ben-Yishai et al., 1995;La Cara and Ursino, 2007;La Cara et al., 2004;Ursino and La Cara, 2004b;Ursino et al., 2007). These models conflict not only to the different importance given to the thalamic input vs. intracortical feedback, but also to the different arrangement used for excitatory and inhibitory cortical connections. Furthermore, among these models, the more detailed ones exhibit some disadvantages, beside their great scientific value: they are complex, computationally onerous, and the analysis of the results is often not intuitive and a clear understanding of the role of intracortical connections is precluded.

Hence, the use of simpler models has also been proposed to describe the main properties of simple cells using just a few mathematical equations. The computer implementation of these models is straightforward, and their results can be easily analyzed. However, they neglect important anatomical and physiological aspects, leading perhaps to oversimplified results.

This scenario suggests that models with an intermediate level of complexity may also be helpful in neurophysiological research: they should maintain the most important anatomical and physiological details of the orientation selectivity process while, at the same time, they should be smoothly simulated on a computer.

Accordingly, the present work was designed with the following main objectives:

(i)   to present mathematical equations for orientation selectivity (as well as for direction and velocity selectivity [section 4] and for the simulation of Tilt Aftereffect [section 3]), of simple cells in the visual cortex which overcome the gap between detailed models and maximally reduced models.

(ii) to demonstrate that the proposed equations can reproduce several different experimental data concerning the response of simple cells in V1 (including orientation selectivity, direction selectivity, velocity selectivity, spatial frequency tuning, temporal frequency tuning, contrast invariance and Tilt Aftereffect).

In the following section a detailed description of the model is provided, both spatially and temporally. First, we focus the study on the orientation selectivity, hence the steady state condition are investigated in depth (i.e., after the end of the transient period, $t \rightarrow \infty$).

2.2. Model Description

In the present model the output of neurons is represented as a continuous quantity describing the firing rate expressed in Spikes/s. The model architecture concerns of a single hypercolumn in order to approach the study of visual information processing at a single point of the retina.

The model consists in N_E excitatory neurons and N_I inhibitory interneurons. The neurons are parameterized by their preferred orientation, identified by the angle ϑ. In general the angle ϑ determines both the preferred orientation and the preferred direction for each neuron: two neurons with preferred orientation that differ by 180° are selective to the same orientation but have opposite preferred directions. In first instance the dynamic response of thalamic cells has been neglected, since in a first set of simulations we use static inputs to the retina (i.e., steady state gratings which do not drift with time), and the dynamic in the model is provided only by recurrent intracortical connections.

A more complete model, including the temporal response of thalamic cells, shall be described in the section 4. For these reasons, in the analysis presented in the present section the orientation angle is restricted to the range 90° - 270° (180° representing the horizontal orientation, 90° and 270° the vertical one).

We assume that orientation selectivity varies gradually and regularly form one neuron to the next in the hypercolumn, in particular excitatory neurons differ in their orientation selectivity by just 1° (N_E=180), while inhibitory neurons differ by 4° (N_I=45). The ratio $N_E/N_I = 4$ agrees with the physiological literature (Troyer et al., 1998;Somers et al., 1995;Gabbott and Somogyi, 1986;McLaughlin et al., 2000).

2.2.1. The Response of Geniculate Cells

First the model describes the response of thalamic cells. The input to the thalamic cells is the intensity of light at the position (i,j) of the retina at the time t ($l(i,j,t)$). Since the cones in the retina are sensitive to local light intensity variations with respect to the average luminance (l_0), we consider a normalized luminance ($R(i,j,t)$) as follows:

$$R(i, j,t) = \frac{l(i, j,t) - l_0}{l_0} \tag{1}$$

Although in this section we do not explicitly provide a temporal characterization for the receptive field of the thalamic cells, we introduce a temporal variable in order to guarantee a continuity in the model description with sections that follow. We chose this approach in order to provide a clearer investigation for each aspect of the model, both in static condition (the present section and section 3) and in dynamic condition (section 4).

We assume that thalamic cells have a separable spatio-temporal RF, that is it can be described as the product of a spatial term and a temporal term, i.e.

$$RF_{xy}(i, j,t) = \varphi_{xy}(i, j) \cdot F_{xy}(t) \tag{2}$$

where $RF_{xy}(i,j,t)$ represents the spatio-temporal receptive field of a thalamic cell centred at position x,y of the retina, $\varphi_{xy}(i, j)$ is its spatial component, and $F_{xy}(t)$ is its temporal component. Since in the present section we only consider static visual stimuli, we have $RF_{xy}(i,j,t)=\varphi_{xy}(i,j)$.

For the sake of simplicity, the model does not consider the response of ON and OFF ganglion cells in the retina, but directly provides a description of activity in LGN cells as a function of $R(i,j,t)$. We assume that thalamic cells have a ON centre or an OFF centre spatial RF, described as the difference of two Gaussian functions having the same space constant in both directions (Linsenmeier et al., 1982;Cheng et al., 1995). Hence, the following function has been used to mimic the spatial RF of a thalamic cell:

$$\varphi_{x,y}(i,j) = A_1 e^{-\left[\left[(i-x)^2 + (j-y^2)\right]/r_1^2\right]} - A_2 e^{-\left[\left[(i-x)^2 + (j-y^2)\right]/r_2^2\right]} \tag{3}$$

where x and y are the coordinates for the centre of the thalamic cell, r_1 and r_2 are the radii of the central and surround regions, and A_1 and A_2 are parameters which set the strength of the response in the centre and surround, respectively. The values of parameters A_1, A_2, r_1 and r_2 in Eq. 3 have been given in order to reproduce the spatial RF of retinal ganglion cells and geniculate cells as measured by (So and Shapley, 1981;Linsenmeier et al., 1982;Cheng et al., 1995) in cats at an eccentricity of about $10°$ (see Figure 1, panel a).

The input to a single LGN cell is computed as the dot product of the normalized luminance $R(i,j,t)$ (Eq. 1) and the receptive field $\varphi_{xy}(i,j)$ (Eq. 3). The spatial response for a thalamic cell can be expressed as follows:

$$g_t(x,y,t) = \iint_{i,j} \varphi_{xy}(i,j) \cdot R(i,j,t) di\, dj \cong \sum_i \sum_j \varphi_{xy}(i,j) \cdot R(i,j,t)\Delta i \Delta j \tag{4}$$

where $g_t(x,y,t)$ represents the input to a LGN cell centred at the position x,y. It is worth noting that this input is excitatory when directed to the ON-centre cells, and inhibitory when directed to the OFF-centre cells (see Eq. 5 below). The last member in Eq. 4 means that, during model numerical implementation, the integral has been approximated by a sum. The steps for Δi and Δj used in all simulations are $0.01°$.

Finally, the output of LGN cells is computed, starting from the input, by considering two non-linear effects: i) the output cannot decrease below zero, and ii) it exhibits progressive saturation if contrast approaches 30-35%.

Accordingly, the following sigmoidal expression has been used to describe the thalamic output as a function of g_t:

$$T(x,y,t) = \left[\frac{B_1}{1 + e^{\pm g_t(x,y,t)/k_t}} + B_2\right]^+ \tag{5}$$

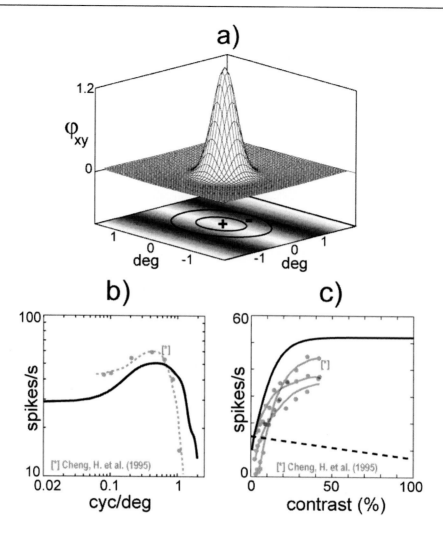

Figure 1. Receptive field and response of the thalamic cells in the lateral geniculate nucleus, at 10° eccentricity, according to the present model. *Panel a)* - Receptive field in the space (equal to the difference of two concentric Gaussian functions) and the visual stimuli, i.e., sine grating with maximal light intensity at the centre of the receptive field (projected in 2D across the visual stimuli). *Panel b)* - Response of an ON-centre cell vs. spatial frequency, simulated using an input grating as in panel a with contrast 0.32. *Panel c)* - Responses of an ON-centre (and an OFF-centre cell, dashed line) to an input grating as in panel a, with spatial frequency 0.7 cyc/deg, at different values of contrast. A comparison with experimental data (gray lines, (Cheng et al., 1995)) is provided.

where the symbol $[\ ]^{+}$ denotes the positive part (i.e., $[y]^{+} = y$ if $y > 0$, otherwise $[y]^{+} = 0$), B_1, B_2 and k_t are constant parameters, to be assigned on the basis of experimental data, and the sign $\pm$ in the exponential function discerns between ON-centre (sign -) and OFF-centre (sign +) cells. In particular, parameter k_t is inversely related to the slope of the curve at low input values (hence, decreasing k_t causes more rapid saturation), while parameters B_1 and B_2 in Eq. 5 are associated with the basal activity of the cell (that is the activity with zero input, say T_0) and with the saturation level (say T_{sat}) through the following relationships: $B_1 + B_2 = T_{sat}$ and

$B_1/2 + B_2 = T_0$. By separately rearranging Eq. 4 for the ON and OFF-centre cells, taking the previous relationships into account, we can write:

$$T_{on}(x,y,t) = \left[\frac{T_{on,sat} + \left(2T_{on,0} - T_{on,sat}\right)e^{-g_t(x,y,t)/k_t}}{1 + e^{-g_t(x,y,t)/k_t}} \right] \tag{6}$$

$$T_{off}(x,y,t) = \left[\frac{T_{off,sat} + \left(2T_{off,0} - T_{off,sat}\right)e^{g_t(x,y,t)/k_t}}{1 + e^{g_t(x,y,t)/k_t}} \right] \tag{7}$$

The values of thalamic outputs in basal condition (i.e., $T_{on,0}$ and $T_{off,0}$) have been given according to (Troyer et al., 1998). Saturation levels ($T_{on,sat}$ and $T_{off,sat}$) and the parameter k_t have been given to simulate the contrast response function of geniculate cells measured by (Cheng et al., 1995) using sinusoidal grating with spatial frequency 0.7 cyc/deg. All parameter values can be found in Table 1.

Table 1. Parameters of the model (Hypercolumn) used in Sections 2, 3 and 4

A_1	10^4		mV/deg^2
A_2	$1/17 \cdot A_1$		mV/deg^2
r_1	0.3		deg
r_2	$4 \cdot r_1$		deg
$T_{on,0}$	10		spikes/s
$T_{off,0}$	15		spikes/s
$T_{on,sat}$	52		spikes/s
$T_{off,sat}$	52		spikes/s
k_t	20kk	208.9	mV
W_{ct0}	0.02		mV/(spikes/s)
Δx	0.5		deg
Δy	0.35		deg
σ_x^2	0.49		deg^2
σ_y^2	0.25		deg^2
f	0.8		cyc/deg
k_c	5		spikes/(s·mV)

Table 1. (Continued)

υ	0.2	mV
τ	2.5	ms
υ_1	0.2	mV
W_{ex0}	0.018	mV/(spikes/s)
W_{in0}	0.005	mV/(spikes/s)
σ_{ex}	200	
σ_{in}	0.4472	
K_1	1.26	
c_{01}	0.19	
t_{01}	8.22	
n_1	-8.52	
K_2	0.46	
c_{02}	0.031	
t_{02}	1.94	
n_2	7.37	

The simulated responses of the geniculate cells (case of an ON-centre cell) are presented in Figure 1. The panel b shows the response of a cell to a sinusoidal grating, with maximal light intensity placed at the centre of the RF and contrast c at 32%, at different values of spatial frequency ranging between 0.01 and 2 cyc/deg. The response exhibits a maximal sensitivity for a spatial frequency in the range 0.3 – 1.0 cyc/deg, and then falls rapidly to zero at frequencies above 2-3 cyc/deg. These results agree with those reported in (Linsenmeier et al., 1982). The panel c displays the activity of the geniculate cell response to sinusoidal gratings with maximal light at the centre of the RF and different values of contrast ranging between 0 (i.e., constant luminance $l(i,j,t) = l_0$) and 1.0. The spatial frequency used in this figure was 0.7 cyc/deg. The results show that activity of the ON cell increases linearly with contrast at low levels, to reach a saturation at contrast values around 35-40%. The results (panel b and c) are compared with those reported in (Cheng et al., 1995).

2.2.2. The Thalamic Input to Simple Cells

After the spatial characterization of the RF of a thalamic cell, we can spatially characterize the RF of simple cells in V1. For the sake of simplicity, in the present model we assume the very simple disposition for thalamic cells shown in Figure 2: the cortical cell receives excitatory synapses from 15 geniculate cells, arranged in a regular lattice (Figure 2, panel a) and oriented along the preferred orientation of the cell. These synapses are weighted according to a Gabor function (Figure 2, panel b). Of course, the horizontal disposition of the RF shown in Figure 2 panel a holds only when $\vartheta = 0$. When $\vartheta \neq 0$, the three subregions of the RF rotate, to simulate cells with different preferred orientations.. The number 15 lies in the lower range reported in the physiological literature (Alonso et al., 2001;Tanaka, 1983)

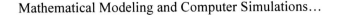

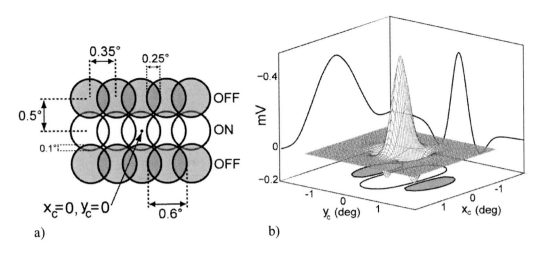

Figure 2. Thalamic input to a simple cell according to the present model. The receptive field of the simple cell arises from 15 thalamic cells arranged in a regular lattice (*panel a*). The synaptic weights from each thalamic cell to the simple cell are assigned according to the Gabor function in Eq. 8. *Panel b)* - RF of the simple cell in the space and its orthogonal sections (as well as its 2D projection). These represent the input to the simple cell computed by moving a single spot of light along the central vertical direction ($x_c=0$) and along the central horizontal direction ($y_c=0$).

By considering an ON centre RF, we can write the following expression for the changes in membrane potential of a simple cell, induced by its thalamic input

$$\Delta V_{ct}^{ON}(\vartheta,t) = \sum_{m=-2}^{+2} \left|W_{ct}(m\Delta x, 0)\right| \cdot T_{on}(m\Delta x \cos\vartheta, -m\Delta x \sin\vartheta, t) + \qquad (8)$$

$$+ \sum_{\substack{l=-1 \\ l\neq 0}}^{+1} \sum_{m=-2}^{+2} \left|W_{ct}(m\Delta x, l\Delta y)\right| \cdot T_{off}(m\Delta x \cos\vartheta + l\Delta y \sin\vartheta, -m\Delta x \sin\vartheta + l\Delta y \cos\vartheta, t)$$

where $T_{on}(x,y,t)$ and $T_{off}(x,y,t)$ represent the activity, at the instant t, of an ON centre or OFF centre thalamic cell centred at position x, y (see Eqs.6 and 7); ϑ establishes the preferred orientation of the target cell; Δx and Δy represent the distance between the centres of the thalamic cells in the preferred and orthogonal orientation respectively, and W_{ct} is the synaptic strength from the thalamic cell to its target cortical cell. The absolute value has been used, in the expression of the synaptic weight, to have only excitatory connections from the thalamus to the cortex, in agreement with physiological knowledge (Ferster and Miller, 2000). The expression for W_{ct} is

$$W_{ct}(x_g - x_c, y_g - y_c) = W_{ct0} \cdot e^{-\left((x_g - x_c)^2 / \sigma_x^2\right)} \cdot e^{-\left((y_g - y_c)^2 / \sigma_y^2\right)} \cos\left(2\pi \cdot f \cdot (y_g - y_c) + \varphi\right) \qquad (9)$$

where (x_c, y_c) are the coordinates of the centre of the cortical cell RF, (x_g, y_g) are the coordinates of the centre of the receptive fields for the geniculate cells ($g = 1, 2, ...15$). Parameters σ_x^2 and σ_y^2 set the dimension of the RF, and the spatial frequency, f, is correlated with the width of the ON and OFF subregions. Finally the phase φ allows simulation of both

ON ($\varphi = 0$) and OFF ($\varphi = \pi$) cortical cells. In the present work we always use $\varphi = 0$ to mimic ON cortical cells.

Equation 8 presupposes the presence of both excitatory and inhibitory synapses from the thalamus to the cortex, depending on the sign of W_{ct}. However, there is no physiological evidence on the existence of inhibitory connections from geniculate cells to cortical cells (Ferster and Miller, 2000). This problem can be overcome thinking that positive values for the synapses in Eq. 9 means *excitatory* connections from ON thalamic cells to the cortical cells, while negative values mean *excitatory* connections from OFF thalamic cells (Reid and Alonso, 1995).

Equation 8 provides an ON centre RF oriented along the direction ϑ. Of course, an OFF centre RF can be computed with an analogous equation in a straightforward way by simply inverting the position of the ON and OFF thalamic cells.

All the parameters in Eqs. 8-9 have been assigned in acceptable accord with physiological data (Troyer et al., 1998;Cai et al., 1997;Ferster et al., 1996;Cheng et al., 1995;Tanaka, 1983;Reid and Alonso, 1995;Alonso et al., 2001;Jones and Palmer, 1987a;Jones and Palmer, 1987b;Gardner et al., 1999) (see Table 1).[1]

As specified in section 1 in the present section attention is focused exclusively on a single hypercolumn, hence the receptive fields of all simulated cortical cells are centred in the same position, and differ only as to their orientation preference. This position can be conventionally assumed at the origin of the x, y axes. Hence, in the following we always set $x_c = 0$ and $y_c = 0$.

A model including several hypercolumns (information processing in more points of the retina, and then different values for x_c and y_c) will be the subject of the extension presented in the following sections (5, 6, 7 and 8).

2.2.3. The Intracortical Circuitry

The model assumes that intracortical excitation arrives from other excitatory neurons in the same hypercolumn whereas inhibition comes from inhibitory interneurons. The latter (as the excitatory cells) are parameterized by their orientation (and direction preference in case of moving stimuli). Furthermore, as illustrated in Figure 3 panel a, which summarizes the arrangement of thalamic and cortical inputs in the model, the activity of inhibitory interneurons is only a function of their thalamic input, i.e., these neurons do not receive intracortical synapses. As a consequence, intracortical inhibition to excitatory cells is arranged according to a feedforward scheme. By contrast, excitation involves a feedback among excitatory cortical cells. The corresponding dynamic is described via a differential equation with time constant τ.

---

[1] Note that the arrangement of the thalamic neurons differs slightly from the one reported in a previous (Ursino and La Cara, 2004b). Such difference, concerning a slight overlapping along the minor axis of the receptive field, produces a more accurate match to experimentally-derived receptive fields in the spatio-temporal domain (see Fig. 3E, page 455 in (DeAngelis et al., 1995) but does not affect any other result in this work.

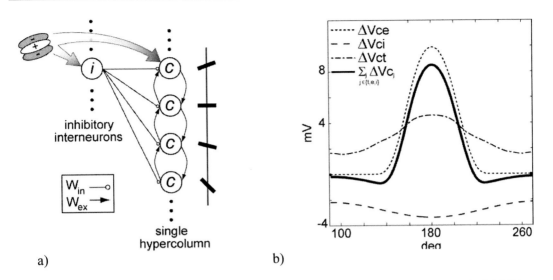

Figure 3. *Panel a)* - Arrangement of thalamic excitatory, cortical excitatory and cortical inhibitory inputs to simple cells according to the model. *Panel b)* - Patterns of the different contributions to membrane potential changes (thalamic excitatory, dot-dashed line; cortical excitatory, dotted line; cortical inhibitory, dashed line; cortical cell membrane potential, continuous line), simulated with the model for a simple cell with 180° preferred orientation at different orientations of the input grating. The sum of the three contributions results in the classical "mexican hat" distribution of excitation and inhibition.

The previous concepts are summarized by the following equations:

$$\Delta V_c^{ON}(\vartheta,t) = \Delta V_{ct}^{ON}(\vartheta,t) + \Delta V_{ce}^{ON}(\vartheta,t) - \Delta V_{ci}^{ON}(\vartheta,t) \tag{10}$$

$$\tau\frac{dc^{ON}(\vartheta,t)}{dt} = -c^{ON}(\vartheta,t) + k_c\left[\Delta V_c^{ON}(\vartheta,t) - \upsilon\right]^{+} \tag{11}$$

where $V_c(\vartheta,t)$ denotes the membrane potential of the cortical cell with orientation preference ϑ at time t, $\Delta V_{ct}(\vartheta,t)$, $\Delta V_{ce}(\vartheta,t)$ and $\Delta V_{ci}(\vartheta,t)$ are the changes in membrane potential caused by the thalamic input (Eq. 8), and by the excitatory and inhibitory intracortical connections, respectively. $c^{ON}(\vartheta,t)$ is the output activity of the cortical cell at time t, ϑ represents the orientation preference. At equilibrium, the value of cortical cell activity is obtained by comparing the variation in membrane potential with a threshold, υ, using a single wave rectifier $[]^{+}$ which cuts negative values (positive part), and multiplying the value so obtained by a gain factor k_c. The gain factor k_c has been assigned to have physiological values for simple cells activity at high contrast (Sclar and Freeman, 1982).

Equation 10 simply signifies that the overall change in membrane potential is the sum of contributions from thalamic and cortical (excitatory and inhibitory) inputs. As a consequence of feedback interaction among cortical cells (described below) the activity of the generic cortical cell exhibits a dynamical time evolution.

In the model we propose, the inhibitory interneurons have the same phase arrangement as excitatory neurons but wider orientation tuning (as in (Somers et al., 1995)), so the model is named "in-phase inhibition model": the inhibitory interneurons receives only the thalamic input with RF of the same phase as the cortical cells. Hence:

$$i^{ON}(\phi,t) = k_c \left[\Delta V_{ct}^{ON}(\phi,t) - \upsilon_l \right]^+ \tag{12}$$

where $i^{ON}(\phi,t)$ is the output activity of the inhibitory interneurons cell at time t, ϕ represents the orientation preference. Also in this case the value of inhibitory interneurons cell activity is obtained by comparing the variation in membrane potential with a threshold for inhibitory interneuron, υ_l, using a single wave rectifier $[]^+$, and multiplying the obtained value by the gain factor k_c.

Without considering any particular adaptive mechanism which sets different values for the parameter υ_l (see the section 3, which deals with the tilt after effect), the threshold υ_l for inhibitory interneuron coincides with the threshold υ for cortical cells.

The model is then completed by the following equations

$$\Delta V_{ce}^{ON}(\vartheta,t) = \sum_{\phi} w_{ex}(\vartheta-\phi)c^{ON}(\phi,t) \tag{13}$$

$$\Delta V_{ci}^{ON}(\vartheta,t) = \sum_{\phi} w_{in}(\vartheta-\phi)i^{ON}(\phi,t) \tag{14}$$

where the symbols $w_{ex}(\vartheta-\phi)$ and $w_{in}(\vartheta-\phi)$ represent the excitatory synapse from a simple cell with orientation ϕ to a simple cell with orientation ϑ and the same spatial phase (ON vs. ON), and $w_{in}(\vartheta-\phi)$ represents the synapse from an inhibitory interneuron (orientation preference ϕ) to a simple cell (orientation preference ϑ).

The strength of excitatory and inhibitory synapses depends on the correlation between cortical cells activity, i.e. it decreases with the distance between the orientation preference of the pre-synaptic and post-synaptic cells. The decrease is implemented by assuming a Gaussian relationship, with assigned variance:

$$W_{ex}(\vartheta,\phi) = W_{ex0} \cdot e^{-\left[\delta(\vartheta-\phi)^2 / 2\sigma_{ex}^2 \right]} \tag{15}$$

$$W_{in}(\vartheta,\phi) = W_{in0} \cdot e^{-\left[\delta(\vartheta-\phi)^2 / 2\sigma_{in}^2 \right]} \tag{16}$$

where the "orientation distance", δ, is computed as follows

$$\delta(\vartheta-\phi) = \begin{cases} |\vartheta-\phi|/90 & \text{if } 1 \le |\vartheta-\phi| \le 90 \\ [180-|\vartheta-\phi|]/90 & \text{if } 90 < |\vartheta-\phi| \le 180 \end{cases} \tag{17}$$

where W_{ex0}, W_{in0}, σ_{ex}^2, σ_{in}^2 are constant parameters, and $\delta(\vartheta - \phi)$ represents the distance between the preferred orientations, normalized between 0 (equal orientation), and 1 (maximal orientation difference = 90°).

Equation 17 calculates the orientation distance when orientation domain is considered to be included in 0-180 degrees, and this is the case of static stimuli. In the case of dynamic conditions, the orientation domain have to be extended to all 360 degrees (see section 4).

Parameters of intracortical connectivity (W_{ex0}, W_{in0}, σ_{ex}^2, σ_{in}^2) and the thresholds (υ and υ_l) have been chosen to have patterns of orientation tuning, spatial frequency tuning, and contrast invariance that agree with experimental data in the literature (Heggelund and Albus, 1978;Sclar and Freeman, 1982;Vidyasagar and Siguenza, 1985;Vidyasagar et al., 1996;Hammond and Pomfrett, 1990). The time constant of neural dynamics, τ, agrees with values used in deterministic mean-field equations [a few milliseconds in conditions when a neuron receives many inputs [see (Chance et al., 1999;Treves, 1993;Ben-Yishai et al., 1995). In particular, this value can be chosen significantly lower than the membrane time constant, that is 2.5 ms (Treves, 1993).

The set of differential equations has been numerically solved using the simple Euler method, with an integration step that warrants the achievement of a final stable equilibrium point. All computations have been performed using the software package MATLAB (The MathWorks Inc©) or C/C++ code on personal computers.

Figure 3 panel b summarizes the thalamic and intracortical contributions to the cortical cells membrane potential (i.e., ΔV_{ct}, ΔV_{ce} and ΔV_{ci} in Eq. 10), and their sum resulting in the classical "mexican hat" distribution of excitation and inhibition, simulated in a simple cell with preferred orientation 180° vs. the orientation of the input grating. The standard deviations of inhibition and excitation can be estimated approximately in 40 deg and 4.5 deg, while the ratio of peak inhibition to peak excitation is about 0.45. Moreover Figure 3 panel b shows that the model provides a thalamic input (ΔV_{ct}) in the range 30-50% of the total input, in agreement with experimental data (Ferster et al., 1996;Ferster and Miller, 2000;Chung and Ferster, 1998).

2.3. Results

The behaviour of the model was first tested against a set of experimental evidences, in particular:

(1) The orientation tuning of simple cells exhibits an half width at half height (HWHH) in the range 18°-28°, although large differences can be found among individual cells (Watkins and Berkley, 1974;Heggelund and Albus, 1978;Sclar and Freeman, 1982;Skottun et al., 1987). Moreover, orientation tuning is quite independent of the contrast of the input stimulus (Sclar and Freeman, 1982;Skottun et al., 1987;Ferster and Miller, 2000);

(2) The response of cortical cells is maximal at an optimal spatial frequency of the input grating (range: 0.3-1.0 cyc/deg) and decreases to zero at higher spatial frequencies (Skottun et al., 1987;DeAngelis et al., 1993).

(3) The HWHH of the tuning curve decreases when the spatial frequency of the input grating is increased (Vidyasagar and Siguenza, 1985;Jones and Palmer, 1987a;Jones and Palmer, 1987b;Hammond and Pomfrett, 1990).

(4) The response of cortical cells saturates when contrast is increased. This saturation level, however, depends on the input stimulus. The response to stimuli with non-optimal spatial frequency and/or non optimal orientation saturates at lower levels compared with the response to an optimal stimulus (Sclar and Freeman, 1982).

(5) Complete inactivation of the cortical circuitry reduces the response of a single cell to 1/3 - 1/2 of the basal one (Chung and Ferster, 1998;Ferster and Miller, 2000;Ferster et al., 1996). The thalamic input exhibits a broader orientation tuning (HWHH $\sim$ 35°-38°) compared with that of simple cells (18°-28°) (Ferster et al., 1996;Carandini and Ferster, 2000).

(6) The response to two gratings (or two bars) with different orientation is lower than the sum of the individual responses, even if the second grating (or bar) cannot evoke any response (or evokes negligible response) if applied alone (Sengpiel and Hubener, 1999;Morrone et al., 1982;Bonds, 1989).

Behaviour of the model - In order to test the properties 1-4, the model has been stimulated with single input gratings of different orientation, contrast and spatial frequency. Results are summarized in Figure 4, where a comparison with some experimental data (shown in bottom row of the figure) is provided (Sclar and Freeman, 1982;Vidyasagar and Siguenza, 1985;DeAngelis et al., 1993;Skottun et al., 1987). The panel a in first row shows the orientation curve (i.e., the cell response vs. orientation of the input grating) at different contrast levels. The spatial frequency was set at 0.8 cyc/deg. This graph can be seen as the response of a single cell (preferred orientation 180°) to different input orientations, or the response of all excitatory cells in the hypercolumn to a single horizontal grating. Panel b shows the response to a grating with optimal orientation and contrast equal to 32%, at different values of spatial frequency. Panel c shows the response of a simple cell vs. contrast of the input grating (i.e., the saturation curve) computed at different orientations (optimal, and 25° from optimal) and different spatial frequencies (0.8 and 0.6 cyc/deg). Finally, panel d shows the HWHH of the tuning curves, computed with a contrast equal to 32% at different values of spatial frequency.

The previous results demonstrate that with suitable parameters for synaptic weights, the model can satisfy properties 1-4 quite well.

Sensitivity analysis on synaptic strength - In order to investigate the impact of cortical (excitatory and inhibitory) connections on the orientation curve, a sensitivity analysis on the parameters characterizing the synaptic strength (i.e., parameters W_{ex0} and W_{in0} in Eqs. 15 and 16), has performed. Results are illustrated in Figure 5. As it is clear from the panel a, a change in the strength of the excitatory synapses does not significantly modify the orientation tuning, but causes a clear change in the peak activity. Conversely a reduction in the strength of inhibitory synapses broadens the orientation curve. Moreover, the peak activity of the orientation curve significantly increases (by about two-fold) after reduction of inhibitory synapses.

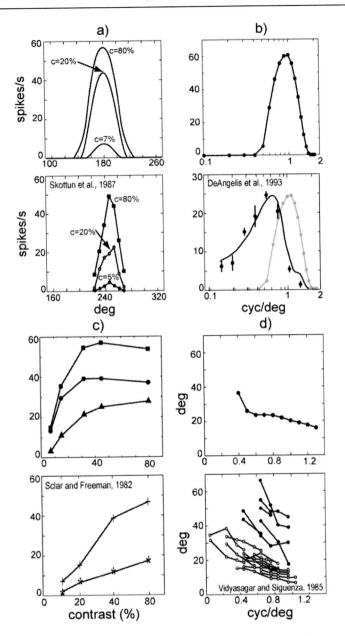

Figure 4. Simulated behaviour of the model in response to gratings with different orientation, contrast and spatial frequency. *Panels a)* - Orientation curve at different values of contrast. The spatial frequency was set at 0.8 cyc/deg. Comparison with experimental data provided by (Skottun et al., 1987). *Panels b)*- Response of one cell to an optimally oriented grating at different values of spatial frequency (contrast 32%). Comparison with experimental data provided by (DeAngelis et al., 1993); the output model was normalized (grey line) to the maximum value provided by experimental data in order to have a direct comparison. *Panels c)* - Response of a simple cell vs. contrast of the input grating. ■ : optimal orientation and optimal spatial frequency (0.8 cyc/deg). ●: optimal orientation and non-optimal spatial frequency (0.6 cyc/deg). ▲: orientation 25° from the optimal one, but optimal spatial frequency. Comparison with experimental data provided by (Sclar and Freeman, 1982); *Panels d)* - HWHH of the orientation curve at different values of spatial frequency (contrast 32%) according to the model. Comparison with experimental data provided by (Vidyasagar and Siguenza, 1985).

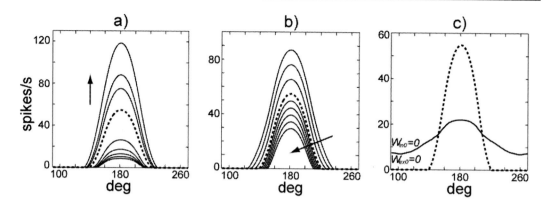

Figure 5. Sensitivity analysis on the strength of excitatory and inhibitory cortical synapses. *Panel a)* - dependence of the orientation curve on the strength of cortical excitatory synapses (W_{ex0} in Eq. 15). *Panel b)* - Dependence of the orientation curve on the strength of cortical inhibitory synapses (W_{in0} in Eq. 16). In the panels parameter increases in the direction of the arrow, while the dashed line represents the orientation curve computed with basal parameter values (i.e., with the values reported in Table 1). *Panel c)* – Comparison of the orientation curve obtained with basal parameter values, with the curve obtained after complete elimination of the cortical circuitry (Contrast 32%; spatial frequency 0.8 cyc/deg). The parameter ranges used for the sensitivity analysis were: $W_{ex0} \in [0.008 - 0.019]$; $W_{in0} \in [0.0068 - 0.009]$ (in mV/(spikes/s)).

Finally, the panel c compares the orientation curves obtained with basal values of cortical synapses, with the response obtained after total elimination of cortical circuitry (i.e., $W_{ex0} = 0$, $W_{in0} = 0$). The peak of cell activity is reduced to 1/3 – 1/2 of basal after total cortical inactivation, while the HWHH increases from 20-25° to 35-38°, in agreement with property 5 above.

Sensitivity analysis on the thalamic input – According to (Ferster and Miller, 2000), the present model, in basal conditions, exhibits a thalamic input to a cortical cell as great as 35-50% of the total input. Other authors, however, provided a smaller estimate for the thalamic input (10-15% of total) (Douglas and Martin, 1991). Hence, it is interesting to analyze how the model is sensitive to a change in this parameter. For this reason, the orientation curve was re-calculated after a reduction of parameter W_{ct0} in Eq. 9. A reduction in thalamic input alone, however, causes a lessening in the overall activity of the cortical cells, and a fall in the peak of the orientation tuning curve (similar to that occurring with a decrease in contrast of the visual input), while the ratio of thalamic input vs. total input remains quite constant. For this reason, the fall in thalamic input was compensated by a small increase in the strength of intracortical excitatory synapses (see the figure legend for parameter numerical values). Results in Figure 6 show that the model provide a satisfactory orientation tuning curve even in the presence of a modest thalamic input: the orientation curve is nearly unaffected (see panel a). The three input components to the cortical cells are represented in panel b, demonstrating that, with the new parameter values, the thalamic component is actually reduced to 10-15% of total.

Suppression by non-optimal stimuli - A common experimental observation is that superimposition of a grating with non-preferred orientation to an optimally oriented grating causes a reduction in the response of most cortical cells, compared with the response to the preferred grating alone (Morrone et al., 1982;Bonds, 1989;Bauman and Bonds, 1991;Sengpiel et al., 1998). This behaviour is evident even if the non-preferred grating evokes no response when applied individually.

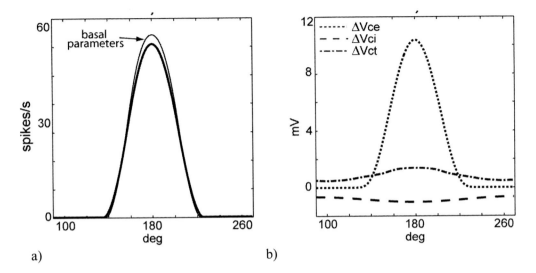

a)   b)

Figure 6. Sensitivity analysis on the strength of the thalamic input. *Panels a)* - Orientation curves obtained with basal parameter values (thin line) and after a reduction of parameter W_{ct0} from 20 mV/(spikes/s) to 6 mV/(spikes/s) (thick line). In order to maintain a constant peak of the orientation curve we augmented the strength of intracortical excitatory synapses ($W_{ex0} = 0.0199$). *Panels b)* - Three contributions to the thalamic input (i.e., the same quantities as in Figure 3) computed with the new parameter values. In this new condition, thalamic input represents just 10-15% of the total input to a simple cell.

In order to analyze this phenomenon, first we simulated the response of the model to a visual input consisting of two simultaneous gratings with identical contrast and spatial frequency (1.0 cycle/deg) separated by a given angle (30°, 60° or 90°). Two different contrast levels were used (32 and 80%) to test the effect of this parameter on suppression. The results are summarized in Figure 7, panels a. Two aspects of this figure deserve attention. First, as in (Carandini and Ringach, 1997), two gratings separated by just 30 degrees produce an orientation curve with a single peak placed at the intermediate orientation. This is simply the consequence of the limited orientation tuning of the cells, which poses a restriction to their effective resolution. Moreover, superimposition of the second non-optimal grating causes a significant reduction in the peak response of the orientation curve and this suppression increases dramatically at low-contrast. Of course, we can reduce the HWHH of the orientation tuning curves by increasing the inhibition strength (see Figure 5). However, in the latter case, application of two orthogonal gratings would cause a total suppression of cortical cell activity (unpublished simulations). Total suppression has been occasionally observed by (Bonds, 1989) in cells with narrow orientation tuning.

The same simulations have been repeated in the case of light bars (width 1 degree) separated by a given angle of 90° at three different contrast levels (20, 35 and 80%). The results are shown in Figure 7, panels b. The effect of suppression by non optimal stimuli is well appreciable also in this scenario and it is possible to note that the cortical cells saturate at minor contrast level with respect to the case of gratings. Moreover, the superimposition of the second non-optimal bar causes a slenderer reduction in the peak response of the orientation curve, also in the case of low-contrast.

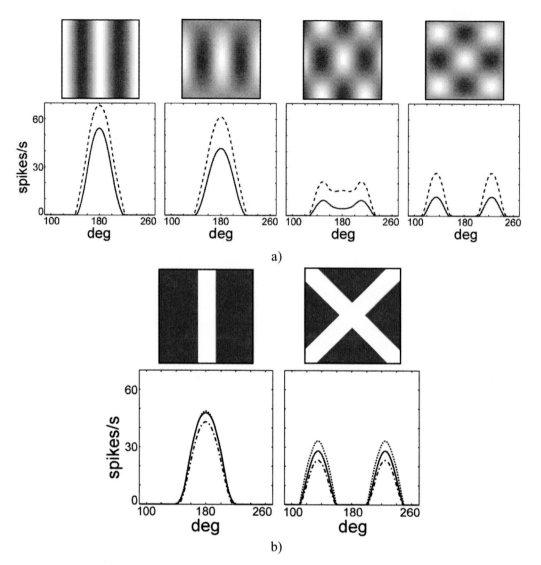

Figure 7. Effect of a second visual input with non-optimal orientation superimposed on a first one. *Panels a)* - The four upper panels show the visual input and, below, the corresponding orientation curves. In order, from left to right, the figure shows the orientation curves in response to: an optimal oriented grating (180°); two gratings separated by 30° (first orientation 165°, second orientation 195°); two gratings separated by 60° (first orientation 150°, second orientation 210°); two orthogonal gratings (first orientation 135°, second orientation 215°). Spatial frequency was 1 cyc/deg, while two different contrast levels were used for each simulation: 32% (continuous line) and 80% (dashed line). *Panels b)* The two upper panels show the visual input and, below, the corresponding orientation curves. The left panel shows the orientation curves in response to an optimally oriented light bar; the right panel shows the orientation curves in response to two orthogonal light bars. The width of bars was 1 deg, while three different contrast levels were used: 20 % (dot-dashed line) 35% (continuous line) and 80% (dashed line).

3. Tilt after Effect

3.1. Introduction

A classic visual illusion, (Mather et al., 1998), is the tilt aftereffect (TAE). If a subject looks at an oriented stimulus for a prolonged time, a subsequent stimulus with similar orientation appears rotated away from the adapting orientation. A common explanation for this phenomenon assumes that neurons in V1 fatigue during prolonged activity. Since the orientation selectivity is a peculiarity of V1 neurons (section 2) (Hubel and Wiesel, 1962), fatigue depends on the particular orientation used in the adapting period. These selective changes may explain the "false" perceived orientation observed during the test phase [see (Jin et al., 2005) for exempla].

However, results of recent physiological experiments performed on anesthetized cats have revealed a more complex scenario (Dragoi et al., 2000). The tuning curve of V1 neurons exhibits depression near the adapting orientation (as assumed by the fatigue theory), but also the position of the peak response (i.e., the preferred orientation) repulsively shifts away from the adapting orientation. Using a simple population coding model, which simulates the changes in the tuning curve of individual neurons in one hypercolumn, Jin et al (2005) have shown that suppression of the tuning curves contribute to the TAE, whereas the repulsive shift of the tuning curves reduces the amount of the TAE, and lessens the orientation error.

Although the model by Jin et al. (2005) is able to characterize TAE in terms of the alterations of the neuron tuning curves, it describes empirically the changes in the neuron tuning curves without entering into possible mechanisms occurring in V1. Hence, it does not investigate which physiological adjustments, induced by adaptation, may explain the observed changes in neuron tuning curves, and the consequent observed TAE.

Since intracortical mechanisms play a fundamental role in determining the tuning curve of V1 cells, it is reasonably to expect that they are also essential during adaptation, and in the development of the consequent TAE.

According to the previous description, alternative scenarios have been proposed in order to explain TAE in terms of physiological mechanisms:

1. First, some models of the TAE were based on the selective suppression of neural response, according to the fatigue hypothesis (Clifford et al., 2000;Wainright, 1999).

2. A second plausible scenario assumes adaptation of the excitatory connections to neurons tuned to the adapting orientation (Felsen et al., 2002;Teich and Quian, 2003). As a consequence of a reduced intracortical excitation, the response of these neurons would be diminished, resulting in the TAE.

3. A third scenario, especially explored by Bednar and Mikkulainen (2000), emphasizes the importance of inhibitory weight changes (i.e., an increase of inhibitory weights to neurons tuned for the adapting orientation). In this case, the suppression of activity for the neurons with preferred orientation proximal to the adapting one would be a consequence of an increased intracortical inhibition from cortical interneurons.

Hence, different mechanisms may thus be responsible for the observed adaptation of V1 neurons to a grating and may be at the basis of TAE. They may include: a fatigue of neurons excited for a long period (1), a depression of intracortical excitation during adaptation (2), a reinforcement of intracortical inhibition during adaptation (3). It is also possible that multiple parameters changes may be involved in adaptation, including a fatigue of inhibitory interneurons or depression (instead of reinforcement) of intracortical inhibition. The latter two changes would counteract the depression in excitation. Although various models have been presented in past years, we are not aware of any study which quantitatively compares the effect of the different hypotheses within a single theoretical framework. The aim of this section is to use the model of orientation selectivity presented in section 2, to investigate the possible physiological mechanisms responsible for adaptation in the primary visual cortex and the consequent TAE.

A specific aspect of this study is that alternative hypotheses are tested within the same model, in order to allow an immediate comparison of their consequences. In particular, three alternative parameter changes, related to the three previous scenarios, are implemented and their capacity to mimic real data is checked vs. existing data in the literature.

1. In a first scenario, we assumed adaptation causes an increase in the threshold of excitatory neurons, proportional to their activity during the adapting period. Eventually, a fatigue of inhibitory interneurons may also be assumed.
2. In the second scenario, we assumed a depression of excitatory synapses, according to an anti-Hebbian learning rule (that is, depression is proportional to the correlation of activity of the presynaptic and post-synaptic neurons).
3. In the third scenario we assumed a reinforcement (or a depression) of inhibitory synapses according to a Hebbian rule.

The results are then compared with data in the literature concerning the TAE, and discussed in terms of the plausibility of the mechanisms proposed. Finally, since a single adjustment is unable to explain all data in the literature, some exempla are presented, assuming a combination of the adjustments delineated above.

3.2. Model Description: Introduction of the Adapting Phase

In order to simulate adaptation, we assumed three different changes caused by prolonged activity of intracortical neurons: i) a fatigue of excitatory neurons, ii) a depression of intracortical excitatory synapses, iii) a reinforcement of intracortical inhibitory synapses. In cases ii and iii we adopted a classic Hebbian (or anti-Hebbian) adaptation rule, Finally, in the last simulation set we will also consider a fatigue of inhibitory interneurons and a depression of intracortical inhibition.

In order to simplify the mathematical treatment, in the following the adapting phase and the test phase are considered as completely separate, i.e., we first modify model parameters (adapting phase) by using the output of neurons in normal conditions, then we use the model with modified parameters to simulate its behaviour in the test phase. Of course, this is a simplification (but commonly used in most neural network models) since, in the reality, the outputs of neurons start to change during the adapting phase.

The three scenarios are mathematically described below:

3.2.1. Fatigue of Excitatory Neurons

In order to simulate a simple fatigue phenomenon, we assumed that the threshold of excitatory cortical cells (that is, parameter υ in Eq. 11) increases proportionally to the activity of the neuron during the adaptation period. By denoting with $\Delta\upsilon$ a parameter which establishes the adaptation strength, we can write:

$$\upsilon_{new}(\vartheta) = \upsilon + \Delta\upsilon \cdot \frac{c^{ON}(\vartheta,\infty)}{c^{ON}(\alpha,\infty)} \tag{18}$$

where $c^{ON}(\vartheta,\infty)$ has the same meaning of Eqs. 10-11, in particular represents the output of the excitatory during the adaptation period in steady state conditions. α is the adapting orientation, and $\upsilon_{new}(\vartheta)$ represents the new threshold of an excitatory cell with preferred orientation ϑ, after adaptation. Hence, the ratio $c^{ON}(\vartheta,\infty) / c^{ON}(\alpha,\infty)$ represents the activity of neurons in the hypercolumn, normalized to the maximal activity during adaptation.

Thanks to this normalization, parameter $\Delta\upsilon$ is equal to the threshold change of the neuron with $\vartheta=\alpha$ (i.e., this parameter represents the threshold change of the neuron with maximal adaptation).

Conditions characterized by greater or smaller adaptation can be simulated by simply acting on this parameter (see section 3.3 Results below).

In a last simulation set (section 3.3.3), an equation analogous to Eq.18 has been applied to the threshold of inhibitory interneurons too (parameter υ_I in Eq. 12)

3.2.2. Depression of the Excitatory Synapses

In this scenario we assumed that the synapses linking two excitatory cortical cells (i.e., the quantities $W_{ex}(\vartheta,\phi)$ in Eq. 15) are modified via an anti-Hebbian rule: the decrease in the synaptic strength depends on the correlation between the presynaptic and postsynaptic activity during the adaptation period. This decrease affects the parameter W_{ex0} in Eq. 15 (originally identical for all neurons). We can write:

$$W_{ex0,new}(\vartheta,\phi) = W_{ex0} - \Delta W_{ex0} \cdot \frac{c^{ON}(\vartheta,\infty)}{c^{ON}(\alpha,\infty)} \cdot \frac{c^{ON}(\phi,\infty)}{c^{ON}(\alpha,\infty)} \tag{19}$$

where $W_{ex0,new}(\vartheta,\phi)$ is the new value of parameter W_{ex0} to be used in Eq. 15 for a synapse linking a presynaptic neuron with preferred orientation ϕ to a post-synaptic neuron with preferred orientation ϑ, ΔW_{ex0} is a parameter which sets the strength of adaptation, and the other quantities have the same meaning as in Eq. 18.

Hence, after adaptation, the excitatory synapse linking two neurons becomes:

$$W_{ex}(\vartheta,\phi) = W_{ex0,new}(\theta,\phi) \cdot e^{-\left[\delta(\vartheta-\phi)^2/(2\sigma_{ex}^2)\right]} \tag{20}$$

The previous rule implies that the sum of all synapses converging to a given neuron (i.e., the quantity $\sum_{\phi=1}^{180} W_{ex}(\vartheta,\phi)$) may vary (in particular may decrease) as a consequence of the adaptation changes.

3.2.3. Reinforcement of Inhibitory Synapses

In the third scenario we assumed that inhibitory synapses, linking a pre-synaptic inhibitory cortical cell to a post-synaptic excitatory cell, reinforce with a Hebbian rule. The increase affects the parameter W_{in0} in Eq. 16 (which was originally identical for all neurons). We can write:

$$W_{in0,new}(\vartheta,\phi) = W_{in0} + \Delta W_{in0} \cdot \frac{c^{ON}(\vartheta,\infty)}{c^{ON}(\alpha,\infty)} \cdot \frac{i^{ON}(\phi,\infty)}{i^{ON}(\alpha,\infty)} \tag{21}$$

where $i^{ON}(\phi,\infty)$, represents the inhibition from an interneuron with preferred orientation ϕ. ΔW_{in0} is a parameter which sets the strength of adaptation, and the other quantities have the same meaning as in previous equations.

After application of the previous rule, the inhibitory synapse linking two neurons becomes:

$$W_{in}(\vartheta,\phi) = W_{in0,new}(\theta,\phi) \cdot e^{-\left[\delta(\vartheta-\phi)^2/(2\sigma_{in}^2)\right]} \tag{22}$$

3.2.4. Simulation of Adaptation with Different Parameter Changes

The adaptation phase consisted in the application of a grating with preferred orientation 80 deg, contrast 30% and optimal spatial frequency 0.7 cyc/deg (see section 2, or also (Ursino and La Cara, 2004b)). Different levels of adaptation were mimicked by assigning different values to the parameters Δv (threshold change of excitatory neurons, Eq. 18), Δv_1 (threshold change of inhibitory interneurons), ΔW_{ex0} (excitatory synapse decrease, Eq. 19) and ΔW_{in0} (inhibitory synapse increase, Eqs. 21).

After adaptation, a test phase was simulated by applying a grating with the same contrast and spatial frequency as the adapting grating and orientation 90 deg. The "population curve" (i.e., the activity of all 180 neurons in the hypercolumn) was then computed. From this curve, TAE was evaluated assuming that the brain "reads out" orientation as the maximum of the population curve.

Subsequently, the analysis has been deepened for some exemplary cases (i.e., for some particular values of parameter adaptation) as follows: i) the minimum perceived contrast was evaluated after adaptation. To this end, we applied a test grating with the same spatial frequency (0.7 cyc/deg), orientation 90 deg, but progressively decreased its contrast, until the maximum of the population curve was reduced to zero. ii) After adaptation, we computed the response of all neurons to gratings with different orientations from 0 to 180 deg. From this analysis, two additional pieces of information were derived: the dependence of TAE on the difference between the test grating and the adapting grating, and the tuning curves of all neurons in the hypercolumn after adaptation.

3.3. Results

Results are summarized in Figure 8, for what concerns an augmentation in threshold (panels in row a), a decrease in excitatory synapses (panels in row b) and an increase in inhibitory synapses (panels in row c) with simple Hebbian plasticity. In this figure, the first column presents the population response for different levels of adaptation; the second column depicts the computed value of TAE; the third column shows the dependence of the minimum perceived contrast on the level of adaptation; the fourth column shows the dependence of TAE on the difference between the test grating and the adapting grating for an exemplary level of adaptation. Finally, the tuning curves of individual neurons are shown in the right column for an exemplary level of adaptation.

3.3.1. Analysis of the Population Curves

Results in Figure 8 show that, with all types of adaptation, the model is able to produce reliable values of TAE with moderate parameter changes. However, a decrease in excitatory synapses (panels in row b) is not able to mimic an increase in the minimum perceived contrast.

An increase in threshold as low as 0.4-0.6 (basal value = 0.2) or a change in excitatory or inhibitory synapses as low as 10-15%, panels in rows a and c respectively, are sufficient to produce values of TAE in the range 5-10 deg in the model.

3.3.2. Analysis of the Tuning Curves of Individual Neurons

The previous analysis was devoted to the population curves, i.e., the response of all neurons in the hypercolumn to a grating with given orientation. Recent experimental results, however (Felsen et al., 2002;Dragoi et al., 2000;Müller et al., 1999), analyze the tuning curves of individual neurons. It is worth noting that, due to symmetry in the normal values of synapses, in our model the population curve and the tuning curve are identical before adaptation, but become different after adaptation, due to a rupture in the initial symmetry of the model.

The results, shown in the right column of Figure 8, can be summarized as follows: the tuning curves of neurons with preferred orientation close to the adapting orientation (orientation difference 10-20 deg) exhibit a reduction in amplitude, while the preferred orientation (i.e., the maximum of the tuning curve) exhibits a moderate repulsive shift.

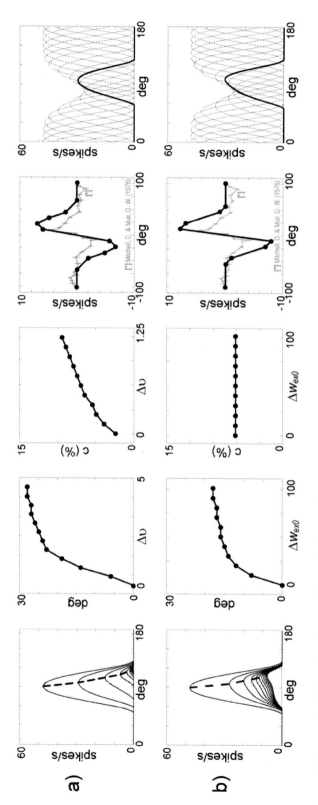

Figure 8. Panels a) - Effect of an increase in threshold of excitatory neurons (parameter $\Delta \upsilon$ in Eq. 18). The exemplary cases in the fourth and fifth panels were obtained with $\Delta \upsilon = 0.4$; Panels b)- Effect of a percentage decrease in excitatory synapses (parameter $\Delta wex,0$ in Eq. 19 expressed as a percentage of its basal values wex,0). The exemplary cases in the fourth and fifth panels were obtained with $\Delta wex,0 = -10\%$ of wex,0; Panels c) Effect of a percentage increase in inhibitory synapses (parameter $\Delta win,0$ in Eq. 21 expressed as a percentage of its basal values win,0). The exemplary cases in the fourth and fifth panels were obtained with $\Delta win,0 = 10\%$ of win,0. The first column shows the population curves; The second column shows the computed aftereffect at different values of parameter change. Aftereffect is computed as the difference between the maximum of the population curves (dashed line in the panels of first column) and 90 deg; the third column shows the minimum perceived contrast as a function of the parameter change. In all these figures, orientation of the adaptation grating was 80 deg, while orientation of the test grating was 90 deg; The fourth column shows the computed aftereffect as a function of the difference between the test grating and the adaptation grating, at an exemplary value of parameter change. In these trials, orientation of the adaptation grating was 80 deg, while orientation of the test grating was given different values between 0 and 180 deg. For these curves a comparison with experimental data is provided (Mitchell and Muir, 1976); The most right column shows the tuning curves of several exemplary neurons (original preferred orientation between 0 and 180 deg, step 10 deg) after adaptation (adaptation grating 80 deg) at the exemplary value of parameter changes. The thick line shows the population response when the test grating was 90 deg, and is used to give an indicative value of TAE.

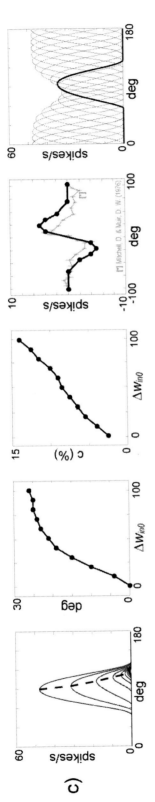

Figure 8. (continued) Panels c) Effect of a percentage increase in inhibitory synapses (parameter $\Delta win,0$ in Eq. 21 expressed as a percentage of its basal values win,0). The exemplary cases in the fourth and fifth panels were obtained with $\Delta win,0 = 10\%$ of win,0. The first column shows the population curves; The second column shows the computed aftereffect at different values of parameter change. Aftereffect is computed as the difference between the maximum of the population curves (dashed line in the panels of first column) and 90 deg; the third column shows the minimum perceived contrast as a function of the change. In all these figures, orientation of the adaptation grating was 80 deg, while orientation of the test grating was 90 deg; The fourth column shows the computed aftereffect as a function of the difference between the test grating and the adaptation grating, at an exemplary value of parameter change. In these trials, orientation of the adaptation grating was 80 deg, while orientation of the test grating was given different values between 0 and 180 deg. For these curves a comparison with experimental data is provided (Mitchell and Muir, 1976); The most right column shows the tuning curves of several exemplary neurons (original preferred orientation between 0 and 180 deg, step 10 deg) after adaptation (adaptation grating 80 deg) at the exemplary value of parameter changes. The thick line shows the population response when the test grating was 90 deg, and is used to give an indicative value of TAE.

This shift is about 2-3 deg for parameter changes which cause a TAE as low as 7-8 deg, and becomes about 4-5 deg for parameter changes which cause a TAE as large as 12-15 deg. A similar repulsive shift in the tuning curves has been observed by Dragoi et al. (2000): however, the repulsive shift observed by these authors is greater, and occurs at higher values of orientation difference.

3.3.3. Simultaneous Change in Several Parameters

Experimental results show that the amplitude of the tuning curves decreases close to the adapting orientation, whereas it increases far from the adapting orientation. As evident in Figure 9, this effect cannot be obtained with a single adjustment (i.e., assuming that just one parameter changes as a consequence of adaptation). In order to have an increase in the amplitude of the tuning curves at large orientation differences, one needs antagonistic combinations of parameter changes: some parameter changes would reduce the tuning curves, whereas other would cause an increase. For instance, (Teich and Quian, 2003) suggested that adaptation can be simulated by depressing both intracortical excitatory and intracortical inhibitory connections. The first change would reduce the tuning curves close to the adapting grating, whereas the second would increase the tuning curves at greater orientation distance.

In order to explore these possibilities, a last set of simulations was performed assuming the simultaneous changes of several parameters, with antagonistic effects on the tuning curves. Besides the decrease in excitatory synapses, and the increase in the threshold of excitatory neurons, in these simulations we also tested the effect of a depression in intracortical inhibitory synapses, and increase in the threshold of inhibitory interneurons (parameter υ_l in Eq. 12).

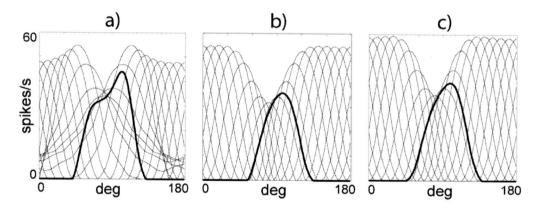

Figure 9. Tuning curves of several exemplary neurons (original preferred orientation between 0 and 180 deg, step 10 deg) after adaptation with different combinations of parameter changes. The simulated adaptation changes (without normalization of synapses) are: *Panel a)* - increase in threshold of excitatory neurons: $\Delta\upsilon = 0$ (no change); increase in threshold of inhibitory interneurons: $\Delta\upsilon_1 = 0$ (no change); percentage decrease in excitatory synapses: $\Delta w_{ex,0} = 50\%$; percentage decrease in inhibitory synapses: $\Delta w_{in,0}$ −90%. *Panel b)* - increase in threshold of excitatory neurons: $\Delta\upsilon = 0.2$; increase in threshold of inhibitory interneurons: $\Delta\upsilon_1 = 0.2$; percentage decrease in excitatory synapses: $\Delta w_{ex,0} = 0$ (no change); percentage increase in inhibitory synapses: $\Delta w_{in,0}$ +10%. *Panel c)* - increase in threshold of excitatory neurons: $\Delta\upsilon = 0.1$; increase in threshold of inhibitory interneurons: $\Delta\upsilon_1 = 0.3$; percentage decrease in excitatory synapses: $\Delta w_{ex,0} = 5\%$; percentage increase in inhibitory synapses: $\Delta w_{in,0}$ +5%.

The latter change was simulated with an equation equivalent to Eq. 18, but using the activity of interneurons i^{ON} to simulate the fatigue phenomenon. A fatigue of interneurons would cause a decrease in inhibition, with the effect of augmenting the amplitude of the tuning curves especially far from the adapting orientation.

Figure 9 shows the effect of three possible combinations of parameter changes on the tuning curves. The panel a shows the effect of a simultaneous decrease in both excitatory and inhibitory synapses (the same assumption as in (Teich and Quian, 2003)). The panel b shows the effect of an increase in inhibitory synapses (the same as in Figure 8 panel c together with a fatigue of both excitatory and inhibitory interneurons. Finally, the panel c shows an exemplum characterized by a decrease in excitatory synapses, an increase in inhibitory synapses, and a fatigue of both excitatory and inhibitory interneurons. The tuning curves show a 20-30% decrease in amplitude close to the adapting orientation, a 10-15% increase in amplitude far from the adapting orientation (indirect TAE) a moderate repulsive shift of the tuning curves as large as 2-4 deg, and a direct TAE as large as 7-12 deg.

4. Direction and Velocity Selectivity of V1 Neurons

4.1. Introduction

It is well-known that cells in V1 do not only exhibit orientation preference, but often exhibit direction and velocity selectivity too; they respond preferentially to a given direction, and only when velocity lies in given range.

A series of models has been proposed to explain direction and velocity selectivity, via learning rule such as Hebbian learning process (Wimbauer et al., 1997a; Wimbauer et al., 1997b) or the BCM learning rule (Blais et al., 2000). Other authors, such as Sabatini and Solari (1999), suggested an alternative hypothesis: according to their model, direction selectivity would emerge merely from asymmetric recurrent intracortical interactions, without any direction bias inherited from the LGN. Similarly, Maex and Orban (1992) emphasized the role of time delays in the intracortical connections, whereas Hillenbrand and von Hemmen (2000; 2001) stressed the role of a feedback from the visual cortex to the geniculate relay cells, to control the spatiotemporal structure of cortical receptive fields.

A popular hypothesis is that direction selectivity in the cat arises from temporal diversity in the response of thalamic cells, whose convergence to simple cells would produce a space-time inseparable receptive field. In other words, the timing differences among the thalamic inputs may be the basis of direction selectivity. The latter hypothesis is supported by the observation of lagged and non-lagged thalamic cells in the cat (Saul and Humphrey, 1990; Saul and Humphrey, 1992). A model which exploits these concepts was proposed by Hamada et al. (1997): in their model cortical activity depends on input coming from lagged and non-lagged thalamic cells as well as from excitatory and inhibitory mutual connections. Despite the great number of experimental studies performed, and mathematical models proposed, the exact intracortical circuit responsible for velocity and direction selectivity is still largely hypothetical.

In this section, the model of orientation selectivity presented in section 2 will be extended, to temporarily characterize the receptive field of simple cells, through the use of thalamic cells with a different delay. In this way, we can account for direction and velocity selectivity, besides orientation selectivity. The model is then used to simulate the response of the thalamic and cortical cells to drifting gratings or bars with different spatial and temporal frequencies (or width in case of bars), velocity, and directions of motion.

The model is based on the assumption that the thalamic input establishes a moderate direction selectivity, thanks to a different time lag of the thalamic responses. This initial moderate bias for one direction is then enhanced and sharpened by intracortical circuitry that, depending on synaptic strength, may lead to various levels of direction preference.

4.2. Temporal Characterization of Thalamic Cells

In the following, the new aspects of the model (compared with those in section 2) are described in detail. The new elements concern the temporal response of thalamic cells, and their spatio-temporal arrangements to constitute an inseparable receptive field. These aspects are essential to establish temporal frequency tuning and direction selectivity.

As in Eq. 2 of section 2, we assume that thalamic cells have a separable spatio-temporal RF, described as the product of a spatial term and a temporal term, i.e.

$$RF_{xy}(i,j,t) = \varphi_{xy}(i,j) \cdot F_{xy}(t) \qquad (2)$$

where $RF_{xy}(i,j,t)$ represents the spatio-temporal receptive field of a thalamic cell centered at position x,y of the retina, $\varphi_{xy}(i,j)$ is its spatial component (already described in Eq. 3), and $F_{xy}(t)$ is its temporal component.

According to (Cai et al., 1997), the temporal component can be described with a biphasic impulse response obtained as the difference of two γ-functions:

$$\gamma(t) = K_1 \times \frac{[c_1(t - t_{01})]^{n_1} e^{-c_{01}(t - t_{01})}}{n_1^{n_1} e^{-n_1}} - K_2 \times \frac{[c_2(t - t_{02})]^{n_2} e^{-c_{02}(t - t_{02})}}{n_2^{n_2} e^{-n_2}} \qquad (23)$$

in which all parameters have been determined by best fitting (Cai et al., 1997) (see Table 1).

However, in order to account for the existence of lagged responses of thalamic cells, we introduced a time delay in the temporal RF. As will be specified below, this time delay depends on the spatial position of the cell. Hence, the following expression has been used to describe the temporal RF

$$F_{xy}(t) = \gamma(t - D(x, y)) \qquad (24)$$

where $D(x, y)$ represents a pure delay for the response of the cell at position x, y.

The response of thalamic cells is computed in two subsequent steps: first, we compute the linear response (i.e., the quantity $g_l(x,y,t)$ to be used in Eqs. 6 and 7).Then, the latter is passed through the sigmoidal relationship (Eqs. 6 or 7).

Thanks to the spatio-temporal separability, computation of the linear response can be further subdivided into two distinct phases: elaboration in the spatial domain, (already exploited in previous sections 2 and 3) and elaboration in the temporal domain, that we are going to present.

Accordingly, the linear response of thalamic cell in temporal domain is computed by performing the convolution of the spatial response with the temporal receptive field, i.e.

$$g_t(x,y,t) = \int_0^\infty F_{xy}(\tau) \cdot s(x,y,t-\tau)d\tau \tag{25}$$

where $s(x,y,t)$ represents the spatial component (computed as in Eq. 4, when the RF was characterized only by its spatial property). Eq. 25 has been numerically computed in the frequency domain using the Fast Fourier Transform algorithm. In particular, we first calculated the transforms of $s(x,y,t)$ and $\gamma(t)$:

$$S(x,y,\omega) = \Im[s(x,y,t)] \tag{26}$$
$$\Gamma(\omega) = \Im[\gamma(t)] \tag{27}$$

where ω represents temporal frequency. Then, $g_t(x,y,t)$ is obtained by reverse transforming

$$g_t(x,y,t) = \Im^{-1}[S(x,y,\omega) \cdot \Gamma(\omega) \cdot \exp(-jD(x,y)\omega)] \tag{28}$$

where the exponential term in the right hand member of Eq. 28 accounts for the presence of a time lag in the response of the thalamic cell.

Finally, the output of a thalamic cell is computed via Eqs 6-7[1] , to account for threshold and saturation non-linearities. The RF of thalamic cell in the spatio-temporal domain is represented in Figure 10 panel a.

A final fundamental aspect of the present extended model concerns the value used for the time lags of each thalamic cell ($D(x, y)$ in Eq. 24). We assume that, to obtain an inseparable spatio-temporal RF for the downstream simple cell, the time lag of thalamic cells increases regularly from one subregion to the next of the RF. This assumption agrees with predictions of recent developmental models (Wimbauer et al., 1997a;Wimbauer et al., 1997b;Blais et al., 2000). This is summarized by the following equation, which sets the time lag, $D(x, y)$, of each LGN cell at position x,y in Eq. 8.

$$D(m\Delta x \cos\vartheta + l\Delta y \sin\vartheta, -m\Delta x \sin\vartheta + l\Delta y \cos\vartheta) = (l+1)D_0 \qquad l=-1,0,1 \tag{29}$$

Eq. 29 can be explained as follows: two variables m and l ($m \in [-2,-1,0,1,2]$; $l \in [-1,0,1]$) are used in Eq. 8 of section 2 to represent the 15 thalamic cells which target onto the same cortical simple cell (see Figure 10 a). In particular, the variable l is used to move from one subregion to the next of the receptive field. When $l = 0$, we are in the central ON subregion, and the time lag of all thalamic cells is D_0. The first OFF subregion (l = -1, bottom subregion

---

[1] It is worth noting that the value of the parameter k_t in this new description differs from that previously calculated in stationary conditions (see section §2.2.1). This difference has been introduced to compensate for the effect of the transfer function of the thalamic neuron, $\Gamma(\omega)$.

OFF$_1$) exhibits a time lag conventionally assumed equal to 0 The time lag in the last OFF subregion (l = +1, upper subregion OFF$_2$) is as great as 2 D_0.

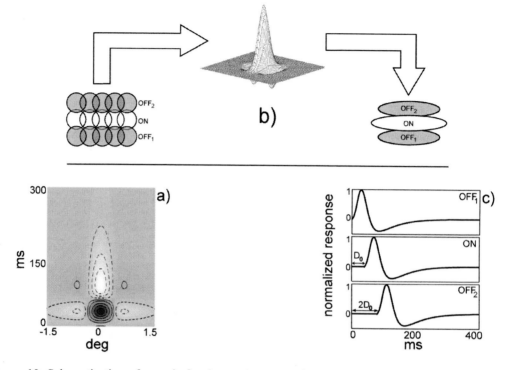

Figure 10. Schematization of genesis for the spatio-temporal organization of simple cells. *Panel a)* - Thalamic input to a simple cell (see also Figure 2, panel a) and thalamic cell's receptive field in the spatio-temporal domain (x-t domain) as yielded by the model: the horizontal axis represents space (x), and the vertical axis represents time (t). Regions of visual space that are sensitive to light spots are shaded black, and are delimited by solid lines; regions that are responsive to dark spots are shaded white, and are delimited by dashed lines. Shade colour saturation is proportional to response strength; *Panel b)* – Spatial RF which filters the thalamic afferents to the simple cells (see Figure 2 panel b for a complete characterization); *Panel c)* - impulse responses of thalamic cells belonging to different receptive field subregions (OFF$_1$, ON, OFF$_2$). The time lag of the response increases regularly from one subregion to the next.

In conclusion, the meaning of Eq. 29 is that the three subregions (OFF$_1$, ON, OFF$_2$, in Figure 10 a) have a different time delay, caused by afferents from thalamic cells. The situation is summarized in Figure 10 panel c, which represents the impulse responses of three thalamic cells: non-lagged neurons ($D(x, y)$ = 0 ms in Eq.24) in the lower subregion, lagged neurons with low delay ($D(x, y)$ = 40 ms) in the middle subregion and lagged neurons with high delay ($D(x, y)$ = 80 ms) in the upper subregion. The simple cell obtained from the convergence of such thalamic responses exhibits an inseparable receptive field, which is characteristic of direction selective cortical cells.

By way of example, Figure 11 shows the RF of a simple cell obtained from the model by using a value D_0 = 0 ms in Eq. 29 (i.e., all thalamic cells are not lagged). The RF is clearly separable. Figure 12 shows the inseparable RF obtained with D_0 = 40 ms. In both figures the

RFs are compared with those obtained from an experimental registration (Fig 3E, pag 455 (DeAngelis et al., 1995)).

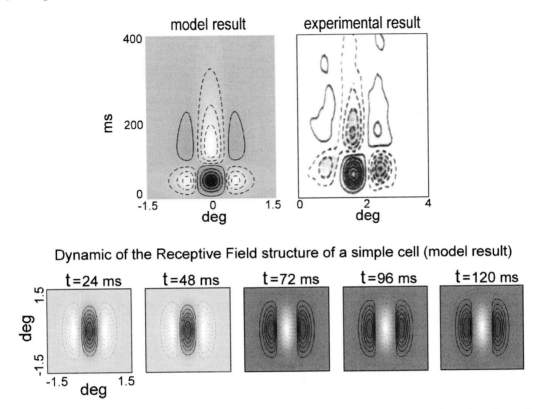

Figure 11. Comparison between simulated (upper left) and experimentally measured (DeAngelis et al., 1995) (upper right) simple cell's receptive fields in the x-t domain (same conventions for colour and lines as in Figure 10 a) with reference to a space-time separable receptive field. Simulations were performed using a zero time lag for all thalamic cells. The lower panels describe the dynamics of the receptive field structure of a simple cell. Each snapshot represents the spatial profile of the receptive field at different times relative to stimulus onset. These receptive fields clearly appear to be separable. From t = 24 ms up to t = 48 ms the receptive field profile shows three subregions: the external two are dark-excitatory while the central one is a light-excitatory. These subregions, from t = 72 ms to t = 120 ms, reverse their polarity. It is possible to notice that the spatial position of the three subregions is motionless.

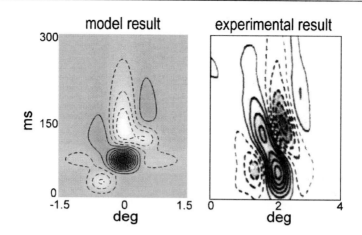

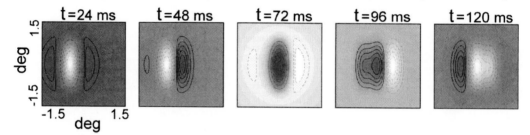

Figure 12. Comparison between simulated (upper left) and experimentally measured (upper right) simple cell's receptive fields in the x-t domain (same conventions for colour and lines as in Figure 10 a) with reference to a space-time inseparable receptive field. Simulations were performed using the values 0 ms, 40 ms and 80 ms for the time lags of the thalamic cells in the three subregions. The lower panels describe the dynamics of the receptive field structure of a simple cell. Each snapshot represents the spatial profile of the receptive field at different times relative to stimulus onset. These receptive fields clearly appear to be space-time inseparable: the spatial organization of the receptive field changes over time. At t = 24 ms the profile is approximately even symmetric (light-excitatory central subregion, dark-excitatory lateral subregions) and then it inverts its polarity although remains even symmetric yet (t = 72 ms). Later, at t = 96 ms and t = 120 ms, the receptive field profile becomes odd symmetric with the light-excitatory subregion on the left. It is important to note that, in this case, the spatial position of the three subregions modifies during time.

4.3. Results

4.3.1. Response to Gratings

First, we performed some simulations to analyze the behaviour of the thalamic input to simple cells (i.e., quantity ΔV_{ct} in Eq. 8). These simulations are aimed at studying the role of the RF organization in the genesis of direction selectivity, by excluding the contribution of the intracortical circuitry.

As described above, in the model direction selectivity, in response to a drifting grating, originates from the superimposition of the activities in the three subfields (OFF-ON-OFF), as a consequence of the different spatial phase and time lag. A typical behaviour is illustrated in Figure 13.

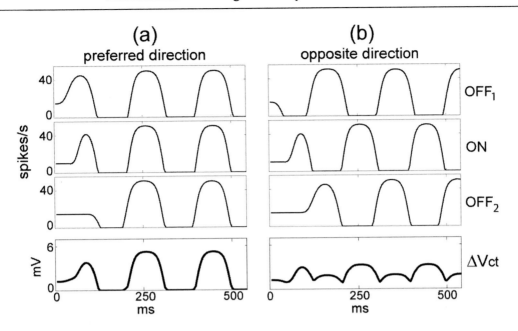

Figure 13. Temporal patterns of three different thalamic contributions to a cortical cell. The panels in the first row show the temporal activity (spikes/s) of a thalamic neuron belonging to the first lateral OFF subregion (no lagged neuron); the panels in the second row show the temporal activity of a thalamic neuron belonging to the central ON subregion (lagged neuron with 40 ms delay); the panels in the third row show the temporal activity of a thalamic neuron belonging to the second lateral OFF subregion (lagged neuron with highest delay, 80 ms). The visual stimulus is an optimal drifting grate (spatial frequency: 0.54 cyc/deg, temporal frequency: 5.5 Hz, contrast 30%) moving in the preferred direction (a) and in the null direction (b). The fourth row shows the sum of the thalamic responses, weighted by the Gabor function (i.e., Eq. 8). As shown in these panels, direction selectivity is explicable through the synchronization of the thalamic neurons response: the panel a shows that the thalamic responses are synchronized in case of preferred direction, resulting in a maximum thalamic input (mV) to the cortical cell; the panel b shows that the thalamic responses are not-synchronized in case of null direction, resulting in a smaller thalamic input to the cortical cell.

The three upper panels in this figure show the response of each subfield (i.e., the activities of thalamic cells with $l = -1$, 0 and $+1$ in Eq. 8) to a sinusoidal grating drifting in the direction of increasing delay (left panels) or in the reverse direction (right panels). The drifting grating was chosen with 30% contrast, optimal orientation and optimal spatial and temporal frequencies ($f_S = 0.54$ cyc/deg; $f_T = 5.5$ Hz). The time lags among adjacent subfields is $D_0 = 40$ ms. These parameter values will be maintained throughout the subsequent simulations, if not differently specified. The bottom panels show the effect of these thalamic inputs on the membrane potential of the target cell (ΔV_{ct}), computed via Eq. 8 as the sum of the thalamic activities weighted via a Gabor function.

As it is clear from Figure 13, if the grating drifts from the subfield with *shorter* time lag ($l = -1$, subfield OFF$_1$) to the subfield with *longer* time lag ($l = +1$, subfield OFF$_2$) the activities of thalamic cells in the three subfields are synchronized, and so the target cortical cell exhibits a maximal response. By contrast, poor synchronization occurs if the grating is shifting in the opposite direction.

A common way to summarize direction selectivity is to calculate the direction index (DI). This is usually defined as follows:

$$\frac{\text{response to the preferred direction } (R_P) - \text{response to the non preferred direction } (R_{NP})}{\text{response to the preferred direction } (R_P)}$$

Since in the present work we are using periodic gratings, DI was computed using the peak response, after the exhaustion of the initial transient period. For instance, in Figure 13 the maxima in periodic regimen are 5.3 mV (preferred direction) and 3.28 mV (non-preferred direction) resulting in a DI for the thalamic input as high as 0.38.

Of course, the synchronization depends on the spatial and temporal frequency of the drifting grating, on the distance between the centres of the subfields, and on the time lags among the subfields (i.e., on parameters Δy and D_0 in Eqs. 8 and 29). In the case of linear superposition, a simple mathematical analysis suggests that maximal direction selectivity occurs when two subfields are separated by a distance $\Delta y = \lambda/4$ (where $\lambda = 1/f_S$ is the spatial wavelength of the drifting grating) and the time lag between two adjacent subfields is $D_0 = T/4$ (where $T = 1/f_T$ is the time period of the drifting grating). The results, however, are modified by the presence of non-linearities, such as those induced by the sigmoidal relationships in Eqs.6 and 7.

By way of example, Figure 14 shows the direction index (DI) computed from knowledge of the thalamic input only, using the same drifting grating as in Figure 13 but different values of the time lag D_0. The left panel shows the result of a linear computation, performed through the Fourier analysis of the RF profile (see (DeAngelis et al., 1993) for details on this method). The right panel shows the DI computed using Eq. 8, which accounts for non-linear terms (i.e., $DI = \left(\Delta V_{ctPD} - \Delta V_{ctNPD}\right)/\Delta V_{ctPD}$, where the subscript PD and NPD stand for preferred and non-preferred direction).

Results in the left panel of Figure 14 demonstrate that maximal direction selectivity, computed via a Fourier analysis, actually occurs when $D_0 \simeq 40$ ms $= T/4$. However, even in the optimal case, DI is lower than 0.5. This result agrees with values of the DI commonly obtained in physiological works using linear prediction (DeAngelis et al., 1993;Reid et al., 1991). Non linearities in the model have two major effects (Figure 14, right panel): they reduce the DI (down to 0.4) and make DI almost independent of the time lag, D_0, in the range 30-60 ms. These differences between the linear analysis (left panel) and the non-linear model (right panel) can be ascribed to the presence of an upper saturation and lower threshold in Eq. 6. As a consequence of these non-linearities, in fact, the maximum of the temporal response is smoothed (saturation) while negative values are set to zero (threshold). These effect reduce the DI and make direction selectivity less dependent on the exact value of time delay employed in the model (hence, less dependent on the value of temporal frequency).

The previous analysis was concerned with the thalamic input only. The subsequent simulations have been performed by including the role of intracortical circuitry. A first example is presented in Figure 15, which shows the DI computed at different values of time lag (i.e., parameter D_0 in Eq. 29 ranging from 0 to 70 ms) by using the basal values for synapses. Parameters of the drifting grating are the same as in the previous Figure 14.

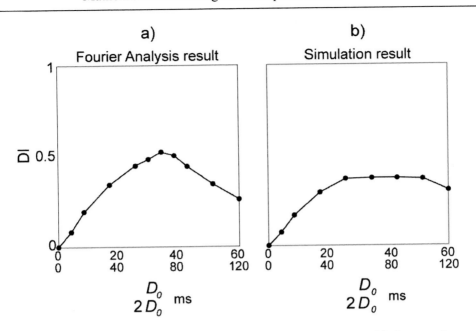

Figure 14. Direction Index (DI) for the thalamic input (i.e., without considering any intracortical circuit) vs. the different couples of temporal lags used to characterize each subregion of the receptive field: the upper index in the x-label identifies the temporal delay for the central ON subfield, whereas the bottom identifies the temporal delay for the distal OFF subfield. a) DI computed on Fourier Analysis of the simple cell's receptive field; b) DI computed through numerical simulations of the non-linear equations of the thalamic input, i.e., including non-linearities.

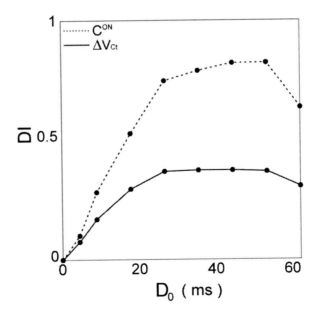

Figure 15. DI computed through numerical simulations of the thalamic input (continuous line), and effect of intracortical circuit (dotted line), vs. the different couples of temporal delays used to characterize each subfield of the receptive field. The index in the x-label identifies the temporal delay for the central ON subfield.

By way of comparison, the DI computed from thalamic input only is also displayed in the same plot. Results of Figure 15 demonstrate that intracortical processing strongly improves direction selectivity. The thalamic DI, which is about 0.38 when D_0 ranges between 30 and 60 ms, is augmented to about 0.8 as a consequence of intracortical processing. The peak value for D_0, which provides a maximum DI, is about 50 ms. As mentioned above, in all subsequent simulations parameter D_0 will be set at 40 ms, if not differently specified.

A more comprehensive description of the cortical cell response in the model is reported in Figure 16. This figure is arranged as follows:

- The part a represents the analysis in the temporal domain by using a grating with a fixed spatial frequency (0.54 cyc/deg) and different values of temporal frequency. The upper row reports the amplitude of the optimal (R_P) and non-optimal (R_{NP}) responses both for thalamic input (in mV) and for cortical output (in spikes/s) vs the temporal frequency; the second row represents the correspondent resulting DI.
- The part b represents the analysis in the spatial domain by using a grating with at fixed temporal frequency (5.5 Hz) and different values of spatial frequency. The meaning of the panels are the same of case a.

In both cases the HWHH is also reported in the panels of the third row. The HWHH remains quite constant in the range 2-10 Hz in the model, and exhibits a moderate decrease with spatial frequency.

DI increases with temporal frequency in the range 5-10 Hz, while with spatial frequency in the range 0.2-0.7 cyc/deg the DI decreases. DI falls to zero (and then becomes negative) at high temporal and spatial frequency, a phenomenon related with the inversion of preferred direction. In the model, the amplitude of the response exhibits a low-pass behaviour with temporal frequency (with a cut-off at about 10-12 Hz), and a band-pass behaviour with spatial frequency (with an optimal response at about 0.5 cyc/deg). The preferred direction reverses at higher values of spatial and temporal frequency (about 12 Hz and about 1.2 cyc/deg). It is worth noting that reversal of direction preference with temporal and spatial frequency is a property of the thalamic input, i.e., it depends on the superposition of lagged and non-lagged thalamic activities. The moderate preference for one direction, which is evident in the thalamic input, is then sharpened and amplified by the intracortical circuitry causing much higher values of DI.

However, the position of the cut-off frequency in the model, and the frequency value at which preferred direction reverses, depend on the choice of temporal delays in Eq. 29. By way of example, the fourth row in Figure 16 shows the amplitude of the response to both directions, by using a time delay as great as 80 ms. In this case, the direction reverses at about 6Hz, while the cut off frequency falls to about 4 Hz.

Our model, in agreement with experimental data (Saul and Humphrey, 1990;Saul and Humphrey, 1992), predict that direction selectivity depends on temporal and spatial frequency. Saul and Humphrey (1992) observed that simple cells are direction selective at low values of frequency, but lose their direction selectivity at higher frequencies. Several cells reverse their direction preference, so that one direction is optimal at low frequencies (1-6Hz, 0-0.8 cyc/deg) and the other direction is optimal at higher frequencies (4-18 Hz, more than 1 cyc/deg) (see Figure 1 in (Saul and Humphrey, 1992)).

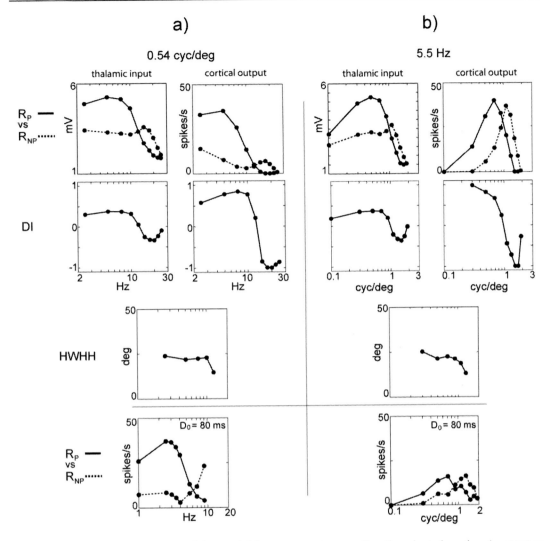

Figure 16. Simulated behaviour of the model in response to an optimally oriented grating (contrast = 30%) vs. temporal frequency (panels in side a; spatial frequency fixed at 0.54 cyc/deg) and spatial frequency (panels in side b; temporal frequency fixed at 5.5Hz). In each panel the continuous line represent the response of the neuron to a grating moving in the preferred direction, the dashed lines represent the response of the neuron to a grating moving in null direction. The two panels in the first row , both for side a and for side b, show the thalamic input, and the simple cells response. These curves show the phenomenon of the inversion of preferred direction. The panels in the second row, both for side a and side b, represents the DI vs. spatial and temporal frequency for thalamic input and cortical output, respectively. The two panels in the third row, both for side a and side b, shows the HWHH of the tuning curve vs. spatial and temporal frequency, when the grating moves in preferred direction. It s worth noting that with the basal value used for the temporal delay (i.e., $D_0 = 40ms$) the preferred direction reverses at high values of spatial and temporal frequency (about 12 Hz and about 1.2 cyc/deg). By using an higher temporal delay (two panels in fourth row, both for side a and side b, $D_0 = 80$ ms), the direction reverses at smaller frequencies (about 6 Hz and about 0.8 cyc/deg).

In order to reach deeper understanding on the role of intracortical synapses, we performed a sensitivity analysis by individually varying the strength of the feedforward intracortical inhibition and of the feedback intracortical excitation (both separately and together). Results on DI are shown in the upper panels of Figure 17.

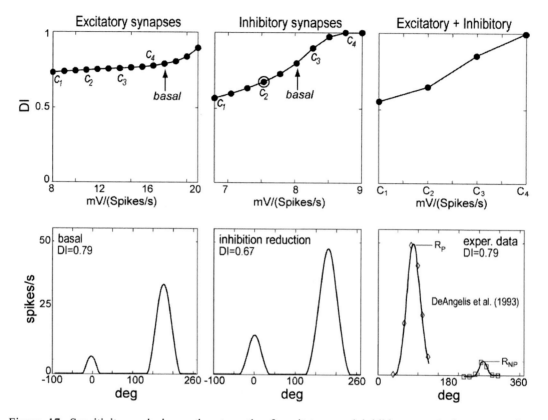

Figure 17. Sensitivity analysis on the strength of excitatory and inhibitory cortical synapses (i.e., parameters W_{ex0} and W_{in0} in Eqs. 15 and 16). First row shows DI dependence on the strength of cortical excitatory synapses, on the strength of cortical inhibitory synapses, and on the simultaneous reduction of excitation and inhibition. The parameters values used to define the four configurations (C_1, C_2, C_3, C_4) are (in $\mu V/(spikes/s)$): C$_1$: [W_{ex0}=8; W_{in0} =6.8] ; C2 : [W_{ex0}=11; W_{in0} =7.5]; C3 : [W_{ex0}=14; W_{in0} =8.3]; C4 : [W_{ex0}=17; W_{in0} =9]. Panels in the second row show the orientation tuning curve of the model: at basal parameters (left panel), and with a change in the inhibitory synapses (right panel). In particular, we used W_{in0} = 7.5 $\mu V/(spikes/s)$ (marked circle in the middle panel on the first row). The most right panel in the second row show the experimental data (DeAngelis et al., 1993), for comparison with model results.

The lower panels show the orientation tuning curves in two exemplary cases (with basal parameter values and after reduction of intracortical inhibition), compared with experimental data (DeAngelis et al., 1993). The model shows a physiological behaviour. The DI can be easily changed by performing moderate changes in the excitatory and inhibitory synapses. In particular, DI in the model is sensitive to the level of intracortical inhibition: changing the inhibition strength by ±10% from the basal value causes a shift in DI from 0.5 to 1.0, without too much affecting the orientation tuning curve (see lower panels in Figure 17). Moreover a simultaneous reduction of excitation and inhibition, depicted in the upper right panel, causes a reduction of DI comparable with that obtained with a reduction of inhibition only. Hence it is possible to assert that in the model the inhibition is more influential than the excitation.

Further simulations have been performed to characterize the spatial scale of direction selectivity in our model, i.e., to determine how small can be a stimulus to still produce a direction selective response. In fact, experimental results suggest that even a stimulation which covers a small portion of the RF (within one sub-region) can exhibit direction selectivity (Baker and Cynader, 1986). To test this behaviour, we used sinusoidal grating patches of decreasing width, from 3 deg (which covers the overall RF) down to 0.5 deg (i.e., inside the central sub-region). It is worth noting that we did not decrease the patch below 0.5 deg, since in this case the response becomes negligible. Results in Figure 18 show that DI increases with a reduction of the patch. In other words, it is sufficient that the stimulus covers just a small portion of the RF to have direction selectivity. This result may be understood thinking that the receptive fields of the LGN cells which target to the simple cells are largely superimposed (Figure 2 a and Figure 10 a). Hence, the response to stimulation of the central subregion in the simple cortical cell is not only determined by the central geniculate neurons, but also by the lateral ones. Their responses exhibit different delays and so give different synchronization if the stimulus moves in one direction or in the other within the central subregion.

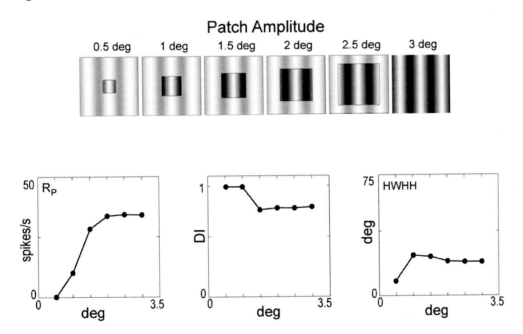

Figure 18. Simulated behaviour of the model vs. the width of a sinusoidal grating patch (30% contrast, and optimal spatial and temporal frequency). The patch dimension extends from 0.5 deg, inside the central sub-region of the RF, to 3 deg, covering the entire RF (upper panels). The panels in the second row show the amplitude response of neuron at optimal direction (R_P) vs. the patch amplitude (left panel), the DI vs the patch amplitude (middle panel) and the HWHH vs the patch amplitude (right panel).

4.3.2. Response to Bars
In a subsequent set of simulations we studied the response to bars (luminance 30% of the background) with different length (4 deg, 0.7 deg and 0.5 deg) and width 0.5 deg.

The first simulations were performed to analyze the velocity tuning curve (i.e., cell activity vs. the velocity of the bar) of the thalamic cells and of simple cells. Figure 19 compares curves obtained using basal parameter values with data in the literature. The curve of a single thalamic cell (upper left panel) and the overall thalamic input (upper middle panel) exhibit a wide band-pass characteristic, extending up to high velocities (almost 100 deg/s).

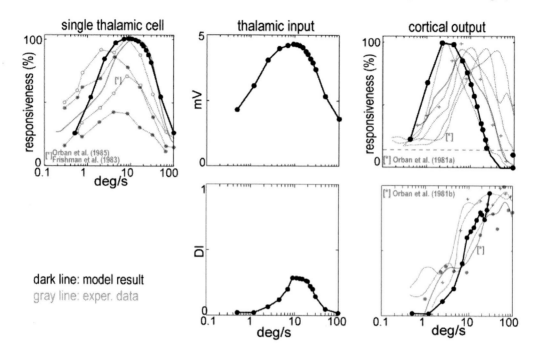

Figure 19. Velocity response curves of the model. First row: *left panel* -normalized velocity tuning curve of a single thalamic cell (at 10 deg of eccentricity) which exhibits a wide band pass characteristic. The model (black line) provides a response comparable with experimental data (data have been redrawn from Figure 1 in (Orban et al., 1985) and from Figure 2 in (Frishman et al., 1983); *middle panel* - velocity tuning curve of the overall thalamic input to a simple cell according to the present model: i.e., the sum, of the response of 15 thalamic cells weighted by a Gabor function (middle panel). *Right panel* - velocity tuning curve of the simple cell. The model provides a velocity curve response comparable with experimental data (grey continuous line: (Orban et al., 1981b), Figure 2a; grey dashed line: (Orban et al., 1981b), 1981 Figure 5a). Second row: *left panel* - direction index (DI) vs. velocity of the light bar computed for the thalamic input; *right panel* - DI vs. velocity computed for a simple cell. The model provides results in accordance with some experimental curves (data have been redrawn from Figure 3b in (Orban et al., 1981a) and from Figure 1b in (Orban et al., 1981a)).

This model prediction agrees quite well with data by Orban et al. (1985) and with some curves by Frishman et al. (1983). The curve of simple cells, exhibits a greater velocity selectivity: the lower cutoff velocity is close to that obtained for thalamic cells (about 1 deg/s); by contrast, the upper cutoff velocity is much smaller in simple cells (approximately 10-15 deg/s) than in thalamic cells, i.e., the intracortical circuitry attenuates the response to higher velocities. The velocity tuning curves approach the variety of curves reported in Orban et al. (1981a;1981b). In the same Figure 19, lower panels, we also show how DI depends on the velocity of the light bar. The left lower panel confirms that the thalamic input exhibits just a moderate preference for one direction. This preference is then sharpened by the intracortical circuitry (right lower panel). In the model DI increases with velocity of the bar and it is possible to observe an high direction preference (DI close to 1) at the upper cutoff velocity (10 deg/s).

In Figure 20 the role of the length of a light bar moving across the RF is investigated. Two different velocities are simulated (4.5 and 11 deg/s). The bar has constant luminance and moves perpendicularly to its long axis at constant velocity: it starts its movement well outside the RF of the cell, and terminates only when the RF has been completely crossed. All 360 different orientations of the bar have been tested.

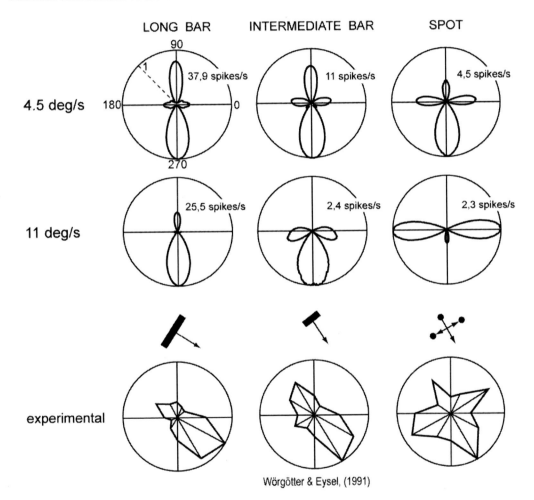

Figure 20. Analysis of the role of the length and of the velocity of a light bar (0.5 deg of width), moving across the receptive field in the direction orthogonal to the long axis of the bar: result. A long bar (4 deg), an intermediate bar (0.7 deg) and a light spot (0.5 deg) are investigated. The velocities simulated was 4.5 deg/s (upper panels) and 11 deg/s (lower panels). The cortical responses are shown in a polar plot: the phase represents the direction of movement for the bar and the modulus represents the strength of the evoked response normalized to the maximum (the maximum firing rate in spikes/s is reported in each polar plot). The last row in this figure presents some panels taken from (Wörgötter and Eysel, 1991), with different bar length.

The responses are presented in the form of a polar plot, where the phase (from 0 to 360 deg) represents the direction of movement for the bar, and the modulus represents the strength of the evoked response, normalized to the maximal one. We assumed that the long axis of the RF for the cell is oriented at 0 deg (or 180 deg).

In the model a reduction in the bar length causes a widening of the orientation tuning curve (we remind that orientation is orthogonal to the direction of movement, i.e., orientation and direction simply differ by 90 deg) but the preferred direction of movement does not change with the bar length. In other words, the orientation tuning curve remains unimodal. This result agrees with observation by Henry et al. (1974a;1974b;1985) .Furthermore, this component exhibits very high direction selectivity (DI close to 1 at high velocity). It is also possible to observe two preferred directions of movement, depending on the bar length. A long bar exhibits its maximal response when the long axis of the bar is oriented optimally, and the bar moves orthogonally to the long axis of the RF (90 deg or 270 deg) (*orientational component*). Moreover, this component exhibits direction preference. However, a reduction in bar length causes the appearance of a second component of movement, which is parallel to the long axis of the RF (0 deg or 180 deg) (*axial component*). At intermediate values of bar length these two components may coexist, and so the orientation tuning curve exhibits a bimodal pattern. When the bar length is reduced to a spot and velocity is high, only the axial component remains. These results partially agree with data reported in Worgotter et al. (Wörgötter et al., 1998;Wörgötter and Eysel, 1989;Wörgötter and Eysel, 1991;Wörgötter et al., 1991;Wörgötter and Koch, 1991;Crook et al., 1994). From Figure 20, it is evident that the axial component is stronger at high values of velocity, a result which agrees with Crook et al. (1994).

An important point, to be noted, is that the axial component in our model does not exceed 2-3 spikes/s, i.e., it is much smaller than the orientational component observed with a long bar (25.5 spikes/s). This result disagrees with some observations by Wörgötter and Eysel (1989). These authors, in fact, observed an increased responsiveness with decreasing bar length, i.e., a behaviour similar to that of end-stopping cells. It is probable that additional mechanisms, not included in our study, may amplify the axial component and account for these differences.

5. Visual Space

5.1. Introduction

In the previous sections, we described a model able to simulate the receptive field of simple cells in V1, and to account for the main properties (orientation, direction and velocity selectivity, as well as adaptation to prolonged inputs) of these cells.

The purpose of the second part of this work (sections 5-8) is to extend the description of V1, in order to include "contextual influences" and to describe how cells in V1 can integrate information coming from a wide portion of space.

As described before, the RFs of V1 cells, as measured by spot stimuli, result quite small and signal just a tiny edge of specific orientation (Hubel and Wiesel, 1962;Ferster and Miller, 2000); however V1 cells have been observed to modify their response depending on the presence of surrounding stimuli, i.e., stimuli located outside their classic RF (Nelson and Frost, 1985;Kapadia et al., 1995;Kapadia et al., 2000). According to Kapadia et al. (1995), in this study we will use the term "contextual influences" to denote "the spatial distribution of excitation and inhibition surround interactions around a neuron RF". A common idea is that the main structures responsible for these contextual influences are long-range horizontal intracortical connections emanating from excitatory cortical pyramidal cells (Gilbert and Wiesel, 1989;Ts'o et al., 1986;Rockland and Lund, 1983) (section 7).

Several additional aspects, however, complicate the response of V1 cells. One is related to "spatial frequency channels" or "psychophysical channels": V1 cells are quite sharply tuned for spatial frequency, i.e., they respond optimally only to elongated stimuli within a narrow spatial frequency range (Hubel and Wiesel, 1977;Palmer, 2002;Webster and De Valois, 1985). This observation led some authors to postulate that V1 cells behave mainly as filters, or wavelets decomposing an image into components at a particular frequency or scale (De Valois and De Valois, 1998). Recent hypotheses suggest that different spatial frequency channels may be involved in different tasks (Oliva and Schyns, 1997;Schyns and Oliva, 1997;Mermillod et al., 2005) and in a coarse-to-fine integration of visual information (section 8).

The aim of this section, and of the following ones, is to propose and validate a model of the visual cortex, which incorporates both connections between neurons in a single hypercolumn (as in Sections 2-4) and connections among hypercolumns (i.e., between neurons with different positions of the RF). The model differs from that developed in the previous sections, in that it not only includes feed-forward input from the LGN, feed-forward inhibition from inhibitory interneurons and excitatory synapses within a hypercolumn, but also long-range excitatory and inhibitory connections which integrate information in a wide spatial region, and realizes "contextual influences".

The present section provides a generic description of the model. In the subsequent sections (6, 7 and 8) the particular model specializations are described depending on the purpose of the model.

Section 6, analyses long-range intracortical synapses, with particular emphasis on intracortical excitation and its role in determining the response properties of V1 cells as simple-like or complex–like functional behaviour; Section 7, shows model's capacity to extract contours of an image and analyzes the role of each type of synaptic connections in the process of contour extraction; Section 8, proposes an improvement in the model by including two additional aspects, i.e., multi-scale decomposition and attention. The latter version of the model incorporates two independent paths for visual processing corresponding to two different scales. Attention from higher hierarchical levels works by modifying different properties of the network: by selecting the portion of the image to be scrutinized and the appropriate scale, by modulating the threshold of a gating mechanism, and by modifying the width and/or strength of lateral inhibition.

The extension of the model implies mathematical forms which may appear slightly different from those in the previous sections, although they refer (qualitatively) to the same terms. By the way, in the model description we will use the same symbols employed in the previous section, when we refer to the same entities.

5.2. Model Description (Intracortical Connectivity)

As originally described by Hubel and Wiesel (1962) the primary visual cortex is composed of "hypercolumns", which consist of cells responding to the same spatial position in the retina, but with different orientation preferences, and "orientation columns" which consist of cells responding to the same orientation but with different positions in the visual space (see Figure 21). In the model we consider an array of (N)x(N) hypercolumns (N=51 or 101), that scrutinize images wide (D)x(D)deg, (in the following D is assuming values up to 20 degrees). In the model the number of distinct orientation preferences for the excitatory neurons in each hypercolumn is equal to 16. Moreover, each hypercolumn includes 4 inhibitory interneurons, which also have a distinct orientation preference. The ratio between excitatory neurons and interneurons is the same used in the previous sections, that is 4. Hence, in the model two consecutive excitatory neurons in the hypercolumn have orientation preferences, which differ by 11.25 deg, while orientation preferences of consecutive interneurons differ by 45 deg.

In the following, the notation (x, y, ϑ) will be used to represent a cell whose RF is positioned at the coordinate x, y of the visual space, with preferred orientation, ϑ. In particular, the subscript c (hence, the notation (x_c, y_c, ϑ_c)) will be used to denote an excitatory cortical cell, while the symbol i (hence, (x_i, y_i, ϑ_i)) a feed-forward inhibitory interneuron. When two excitatory cells are connected with an intracortical synapse, we will denote with the subscripts c and h (hence, with coordinates (x_c, y_c, ϑ_c) and (x_h, y_h, ϑ_h)) the post-synaptic and pre-synaptic cells, respectively.

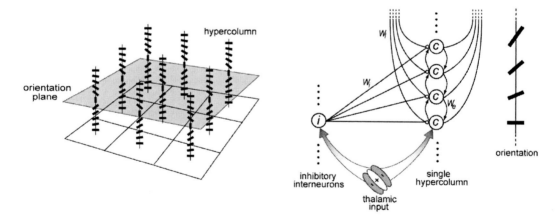

Figure 21. Functional architecture of the visual cortex adopted in the model. The left panel represents the disposition of different hypercolumns. The right panel shows the main synaptic connections used in the model. Each neuron receives a thalamic input, according to an even Gabor function, a feed-forward inhibition from interneurons, confined within the hypercolumn (synapses Wi), a feedback excitation (synapses W_e) which can be confined within the hypercolumn or spread out to other hypercolumns, and long-range inhibition, which in our model is realized via lateral synapses (W_l) but actually should originate from other cortical areas (V2, V3 or MT).

5.2.1. The Geniculate Input

As analyzed in previous sections, cortical cells receive their afferent inputs from cells in the lateral geniculate nucleus. In the present model, we considered a simplified version of these afferents, to realize a "simple-like" feed-forward RF, with a central ON region (excited by light) surrounded by two lateral OFF regions (excited by darkness). Each region is elongated along the same preferred orientation, and is reproduced using a Gabor function (Jones and Palmer, 1987a;Jones and Palmer, 1987b).

Hence, by considering a cortical cell whose RF is centred at the position x_c, y_c of the visual input, with preferred orientation ϑ_c, the feed-forward RF assumes the following expression

$$FF(x - x_c, y - y_c, \vartheta_c) = FF_0 \cdot G \cdot \exp\left(\frac{v_1^2}{-2(\sigma_1/\alpha_G)^2}\right) \exp\left(\frac{v_2^2}{-2(\sigma_2/\alpha_G)^2}\right) \cos(2\pi \cdot \alpha_G \cdot f \cdot v_1) \tag{30}$$

where

$$v_1(x - x_c, y - y_c, \vartheta_c) = (x - x_c)\cos\vartheta_c + (y - y_c)\sin\vartheta_c \tag{31}$$

$$v_2(x - x_c, y - y_c, \vartheta_c) = -(x - x_c)\sin\vartheta_c + (y - y_c)\cos\vartheta_c \tag{32}$$

Equation 30 represents the Gabor function; Eqs. 31 and 32 describe a rotation of the RF by an angle θ_c around the central point of coordinate (x_c, y_c). x, y represent a generic coordinate in the input image, $(\sigma_1/\alpha_G)^2$ and $(\sigma_2/\alpha_G)^2$ are spatial variances, which establish the dimension of the RF in the preferred and non-preferred orientations, and $f \cdot \alpha_G$ is a spatial frequency, which determines the width of the ON and OFF subregions. Hence, both the dimensions of the RF, and the spatial frequency depend on the parameter α_G. For instance, by doubling α_G, the spatial frequency is doubled, whereas the dimensions of the RF are halved in both directions (this aspect will be described in depth in section 8). Parameter G (also discussed in section 8) represents a multiplicative factor for the gain of the Gabor function FF_0. In first instance we use $G = \alpha_G = 1$.

Parameters G and α_G have been introduced to account for the presence of different spatial frequency channels, as will be described in Section 8.

Starting from Eqs. 30-32, the geniculate input to the cortical cell (say $g_t(x_c, y_c, \theta_c)$) is obtained, following the same approach provided in Eq. 3, i.e., by performing the inner product of the visual input, $I(x,y)$, and the RF, i.e.,

$$g_t(x_c, y_c, \theta_c) = \left[\iint I(x, y)FF(x - x_c, y - y_c, \theta_c)dxdy\right]^+ \cong \left[\sum_{m=1}^{M}\sum_{n=1}^{N} I(m\Delta x, n\Delta y)FF(m\Delta x - x_c, n\Delta y - y_c, \theta_c)\Delta x\Delta y\right]^+ \tag{33}$$

In Eq. 33 the two-dimensional integral has been approximated with the histogram method, and Δx, Δy represent the dimensions of the single pixel in the input image. N and M are the number of pixels in the horizontal and vertical directions. In this work, input images with 101x101 pixels were used. The symbol []$^+$ denotes the positive part, as in the previous sections.

5.2.2. The Intracortical Synapses

In the model we considered three kinds of intracortical synapses that assume a different role:

    (i) a short-range feed-forward inhibition (synapses $W_i < 0$);
    (ii) a long-range feedback intracortical excitation (synapses $W_e > 0$);
    (iii) a long-range feedback intracortical inhibition (synapses $W_l < 0$).

Synapses at point i) have been already considered in sections 2-4. Synapses at point ii includes both excitation within a hypercolumn, and excitation among different hypercolumns (i.e., among different points in the retina). The first aspect has been already accounted for in sections 2-4, whereas the second represents an extension not considered in those sections. Similarly, long range inhibition is also a new aspect, not considered before.

The three kinds of connections aspire to reproduce the spatial distribution of contextual interactions in V1, according to data reported in Kapadia et al. (1995;2000).Relationships with anatomical data will be discussed in the sections 6.4 and 7.3.

In the following, the general structure of synapses is first presented. Subsequently, each kind of synapse is described and justified in detail.

5.2.2.1. The General Form of Synapses

As a general rule, we assume that the synaptic strengths decrease with the distance between the centres of the RFs of the pre-synaptic and post-synaptic cells. Moreover, we assume that the strength of the synapses also depends on the angle between the preferred orientation of the post-synaptic cell (ϑ_c) and the line connecting the centres of the RFs (see Figure 22). In other words, the strength of synapses may be different along the orientation of the receptive field compared with the orthogonal orientation. This choice implements the co-axial (or trans-axial) specificity principle. Looking at Figure 22, we can write

$$W_j = W_{0,j} \exp\left(\frac{d_\vartheta^2}{-2\sigma_{\vartheta,j}^2}\right) \exp\left(\frac{d_{\vartheta+\pi/2}^2}{-2\sigma_{\vartheta+\pi/2,j}^2}\right) \tag{34}$$

where (see also Figure 22)

$$d = \sqrt{(x_c - x)^2 + (y_c - y)^2} \quad \varphi = arctg\left((y_c - y)/(x_c - x)\right) \tag{35}$$

$$d_\theta = d\cos(\varphi - \vartheta_c) ; \; d_{\vartheta+\pi/2} = d\sin(\varphi - \vartheta_c) \tag{35''}$$

W_j is a generic synapse, φ is the orientation of the line connecting the pre-synaptic and post-synaptic cells and x, y are the coordinates of the pre-synaptic cell. d represents the distance between the centres of the RFs, and d_ϑ, $d_{\vartheta+\pi/2}$ represent the projections along the preferred and non-preferred orientations of the post-synaptic cell. The subscript j indicates the kind of synapse (either $j = i$, e or l for the three types of synapses).

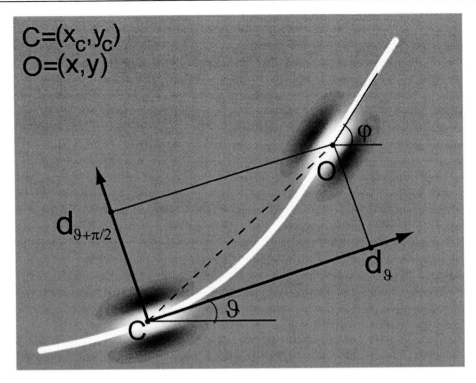

Figure 22. Computation of the horizontal connectivity between a pre-synaptic and a post-synaptic (target) cell, located in two different hypercolumns. The point labelled C represents the centre of receptive field of the target cell, while O represents the position of the receptive field of the pre-synaptic cell. ϑ: preferred orientation of the target cell; φ: orientation of the line connecting the two receptive fields; d: distance between the two receptive fields; d_ϑ and $d_{\vartheta+\pi/2}$: projection of the distance along the preferred and non-preferred directions, respectively.

It is worth noting that the present model does not include self-coupling terms, i.e., a neuron is not connected with itself.

Equation 34 implies that the synaptic strengths decrease with distance according to a classical Gaussian function, with a different variance (σ_ϑ^2 and $\sigma_{\vartheta+\pi/2}^2$) in the preferred and non-preferred directions. Equation 34 applies to all intracortical synapses, but with different choices of parameters σ_ϑ^2 and $\sigma_{\vartheta+\pi/2}^2$, and consider only the *distance between hypercolumns* (i.e., the distance between the centres of the RFs) and implements the axial specificity.

In order to implement the modular specificity, the quantity $W_{0,j}$ in Eq. 34 may not be constant, but may depend on the difference between the orientation preferences of the presynaptic and postsynaptic cells (i.e., the *distance inside the hypercolumn*).

In the following, the maps of the different synapses are described in detail.

5.2.2.2. The Feed-Forward Inhibition

As demonstrated in previous sections, an inhibitory input should be added to the input from relay cells, in order to suppress non-optimal stimuli and to provide contrast invariance: without feed-forward inhibition, in fact, a stimulus with high-contrast but not-optimal orientation would evoke a suprathreshold response, i.e., the width of the orientation tuning curve of cortical neurons would increase with contrast (Troyer et al., 1998;Somers et al., 1995), resulting so named "iceberg effect" (Carandini, 2007). Since synapses from the LGN to the cortex are only excitatory, this inhibition should reach simple cells via intracortical inhibitory interneurons, located in the same hypercolumn or in close hypercolumns. As proposed and analyzed in depth in the previous sections, we adopted an in-phase arrangement for inhibition.

In order to compute the feed-forward inhibitory input to cortical cells, we consider that the interneurons receive just the thalamic input and their output pass through a sigmoidal relationship. By denoting with $\rho(x_i, y_i, \vartheta_i)$ the firing rate of the interneuron at position x_i, y_i and preferred orientation ϑ_i, we have

$$\rho(x_i, y_i, \vartheta_i) = S\left[\left(1 - e^{-2g_t(x_i, y_i, \vartheta_i)/S}\right) \Big/ \left(1 + e^{-2g_t(x_i, y_i, \vartheta_i)/S}\right)\right]^+ \tag{36}$$

where S represents the upper saturation of neural activity, g_t is the geniculate input (Eq. 33) and the symbol $[]^+$ denotes the positive part. According to Eq. 36, the output of an interneuron is equal to the input at low values of excitation, whereas it saturates toward S at high excitation levels.

Starting from Eq. 36, the feed-forward inhibition to the target cell (say $i(x_c, y_c, \vartheta_c)$) is computed as follows:

$$i(x_c, y_c, \vartheta_c) = \sum_{\vartheta_i} \sum_{x_i} \sum_{y_i} W_i\left(x_c, y_c, \vartheta_c, x_i, y_i, \vartheta_i\right) \cdot \rho(x_i, y_i, \vartheta_i) \tag{37}$$

The synaptic link $W_i(x_c, y_c, \vartheta_c, x_h, y_h, \vartheta_h)$ between interneuron and postsynaptic cortical cell shall be described in detail in the following sections, depending on the scenario in which the model is applied.

5.2.2.3. The Feedback Intracortical Excitation

This type of synapses realize a feedback mechanism within the visual cortex, which improves and sharpens the information coming from feed-forward inputs.

The excitatory input to a cortical cell (say $e(x_c, y_c, \vartheta_c)$), coming from all other cells in the model, is computed as follows:

$$e(x_c, y_c, \theta_c) = \sum_{\theta_h} \sum_{x_h} \sum_{y_h} W_e\left(x_c, y_c, \theta_c, x_h, y_h, \theta_h\right) \cdot r(x_h, y_h, \theta_h) \tag{38}$$

where $W_e(x_c, y_c, \vartheta_c, x_h, y_h, \vartheta_h)$ is the strength of the intracortical excitatory synapse (described in detail in the following sections), and the function $r(x, y, \vartheta)$ represents the firing rate (i.e., the output) of a cortical cell (see point 5.2.2.5 below).

5.2.2.4. The Map of the Inhibitory (Long-Range) Synapses

According to various authors (Kapadia et al., 2000;Angelucci et al., 2002;Angelucci and Bullier, 2003) a large weak field of diffuse inhibition is evident in the contextual map of V1 neurons. Recent experimental results suggest that this broad inhibition is not within V1, but originates from neurons in V2, V3 or MT (Angelucci et al., 2002;Angelucci and Bullier, 2003). Since these cortical areas are not included in the present model for the sake of simplicity, long range inhibition was realized by means of intracortical inhibitory synapses (say W_l, with $W_l < 0$), which directly link excitatory cells. Of course, this choice disagrees with physiological knowledge, and was adopted merely to reduce the number of cells in the model, to facilitate computations. Hence, the negative synapses W_l may be considered representative of a possible feedback with cells in V2, V3 or MT: for instance, a bi-synaptic connection from an excitatory cell in V1 to a inhibitory interneuron in V2, and then back from the inhibitory interneuron in V2 to an excitatory cell in another hypercolumn in V1.

Accordingly, the inhibitory input arriving to a cortical cell via these lateral inhibitions (say $l(x_c, y_c, \theta_c)$) is computed as follows:

$$l(x_c, y_c, \theta_c) = \sum_{\theta_h} \sum_{x_h} \sum_{y_h} W_l(x_c, y_c, \theta_c, x_h, y_h, \theta_h) \cdot r(x_h, y_h, \theta_h) \qquad (39)$$

where the meaning of the function $r(x, y, \vartheta)$ is the same as in Eq. 38 and lateral inhibition $W_l(x_c, y_c, \vartheta_c, x_h, y_h, \vartheta_h$) will be described in detail in the following sections depending on the scenario in which the model is applied.

5.2.2.5. The Response of the Cortical Excitatory Cells

Finally, the response of a generic excitatory cortical cell is obtained by computing the sum of its input quantities and passing it through a sigmoidal relationship (similar to Eq. 36) with lower threshold and upper saturation. Moreover, as a consequence of feedback interactions, the activity of a generic cortical cell exhibits time evolution. This is summarized by means of a first-order differential equation with time constant τ.

Hence, we can write:

$$u(x_c, y_c, \theta_c) = g_t(x_c, y_c, \theta_c) + i(x_c, y_c, \theta_c) + e(x_c, y_c, \theta_c) + l(x_c, y_c, \theta_c) \qquad (40)$$

$$\tau \frac{dr(x_c, y_c, \theta_c)}{dt} = -r(x_c, y_c, \theta_c) + S\left[\left(1 - e^{-2u(x_c, y_c, \theta_c)/S}\right)\Big/\left(1 + e^{-2u(x_c, y_c, \theta_c)/S}\right)\right]^+ \qquad (41)$$

where the input quantities g_t, i, e and l are provided by Eqs. 33, 37, 38 and (39), u is the global input to the cortical cell, S is the upper saturation level of cortical cell activity, and τ is the time constant characteristic of the time evolution.

6. Role of Intracortical Circuitry in the Genesis of Complex Cell Behaviour

6.1. Introduction

Cells in the primary visual cortex are usually classified (Hubel and Wiesel, 1962) into two fundamental functional types: i.e., simple and complex. According to this traditional classification, simple cells evoke a response only if a bar with optimal orientation is positioned exactly at the centre of their receptive field and exhibit well segregated ON and OFF subregions. By contrast, complex cells do not exhibit a clear distinction between ON and OFF subregions, and give out a response to an optimally oriented bar independently of its spatial position within the RF. Moreover the simple and complex cells differ in their response to drifting or counterphase gratings, in particular in the temporal modulation of the response(Alonso and Martinez, 1998;Movshon et al., 1978a;Movshon et al., 1978b;Skottun et al., 1991).

However, the arrangement of the intracortical circuitry able to generate this distinction and the specific role of these cells in vision processing are still a matter of debate in the neurophysiologic literature.

Indeed, although the distinction between simple and complex cells is generally well accepted in the literature, several difficulties can be encountered to practical discriminate complex vs. simple cells in a rigorous way. Hence, alternative more quantitative criteria have been suggested: these include quantification of the spontaneous activity level of the cell (Pettigrew et al., 1968), the amplitude of the cells response, the size of the receptive field (Hubel and Wiesel, 1962) (Schiller et al., 1976) the HWHH of orientation selectivity (Heggelund and Albus, 1978;Schiller et al., 1976). Furthermore, other authors proposed to examine the temporal modulation of cell activity in response to drifting or counterphase sinusoidal gratings to discriminate simple vs. complex cells (Alonso and Martinez, 1998;Movshon et al., 1978a;Movshon et al., 1978b;Skottun et al., 1991): the response of simple cells to a drifting grating is characterized by a ratio between amplitude of the first harmonic and mean spike rate activity (F1/F0) greater than 1; by contrast, the response of the complex cells is relatively unmodulated by the sinusoidal component, resulting in a ratio of the first harmonic to a mean level much smaller than 1. Similarly, the response to a counterphase grating (that is, a grating which remains stationary in space, and whose contrast varies sinusoidally in time) is also significantly different in the two cell types: complex cells exhibit a significant second harmonic, i.e., activity of these cells reveals a clear component at twice the frequency of the input grating, whereas the response of simple cells displays just the same frequency as the input sinusoid.

The original hypothesis formulated by Hubel and Wiesel (1962) presumes that simple and complex cells represent two subsequent stages in the vision processing system (that is, two distinct hierarchical levels): the RF of simple cells would be produced by the convergence of thalamic cells aligned along the preferred orientation, whereas the RF of complex cells would derive from the convergence of several simple cells, which share the same orientation preference but whose RF exhibits different positions. Although this hypothesis has received some experimental support recently (Alonso and Martinez, 1998;Martinez and Alonso, 2003), it has also been questioned by various authors (Chance et al., 1999;Tao et al., 2004;Mechler and Ringach, 2002).These assume that simple and complex cells originate from the same basic intracortical circuit, but with different values of some intracortical parameters. For example, Chance et al. (1999), using a simple model of recurrent connections in V1, demonstrated that the same basic feedback intracortical circuit can mimic the temporal modulation of the response both in simple and complex cells: simple cells would be characterized by a low value of intracortical synapses, thus maintaining the basic properties of their input; complex cells would receive strong intracortical synapses, thus showing an emergent property independent of the spatial position of the input.

Despite its evident importance, the model by Chance et al. has some simplifications: all neurons exhibit the same orientation preference and they are parameterized only by their spatial phase and spatial frequency, and so it is not possible to construct a two-dimensional RF. Moreover, the role of intracortical inhibition is not considered. Finally, Chance et al. assumed that input to their neurons is provided by simple cells (as in the classical hierarchical model), whereas recent data suggest that at least some complex cells may receive direct LGN input (Malpeli, 1983;Malpeli et al., 1986;Martinez and Alonso, 2001).

The aim of the present work is to further corroborate the assumption by Chance et al. (1999), by using the model of the visual cortex described in section 5, which incorporates long-range excitatory and inhibitory synapses. For the sake of simplicity, we did not consider neurons with different spatial frequency, assuming, according to Chance et al. (1999), that only neurons with close spatial frequency are connected. Hence, just a single spatial frequency is considered (an extension of the model including more spatial frequency channels is the object of section 8). With this model, we will show that a progressive conversion of cell behaviour from simple to complex can be achieved by changing the strength and/or extension of excitatory intracortical synapses which link different hypercolumns (feedback intracortical excitation, section 5.2.2.3). The difference of complex vs. simple cells in the model is tested not only with respect to the response to drifting and counterphase gratings, but also for what concerns the width of the RF, the independence of the response to position of a bar, and the amplitude and width of the orientation tuning curve.

Finally we will compare predictions of the present model (named "the recurrent model" throughout the present section) with predictions of the classical "hierarchical model". To this end, a hierarchical model was also implemented, assuming that a complex cell originates from the convergence of different simple cells with the same orientation preference but different position in space (neurons belonging to the same orientation plane). The behaviour of the two models was then compared in response to drifting and counterphase gratings, as well as bars with different position in the RF, or drifting grating patches with different sizes, in order to suggest possible experiments able to discriminate between the recurrent and hierarchical mechanisms.

6.2. Intracortical Connectivity

In this section we explicit and describe in details, the arrangement of intracortical synapses for the model described by Eqs. 30-41 presented in section 5.

6.2.1. The Feed-Forward Inhibition

As specified in section 5, in this scenario we assumed that the feed-forward inhibition was confined within the hypercolumn, i.e., it did not involve connections among different hypercolumns. Interactions among different hypercolumns would be adopted for the feedback intracortical excitation and inhibitory (long-range) synapses.

The Eq. 37 is specialized as follows:

$$i(x_c, y_c, \vartheta_c) = \sum_{\theta_i} W_i(\vartheta_c, \vartheta_i) \cdot \rho(x_i, y_i, \vartheta_i) = \sum_{\theta_i} W_{0,i} \cdot \rho(x_i, y_i, \vartheta_i) \qquad (42)$$

where $W_i(\vartheta_c, \vartheta_i)$ denotes the short range inhibitory synapse linking the presynaptic interneuron with orientation preference ϑ_i to the postsynaptic cortical cell with orientation preference ϑ_c, both located in the same hypercolumn (at position (x_c, y_c)). This inhibition exhibits a broad dependence on the orientation difference, $\vartheta_c - \vartheta_i$, of the presynaptic and the post-synaptic cells (Somers et al., 1995;Troyer et al., 1998;Ursino and La Cara, 2004b). This assumption is further supported by the observation that the response to a grating of optimal orientation was suppressed by a second non-optimally oriented grating, and this inhibition was quite similar in magnitude for all orientations of the superimposed grating (DeAngelis et al., 1992) (see section 2.3 and 7.4). Hence, for the sake of simplicity we further simplify the model and assume that inhibitory synapses from interneurons are independent of the orientation difference. Hence, the term W_i in the present model is assumed to be constant and equal $W_{0,i}$. In Eq. 42 the term $\rho(x,y,\vartheta)$ represents the firing rate of interneuron at position (x,y) with preferred orientation ϑ, as described in section 5.2.2.2.

6.2.2. The Feedback Intracortical Excitation

According to several experimental studies (Field et al., 1993;Gilbert and Wiesel, 1989;Kapadia et al., 1995), we assumed the excitatory synaptic strength decreases with the difference in the orientation preference between the pre-synaptic and the post-synaptic neurons, i.e., synapses may link only intracortical neurons which share similar orientation preference. Furthermore, we assumed that the synaptic strength decreases with the distance between the centres of the RFs of the pre-synaptic and post-synaptic cells, i.e., with the distance d between hypercolumns in an isotropic way (see Eqs 35' and 35''). Hence, we can write:

$$W_e(x_c, y_c, \vartheta_c, x_h, y_h, \vartheta_h) = W_{0,e} \exp\left(\frac{(\vartheta_c - \vartheta_h)^2}{-2\sigma_{\Delta\vartheta,e}^2}\right) \cdot \exp\left(\frac{d^2}{-2\sigma_{d,e}^2}\right) \tag{43}$$

where $W_{0,e}$ is a constant parameter and $\sigma_{\Delta\vartheta,e}^2$, $\sigma_{d,e}^2$ are the variances describing the fall in connectivity with orientation difference and with spatial distance, respectively. Equation 43 takes the place of Eq. 38 providing a complete description for excitatory input to cortical cell. It is worth-noting that, at $d = 0$ (i.e., within the same hypercolumn), Eq. 43 provides the same excitatory pattern used in sections 2-4.

6.2.3. The Map of the Long-Range Inhibitory Synapses

According to Kapadia et al. (2000) we assumed that this inhibition has no specific arrangement, either in the visual space or within the hypercolumn. The only characteristic is a decrease with distance in the visual space (see Figure 29, column b). Intracortical inhibitory synapses obey to Eq. 34, but with $\sigma_\vartheta^2 = \sigma_{\vartheta+\pi/2}^2 = \sigma^2$. Hence:

$$W_i(x_c, y_c, \theta_c, x_h, y_h, \theta_h) = W_{0,i} \exp\left(-d^2/\sigma_i^2\right) \tag{44}$$

where $W_{0,i} < 0$ and d the distance between hypercolumns.

According to physiological knowledge, feedback inhibitory input should reach the cortical cells via additional inhibitory interneurons (basket cells). It is worth noting that, in the present study, we did not use inhibitory interneurons to realize long-range inhibition, but assumed that inhibitory synapses come directly from excitatory neurons (see section 5.2.2.4). The negative synapses W_l must be considered representative of a bi-synaptic connection: from the excitatory neuron to a cortical inhibitory interneuron (which is not explicitly described in the model) and then to excitatory cells.

Equation 44 takes place in Eq. 39 providing a complete description for lateral inhibitory input to cortical cell.

6.3. The Hierarchical Model

An important objective of this section is to discriminate the present (recurrent) model from the classical hierarchical model on the basis of the respective output responses. This analysis may be useful to design new ad hoc experiments, able to validate the models and distinguish among them.

To this end, in the present section we implemented a classical hierarchical model too. In the hierarchical model Eqs. 30-41 are used to build a layer of simple cells with different positions and orientation preference (it is worth noting that simple cells are constructed by assuming negligible long-range connections in the previous equations). The output from simple cells, which belong to the same orientation plane (i.e., all simple cells which share the same preferred orientation), is sent to a cell at a subsequent hierarchical level via excitatory synapses. These excitatory synapses were chosen according to a Gaussian function with the same standard deviation in both directions. Finally, the response of the complex cell exhibits the same sigmoidal non-linearity (with lower threshold and upper saturation) as in Eqs 37 and 41 (see Figure 23).

These aspects are described via the following equations:

$$u(x_c, y_c, \vartheta) = \sum_{x_h} \sum_{y_h} W_c(x_c, y_c, x_h, y_h) \cdot r(x_h, y_h, \vartheta) \tag{45}$$

$$W_c(x_c, y_c, x_h, y_h) = W_{0,c} \exp\!\left(-d^2/\sigma_c^2\right) \tag{46}$$

$$r_c(x_c, y_c, \vartheta) = S\left[\left(1 - e^{-2u(x_c, y_c, \vartheta)/S}\right)\!/\!\left(1 + e^{-2u(x_c, y_c, \vartheta)/S}\right)\right]^+ \tag{47}$$

where $r_c(x_c, y_c, \vartheta)$ is the output of a complex cell at the second hierarchical level, $W_{0,c}$ sets the strength of synapses, σ_c is the spatial standard deviation, and d is the spatial distance between the presynaptic and postsynaptic cells (Eqs. 35). The output of simple cells, $r(x_h, y_h)$, is obtained assuming negligible long-range connections.

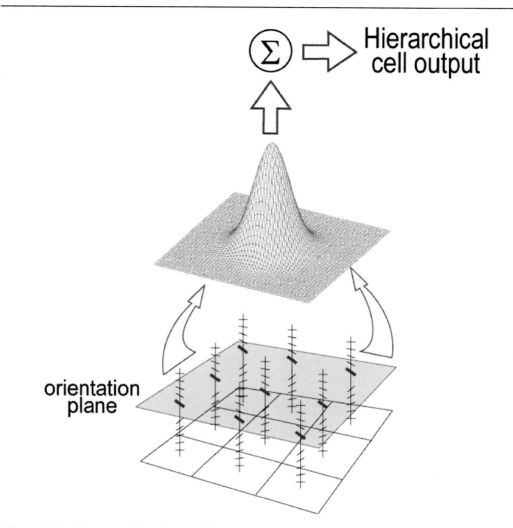

Figure 23. Architecture of the classical hierarchical model. All Simple cells with different positions in the same orientation plane (i.e., all simple cells which share the same preferred orientation) send theirs output to a cell at a subsequent hierarchical level via excitatory synapses. The excitatory synapses were chosen according to a Gaussian function with the same standard deviation in both directions.

6.4. Parameter Assignment

Parameters in the model in basal conditions were given on the basis of various complementary criteria:

(1) *Lateral geniculate input* - Parameters which describe the classic RF of V1 simple cells were given as defined in Section 5.2.1. Since a large variability of results is obtained experimentally, the present parameters are just within the range of values reported in the literature. In particular, in this section just a single value of spatial frequency f is used.

(2) *Cortical cell saturation and dynamics* - The value of saturation S for cortical cell activity (50 spikes/s) agrees with values reported by several authors (Somers et al., 1995;Skottun et al., 1991) although a large variability can be found in the literature regarding this parameter. The time constant has been chosen as defined in section 5.2.2.5.

(3) *Feed-forward short-range intracortical inhibition* - The strength of the feed-forward inhibition (i.e., the constant parameter $W_{0,i}$ in Eq. 42) was given to ensure contrast invariance of the orientation tuning curve.

(4) *Intracortical excitation* - A value to the parameter which represents the fall in excitatory connectivity with orientation difference (i.e., $\sigma_{\Delta\vartheta,e}$ in Eq. 43) was given according to data reported in (Field et al., 1993;Kapadia et al., 1995). These data suggest that the connection falls close to zero if orientation difference is greater than 40-60 deg. Since a Gaussian function is close to zero after two-three standard deviations, we have $\sigma_{\Delta\vartheta,e} = 22.5\,\mathrm{deg}$. The parameter which represents the fall of connectivity with spatial distance (i.e., $\sigma_{d,e}$ in Eq. 43) was given different values, to mimic a progressive shift from simple to complex cells. The value is taken close to zero as to simple cells, to mimic the absence of interactions among hypercolumns. A basal value for complex cells was assigned assuming that horizontal excitatory connections extend by about 1 deg, which is within the range of lateral excitatory connections in V1 (Angelucci and Bullier, 2003;Angelucci et al., 2002;Gilbert and Wiesel, 1989;Kapadia et al., 2000;Chance et al., 1999;Kisvarday et al., 2000).

(5) Finally, the strength of excitation ($W_{0,e}$ in Eq. 43) was given to obtain a pattern of orientation tuning curve (both regarding orientation half width at half height, and maximum activity) in agreement with physiological data (Henry, 1985;Skottun et al., 1987).

(6) *Isotropic long-range inhibition* – The parameter which establishes the extension of surrounding inhibition in complex cells (i.e., σ_l in Eq. 44) was given according to data reported in (Angelucci and Bullier, 2003;Angelucci et al., 2002;Kapadia et al., 2000). These authors suggest that long-range inhibition can extend for several degrees. The strength of this suppression (i.e., parameter $W_{0,l}$ in Eq. 44) was given a low value, assuming that this isotropic suppression is weak. This value was chosen just to guarantee stability of the network, i.e., to avoid instability due to excitatory recurrent connections among neurons.

(7) *Hierarchical model* – The strength of the synapses which link the first to the second layer in the hierarchical model (i.e., parameter $W_{0,c}$ in Eq. 46) was given to ensure that the average responses to a drifting grating with moderate contrast (25%), in the hierarchical and recurrent models, were comparable (34-35 spikes/s). The standard deviation of the synapses (i.e., parameter σ_c in Eq. 46) was given to have a dimension of the RF for the complex cell in the hierarchical model, computed with a bar, similar to that of the recurrent model.

The basal values of parameters can be found in Table 2.

Table 2. Parameters for the models presented in Section 6 (the first 6 rows of the table provide a set of basal parameters used through Sections 6, 7 and 8)

FF_0	180	
σ_1	0.42	deg
σ_2	0.6	deg
f	1.2	cyc/deg
S	50	spikes/sec
τ	3	ms
Feed-forward inhibition		
$W_{0,i}$	-0.15625	
Basal parameters for type I (SIMPLE) cells		
Excitatory intracortical synapses		
$W_{0,e}$	0.04	
$\sigma_{d,e}$	0.03	deg
$\sigma_{\Delta\vartheta,e}$	22.5	deg
Inhibitory long-range synapses		
$W_{0,l}$	$-3.125 \cdot 10^{-5}$	
σ_l	0.03	deg
Parameters for Receptive Field of HIERARCHICAL COMPLEX cells		
$W_{0,c}$	1/300	
σ_c	1.5	deg
Basal parameters for type II (COMPLEX) cells		
Excitatory intracortical synapses		
$W_{0,e}$	0.04	
$\sigma_{d,e}$	0.4	deg
$\sigma_{\Delta\vartheta,e}$	22.5	deg
$W_{0,l}$	$-3.125 \cdot 10^{-5}$	
σ_l	4	deg

6.5. Results

6.5.1. Differences between Simple and Complex Cells in the Recurrent Model

The first simulations were performed to assess the RFs, orientation tuning curves, and the response to drifting and counterphase gratings obtained with the model using two different sets of parameters for the synapses:

(a) type I (simple cells) – In order to simulate the behaviour of simple cells, we assumed that synapses (both excitatory and inhibitory) linking different hypercolumns were negligible. This condition was achieved by giving very small values to standard deviations $\sigma_{d,e} = \sigma_l = 0.03$ deg. According to Eqs 43 and 44, with these values synapses W_e and W_l were close to zero at the distance ($d = 0.2$ deg) between two proximal hypercolumns in the model.

(b) type II (complex cells) - In order to simulate the behaviour of a complex cell, we assumed a value $\sigma_{d,e} = 0.4\,\text{deg}$ in Eq. 43 and $\sigma_l = 4\,\text{deg}$ in Eq. 44, to establish synapses among hypercolumns. These values provide a map of horizontal excitation extending by about 1 deg and a map of long range suppression extending by 8-10 deg. These dimensions agree with data reported in (Angelucci et al., 2002;Angelucci and Bullier, 2003;Gilbert and Wiesel, 1989;Kapadia et al., 2000;Kisvarday et al., 2000) (see also "parameter assignment).

Figure 24 shows the results obtained by using a light bar (length 3 deg, width 0.1 deg) as input to the model, positioned at the central point of the network and rotated to simulate all possible orientations. The panels a show the orientation tuning curves in the two cases of simple and complex cells. The two curves are compared with experimental data from Henry (1985). The complex cell maintains orientation preference, but with a reduced orientation selectivity. In these simulations the half width at half height (HWHH) of the orientation curve is about 19 deg in the simple cell, but rises to about 29 deg in the complex one. These results also agree with observations by others (Skottun et al., 1991).

The panels b of Figure 24 show a plot of the RF. This was obtained by applying the vertical bar at the central point of the image, and computing the response of all neurons in different hypercolumns with vertical optimal orientation. By way of comparison, two experimental RFs (taken from (DeAngelis et al., 1995)) are plotted in the panels c). As it is clear from these figures, the RF of the type I cells exhibits the typical characteristic of simple cell RF. By contrast, the RF of type II cells is larger, without a clear distinction between ON and OFF subregions, and responds to the bar independently of a shift by 1-2 deg. The latter result means that the cell is not selective to the spatial phase.

The temporal responses of the two types of cells to optimally oriented drifting and counterphase gratings, at 100% contrast, are shown in Figure 25 a. The zero phase of the counterphase grating is exactly positioned at the centre of the RF and the cell is strongly activated and works close to its saturation (50 Hz).

In the case of type I cells (upper panels), the response to both drifting and counterphase gratings are highly modulated by the first harmonic, i.e., the ratio between the amplitude of the first harmonic and the mean level (F_1/F_0) is higher than 1. By contrast, the response of the type II cells is dominated by the mean value (the ratio F_1/F_0 is lower than 1). Moreover, in the type II cell the response to a counterphase grating reveals a significant second harmonic which is almost absent in the response of type I cells.

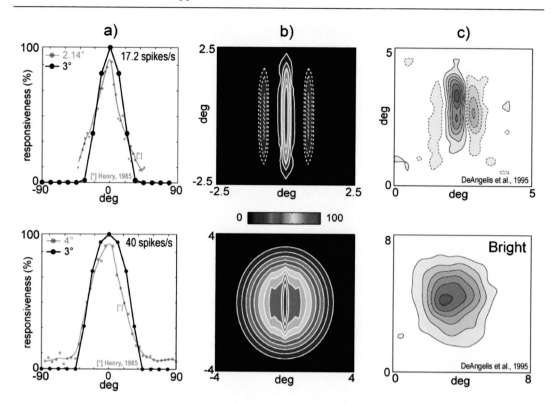

Figure 24. Comparison between model simulation results obtained with application of bars, and experimental data. The upper rows refer to type I cells (simple cells); the bottom rows to type II cells (complex cells).*Panels a)* orientation tuning curves simulated with the model (black thick line) by applying a bar (length 3 deg, width 0.1 deg) with vertical orientation, and computing the response of all neurons in the hypercolumn. The x-axis represents the orientation preference, the y-axis the activity of the cells, normalized to the peak value. By way of comparison, experimental results by Henry (1985) are shown as grey lines. *Panels b)* show an example of the RF. The figure was obtained by applying a bar, with vertical orientation, at the central point of the visual space, and computing the response of all neurons in different hypercolumns with vertical optimal orientation. Due to the symmetry of synapses, this figure can be interpreted equally well as the response of the central neuron, with vertical optimal orientation, to a vertical bar moved at different points of the visual space. *Panels c)* show two examples of RFs observed experimentally, in simple and complex cells (DeAngelis et al., 1995).

To better appreciate the temporal modulation, it is interesting to observe the activity of type II neurons with sub-optimal orientations, i.e. ± 11.25 and ± 22.5 deg (Figure 25 b), which exhibit reduced activity, but reveal an increased modulation by the second harmonic (i.e., the ratio of the second harmonic to the first harmonic, F_2/F_1, increases at the border of the orientation tuning curve). Cells, whose optimal orientation is far from 0 deg (range ±33.75 ÷ ±90 deg), exhibit a null response. Moreover, if we observe the response of cells in the same hypercolumn at optimal spatial position, but in response to a counterphase grating with only 20% contrast (Figure 25 c), the average activity is reduced, and temporal modulation by the second harmonic becomes much more evident. A similar behaviour is appreciable from cells in a different hypercolumn, whose RFs are not exactly centred in the region of maximal luminance: they exhibit reduced activity, but the ratio F_2/F_1 increases (see (Ursino and La Cara, 2005)).

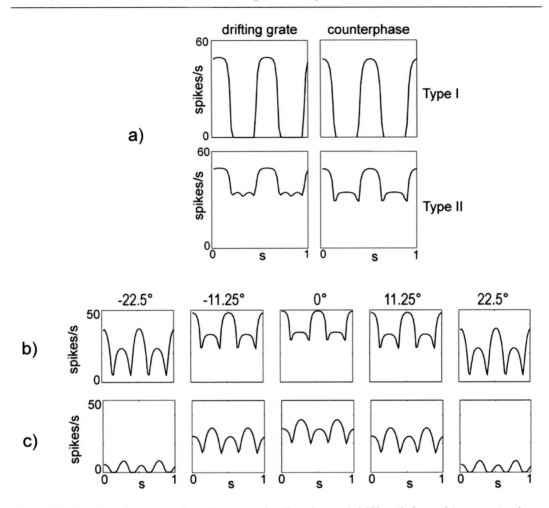

Figure 25. *Panels a)* Response of a cell to an optimally orientated drifting (left panels) or counterphase (right panels) grating with contrast 100%. The upper panel reports the response of type I cell (simple cell), the bottom panels the response of a type II cell (complex cell). The spatial frequency of gratings is 1.2 cyc/deg, temporal frequency 2 Hz. *Panels b)* Response of type II cells (complex cells) belonging to the same hypercolumn to a vertical counterphase grating with 100% contrast. The hypercolumn is positioned in the zone of maximal/minimal luminance. The response of cells with optimal orientation greater than 30 deg is close to zero, hence it is not shown. It is worth noting the increase in the ratio F2/F1 in response to a counterphase grating for cells with sub-optimal orientation preference (i.e., cells located at the boundary of the orientation tuning curve of Figure 24). The spatial frequency of gratings is 1.2 cyc/deg, temporal frequency 2 Hz. *Panels c)* Response of cells in the same hypercolumn as in the panels b) (optimal spatial position) in response to a counterphase grating with only 20% contrast. It is worth noting that, the lower the average activity of the cell the more evident the temporal modulation by the second harmonic.

In conclusion, type II cells exhibit an evident temporal modulation, with a marked contribution by the second harmonic, in conditions of reduced activity far from saturation. In order to better unmask the role of excitatory lateral synapses in the genesis of complex cell behaviour, in a subsequent set of simulations we performed a sensitivity analysis in type II cells, first on the parameter $\sigma_{d,e}$ which establishes the spatial extension of these synapses (Figure 26), and then on parameter $W_{o,e}$, which sets the synaptic strength (Figure 27).

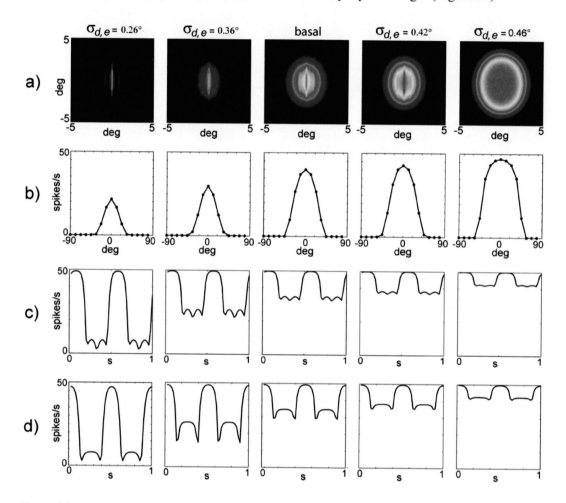

Figure 26. Sensitivity analysis on parameter $\sigma_{d,e}$ (i.e., on the extension of excitatory synapses among different hypercolumns) in the case of type II cells (complex cells). The first row (a) shows the receptive field at different values of $\sigma_{d,e}$. The second row (b) shows the orientation tuning curves computed with application of a vertical bar (the same as in Figure 24). The third (c) and fourth (d) rows show the temporal response of an optimally oriented neuron to application of a drifting grating and of a counterphase grating, respectively (the same as in Figure 25). It is worth noting that the cell shifts from simple to complex by increasing the parameter value, and that an abrupt change occurs around the value $\sigma_{d,e} = 0.36 \deg$.

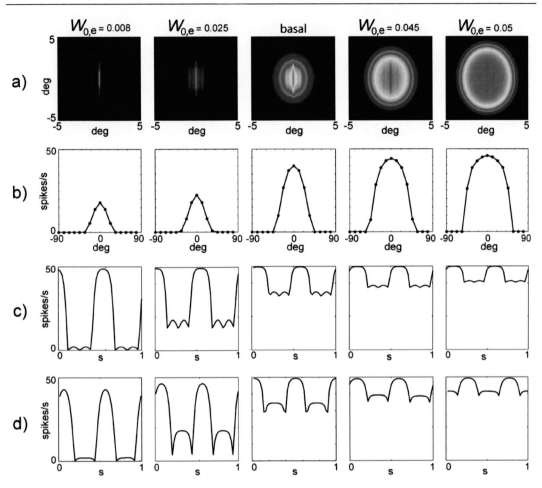

Figure 27. Sensitivity analysis on parameter $W_{0,e}$ (i.e., on the strength of excitation, confined within the hypercolumn) in the case of type I cells (simple cells). The figure shows the orientation tuning curve, computed with application of a light bar, at different values of parameter $W_{0,e}$. In case of very high values of synapses ($W_{0,e} = 2.5$) a certain enlargement of the orientation curve can be counteracted by increasing feed-forward inhibition (i.e., raising parameter $W_{0,i}$). The meaning and disposition of the panels is the same as in Figure 26.

Figure 26 shows the RF obtained with optimally oriented bars (first row), the orientation tuning curve obtained with bars of different orientations (second row), and the temporal response to drifting (third row) and counterphase (fourth row) gratings at different values of $\sigma_{d,e}$. The width of the RF, the amplitude of the response and the ratio F_1/F_0 all increase monotonically with $\sigma_{d,e}$. An acceptable independence of spatial phase is achieved for values of $\sigma_{d,e} > 0.36$ deg. This can be considered as a boundary value between a behaviour more similar to that of a simple cell, and a behaviour more similar to that of a complex cell. The response to a counterphase grating exhibits a marked second harmonic component especially at values of $\sigma_{d,e} \cong 0.36 \deg$.

The results obtained by changing the synaptic strength, $W_{0,e}$ (Figure 27) were quite similar. It is worth noting that a small change in this parameter, around 0.04, caused a significant increase in the RF size and in cell activity.

A sensitivity analysis for $W_{0,e}$ has also been executed in type I cells. The rational is that, in the previous simulations, complex cells received a greater amount of synapses compared with simple cells. By contrast, recent development theories suggest that the number of excitatory synapses to a cell is quite constant [see (Miller, 1996;Miller and MacKay, 1994)]. The sensitivity analysis suggests that increasing the strength of synapses to a simple cell does not modify the orientation selectivity (i.e., the HWHH) in response to a light bar, but just increases the maximal activity. Moreover, the shape and extension of the RF is also unaffected (unpublished simulations).

6.5.2. Comparison between the Recurrent and the Hierarchical Model

In order to compare the two models, we performed various simulation trials, using both drifting and counterphase gratings, as well as optimally oriented bars. In the following, the output response of the two models is shown, to underline the main differences.

1) *Response to large gratings* – Figure 28 (upper panels) compares the response of the two models to drifting and counterphase gratings with 25% contrast (to warrant both models work in their linear region and provide similar average response to drifting gratings). Results show that the response of the *hierarchical model* to a drifting grating is quite constant with only negligible residuals from the first harmonic (i.e., the ratio F_1/F_0 is close to zero). The response to a counterphase grating exhibits only the component at twice the frequency of the input grating (i.e., $F_1 << F_2$, with a suppression of the first harmonic). Moreover, the average response to a counterphase grating is significantly smaller than the average response to a drifting grating (16 spikes/s vs 35 spikes/s), due to the presence of significant minima in the temporal pattern.

By contrast, in the *recurrent model* the ratio F_1/F_0 with drifting grating is clearly greater than 0 (although less than 1), i.e., we can observe a significant residual from the first harmonic. The response to a counterphase grating also exhibits a significant first harmonic, together with the clear presence of the second harmonics at twice the fundamental frequency. The differences between the first and second harmonic are especially evident in the maxima of the temporal patterns. The average response to the counterphase grating is only moderately reduced compared with the average response to drifting grating, since minima are less accentuated.

2) *Response to optimally oriented bars* – Figure 28 (lower panels) depicts the temporal response to an optimally oriented bar (maximal luminance 200% of the background) in the two models. Two different inputs are considered for each model: a bar placed at the centre of the RF of the complex cell, and a bar placed at a distal portion of the RF (about 1.5 deg from centre). Two aspects deserve attention. First, the final response to the central bar in the recurrent model (about 41 spikes/s) is stronger than the response to the same bar in the hierarchical model (about 13.5 spikes/s), although the two models have comparable average responses to a drifting grating. In other words, the bar is less effective at inducing a response compared to the grating in the hierarchical model, whereas this "loss of effectiveness" is not manifest in the recurrent model. The second fundamental aspect of the response to a bar concerns its temporal dynamic. In the hierarchical model the response of the complex cell to a bar exhibits the same dynamic, independently of whether the bar is applied at the centre or at

the periphery of the RF (a possible time lag induced by the synaptic link from the first to the second hierarchical level, not included in our model, should delay both responses in a similar way). By contrast, in the recurrent model the response to a bar placed at the centre of the RF is much prompter than the response to a peripheral bar (settling time as short as 30 ms vs. more than 75 ms).

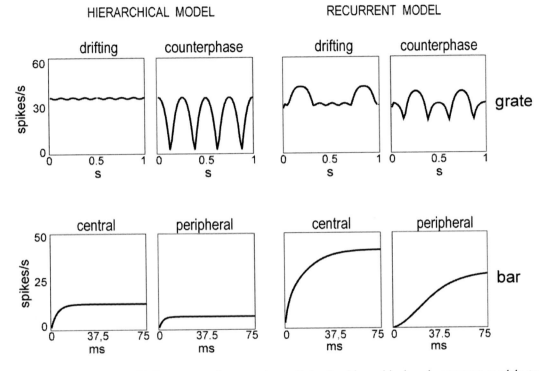

Figure 28. *Upper panels)* Response of a complex cell in the hierarchical and recurrent models to drifting and counterphase gratings with 25% contrast and optimal orientation. The spatial frequency of the grating was 1.2 cyc/deg, the temporal frequency was 2 Hz.. *Bottom panels)* Temporal response of a complex cell in the hierarchical and recurrent models to an optimally oriented bar (luminance 200% of the background). The bar width was 0.1 deg, its length was 3 deg. The bar was applied at the instant t = 0 s, starting from a condition of uniform luminance. Two different inputs are considered: a bar applied at the centre of the receptive field of the complex cell and a bar applied at the periphery of the RF (1.5 deg from the centre).

The latter results are a consequence of the intracortical feedback working in the recurrent model. In fact, the initial response to a bar, induced by the feed-forward from the LGN to the cortex, is amplified by long-range intracortical excitatory synapses. This amplification makes the response to a bar almost as effective as the response to grating. Moreover, this "amplification" requires more time for a peripheral bar, since excitation must propagate across a longer distance, from the periphery to the centre of the RF. These results suggest that the two theories for the generation of complex cells (recurrent and feedforward) could be discriminated quite easily on the basis of "ad hoc" experiments.

7. Contextual Interactions and Contour Detection

7.1. Introduction

Simple cells in the primary visual cortex, due to the elongated receptive fields (and their optimal response to optimally oriented edges or bars), are classically defined as "edge detector". It is generally assumed that contours can "pop out" from noisy environment if they satisfy some Gestalt (Koffka, 1935;Wertheimer, 1938) psychology criteria, which govern the organization of perception: among the others the contiguity and continuity criteria: if successive elements in the contour are closed together and share similar orientations they are perceived as a global entity.

In this context the contextual influences (see also section 5) assume the following meaning: a V1 neuron, excited by an optimally oriented bar within its RF, receives facilitation by a second bar located proximally but outside its RF. The second bar, however, must be aligned with the RF and exhibit similar dependency on orientation (Ito and Gilbert, 1999;Kapadia et al., 1995;Kapadia et al., 2000;Allman et al., 1985). A bar which does not satisfy these criteria may cause inhibition instead of facilitation (Kapadia et al., 1995;Nelson and Frost, 1985). The contextual influences have been implicated in contour saliency (Field et al., 1993;Kapadia et al., 1995;Wertheimer, 1938). The problem has been analyzed by several mathematical models supporting the idea that detection of boundaries between regions and extraction of smooth contours are fundamental tasks performed by V1 cells (Grossberg and Mingolla, 1985;Yen and Finkel, 1998;Ursino and La Cara, 2004a). Other models (Li, 1999b;Li, 1999a;Thielscher and Neumann, 2006;de Brecht and Saiki, 2006) exploit similar mechanisms to pop-out targets against background.

Various recent physiological studies provide indications on the possible spatial arrangement of the facilitatory synapses. Field et al.(1993) observed that detection of a contour depends primarily on the relative orientation of its elements (continuity Gestalt rule), and suggested the existence of an "association field" linking neurons proximally located and with close orientation preference (see also (Rockland and Lund, 1983;Ts'o et al., 1986;Gilbert and Wiesel, 1989)). This property has also been named "modular specificity" (Shouval et al., 2000).

A second important property of excitatory synapses, named "axial specificity", implicates that two neurons are connected by excitatory synapses only if their RFs are approximately displaced along an axis in visual space which correspond to the preferred orientation (Schmidt et al., 1997;Shouval et al., 2000). This property implies that the response of a neuron to an optimally oriented bar is facilitated by a collinear bar placed outside its RF (Nelson and Frost, 1985;Polat and Sagi, 1993). This effect decreases with the distance between the RFs (Polat and Sagi, 1993;Polat and Sagi, 1994;Kapadia et al., 1995;Kapadia et al., 2000) and with the misalignments between the preferred orientations (Kapadia et al., 1995).

Besides the facilitatory influences mentioned above, inhibitory surrounding effects have also been demonstrated for V1 neurons (Hubel and Wiesel, 1965;Bishop et al., 1973;Li and Li, 1994). These inhibitory effects are especially located in regions orthogonal to the RF, although a large weaker field of diffuse isotropic inhibition is also well evident (Kapadia et al., 2000). While the excitatory links are thought to play a role in the contextual "pop out" of smooth contours, inhibitory synapses may be important for noise suppression and to avoid the propagation of uncontrolled excitation in the network, i.e., instability.

Recent models exploit the presence of co-axial excitatory connections, including some kind of modular and axial specificity to emphasize smooth contours, while an inhibitory normalization rule obliges the network to converge (Yen and Finkel, 1998;Li, 1998;Pettet et al., 1998). These models are able to simulate various psychophysical and physiological effects, and succeed in identifying and enhancing salient contours. The models by Yen and Finkel (1998) and Li (1998) use both oscillatory neurons, which synchronize over a fast time scale, to represent contours, but differ as the disposition for intracortical synapses: Li assumes that cells with orthogonal preferred orientation are connected by inhibitory synapses, whereas Yen and Finkel assume a facilitatory connection, that they call "tran-axial", between orthogonal cells. By contrast vanRullen et al. (2001) realized contour integration using spike generating neurons and feed-forward mechanisms, avoiding iterative feedback mechanisms.

A recent model was developed by Ross et al. (2000), based on a previous sketch of possible intracortical circuits provided by Grossberg et al. (1997). This is probably the most sophisticated and advanced model of perceptual grouping presently available. However, it differs from the others, and from the present one, since the focus is on the laminar organization of the visual cortex, including interlaminar cortical circuits, a corticogeniculate feedback and the cortical area V2.

However, none of the previous models investigated the effect of changes in excitatory and inhibitory synapses on contour saliency. In particular, some models emphasize just feedback (Yen and Finkel, 1998;Pettet et al., 1998;Li, 1998) or feed-forward (vanRullen et al., 2001), without caring the concurrent action of the two mechanisms and also assume that cells extract orientation without a spatial description of their RF (Yen and Finkel, 1998). A further problem, raised by vanRullen et al. (2001), concerns the time required for a feedback mechanism to converge. Is this time compatible with psychological results on object recognition? How feedback and feed-forward mechanisms participate in this process?

In this section we present a model of contour enhancement in V1, based on recent physiological data, which overcomes some of the limitations mentioned above and aspires to analyze the previous problems. The model represents a further realization of the generic schema presented in section 5. The model implements both a feed-forward, which sets an initial enhancement, and a feedback intracortical which exploit a narrow coaxial excitation but a broader non-axial inhibition. Simulations are aimed at investigating how feed-forward and feedback synapses may affect the characteristics of extracted contours and influence the convergence time. The results may be useful to provide indications on the possible mechanisms (feed-forward + feedback) implemented in V1, and may provide useful suggestions for contour extraction tools in artificial vision.

7.2. Intracortical Connectivity

As in section 6.2, in the present section we specify the arrangement of intracortical synapses described by Eqs. 30-41 (section 5) for the particular application of the model.

7.2.1. The Map of Feed-Forward Inhibition

As mentioned in 6.2.1 the feed-forward inhibitory synapses from interneurons are approximately independent of the orientation difference (i.e., $\vartheta_c - \vartheta_i$). As a new rule, here we assume that they depend only on the distance between the hypercolumns (Ursino and La Cara, 2004a;Ursino and La Cara, 2005).

A value to the parameters σ_ϑ^2 and $\sigma_{\vartheta+\pi/2}^2$ in Eq. 34 can be assigned by considering data published by Kapadia et al. (2000). According to these authors, V1 neurons receive a strong inhibitory contextual interaction preferentially along a direction in the visual space orthogonal to the preferred orientation of the post-synaptic cell (i.e., $\sigma_\vartheta^2 < \sigma_{\vartheta+\pi/2}^2$ in Eq. 34). The map is illustrated in Figure 29, panels a. This contextual arrangement, beside warranting contrast invariance of the orientation tuning, also plays a functional role in the contour extraction mechanism: the feed-forward inhibition from interneurons may inhibits the response of cortical cells which have a poorer probability of belonging to a smooth contour.

Hence, in order to compute the feed-forward inhibition to the target cell (say $i(x_c, y_c, \vartheta_c)$), the Eq. 37 shall be specialized as follows:

$$i(x_c, y_c, \vartheta_c) = \sum_{\vartheta_i} \sum_{x_i} \sum_{y_i} W_{0,i} \cdot \exp\left(\frac{-d_\vartheta^2}{2\sigma_{\vartheta,i}^2}\right) \cdot \exp\left(\frac{-d_{\vartheta+\pi/2}^2}{2\sigma_{\vartheta+\pi/2,i}^2}\right) \cdot \rho(x_i, y_i, \vartheta_i) \qquad (48)$$

where $W_{0,i} < 0$ (see Tab.2). and $\rho(x,y,\vartheta)$ represents the firing rate of interneuron at position (x,y) with preferred orientation ϑ, as described in section 5.2.2.2.

7.2.2. The Map of Feedback Intracortical Excitation

According to results reported in various physiological and psycophysical experiments (summarized in the Introduction of the present section), we assume that excitation among cortical cells is maximal if the pre-synaptic cell lies along the preferred orientation of the post-synaptic cell (co-axial specificity). In other words, individual neurons in the cortex receive excitation from other neurons whose RF centre is located along an axis in the visual space that coincides with the preferred orientation (hence, we have $\sigma_\vartheta^2 > \sigma_{\vartheta+\pi/2}^2$ in Eq. 34).

The map is illustrated in Figure 29, panels a, and corresponds to the criterion named "axial specificity" in Shouval et al. (2000).

Moreover, excitatory intracortical synapses also satisfy the second criterion, named "modular specificity" (Shouval et al., 2000). This means that excitatory synapses may link only intracortical neurons which share similar orientation preference; i.e., the synaptic strength decreases with the difference in the orientation preference between the pre-synaptic and the post-synaptic neurons.

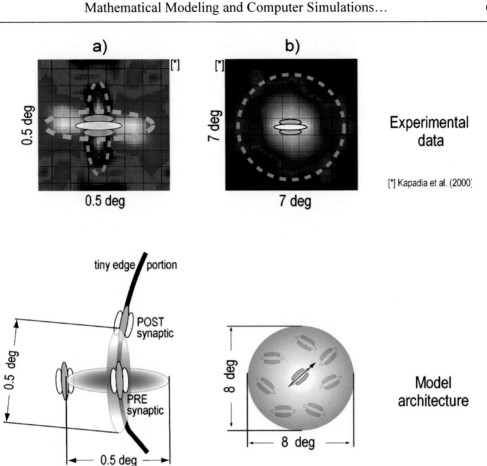

Figure 29. Maps of the intracortical synapses used in the present model (bottom rows), compared with experimental data from (Kapadia et al., 2000) (upper rows). *Panels a) bottom*: map of the intracortical feed-forward inhibitory synapses (W_i) elongated along the orthogonal direction of the target cell, and of the intracortical feedback excitatory synapses (W_e) elongated along the preferred direction of the target cell (co-axial specificity) but also respecting co-modularity specificity (the latter is not shown for the sake of simplicity). *Panels b)*: map of long-range isotropic inhibitory synapses (W_l) which extend for a long distance.

The two previous rules for intracortical excitatory synapses can be summarized by the following equation, which is a particular specialization of Eq. 34.

$$W_e(x_c, y_c, \vartheta_c, x_h, y_h, \vartheta_h) = W_{0,e} \exp\left(\frac{(\vartheta_c - \vartheta_h)^2}{-2\sigma_{\Delta\vartheta,e}^2}\right) \cdot \exp\left(\frac{d_\vartheta^2}{-2\sigma_{\vartheta,e}^2}\right) \exp\left(\frac{d_{\vartheta+\pi/2}^2}{-2\sigma_{\vartheta+\pi/2,e}^2}\right) \qquad (49)$$

where ϑ_c and ϑ_h are the orientation preferences of the post-synaptic and pre-synaptic cells, respectively. The first exponential in the right hand member of Eq. 49 means that the strength of the synapses decreases with the difference of the orientation preference. $\sigma_{\Delta\vartheta,e}^2$ establishes the decrease in the synaptic strength with the difference in the orientation preference. Since these synapses are excitatory, we have $W_{0,e} > 0$.

It is worth noting that Eq. 49 describes both the excitatory connections within an orientation column (i.e., when $\vartheta_c = \vartheta_h$) and the connections within an hypercolumn (i.e., when $d_\vartheta = d_{\vartheta+\pi 2} = 0$). In the first case, Eq. 49 reduces to Eq. 34. In the second case, the synaptic strength decreases exponentially along the hypercolumn, according to experimental evidences (Ferster, 1986).

Equation 49 has a functional role to improve extraction of smooth contours. According to this equation, in fact, excitation is high only among neurons which concur to the formation of a smooth contour, since only in this case both axial and modular specifity rules are simultaneously satisfied. By contrast, neurons which do not concur to the formation of the same smooth contour are linked only by a weak reciprocal excitation.

Hence, the feed-forward excitatory input to the target cortical cell $e(x_c, y_c, \vartheta_c)$, is described by Eq. 38 with the term $W_e(x_c, y_c, \vartheta_c, x_h, y_h, \vartheta_h)$ expressed by Eq. 49 (see Table 3 for parameter values).

7.2.3. The Map of the Inhibitory (Long-Range) Synapses

The inhibitory long-range synapses follows the same approach provided in the previous section 6.2.3 (see Figure 29, panels b). It is worth highlighting that this additional inhibition works to improve noise elimination, by realizing a competitive mechanism among cortical neurons, i.e., neurons which form a smooth contour, and which are mutually excited, through intracortical excitatory synapses, inhibit all other adjacent neurons.

7.2.4. The Response of the Cortical Excitatory Cells

The response of an excitatory cortical cell is obtained by computing the sum of its input quantities and passing it through a sigmoidal relationship with lower threshold and upper saturation, as expressed in section 5.2.2.5 (Eqs 40 and 41). The input quantities g_t, i, e and l are calculated making use of the synaptic specialization expressed in this section.

Finally, the output from the network at position (x_c, y_c), is computed as the sum of all activities in the same hypercolumn. By denoting with $z(x_c, y_c)$ this output, we have

$$z(x_c, y_c) = \sum_{\vartheta_c} r(x_c, y_c, \vartheta_c) \tag{50}$$

7.3. Parameter Assignment

In this section we specify the method to assign parameters only for those cases which are different with respect to the previous model. For what concerns the *Lateral geniculate input (1)*, and the *Cortical cell saturation and dynamics (2)* the parameter assignment follows the rules described in 6.4, in the corresponding sub-section.

For what concerns the *Feed-forward short-range intracortical inhibition (3)*, the *Intracortical excitation (4)* and the *Isotropic long-range inhibition (5)* a description is given in the following

The values to the standard deviations of the synaptic maps linking different hypercolumns (i.e., parameters $\sigma_{\vartheta,j}$ and $\sigma_{\vartheta+\pi/2,j}$ in Eq. 34), with $j = i$, e or l) have been given to mimic results of physiological and psycophysical experiments reported in (Kapadia et al., 2000).

Synapses extension - results of Kapadia et al. (2000) suggest that excitation develops mainly along the preferred direction of the target cell, whereas short-range inhibition is mainly located along the orthogonal direction. Moreover, excitation extends along a distance which is approximately three or four-fold longer than inhibition (see Figs. 5-8 in (Kapadia et al., 2000) and Figure 29 in the present section). The exact value of extension, however, (which describes the range of contextual influences) depends on the eccentricity in the retina. In the case of foveal stimuli, the excitatory map extends for about 0.5 deg in the preferred orientation, while the short range inhibitory map extends for about 0.1-0.2 deg. By contrast, in the near periphery, at an eccentricity of about 4 deg, the excitatory and inhibitory maps have greater extension (about 1 deg and 0.5 deg, respectively). In the present study, we used the standard deviations reported in Table 3. Since the Gaussian function is almost zero after three standard deviations, the excitatory and inhibitory maps in our model extend by about 0.6 deg and 0.15 deg, respectively.

Synapses Strength - It is not easy to assign a numerical value to the strength of the synapses (i.e., to parameters $W_{0,j}$ in Eq. 34)) on the basis of physiological and psychophysical experiments. Only the ratio among these synapses can be approximately deduced. A clear indication is that excitation is stronger than inhibition at short distances, while long range inhibition is even weaker (Kapadia et al., 2000). Hence, a value to these synapses has been given, in accordance with the previous constraint, using an *a posteriori* criterion: More precisely, we chose: i) values for feed-forward inhibitory synapses which warrant an orientation tuning curve in accordance with experimental results; ii) values of feedback synapses which warrant a good contour extraction for some exemplary images, in the presence of wide random noise (see section results).

Table 3. Parameters for the models presented in Section 7 and 8

Feed-forward inhibition		
$W_{0,i}$	-0.08	
$\sigma_{\vartheta,i}$	0.03	deg
$\sigma_{\vartheta+\pi/2,i}$	0.2	deg
Excitatory intracortical synapses		
$W_{0,e}$	0.6	
$\sigma_{\vartheta,e}$	0.2	deg
$\sigma_{\vartheta+\pi/2,e}$	0.05	deg
$\sigma_{\Delta\vartheta,e}$	22.5	deg

Table 3. (Continued)

Coarser scale		
α_G	1	
G	1	
E_m, E_n	20 (10 on Figure 30 and Figure 31)	deg
$\Delta x, \Delta y$	0.2 (0.1 on Figure 30 and Figure 31)	deg
Inhibitory intracortical synapses		
$W_{0,I}$	-0.00125	
σ_I	4	deg
Finer scale		
α_G	5	
G	25	
E_m, E_n	4	deg
$\Delta x, \Delta y$	0.04	deg
Inhibitory intracortical synapses		
$W_{0,I}$	-0.00125	
σ_I	4	deg

For what concerns the isotropic long-range inhibition (the value of which is assigned as in section 6.4 sub-section 5 *"Isotropic long-range inhibition"*), it is worth noting that in this scenario excessive long range inhibition may disrupt proximal contours and, moreover, may be questionable on the basis of anatomical data.

7.4. Results

In order to verify model's capacity to extract contours in the presence of noise, we first used three exemplary images with different geometrical characteristics: i) a square, characterized by only two orientations and sharp corners; ii) a circle, characterized by all orientations without corners; iii) a generic form, which exhibits all possible orientations but with different curvature and rounded corners. In all cases we used images with 50% contrast and superimposed noise. Assuming that $I = 0$ represents the average luminance of the environment, we have $I(x,y) = 0.5 + v_n(x, y)$, in bright regions and $I(x,y) = -0.5 + v_n(x, y)$ in dark regions. v_n is a Gaussian random noise with zero mean value and standard deviation 0.4.

In these first simulations we use a network of 51x51 neurons (N= 51, see section 5). The simulation results are shown in Figure 30. The first column displays the input images; the second column displays network output resulting from the feed-forward input only; the subsequent columns displays the network output at three different steps of the numerical integration, when feedback mechanisms are operating.

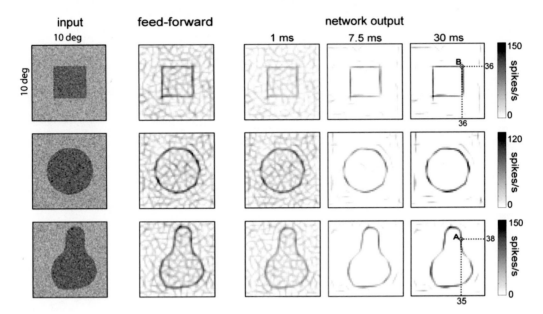

Figure 30. Model response to noisy input images (left column): square, circle and generic form. The original contrast of the images is 0.5 (inner region: I=0.5; external region: I = -0.5). Random noise has a Gaussian distribution with zero mean value and standard deviation 0.4. The second left column represents network outputs (i.e., the quantities $z(x,y)$ in Eq. 50) in response to the feed-forward mechanism only. The panels in the subsequent columns show the time evolution of network's output, for each input, in three time steps during numerical integration (in the last right panels the network is practically in the final equilibrium state).

Results show that the model can extract the contour quite exactly despite the very large amount of noise superimposed on the image. Moreover, the response of the feedback mechanisms converges to a steady state solution in about 30-40 ms.

Examples of the orientation tuning curve of single hypercolumns are shown in Figure 31, together with a representation of the network activity at steady state (after 30 ms); in particular the figure shows the activity of the neurons at position (x,y) for each orientation ϑ. In this space-orientation domain (x,y,ϑ) it is possible to appreciate how the contour extraction is "naturally" accomplished by the network. The coloured segments represent the level activity (in spikes/s) of the neurons revealing contour portions with a particular orientation. Hence, in the case of the square only the neurons responding to 0, 90 and 180 deg (line defining the square contour) have a remarkable activity whereas the others remain silent. In the case of circle, it is possible to appreciate two semi-spirals representing the decomposition of the circle contour along the orientation ϑ (depending on the visual space position (x,y)).

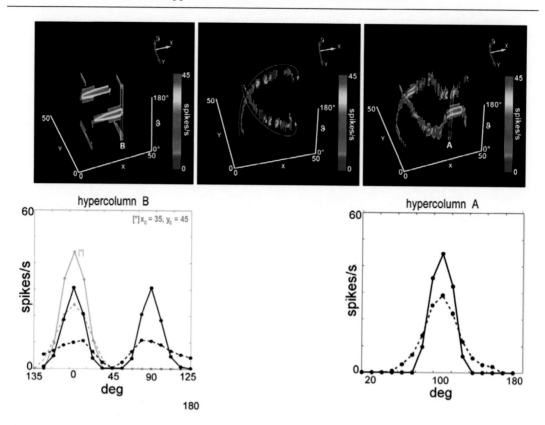

Figure 31. Examples of neurons responses in different hypercolumns, in the three cases of Figure 30. *Upper panels*: representation of the network activity for each neurons in position *(x,y)* with preferred orientation ϑ (domain *x,y, ϑ*). The coloured segments represent the activity (in spikes/s) of the neurons which reveal contour portions with a particular orientation. In the square image (upper left panel) activity is only confined close to orientations 0 deg and 90 deg. In the "circle" input (upper middle panel), two semi-spirals representing the decomposition of circle contour along the orientation ϑ are visible. More complex orientation patterns emerge from the "general figure" (upper right panel). *Lower panels*: Orientation tuning curves corresponding to hypercolumns A e B. Two hypercolumns are considered (labelled A at position (x_c=35, y_c=38) in "generic form", labelled B at position (x_c=36, y_c=36) in "square"). The dashed-line is the curve resulting from the feed-forward mechanisms only. The continuous line is the final effect of feedback mechanisms. For "square" input, two tuning curves are compared: one responding to two simultaneous edges (labelled B), with orientation 0 and 90 deg, and one responding only to a vertical edge (0 deg, position x_c= 35 y_c=45). In this figure one can appreciate the suppression of neuron response to two edges compared with the response to a single optimal stimulus (suppression by non optimal stimuli).

In the case of generic form, the active neurons through the contour follow a more complicated distribution vs. the orientation. However, if this graph is seen along ϑ (z-axis) it is possible to observe the contour of the generic form (as in the case of the square and the circle), in a planar way such as shown in Figure 30 (quantity *z(x,y)*, Eq. 50).

In this 3D representation the point A (position x_c = 35, y_c = 38 in generic form) and B (position x_c = 36, y_c = 36 in the square) highlighted in Figure 30, represent two hypercolumns, each composed of 16 neurons responding to all 16 orientations at the points located at (x_c, y_c), as indicated in Figure 31. The population curve is represented by the activity of all 16 excitatory neurons belonging to the column, B e A respectively, depicted in the two bottom panels of Figure 31. The population curve exhibits a half width at half height of about 20 deg, in agreement with physiological data (Heggelund and Albus, 1978; Vidyasagar and Siguenza, 1985). Moreover, the orientation curves resulting from feed-forward mechanisms are wider and smaller compared with the final ones emerging from feedback, i.e., feedback mechanisms play a major role in sharpening orientation tuning of simple cells.

Furthermore, the hypercolumn B placed in a corner of the square (the neurons are stimulated by two edges, with orientations 0 (180) and 90 deg) presents a population curve in which it is possible to appreciate the phenomenon of suppression by non optimal stimulus analyzed in section 2.3. In fact, due to the symmetry of synapses, the population curve can be interpreted equally well as the response of the central neuron, with 0 deg optimal orientation, to two orthogonal stimuli (corner of the square) placed at 0 and 90 degrees. In the same figure, this curve is compared with another population curve concerning an hypercolumn stimulated by an edge with 0 degrees of orientation, but placed in the middle of the side square (for example, xc =35,yc =45, grey line in Figure 31): it is possible to appreciate a suppression in the level activity by almost 40%.

The parameters characterizing the intracortical synapses (i.e., $W_{0,l}$ and σ_l in Eq. 44 and $W_{0,e}$, $\sigma_{\vartheta,e}$ and $\sigma_{\vartheta+\pi/2,e}$ in Eq. 49) were not assigned on the basis of physiological experiments, but using empirical a posteriori criteria. A deeper insight into the role of intracortical synapses, can be found in our previous work (Ursino and La Cara, 2004a) where a detailed sensitivity analysis is presented. In the following, we will focus particularly on the role of long range inhibition.

In order to investigate the role of long-range inhibition, we processed some real black and white photographs, which exhibit multiple close contours. The real images depict the face of a girl, a flower, a clay sculpture on a black background, an MRI of a knee and, finally, the same girl of the first image in a profile view.

The results are summarized in Figure 32. As it is clear from this figure, the model, with basal parameter values, can recognize the strongest contours of the real images quite well, but it partially eliminates small contours or portions with great curvature. We think that this effect is a consequence of the wide extension used for long-range inhibition (several degrees) which helps noise elimination but may also cause competition between close contours. Hence, the simulations have been repeated with a significant reduction in the extension of long-range inhibition. In this condition, the model is able to detect also the secondary contours of the images quite well. However, if the extension of inhibition is further reduced, we can observe a significant noise superimposed on the image (in particular in the MRI knee, fourth left input in Figure 32).

In conclusion, our simulations demonstrate a conflict between noise elimination (which requires a wide inhibition) and detection of proximal contours (which may benefit from a shorter inhibition). This drawback will be further discussed in depth in the final section 8 of this paper.

Finally, Figure 33 shows the network output in the space-orientation domain *(x,y, ϑ)* using the left panel of Figure 32 as input to the model. In this figure, one can appreciate the main contours of the real input decomposed in their orientation components (as in Figure 31, upper panels).

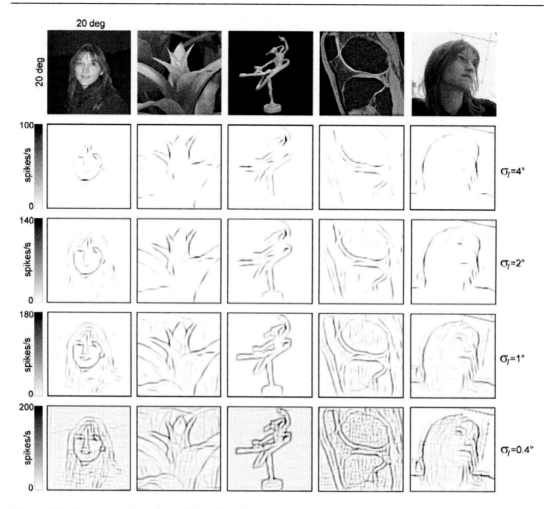

Figure 32. Five examples of model application to real black and white photographs (the photos have been realized with a digital camera by G.E. La Cara, with exception to MRI image). The panels in the upper row represent the original images. The panels in the second row represent model results with basal parameters values. As it is clear, only thick contours are perceived, whereas small contours are suppressed by competitive mechanisms. The panels in the subsequent rows represent model results, obtained by decreasing the standard deviation of inhibition (i.e., parameter σ_l in Eq. 44) from 4 to 0.4 deg passing through 2 and 1 deg. In this condition, multiple contours can co-exist, providing better analysis of details in the images.

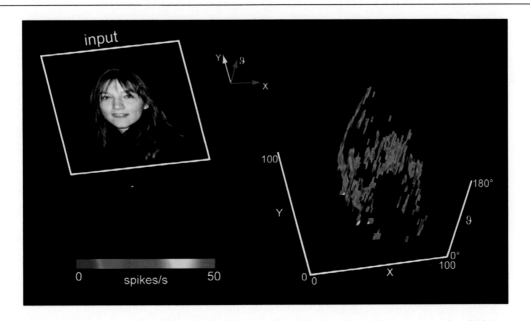

Figure 33. Network output in the space-orientation domain (x, y, ϑ), as in upper panels of Figure 31, when the input is the image depicted in the first left panel of Figure 32. In this representation it is possible to appreciate how the main contours of the visual input have been decomposed in their orientation components.

8. Multiscale Analysis

8.1. Introduction

As it is well known, V1 cells are tuned for spatial frequency, i.e., they respond optimally only to elongated stimuli within a narrow spatial frequency range (Hubel and Wiesel, 1977;Palmer, 2002;Webster and De Valois, 1985). Recent hypotheses suggest that different spatial frequency channels may be involved in different tasks (Oliva and Schyns, 1997;Schyns and Oliva, 1997;Mermillod et al., 2005) and in a coarse-to-fine integration of visual information. Moreover, the response of V1 cells is further enriched by top-down influences from higher visual areas, namely attention. Several results emphasize that cortical activity may be modulated by an attention mechanism operating at early visual stages, such as V1 or V2 (Brefczynski and De Yoe, 1999;Ito and Gilbert, 1999;Zhaoping, 2005;Slotnick et al., 2002;Slotnick et al., 2003;Tootell et al., 1997). In general, attention is assumed to operate both through facilitation of visual processing at the attended position and by inhibition of unattended locations. This attentional active selection is often compared with a spotlight highlighting a definite region in space, where information processing is facilitated to the detriment of information at other locations (Posner and Petersen, 1990;Posner and Gilbert, 1999). The so-called "spotlight" psychophysical model of visual attention (Castiello and Umilta, 1990;Crick, 1984;Eriksen and Yeh, 1985;Eriksen and St.James, 1986;Treisman, 1982) entails a trade-off between the size of the circumscribed region and processing efficiency in the same region (Castiello and Umilta, 1990;Duncan, 1984;La Berge, 1983).

In addition to the classical interpretation of selective attention as a spotlight, some neuropsychological, neurophysiological and neurobiological evidence (Badcock et al., 1990;Shulman and Wilson, 1987;Wörgötter et al., 1998;Yeshurun and Carrasco, 1998;Yeshurun and Carrasco, 1999) stresses the so-called "Resolution theory". This theory supposes that the attentional spotlight also enhances the spatial resolution with which the 'illuminated' local region is further processed to disclose finer details in that region.

In the previous section 7, (see also (Ursino and La Cara, 2004a)) we showed that our model of V1 neurons can extract information on smooth contours by exploiting intracortical excitatory and inhibitory synapses implementing contextual influences. However, the model did not consider the presence of different "spatial frequency channels" (i.e., all neurons were tuned to the same spatial frequency range) nor did it address the possible effect of spatial attention.

In this section we investigate the possibility of including the previous two main topics in the model by considering the role of different spatial frequencies and their possible modulation by attention according to the "resolution theory" (Figure 34).

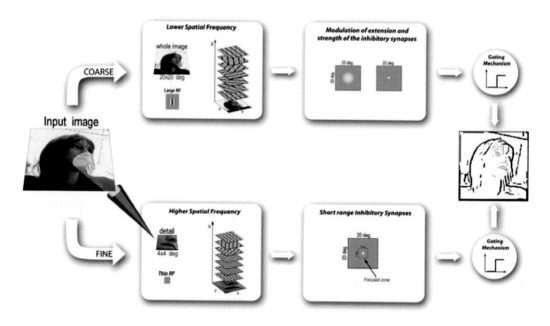

Figure 34. The two parallel computational streams assumed in the present model to scrutinize images at different levels of detail. Two different spatial-frequency channels are used. Attention selects the appropriate portion of the image (spotlight), the spatial-frequency and the extension of lateral inhibition. Finally, a gating mechanism (under the effect of attention too) ensures that only activity above a given threshold is transmitted to subsequent layers.

A further important hypothesis investigated in this section deals with the possibility that spatial attention may work by modifying the disposition of surround inhibition to V1 cells. In fact, our previous results disclosed that excessive long-range inhibition may conceal small contours due to excessive competition with greater contours (section 7, see also (Ursino and La Cara, 2004a)). The hypothesis underlying this computer simulation study is that, besides choosing the appropriate frequency channel and causing facilitation of the selected region, attention modulates long-range inhibition to analyze an image at different scales and at different levels of detail.

8.2. Intracortical Circuitry

The arrangement of intracortical circuitry is architecturally the same presented in section 7.2, with exception for some parameter values, the choice of which will be described in depth in the following sections. Hence, for the main equation describing the model we refer to section 5.2 and section 7.2.

8.3. Multi Scale Approach and Attention

A fundamental aspect of this work is that the image may be scrutinized at different scales. For the sake of simplicity, just two scales are used in this work, but the model may be easily extended to comprise a larger number of scales. In the larger scale we assume that an array of 101x101 (N=101, see section 5) neural clusters scrutinize an image with dimension 20x20 deg (D=20 see section 5, two proximal clusters away 0.2 deg). In this scale, we assume that the RF of the simple cells is obtained using $\alpha_G = G = 1$ in Eq. 30, i.e., the RF has the same dimension (~1.8 deg x 1.0 deg,) of that used in previous section 7 (see also (Ursino and La Cara, 2004a)). In general the relationship between α_G and G (Eq. 30) is summarized as $G = \alpha_G^2$. This choice was adopted to have the same strength of the response independently of the size of the receptive field (in fact, the size of the RF is approximately proportional to $1/\alpha_G^2$). In the smaller scale, we used $\alpha_G = 5$ and $G = 25$. In other words, we assume the existence of other arrays of neurons (which work in parallel with the first) whose RFs are fivefold smaller. Since the finer scale is fivefold smaller than the coarser one, we must assume the existence of $5^2 = 25$ neural arrays at the finer scale for each array at the coarser scale. In the latter case the distance between the RF centres is reduced to 0.04 deg and this array scrutinizes a portion of the image with dimension 4x4 deg (D=4 in section 5).

As specified above, we assume that the shift from one scale to another is caused by an attention mechanism. However, the attention mechanism not only selects the portion of the image to be scrutinized, and neurons corresponding to an appropriate scale, but it also modulates the strength of long range inhibitory synapses. This is simulated acting on parameters σ_l and $W_{0,l}$ of Eq. 44.

8.3.1. Gating Mechanism

Finally, we assume that information on contours reaches the higher visual centres according to a gating mechanism. This means that a significant contour of the image is detected, at a given spatial coordinate, and at a given level of scale, only if activity in the cluster overcomes a threshold (see Figure 34). To this end, the output from the network at position (x_c, y_c), is obtained by computing the sum of all activities in the neurons belonging to the same cluster and subsequently comparing this sum with a threshold ζ_z. The output is then given the value 1 if the threshold is overcome; otherwise it is set to zero. Hence, rearranging Eq. 50 the network output $z(x_c, y_c)$, assumes the following form

$$z(x_c, y_c) = \begin{cases} 1 & \text{if } \sum_{\theta_c} r(x_c, y_c, \theta_c) > \zeta_z \\ 0 & \text{if } \sum_{\theta_c} r(x_c, y_c, \theta_c) \le \zeta_z \end{cases} \qquad (51)$$

Equation 51 may be realized with a third layer of binary neurons, which receive the output of neurons in the same cluster (Figure 34). The usefulness of Eq. 51, however, is simply to switch ON only those positions of the image (i.e., only those clusters) whose activity is sufficiently elevated. By varying the value of the threshold it is possible to recruit clusters at different levels of activity in the disclosure of salient features in the visual input. Hence, parameter ζ_z may also be under control of higher centres.

A list of all model parameters is shown in Table 3.

8.3.2. Details on the Numerical Implementation

The set of differential equations was numerically solved in C++ (using VxL library) on Pentium-based personal computers, using the Euler integration method with all boundary conditions set to zero. The integration step was chosen small enough to ensure negligible error.

In the numerical resolution of Eq. 33 (see section 5.2), N and M are invariants at each scale level of the input analysis, therefore the pixel dimensions in the input image change with the extension of the scrutinized portion of the image. In other words, the pixel dimension depends on the extension of the portion of the image spotlighted by the attention mechanism. Let us identify the horizontal and vertical extensions of the analyzed input image, expressed in degrees, with the symbol E_m and E_n, respectively. Hence we can write: $M\Delta x = E_m$, and $N\Delta y = E_n$, and then

$$g_t(x_c, y_c, \theta_c) \cong \frac{1}{MN} \left[\sum_{m=1}^{M} \sum_{n=1}^{N} I(m\frac{E_m}{M}, n\frac{E_n}{N}) FF(m\frac{E_m}{M} - x_c, n\frac{E_n}{N} - y_c, \theta_c) E_m E_n \right]^+ \qquad (52)$$

8.4. Results

First of all, we analyzed the role of intracortical inhibitory synapses in the model, in order to critically discuss the hypothesis that intracortical inhibition is modulated by an attention mechanism operating at V1 level. Starting from the basal parameter values (Table 2), we stimulated the network with the visual input depicting the profile of the girl (right panel in Figure 32) by modifying the values of σ_l and $W_{0,l}$ (Eq. 44). The results are shown at different values of the threshold ζ_z (Eq. 51) under the assumption that attention can also modulate the gating mechanism. In the following, this input, which covers a visual area extending 20x20 deg, will be named input A.

In these simulations we did not modify the spatial frequency of the RF, i.e., we used the same spatial frequency channels adopted in the previous section (see also (Ursino and La Cara, 2004a)). Results are illustrated in Figure 35 - Figure 37.

The figures display the input image in the upper panel; the lower panels show the network output (i.e., quantity $z(x_c, y_c)$ in Eq. 51), once feedback system has reached a final steady state, for different values of the analyzed parameter (i.e., σ_l or $W_{0,l}$) (rows) and for different values of the gating threshold ζ_z (columns).

First of all, Figure 35 considers a progressive reduction in the standard deviation σ_l, which establishes the extension of the lateral inhibition. If the inhibition is too wide (upper rows) a contour of the image interferes with another contour placed in a not-too-distant position. As a consequence, only the main contours (for instance the contour of the overall face) may emerge. A decrease of the inhibition extension (bottom rows) progressively reveals the secondary features of the image, but concomitant noisy spurious components also appear. This drawback is exacerbated as the threshold assumes low values, but may be attenuated increasing the gating threshold.

Figure 36 describes the effect of a change in the inhibition strength $W_{0,l}$. A reduction in $W_{0,l}$, with a concomitant reduction in the threshold, causes a moderate disclosure of some details. By contrast, an increase in $W_{0,l}$ does not induce significant variations. The reason is that the basal values of strength and extension adopted in the previous work were already high enough to cause a broad inhibition of proximal contours, located close to thick contours.

Hence, we repeated the sensitivity analysis for $W_{0,l}$ using a narrower extension for the inhibition (i.e $\sigma_l = 0.8$ deg). The results reported in Figure 37 suggest that, in this condition, a reduction in the inhibition strength leads to the appearance of small details of the image. However, excessive reduction in the inhibition strength causes a superposition of a myriad spurious components on the salient contours of the image, and eventually instability for the network. In fact for stable behaviour inhibition must be strong enough to avoid an uncontrolled propagation of excitatory activity among proximal neurons. If inhibition is excessively reduced, excitation spreads throughout the network, causing a paroxysmal activity which becomes almost independent of the input, as mentioned in the previous section 7 (see also (Ursino and La Cara, 2004a)).

Of course, the effects of these individual parameter changes on the image are not independent, but may be complementary (in other words, the same final effect might be obtained using different combinations of multiple parameter changes). In order to study this aspect, we performed several simulations in which we systematically varied parameters $W_{0,l}$, σ_l and ζ_z. The effects of different parameter changes were compared by computing the correlation among the images.

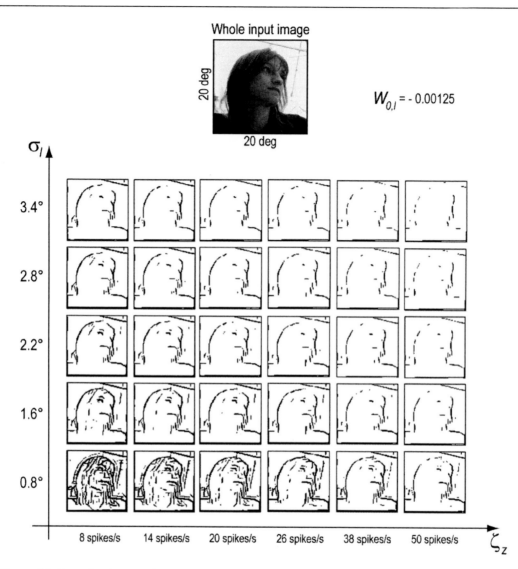

Figure 35. Investigation on the extension of the feedback inhibitory synapses. *Upper panel:* visual input; *lower panels:* simultaneous effect of decreasing the standard deviation of the inhibitory synapses (i.e., parameter σ_l in Eq. 44) and of increasing threshold (i.e., parameter ζ_z in Eq. 51) in the analysis of input A. The strength of the inhibitory synapses was given the value -0.00125, as in (Ursino and La Cara, 2004a). For each value of σ_l (rows) the network output (quantity $z(x_c, y_c)$ in Eq. 51) is shown as the threshold value increases (columns). All network outputs have been computed after 30 ms of the temporal evolution, when the network reached a steady state condition. In these simulations: $E_m=E_n=20$ deg in Eq. 52, while $\alpha_G = 1$ and $G = 1$ in Eq. 30 (coarse scale resolution).

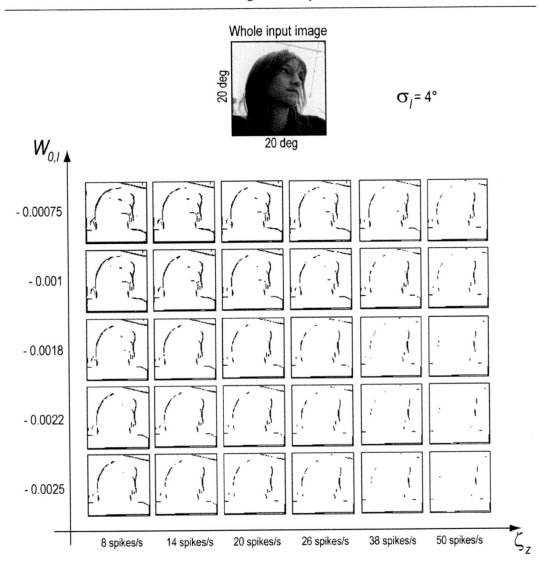

Figure 36. Investigation on the strength of feedback inhibitory synapses. *Upper panel*: visual input; *lower panels*: simultaneous effect of changing the strength of the inhibitory synapses (i.e., parameter $W_{0,I}$ in Eq. 44) and of increasing the threshold (parameter ζ_z in Eq. 51) in the analysis of input A. The extension of the inhibitory synapses was given the value 4 deg, as in (Ursino and La Cara, 2004a). For each value of the strength of the inhibitory synapses (rows) the network output (quantity $z(x_c, y_c)$ in Eq. 51) is shown as the threshold value increases (columns) All network outputs were computed after 30 ms temporal evolution, when the network reached a steady state condition. $E_m = E_n = 20$ deg in Eq. 52, while $\alpha_G = 1$ and $G = 1$ in Eq. 30 (coarse scale resolution).

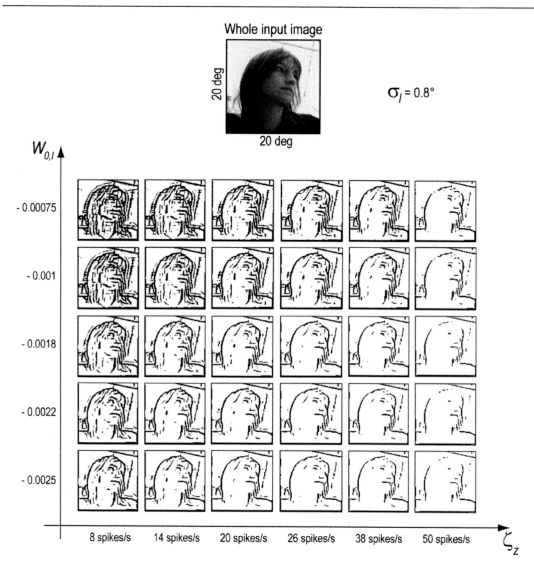

Figure 37. The same investigation as in Figure 36, but performed using a narrower extension of inhibitory synapses ($\sigma_l = 0.8$ deg) to emphasize the role of inhibitory synapses strength. The disposition of the figure and the meaning for the snapshots are as in Figure 36. Weaker inhibition strength causes higher settling time for the intracortical feedback mechanism, and instability can sometimes emerge.

An example of the obtained results is portrayed in Figure 38. This figure demonstrates that a high correlation (close to 1, which means almost identical details) can be achieved by linearly increasing the gating threshold ζ_z from 10 to 80 spikes/s, while σ_l is reduced from 3.4 to 0.6 deg (i.e., the effect of more focused inhibition can be compensated by threshold elevation in the gating mechanism). Similarly, a high correlation among the images is obtained if the gating threshold is increased from 10 to 80 spikes/s, while $W_{0,l}$ changes from -0.0025 to -0.00075 (also in this case, a reduction in inhibition can be compensate by threshold increase). The previous results suggested that disclosure of small details of the image, or focus on larger components only, can be quite finely tuned by acting on both parameters determining the entity of inhibition, and on the gating threshold.

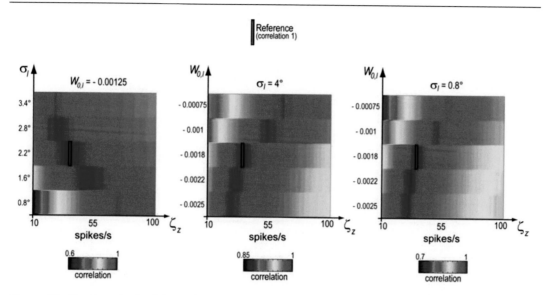

Figure 38. Results obtained by using different combinations of multiple parameter changes in the analysis of input image (the same used in Figs. 35 - 37). The varied parameters are $W_{0,l}$, σ_l and ζ_z. The effects of different parameter changes were compared by computing the correlation among the resulting images (correlation equal to 1 means identical details). The results demonstrate that similar effect can be achieved by linearly increasing the gating threshold ζ_z while reducing σ_l, or by linearly increasing the gating threshold while reducing $W_{0,l}$ (both for large and short inhibition - σ_l).

Hence, results support the idea that these parameters may be modulated by attention mechanisms. This idea is further illustrated by two different examples in Figure 39. The first image is the same as that used in the sensitivity analysis performed in Figure 35 - Figure 37 (input A), the second is a photograph of Bernini's "River Fountain" in Rome (Piazza Navona) taken with a digital camera in the late evening, then with a remarkable superimposed noise (named input B).

Figure 39 portrays the effect of two exemplary configurations for the intracortical inhibition: the first characterized by basal parameters (the first row for each analyzed image), the second by reduced inhibition (the second row for each analyzed image) as the threshold assumes increasing values. The results confirm that a possible attentive modulation of intracortical inhibition in V1 could regulate the sensitivity to stimulus details. However, if the attention mechanism operates only at the level of inhibition, the visual input cannot be scrutinized at a very fine detail level. For example, concerning input A in Figure 39, the network can reveal the mouth of the girl as a single 'macroscopic' feature of the image but without distinctly outlining the two lips.

To overcome this limitation, a second assumption is that, when revealing fine details, a limited area in the visual input is spotlighted together with a concurrent enhancement in spatial resolution, i.e., the focused region is processed using neurons at a higher spatial scale. This assumption agrees with the "resolution theory".

Accordingly, we provided the network with a restricted input and we modified parameters G and α_G, which set the scale of the RF (see Eq. 30 and section 8.3). In particular, we have $G = \alpha_G^2$ and $\alpha_G = 5$. Two examples are shown in Figure 40 where two restricted areas for two whole images presented above are analyzed. For what concerns input A the focused zones include an eye and the mouth; for input B the focused zones are a hand and an ear, the latter hidden in thick beard and hair.

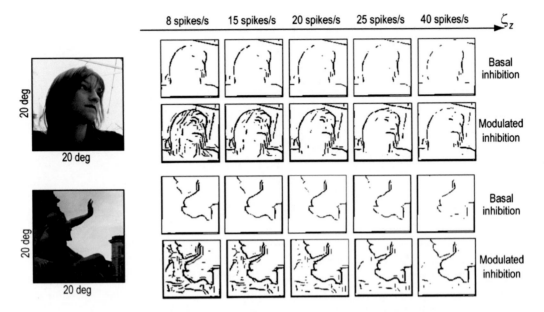

Figure 39. Comparison between two sets of parameters for the intracortical inhibition: the set used in (Ursino and La Cara, 2004a), labelled 'basal inhibition' ($W_{0,l}$ = -0.00125; σ_l = 4 deg; first row for each input), and a set characterized by narrower and stronger inhibition labelled 'Modulated inhibition' ($W_{0,l}$ = -0.0025; σ_l = 0.8 deg; second row for each input). Two visual inputs are presented: input A - face of a girl (the same of Figs 35 - 37); input B- a digital photograph of Bernini's "river fountain" in Piazza Navona, Rome. The network outputs (quantity $z(x_c, y_c)$ in Eq. 51) are presented as the threshold value increases (ζ_z in Eq. 51). All network outputs have been computed after 30 ms of temporal evolution when the network reached a steady state condition. $E_m = E_n = 20$ deg (Eq.52), while $\alpha_G = 1$ and $G = 1$ in Eq. (30) (coarse scale resolution).

All the focused zones cover an attended area of 4x4 degrees. Figure 40 displays the visual inputs with the highlighted focused zones (upper panels), the zones selected by the spotlight (first left column), the first elaboration accomplished by the thalamic neurons (second left column), i.e., quantity g_t in Eq. 33, and the output network as the threshold increases its value (last five columns). The values used for intracortical inhibition are $W_{0,l}$ = -0.0025 and σ_l = 0.8 deg, which are the same used in the lower row of Figure 37. The results clearly show that the attentive modulation of the intracortical inhibition, in synergy with the enhancement of spatial resolution in the focused zone, can disclose the details of the original image at a finer level. For example, the network is now able to distinguish the girl's lips in input A and to isolate the fingers of the hand in input B despite the superimposed noise on the image, and to disclose the salient elements in the entangled background where the ear is placed.

The previous simulations assumed two separate processing streams: one at a coarser scale, which detects the major aspects of a figure, and one at a finer scale (higher spatial frequency) which discloses fine details.

A last aspect deserving attention is the possibility to merge information coming from the broader and finer scale streams. Examples are shown in Figure 41 combining the outputs of the two streams. We can see that the coarser scale stream reveals the major aspects of the figure in the areas not selected by the spotlight, while more subtle details pop out in the two focused zones scrutinized at a finer scale.

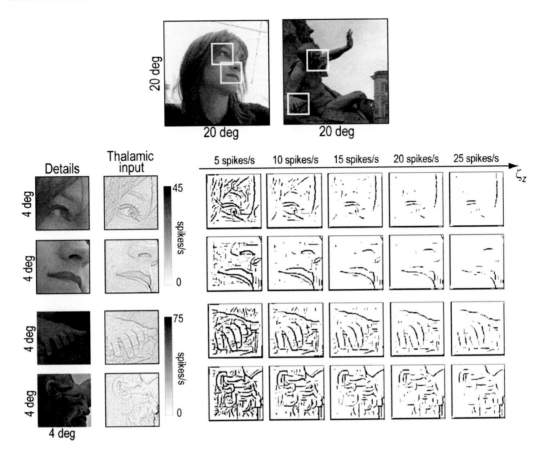

Figure 40. Analysis of two details for input A and input B. For input A: the mouth and an eye; B: a hand and an ear hidden in thick beard and hair. *Upper panels*: visual inputs with the two highlighted focused zones; *lower panels*: first left column depicts a zoom of the spotlighted zones; the second left column represents the thalamic input (quantity g_t in Eq. 33); the subsequent columns represent the network outputs (quantity $z(x_c, y_c)$ in Eq. 51) computed after 30 ms temporal evolution, when the network reached a steady state condition, at different values of the threshold ζ_z. $E_m = E_n = 4$ deg (Eq. 52), while $\alpha_G = 5$ and $G = 25$ in Eq. 30 (fine scale resolution). Parameters for the inhibitory synapses were $W_{0,I} = -0.0025$; $\sigma_I = 0.8$ deg.

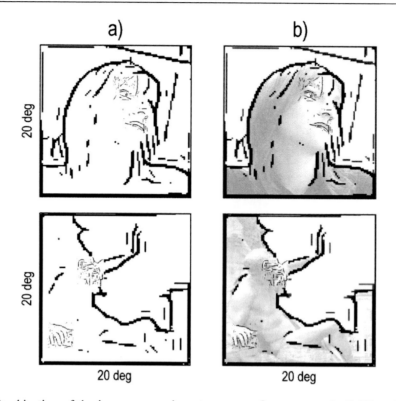

Figure 41. Combination of the image processing at a coarser frequency scale (LSF) and at the finer scale (HSF). Input A and input B are processed. a) Network output (quantity $z(x_c, y_c)$ in Eq. 51; b) superposition of network output on original images. We used a modulated inhibition and $G = \alpha_G = 1$ for the LSF analysis, and $G = 25$, $\alpha_G = 5$ for he HSF analysis. The network outputs were computed after 30 ms of the temporal evolution and the threshold ζ_z (Eq. 51) was set at 15 spikes/s.

9. Discussion

Vision processing, in men and superior animals, requires that different tasks are simultaneously performed and a multitude of data managed all together, with often opposite or contradictory requirements. For instance, one needs to precisely know the position of objects, and their direction of movement, in order to perform motor tasks (such as reaching or grasping), but, at the same time, needs to know that abstract features of objects are correctly detected independently of their position. Some tasks require perception of the global object without caring for details, others require that attention is focused on specific details of an image in a limited portion of space. All these aspects, and many others not listed here for briefness, require a trade off between opposite requirements, and the choice of alternative solutions. This implies the use of alternative neural circuits to manage different aspects of images, avoiding interference with other simultaneous processing steps. It is well known that vision processing, as well as other aspects of neural computation in the brain, is largely distributed in nature and is performed in a massively parallel way.

Then, a fundamental question is: how does the brain process visual information at the early stages, in order to extract the most useful information from images, to be transmitted to subsequent higher hierarchical areas? It is well known that the primary visual cortex, in mammals, is implicated in many different tasks, which comprehend orientation, velocity, direction and spatial frequency tuning, contrast invariance, contour extraction (as demonstrated by the effect of contour illusions on the activity of V1 cells), multi-scale decomposition, adaptation to prolonged stimuli, etc. Do these tasks require the use of different neural circuits, with a hierarchical organisation (as suggested by some authors, for instance to distinguish between simple, complex and hypercomplex cells) or is it possible to build a single comprehensive theory to unify all these qualities?

Several models of vision processing in V1 have been proposed in the past decades, with different purposes: some of them share similar characteristics with the present ones, other are based on different ideas. For briefness, we do not intend to summarize these models here: the interested reader can find several details and comments in our previous papers on the subject (La Cara and Ursino, 2007;La Cara and Ursino, 2008;Ursino and La Cara, 2004b;Ursino and La Cara, 2004a;Ursino and La Cara, 2005;Ursino et al., 2007). We just wish to discuss here the general philosophy of our models, and to emphasize the effort to unify data into a possible single neural network organisation.

In this work we presented several modular models of the primary visual cortex, with the aim of clarifying the possible circuits implicated in signal processing at the early stages of the visual processing pathway. A characteristic of these models is that they are based on physiological arrangements of synapses, which try to mimic those experimentally found in V1 as closely as possible. The rational behind these models is that a single flexible structure can be gradually extended and modified (maybe as a consequence of developmental learning) to account for different properties of vision processing. Accordingly, we started our analysis with a minimal model of a single hypercolumn, able to account for the main properties of simple cells in the mammalian striate cortex, including orientation, direction, velocity and spatial frequency selectivity. In this model, intracortical synapses are confined with the hypercolumn, and their function is that of emphasizing an initial bias (in orientation and direction selectivity) coming from the thalamic input, and to make the response independent of the contrast of the input image.

The model was then complicated and extended to account for the distinction between simple and complex cells. Our basic idea, in accordance with previous recent works (Ursino and La Cara, 2005) is that such a distinction does not imply the existence of two distinct classes of neurons, placed at a different hierarchical level in the processing pathway, but rather this distinction arises from a different connectivity strength among hypercolumns. The result of a poor connectivity among hypercolumns is that of leaving the properties of simple cells unaffected, i.e., these cells respond only to a bar or grating with optimal position in space and optimal orientation, without influences from the surround. By contrast, strong connectivity with neurons in other hypercolumns (but similar preferred orientation) naturally leads to the appearance of a "complex cell" behaviour: the cells respond to an optimally oriented bar independent of its position in a large portion of the visual space.

Subsequently, we argued that the same basic rationale (i.e., different surround connectivity may induce a different cell behaviour and different processing features) may be used to explain not only the distinction between simple and complex cells, but also to account for other fundamental attributes of the primary visual cortex, such as extraction of smooth contours and figure-ground segregation. In order to reach this objective, we modified the previous model by differentiating long-range connections among hypercolumns. In particular, in order to extract smooth contours, excitatory synapses must satisfy the co-axial and modular specificity. It is worth noting that this synapse arrangement corresponds to a neural implementation of some elementary Gestalt rules for figure grouping (such as proximity, smoothness, good continuity).

In this regard, it is interesting to observe that the model for complex cell representation, and the model for contour extraction, share the same structure of thalamo-cortical and intracortical connectivity: a biased input from the thalamic cells, a feed forward inhibition with poor orientation selectivity (which ensures contrast invariance), an intracortical excitation with a clear spatial and/or orientation anisotropy, and an isotropic long-range inhibition. The distinction between different cell behaviour and the specific processing properties of the individual circuits originate almost entirely from changes in the weights and in the orientation/spatial properties of intracortical excitation linking different hypercolumns. Hence, a single basic structure, but with different parameter values, can account for disparate properties of V1 cells, and for eventually complementary functions of processing circuits.

In the last section of this work we further explored the same idea, showing that the model, with different parameter values and a parallel arrangement of two networks, can also be used to account for multi scale decomposition, coarse to fine representation, and to incorporate a flexible attentive mechanism which allows an image to be scrutinized at different detail levels.

In conclusion, the main idea we wish to emphasize is that different visual processing properties can be attained using the same neural circuitry, i.e., without the necessity to hypothesize neither alternative neural network architectures nor different hierarchical levels for the cells. Experimental differences may simply emerge as a consequence of a different plasticity for intracortical synapses, and, perhaps, as in the case of long-range inhibition in section 8, from a modulation of some network parameters from higher visual centres. In perspective, a further step of these models may be to obtain the same results using physiological learning rules for synapses (especially for those describing intracortical excitation). In the present work, learning rules have been used only to account for the phenomenon of adaptation and tilt aftereffect. It may be of the greatest value, in forthcoming works, to study whether the different properties of V1 cells described in this study (simple vs. complex cells, direction selectivity, specialisation for contour extraction and figure-ground segregation, coarse vs. fine representation, focus on details vs. main features of an image) can spontaneously emerge from the same basic circuit, with a moderately different initial bias for synapses and using physiological learning rules and a natural choice for images. This may allow the construction of a unified theory of visual processing in V1, including developmental properties, and the summary of disparate data in the literature into a single, comprehensive theoretical structure.

References

Allman,J., Miezin,F., McGuinness,E. (1985). Stimulus specific responses from beyond the classical receptive field: neurophysiological mechanisms for local-global comparisons in visual neurons. *Annual Review of Neuroscience, 8*, 407-430.

Alonso,J.M., Martinez,L.M. (1998). Functional connectivity between simple cells and complex cells in cat striate cortex. *Nature Neuroscience, 1*, 395-403.

Alonso,J.M., Usrey,W.M., Reid,R.C. (2001). Rules of connectivity between geniculate cells and simple cells in cat primary visual cortex. *Journal of Neuroscience, 21*, 4002.

Angelucci,A., Bullier,J. (2003). Reaching beyond the classical receptive field of V1 neurons: horizontal or feedback axons? *Journal of Physiology (Paris), 97*, 141-154.

Angelucci,A., Levitt,J.B., Walton,J.S.E., Hupé,J.M., Bullier,J., Lund,J.S. (2002). Circuits for Local and Global Signal Integration in Primary Visual Cortex. *The Journal of Neuroscience, 22*, 8633-8646.

Badcock,J., Whitworth,F., Badcock,D., Lovegrove,W. (1990). Low frequency filtering and the processing of local-global stimuli. *Perception*617-629.

Baker,C.L., Cynader,M.S. (1986). Spatial receptive-field properties of direction-selective neurons in cat striate cortex. *Journal of Neurophysiology, 55*, 1136-1152.

Bauman,L.A., Bonds,A.B. (1991). Inhibitory refinement of spatial frequency selectivity in single cells of the cat striate cortex. *Vision Research, 31*, 933-944.

Bednar,J., Mikkulainen,R. (2000). Tilt Aftereffects in a Self-Organizing model of the primary visual cortex. *Neural Computation, 12*, 1721-1740.

Ben-Yishai,R., Bar,O., Sompolinsky,H. (1995). Theory of orientation Tuning in Visual Cortex. *Proceedings of the National Academy of Science (USA), 92*, 3844-3848.

Bishop,P.O., Coombs,J.S., Henry,G.H. (1973). Receptive fields of simple cells in the cat striate cortex. *Journal of Physiology, 231*, 31-60.

Blais,B., Cooper,L.N., Shouval,H.Z. (2000). Formation of direction selectivity in natural scene environments. *Neural Computation, 12*, 1057.

Bonds,A.B. (1989). Role of inhibition in the specification of orientation selectivity of cells in the cat striate cortex. *Visual Neuroscience, 2*, 41-55.

Brefczynski,J.A., De Yoe,E.A. (1999). A physiological correlate of the "spot-light" of visual attention. *Nature Neuroscience, 2*, 370-374.

Cai,D., DeAngelis,G.C., Freeman,R.D. (1997). Spatiotemporal receptive field organization in the lateral geniculate nucleus of cats and kittens. *Journal of Neurophysiology, 78*, 1045.

Carandini,M. (2007). Melting the Iceberg: Contrast Invariance in Visual Cortex. *Neuron, 54*, 11-13.

Carandini,M., Ferster,D. (2000). Membrane potential and firing rate in cat primary visual cortex. *Journal of Neuroscience, 20*, 470-484.

Carandini,M., Ringach,D.L. (1997). Predictions of a recurrent model of orientation selectivity. *Vision Research, 37*, 3061-3071.

Castiello,U., Umilta,C. (1990). Size of the attention focus and efficiency of processing. *Acta psychologica, 73*, 195-209.

Chance,F.S., Nelson,S.B., Abbott,L.F. (1999). Complex cells as cortically amplified simple cells. *Nature Neuroscience, 2*, 277-282.

Cheng,H., Chino,Y.M., Smith,E.L., Hamamoto,J., Yoshida,K. (1995). Transfer Characteristics of Lateral Geniculate Nucleus X in the Cat:Effects of Spatial Frequency and Contrast. *Journal of Neurophysiology, 74*, 2548-2557.

Chung,S., Ferster,D. (1998). Strength and orientation tuning of the thalamic input to simple cells revealed by electrically evoked cortical suppression. *Neuron, 20*, 1177-1189.

Clifford,C.W., Wenderoth,P., Spehar,B. (2000). A functional angle on some aftereffects in cortical vision. *Proceedings of the Royal Society of London B, 267*, 1705-1710.

Crick,F. (1984). Function of the thalamic reticular complex: the searchlight hypothesis. *Proceedings of the National Academy of Science (USA), 81*, 4586-4590.

Crook,J.M., Wörgötter,F., Eysel,U.T. (1994). Velocity invariance of preferred axis of motion for single spot stimuli in simple cells of cat striate cortex. *Experimental Brain Research*, *102*, 175.

de Brecht,M., Saiki,J. (2006). A neural network implementation of a saliency map model. *Neural Networks*, *19*, 1467-1474.

De Valois,R., De Valois,K. (1998). Spatial Vision. New York.

DeAngelis,G.C., Ohzawa,I., Freeman,R.D. (1993). Spatiotemporal organization of simple-cell receptive fields in the cat's striate cortex. II. Linearity of temporal and spatial summation. *Journal of Neurophysiology*, *69*, 1118-1135.

DeAngelis,G.C., Ohzawa,I., Freeman,R.D. (1995). Receptive-field dynamics in the central visual pathways. *Trends in Neurosciences*, *18*, 451.

DeAngelis,G.C., Robson,J.G., Ohzawa,I., Freeman,R.D. (1992). Organization of suppression in receptive fields of neurons in cat visual cortex. *Journal of Neurophysiology*, *68*, 144-163.

Douglas,R.J., Martin,K.A. (1991). A functional microcircuit for cat visual cortex. *Journal of Physiology*, *440*, 735-769.

Dragoi,V., Sharma,J., Sur,M. (2000). Adaptation-induced plasticity of orientation tuning in adult visual cortex. *Neuron*, *28*, 287-298.

Duncan,J. (1984). Selective attention and the organization of visual information. *Journal of experimental psychology General*, *113*, 501-517.

Eriksen,C.W., St.James,J.D. (1986). Visual attention within and around the field of focal attention: a zoom lens model. *Perception and psychophysics*, *40*, 225-240.

Eriksen,C.W., Yeh,Y.Y. (1985). Allocation of attention in the visual field. *Journal of experimental psychology Human perception and performance*, *11*, 583-597.

Felsen,G., Shen,Y.S., Yao,H., Spor,G., Li,C., Dan,Y. (2002). Dynamic modification of cortical orientation tuning mediated by recurrent connections. *Neuron*945-954.

Ferster,D. (1986). Oientation Slectivity of synaptoic potentials in neurons of cat primary visual cortex. *Journal of Neuroscience*, *6*, 1284-1301.

Ferster,D., Chung,S., Wheat,H. (1996). Orientation Selectivity of Thalamic Input to Simple Cells of Cat Visual Cortex. *Nature*, *380*, 441.

Ferster,D., Miller,K.D. (2000). Neural Mechanisms of Orientation in the Visual Cortex. *Annual Review of Neuroscience*, *23*, 441.

Field,D.J., Hayes,A., Hess,R.F. (1993). Contour integration by the human visual system: evidence for a local associative field. *Vision Research*, *33*, 173-193.

Frishman,I.J., Schweitzer-Tong,D.E., Goldstein,E.B. (1983). Velocity tuning of cells in dorsal lateral geniculate nucleus and retina in the cat, *J. Neurophysiol* 50, 1393 (1983).

L.J.Frishman, D.E.Schweitzer-Tong, and E.B.Goldstein. *Journal of Neurophysiology*, *50*, 1393.

Gabbott,P.L., Somogyi,P. (1986). Quantitative distribution of GABA-immunoreactive neurons in the visual cortex (area 17) of the cat. *Experimental Brain Research*, *61*, 323-331.

Gardner,J.L., Anzai,A., Ohzawa,I., Freeman,R.D. (1999). Linear and Nonlinear Contributions to Orientation Tuning of Simple Cells in the Cat's Striate Cortex. *Visual Neuroscience*, *16*, 1115-1121.

Gilbert,C.D., Wiesel,T.N. (1989). Columnar specificity of intrinsic horizontal and corticocortical connections in cat visual cortex. *Journal of Neuroscience*, *9*, 2432-2442.

Grossberg,S., Mingolla,M. (1985). Neural dynamics of perceptual grouping: textures, boundaries, and emergent segmentation. *Perception and psychophysics*, *38*, 141-171.

Grossberg,S., Mingolla,M., Ross,W.D. (1997). Visual brain and visual perception: how does the cortex do perceptual grouping? *Trends in Neurosciences*, *20*, 106-111.

Hamada,T., Yamashima,M., Kato,K. (1997). A ring model for spatiotemporal properties of simple cells in the visual cortex. *Biological Cybernetics*, *77*, 225-233.

Hammond,P., Pomfrett,C.J. (1990). Influence of spatial frequency on tuning and bias for orientation and direction in the cat's striate cortex. *Vision Research*, *30*, 359-369.

Heggelund,P., Albus,K. (1978). Orientation selectivity of single cells in striate cortex of cat: the shape of orientation tuning curves. *Vision Research*, *18*, 1067-1071.

Henry,G.H. (1985). Physiology of cat striate cortex, in: "Cerebral Cortex. Vol. 3: visual cortex". New York.

Henry,G.H., Bishop,P.O., Dreher,B. (1974a). Orientation, axis and direction as stimulus parameters for striate cells, Vision Res 14, 767 (1974). *Vision Research*, *14*, 767.

Henry,G.H., Dreher,B., Bishop,P.O. (1974b). Orientation specificity of cells in cat striate cortex. *Journal of Neurophysiology*, *37*, 1394.

Hillenbrand,U., van Hemmen,J.L. (2000). Spatiotemporal adaptation through corticothalamic loops: a hypothesis. *Visual Neuroscience*, *17*, 107-118.

Hillenbrand,U., van Hemmen,J.L. (2001). Does corticothalamic feedback control cortical velocity tuning? *Neural Computation*, *13*, 327-355.

Hubel,H.D., Wiesel,T.N. (1962). Receptive fields, binocular interaction and functional architecture in the cat's visual cortex. *Journal of Physiology*, *160*, 106-154.

Hubel,H.D., Wiesel,T.N. (1965). The receptive fields and functional architecture in two nonstriate visual areas (18 and 19) of the cat. *Journal of Neurophysiology*, *28*, 229-289.

Hubel,H.D., Wiesel,T.N. (1977). Ferrier lecture: Functional architecture of macaque monkey visual cortex. *Proceedings of the Royal Society of London B*, *198*, 1-59.

Ito,M., Gilbert,C.D. (1999). Attention modulates contextual influences in the primary visual cortex of alert monkeys. *Neuron*, *22*, 593-604.

Jin,D.Z., Dragoi,V., Sur,M., Seung,S. (2005). The tilt aftereffect and adaptation- induced changes in orientation tuning in visual cortex. *Journal of Neurophysiology*, *94*, 4038-4050.

Jones,J.P., Palmer,L.A. (1987a). An evaluation of the two-dimensional Gabor filter model of simple receptive fields in cat striate cortex. *Journal of Neurophysiology*, *58*, 1233.

Jones,J.P., Palmer,L.A. (1987b). The two-dimensional spatial structure of simple receptive fields in cat striate cortex. *Journal of Neurophysiology*, *58*, 1187.

Kapadia,M., Ito,M., Gilbert,C.D., Westheimer,G. (1995). Improvement in visual sensitivity by changes in local context: parallel studies in human observers and in V1 of alert monkeys. *Neuron*, *11*, 843-856.

Kapadia,M., Westheimer,G., Gilbert,C.D. (2000). Spatial distribution of contextual interactions in primary visual cortex and in visual perception. *Journal of Neurophysiology*, *84*, 2048-2062.

Kisvarday,Z., Crook,J.M., Buzas,P., Eysel,U.T. (2000). Combined physiological-anatomical approaches to study lateral inhibition. *Journal of Neuroscience Methods*, *103*, 91-106.

Koffka,K. (1935). Principles of Gestalt Psychology. New York: Harcourt.

La Berge,D. (1983). Spatial extent of attention to letters and words. *Journal of experimental psychology Human perception and performance*, *9*, 371-379.

La Cara,G.E., Ritrovato,M., Ursino,M. (2004). A neural network for detection of orientation, velocity and direction of movement, based on physiological rules. *WSEAS Transactions on SYSTEMS, 3,* 533-539.

La Cara,G.E., Ursino,M. (2007). Direction Selectivity of Simple Cells in the Primary Visual Cortex: Comparison of Two Alternative Mathematical Models. II: Velocity Tuning and Response to Moving Bars. *Computers in Biology and Medicine, 37,* 598-610.

La Cara,G.E., Ursino,M. (2008). A model of contour extraction including multiple scales, flexible inhibition and attention. *Neural Networks, In press.*

Li,C.Y., Li,W. (1994). Extensive integration field beyond the classical receptive field of cat's striate cortical neurons - classification and tuning properties. *Vision Research, 18,* 2337-2355.

Li,Z. (1998). A neural model of contour integration in the primary visual cortex. *Neural Computation, 10,* 903-940.

Li,Z. (1999a). Contextual influences in V1 as a basis for pop out and asymmetry in visual search. *Proceedings of the National Academy of Sciences, 96,* 10530-10535.

Li,Z. (1999b). Visual segmentation by contextual influences via intracortical interactions in primary visual cortex. *Network: Computation in Neural System, 10,* 187-212.

Linsenmeier,R., Frishman,I.J., Jakiela,H.G., Enroth,C. (1982). Receptive Filed Properties of x and y cells in the cat retina derived from contrast sensitivity measurement. *Vision Research, 22,* 1173-1183.

Maex,R., Orban,G.A. (1992). A model circuit for cortical temporal low-pass filtering. *Neural Computation, 4,* 932-945.

Malpeli,J.G. (1983). Activity of cells in area 17 of the cat in absence of input from layer A of lateral geniculate nucleus. *Journal of Neurophysiology, 49,* 595-610.

Malpeli,J.G., Lee,C., Schwark,H.D. (1986). Cat area 17. I. Pattern of thalamic control of cortical layers. *Journal of Neurophysiology, 56,* 1062-1073.

Martinez,L.M., Alonso,J.M. (2001). Construction of complex receptive fileds in cat primary visual cortex. *Neuron, 32,* 515-525.

Martinez,L.M., Alonso,J.M. (2003). Complex receptive fields in primary visual cortex. *The Neuroscientist, 9,* 317-331.

Mastronarde,D.N. (1987a). Two classes of single input X cells in cat lateral geniculate nucleus. I: Receptive field properties and classification of cells. *Journal of Neurophysiology*357.

Mastronarde,D.N. (1987b). Two classes of single input X cells in cat lateral geniculate nucleus. II: Retinal inputs and the generation of receptive field properties. *Journal of Neurophysiology, 57,* 381.

Mather,G., Verstraten,F., Anstis,S. (1998). *The motion aftereffects:a modern perspective.* Cambridge (MA): MIT Press.

McLaughlin,D., Shapley,R., Shelley,M., Wielaard,J. (2000). A neural network model of macaque primary visual cortex (V1): orientation selectivity and dynamics in the input layer 4Calpha. *Proceedings of the National Academy of Science (USA), 97,* 8087-8092.

Mechler,F., Ringach,D.L. (2002). On the classification of simple and complex cells. *Vision Research, 42,* 1017-1033.

Mermillod,M., Guyader,N., Chauvin,A. (2005). The coarse-to-fine hypothesis revisited: Evidence from neuro-computational modeling. *Brain and Cognition, 57,* 151-157.

Miller,K.D. (1996). Synaptic Economics: Competition and Cooperation in Synaptic Plasticity. *Neuron, 17,* 367-370.

Miller,K.D., MacKay,D. (1994). The role of constraints in hebbian learning. *Neural Computation, 6,* 100-126.

Mitchell,D., Muir,D.W. (1976). Does the tilt aftereffect occur in the oblique meridian? *Vision Research, 16,* 609-613.

Morrone,M.C., Burr,D.C., Maffei,L. (1982). Membrane potential and firing rate in cat primary visual cortex. *Proceedings of the Royal Society of London B, 216,* 335-354.

Movshon,J.A., Thompson,I., Tolhurst,D. (1978a). Receptive field organization of complex cells in cat's striate cortex. *Journal of Physiology, 283,* 79-99.

Movshon,J.A., Thompson,I., Tolhurst,D. (1978b). Spatial summation in the receptive fields of simple cells in the cat's striate cortex. *Journal of Physiology, 283,* 53-77.

Müller,J.R., Metha,A.B., Krauskopf,J., Lennie,P. (1999). Rapid adaptation in visual cortex to the structure of images. *Science, 285,* 1405-1408.

Nelson,J.I., Frost,N.J. (1985). Intracortical facilitation among co-oriented, co-axially aligned simple cells in cat striate cortex. *Experimental Brain Research, 61,* 54-61.

Oliva,A., Schyns,P.G. (1997). Coarse Blobs or Fine Edges? Evidence That Information Diagnosticity Changes the Perception of Complex Visual Stimuli. *Cognitive Psychology, 34,* 72-107.

Orban,G.A., Hoffman,K.P., Duysens,J. (1985). Velocity selectivity in the cat visual system. I. responses of LGN cells to moving bar stimuli: a comparison with cortical areas 17 and 18. *Journal of Neurophysiology, 54,* 1026.

Orban,G.A., Kennedy,H., Maes,H. (1981a). Response to movement of neurons in areas 17 and 18 of the cat: direction selectivity. *Journal of Neurophysiology, 45,* 1058.

Orban,G.A., Kennedy,H., Maes,H. (1981b). Response to movement of neurons in areas 17 and 18 of the cat: velocity sensitivity. *Journal of Neurophysiology, 45,* 1043.

Palmer,S.E. (2002). Vision science: Photons to Phenomenology. Cambridge, MA: The MIT Press.

Pettet,M.W., McKee,S.P., Grzywacz,N.M. (1998). Constraints on long range interactions mediating contour detection. *Vision Research, 38,* 865-879.

Pettigrew,J.D., Nikara,T., Bishop,P.O. (1968). Responses to moving slits by single units in cat striate cortex. *Experimental Brain Research, 6,* 373-390.

Polat,U., Sagi,D. (1993). Lateral interactions between spatial channels: suppression and facilitation revealed by lateral masking experiments. *Vision Research* 993-999.

Polat,U., Sagi,D. (1994). The architecture of perceptual spatial interactions. *Vision Research, 34,* 73-78.

Posner MI, Gilbert CD (1999) Attention and primary visual cortex. pp 2585-2587.

Posner,M.I., Petersen,S.E. (1990). The attention system of the human brain. *Annual Review of Neuroscience, 13,* 25-42.

Reid,R.C., Alonso,J.M. (1995). Specificity of monosynaptic connections from thalamus to visual cortex, Nature. *Nature, 378,* 281.

Reid,R.C., Soodak,R.E., Shapley,R. (1991). Directional selectivity and spatiotemporal structure of receptive fields of simple cells. I: cat striate cortex. *Journal of Neurophysiology, 66,* 505.

Ringach,D.L., Hawken,M.J., Shapley,R. (1997). Dynamics of orientation tuning in macaque primary visual cortex. *Nature, 387,* 281-284.

Rockland,U., Lund,J.S. (1983). Intrinsic laminar lattice connections in primate visual cortex. *The Journal of Comparative Neurology, 216*, 303-318.

Ross,W.D., Grossberg,S., Mingolla,M. (2000). Visual Cortical Mechanisms of Perceptual Grouping: Interacting Layers, Networks, Columns, and Maps. *Neural Networks, 13*, 571-588.

Sabatini,S.P., Solari,F. (1999). An architectural hypothesis for direction selectivity in the visual cortex: the role of spatially asymmetric intracortical inhibition. *Biological Cybernetics, 80*, 171-183.

Saul,A.B., Humphrey,J. (1990). Spatial and temporal response properties of lagged and nonlagged cells in cat lateral geniculate nucleus. *Journal of Neurophysiology, 64*, 206.

Saul,A.B., Humphrey,J. (1992). Temporal-frequency tuning of direction selectivity in cat visual cortex. *Visual Neuroscience, 8*, 365.

Schiller,P.H., Finlay,B.L., Volman,S.F. (1976). Quantitative studies of single-cell properties in monkey striate cortex. II. Orientation specificity and ocular dominance. *Journal of Neurophysiology, 39*, 1320-1333.

Schmidt,K.E., Goebel,R., Lowel,S., Singer,W. (1997). The perceptual grouping criterion of colinearity is reflected by anisotropies of connections in the primary visual cortex. *European Journal of Neuroscience, 9*, 1083-1089.

Schyns,P.G., Oliva,A. (1997). Flexible, diagnosticity-driven, rather than fixed, perceptually determined scale selection in scene and face recognition. *Perception, 26*, 1027-1038.

Sclar,G., Freeman,R.D. (1982). Orientation selectivity in the cat's striate cortex is invariant with stimulus contrast. *Experimental Brain Research, 46*, 457-461.

Sengpiel,F., Baddeley,R.J., Freeman,T.C., Harrad,R., Blakemore,C. (1998). Different mechanisms underlie three inhibitory phenomena in cat area 17. *Vision Research, 38*, 2067-2080.

Sengpiel,F., Hubener,M. (1999). Visual attention: spotlight on the primary visual cortex. *Current Biology, 9*, 318-321.

Shouval,H.Z., Goldberg,D.H., Jones,J.P., Beckerman,M., Cooper,L.N. (2000). Structured long-range connections can provide a Scaffold for orientation maps. *Journal of Neuroscience, 20*, 1119-1128.

Shulman,G., Wilson,J. (1987). Spatial frequency and selective attention to local and global information. *Perception, 16*, 89-101.

Skottun,B.C., Bradley,A., Sclar,G., Ohzawa,I., Freema,R.D. (1987). The Effects of constrast on visual orientation and spatial frequency discrimination: a comparison of single cells and behaviour. *Journal of Neurophysiology, 57*, 773-786.

Skottun,B.C., De Valois,R., Grosof,D.H., Movshon,J.A., Albrecht,D.G., Bonds,A.B. (1991). Classifying simple and complex cells on the basis of response modulation. *Vision Research, 31*, 1079-1086.

Slotnick,S.D., Hopfinger,J.B., Klein,S.A., Sutter,E.E. (2002). Darkness beyond the light: attentional inhibition surrounding the classical spotlight. *Neuroreport, 13*, 773-778.

Slotnick,S.D., Schwarzbach,J., Yantis,S. (2003). Attentional inhibition of visual processing in human striate cortex and extrastriate cortex. *Neuroimage, 19*, 1602-1611.

So,Y.T., Shapley,R. (1981). Spatial Tuning of cells in and around lateral geniculate nucleus of the cat: X and Y relay cells and perigeniculate interneurons. *Journal of Neurophysiology, 45*, 107-120.

Somers,D.C., Nelson,S.B., Sur,M. (1995). An Emergent Model of orientation selectivity in cat visual cortical simple cells. *Journal of Neuroscience, 15*, 5448-5465.

Tanaka,K. (1983). Cross-correlation analysis of geniculostriate neuronal relationships in cats. *Journal of Neurophysiology, 49*, 1303.

Tao,L., Shelley,M., McLaughlin,D., Shapley,R. (2004). An egalitarian network model for the emergence of simple and complex cells in visual cortex. *Proceedings of the National Academy of Science (USA), 101*, 366-371.

Teich,A.F., Quian,N. (2003). Learning and adaptation in recurrent model V1 orientation selectivity. *Neurophysiol, 89*, 2086-2100. *Journal of Neurophysiology, 89*, 2086-2100.

Thielscher,A., Neumann,H. (2006). A computational model to link psychophysics and cortical cell activation patterns in human texture processing. *Journal of Computational Neuroscience, in print.*

Tootell,R.B., Hadjikhani,N., Hall,E.K., Ledden,P.J., Liu,A.K., Reppas,J.B., Sereno,M.I., Dale,A.M. (1997). Functional analysis of V3A and related areas in human visual cortex. *Journal of Neuroscience, 17*, 7060-7078.

Treisman,A. (1982). Perceptual grouping and attention in visual search for features and for objects. *Journal of experimental psychology Human perception and performance, 8*, 194-214.

Treves,A. (1993). Mean-field analysis of neuronal spike dynamics. *Network, 4*, 259-284.

Troyer,T.W., Krukowsky,A.E., Priebe,N.J., Miller,K.D. (1998). Contrast-invariant orientation tuning in cat visual cortex: thalamocortical input tuning and correlation-based intracortical connectivity. *Journal of Neuroscience, 18*, 5908-5927.

Ts'o,D.Y., Gilbert,C.D., Wiesel,T.N. (1986). Relationships between horizontal interactions and functional architecture in cat striate cortex as revealed by cross-correlation analysis. *Journal of Neuroscience, 6*, 1160-1170.

Ursino,M., La Cara,G.E. (2004a). A Model Of Contextual Interactions And Contour Detection In Primary Visual Cortex. *Neural Networks, 17*, 719-735.

Ursino,M., La Cara,G.E. (2004b). Comparison Of Different Models Of Orientation Selectivity Based On Distinct Intracortical Inhibition Rules. *Vision Research, 44*, 1641-1658.

Ursino,M., La Cara,G.E. (2005). Dependence of Visual Cell Properties on Intracortical Synapses Among Hypercolumns: Analysis by a Computer Model. *Journal of Computational Neuroscience, 19*, 291-310.

Ursino,M., La Cara,G.E., Ritrovato,M. (2007). Direction Selectivity of Simple Cells in the Primary Visual Cortex: Comparison of Two Alternative Mathematical Models. I: Response to Drifting Gratings. *Computers in Biology and Medicine, 37*, 398-414.

vanRullen,R., Delorme,A., Thorpe,S.J. (2001). Feed-forward contour integration in primary visual cortex based on asynchronous spike propagation. *Neurocomputing, 38-40*, 1003-1009.

Vidyasagar,T.R., Pei,X., Volgushev,M. (1996). Multiple mechanisms underlying the orientation selectivity of visual cortical neurones. *Experimental Brain Research, 19*, 272-277.

Vidyasagar,T.R., Siguenza,J.A. (1985). Relationship between orientation tuning and spatial frequency in neurones of cat area 17. *Experimental Brain Research, 57*, 628-631.

Wainwright,M. (1999). Visual adaptation as optimal information transmission. *Vision Research* 3960-3974.

Watkins,D.W., Berkley,M.A. (1974). The orientation selectivity of single neurons in cat striate cortex. *Experimental Brain Research, 19*, 433-446.

Webster,M.A., De Valois,R. (1985). Relationship between spatial-frequency and orientation tuning of striate-cortex cells. *Journal of the Optical Society of America A, Optics and image science, 2*, 1124-1132.

Wertheimer,M. (1938). Laws of organisation in perceptual forms. London: Harcourt Brace Jovanovich.

Wimbauer,S., Wenish,O.G., Miller,K.D., van Hemmen,J.L. (1997a). Development of spatiotemporal receptive fields of simple cells. I: Model formulation. *Biological Cybernetics, 77*, 453-462.

Wimbauer,S., Wenish,O.G., van Hemmen,J.L., Miller,K.D. (1997b). Development of spatiotemporal receptive fields of simple cells. II: Simulation and analysis. *Biological Cybernetics, 77*, 463.

Wörgötter,F., Eysel,U.T. (1989). Axis of preferred motion is a function of bar length in visual cortical receptive fields. *Experimental Brain Research, 76*, 307.

Wörgötter,F., Eysel,U.T. (1991). Axial responses in visual cortical cells: spatio-temporal mechanisms quantified by Fourier components of cortical tuning curves. *Experimental Brain Research, 83*, 656.

Wörgötter,F., Koch,G. (1991). A detailed model of the primary visual pathway in the cat: comparison of afferent excitatory and intracortical inhibitory connection schemes for orientation selectivity. *Journal of Neuroscience, 11*, 1959-1979.

Wörgötter,F., Muche,T., Eysel,U.T. (1991). Correlations between directional and orientational tuning of cells in cat striate cortex. *Experimental Brain Research, 83*, 665.

Wörgötter,F., Suder,K., Zhao,Y., Kerscher,N., Eysel,U.T., Funke,K. (1998). State-dependent receptive field restructuring in the visual cortex. *Nature, 396*, 165-168.

Yen,S., Finkel,L.H. (1998). Extraction of perceptually salient contours by striate cortical networks. *Vision Research, 38*, 719-741.

Yeshurun,Y., Carrasco,M. (1998). Attention improves or impairs visual performance by enhancing spatial resolution. *Nature, 395*, 72-75.

Yeshurun,Y., Carrasco,M. (1999). Spatial attention improves performance in spatial resolution tasks. *Vision Research, 38*, 293-305.

Zhaoping,L. (2005). Border Ownership from Intracortical Interactions in Visual Area V2. *Neuron, 47*, 143-153.

In: Visual Cortex: New Research
Editors: T.A. Portocello and R.B. Velloti

ISBN 978-1-60456-530-0
© 2008 Nova Science Publishers, Inc.

Chapter 2

The Ventral Visual Path: Moving Beyond V1 with Computational Models

Alessio Plebe[*]
Deptartment of Cognitive Science, University of Messina – Italy

Abstract

This chapter addresses the ventral visual processing stream beyond V1. This part of the visual system is known to be essential for recognition, the most important visual task for humans. In recent years, important progress has been made in regards to two particular areas of the ventral path, namely V2 and LOC (Lateral Occipital Complex), that will be addressed in detail here. There are several reasons for this choice. In the hierarchy of the occipital visual cortex, V2 is the second area and is similar in size to that of V1, and therefore holds a weight in the economy of the visual process that is comparable to V1. The network of areas grouped under the name LOC is human-specific, and is held to be the first area specifically involved in object recognition. While standard neurological research and neuroimaging, in particular, have been essential in advancing the knowledge of the ventral visual system, a thorough understanding of the mechanisms underlying visual object recognition requires assessing the computational functions performed by the cortical maps. In this effort, computational models are extremely helpful and a section of this chapter deals with the achievements obtained in modeling, in the interpretation of the functional role of V2, and in the simulation of object recognition with cortical maps in the ventral stream up to LOC.

1. Introduction

Primary visual cortex, otherwise known as V1, is one of the most researched areas of the brain. The computational functions performed by its neural circuits are those best understood. Considering that V1, though being essential to the task of seeing, makes up less than one-fifth of the human visual cortex, we are unfortunately left with an unclear picture of what the functions of the other areas are. While studies on V1 continue to outnumber those

---

[*]E-mail address: alessio.plebe@unime.it

that focus on other areas of human visual cortex, new research endeavors are beginning to shed light on the role played by areas beyond V1. This chapter focuses on areas in the ventral path, which according to the traditional division of the cortical visual system into dorsal and ventral areas introduced by Ungerleider and Mishkin (1982), is mainly responsible for shape and object recognition. Object recognition is one of the most important as well as puzzling capabilities of human vision. It is easy to acknowledge the importance of this function, since it is the basic way of ascribing meaning to perceptual phenomena. It leads to the development of symbolic representations and raises vision from being a purely optical process, to being a fundamental cognitive activity. Recognition is such an important and pervasive aspect of our ability to see, that most of the time we cannot avoid it, even in tasks where it is not required (James & Gauthier, 2004).

Among the areas in the visual path, special attention will be given to two particular areas of the ventral path, namely V2 and LOC (Lateral Occipital Complex) and the important progress that has been made in this line of research in recent years will be discussed. In the hierarchy of the occipital visual cortex, V2 is the second area and is similar in size to that of V1. Due to its size and position, it is certainly as important as V1 in the visual process, but it is much less understood. One piece of evidence that has emerged from recent studies is that V2's main contribution to vision is the detection of slightly more complex features than those processed in V1. The network of areas grouped under the name LOC is human-specific, and has no obvious homologues in the macaque monkey. It has gained attention as being the first area in the visual processing stream, and is strongly involved in object recognition. The response properties of cells in this area seem to fulfill the requirements for an object-recognition area: sensitivity to moderately complex and complex visual stimuli; reasonable invariance to size, specific visual cues, and some perspective transformation; perceptual filling-in and grouping capabilities.

In the understanding of vision, especially in the ventral path, an important aspect is the grasping of what kind of computational functions are performed, from the sensorial stimuli stage, up to that of recognition. In this respect, several basic concepts that merge functional and anatomical aspects are important, such as that of "receptive field", first introduced by Hartline (1938), and that of "cortical maps", used by Mountcastle (1957). These and other key concepts will be introduced in the second section of the chapter. In the third section the whole ventral cortical pathway beyond V1 will be described, with special emphasis on V2 and LOC. Having said that the enterprise of uncovering the mechanisms underlying the ventral visual process requires understanding its computational functions, it is clear that computational models are important tools of investigation, and will be fleshed out in the fourth section of the chapter. Special emphasis will be given to recent models where the effort has been that of reproducing the development of cortical circuits in the visual areas.

2.   Key Concepts in the Organization of the Visual Cortex

In this section several concepts will be introduced that will serve as the basis of the explanations and the models discussed in this chapter. Several of these concepts are quite general, not only applicable to visual areas other than those here addressed, but also common to the behavior of the cortex as a whole. Though these concepts were later proven valid for the cortex, many of them were first found to be true in the study of vision. They come from empirical neuroscience, but their reach is much wider, enlightening our understanding of the organization of the mind, and grounding the design of modern computational models of the cortex.

2.1. What a Neuron Fires for

Perhaps the most useful concept in current vision science is that of "receptive field", first introduced by Keffer Hartline in 1938, as the area in the retina which must be illuminated in order to obtain a response in a given neuron. Yet, as early as 1928, Hartline was able to exploit the just introduced technology of single cell readings (Adrian & Matthews, 1927b, 1927a) in vision, by examining a very suitable animal, the xiphosuran arachnoid *Limulus polyphemus*, commonly called "horseshoe crab". Its lateral compound eyes are coarsely faceted, and receptor cells project to the brain by long optic nerves, in which single axons can be separated rather easily. The relation between the eye stimulus and the neural discharge is relatively simple, with each omnatidum having its own single neuron. Illuminating a single omnatidum, therefore, elicits firing of its connected neuron. The case of *Limulus* however, turned out to be not so simple after all. When neighbor omnatida are also illuminated, the discharge decreases, revealing inhibitory interactions, an intriguing effect that Hartline went back to study further several years later, and which won him the Nobel Prize(1967). The need for an idea like that of receptive fields become necessary when Hartline, in 1938, after his initial success with the *Limulus*, undertook the same single axon analysis of the more complex optic responses of cold-blooded vertebrate retina. When recording from single axons Hartline found other behaviors, in addition to discharges similar to those in the *Limulus*, in which there was firing for the duration of the light stimulus. What he found was activity appearing when a light stimulus was withdrawn, as well as activity correlated to the onset and cessation of illumination. Moreover, he was able to define the precise configuration of a receptive field, by charting the boundaries of an area over which a spot of light sets up impulses in a ganglion cell axon.

His results were replicated in mammals by Stephen Kuffler (1953), who refined the definition of receptive field, by differentiating its anatomical and functional meaning. The anatomical configuration of a receptive field is the pathway of all receptors actually connected to a ganglion cells, and is fixed at a certain stage of maturation of the organism. The functional meaning includes not only the areas from which responses can actually be elicited by retinal illumination, but also all those areas which show a functional connection, by an inhibitory or excitatory effect on a ganglion cell. In this respect, the field size may change depending on the illumination pattern, involving areas which are not in the immediate neighborhood of the ganglion cell and that by themselves do not induce discharges.

In 1959 the seminal works of David Hubel and Torsten Wiesel extended the concept of receptive fields from neurons in the retina up to neurons in the cortex, discovering the now well-known selectivity to line orientation in the primary visual area. Their studies increasingly spread the double use of the receptive field concepts: taken to mean, the definition of an area on the retina that excites a neuron, or the specific properties of the input pattern that evokes the strongest activity in the neuron. This last use of receptive field is, for example, the one relevant for Hubel and Wiesel in the differentiation of cells in the striate cortex as

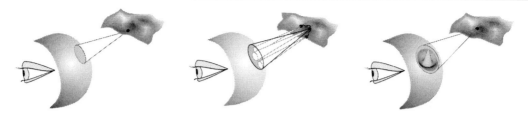

Figure 1. The evolution in the meaning of the expression "receptive field", illustrated by a sketch of the retina and a cortical neuron. On the left, the receptive field as originally introduced by Hartline, in the middle, including lateral connections, on the right, accounting for the shape of the field function.

"simple" or "complex", and is used to further classify several distinct behaviors in complex cells (1962). The focus on the shape of receptive fields, and the new picture given by Hubel and Wiesel, stimulated research efforts to find mathematical formulations that could characterize receptive fields in a concise and readable form . Examples are the difference of Gaussians for ganglion cells and neurons in LGN (*Lateral Geniculate Nucleus*) (Rodieck, 1965; Rose, 1979), or Gabor functions (Gabor, 1946) for simple cells in V1 (Daugman, 1980, 1985). A sort of "evolution" in how the notion of receptive field has been used and interpreted is given in Fig. 1.

It is interesting to point out that the concept of receptive field is not only of practical use in characterizing the specific behavior of cells in visual systems, it is first and foremost, a possible answer to a fundamental question in neuroscience and philosophy as well: what is it exactly a neuron fires for? That question is the essence of an epistemological transition from the understanding of the physics of the neuron, to the explaining of how neural systems can be representational devices of the external world (P. S. Churchland & Sejnowski, 1990, 1994; deCharms & Zador, 2000; P. S. Churchland & Churchland, 2002). When the receptive field concerns ganglion cells, or thalamic cells in LGN, the answer become relatively simple: the neuron activity signals a specific sensorial experience, that takes place in a narrow area of the retina. A direct causal connection, of a topological nature, between facts in the external world and neural behavior can be established. Moving into the cortex, the receptive field of cells in V1 can still be a good explanation of contents or representations: the peculiar shape of objects in the external world on which cells are tuned, together with the topological constraints of where in the retina the stimulus of this object is projected. But as soon as areas in the visual cortex depart from sensorial inputs, the shape of receptive fields become highly complex, and the connections with sensorial input weaker. The receptive field concepts by themselves are not enough to account for neural contents, and need to be integrated with other concepts.

The main factor making receptive fields complex and not as easy to identify as their definition would suggest, was already present in the first studies done by Hartline on the *Limulus*: the effect of lateral interactions (Hartline et al., 1961). In the case of *Limulus* each ommatidium has only inhibitory connections with its immediate neighbors, and still the resulting effects were not straightforward, for the recurrent property of this interaction. In the cortex, lateral interactions become dominant for two main reasons. First, there is an overlapping mechanism of inhibitory and excitatory connections as well, and second, lateral connections from a cell extend over a long range, reaching for example, in V1, up to 7 mm (Gilbert & Wiesel, 1983; Stettler et al., 2002). Lateral interactions seem to play a fundamental role in the computational properties of the cortex, in a way that is yet far from being well understood (Sirosh et al., 1996). Due to lateral interactions the shape of receptive fields in the cortex is less influenced by the afferent pathway of thalamic connections and therefore, the relationship between neural firing and retinal stimulus might be highly complex. In practice, the recurrent mechanism of lateral interactions, replicated over multiple layers of processing, makes it almost impossible to derive mathematical formulations for receptive fields in visual areas beyond V1.

2.2. A Legitimate Partitioning Criterion for the Cortex

A widespread notion about the organization of the cerebral cortex is that of "cortical maps", whose origin can be traced back to Vernon Mountcastle (1957). He discovered the columnar organization of the cortex, reporting that in the vertical dimension cortical cells tend to respond to the same peripheral stimuli. Therefore, it is along the 2-dimensional surface of the cortex that the firing of neurons signals the occurrence of a stimulus on a spot in a sensorial area, and the topological mapping is the first fundamental correlation between sensorial space and cortical space. Mountcastle obtained these results during his investigations of the cat somatosensory cortex, but he speculated that what he saw before him might be a more general, possibly fundamental, architectural principle of the mammalian cortex as a whole. Shortly after, solid confirmation arrived from the above-mentioned studies of Hubel and Wiesel on the visual cortex, and the term "cortical maps" made its appearance as a reference notion for most of the studies on the cortex, and has been used since then. In fact, cortical maps have been found in nearly all of the sensory and motor areas of the brain (Felleman & Van Essen, 1991), and the difficulty in characterizing other areas as maps also, lies in the lack of a direct meaning of the space dimensions in the cortex. A theoretical advantage in the notion of "cortical maps" is the empirical criteria for identifying a portion of the cortex, unified functionally as a specific neural circuit: the consistent responsiveness of the cells in that part to contiguous sensorial stimulations.

The appeal to the spatial correspondence with sensorial periphery has not been the only criteria for partitioning the cortex into meaningful neural aggregates. At the beginnings of the enterprise of understanding the functions of cortical areas, anatomical methods dominated. In some fortunate cases, anatomy was in fact, sufficient for the precise identification of functional maps to be done. This is the case of V1, which can be easily identified by its heavy myelination in layer 4C, using a light microscope in post-mortem material. This was known since the eighteen century as *lineola albidior* (Gennari, 1782). The anatomical approach continues to be extremely useful today supported by sophisticated methods, such as the combination of connectivity patterns and myeloarchitecture (Maunsell & Van Essen, 1983; Felleman & Van Essen, 1991), [2-14C]deoxyglucose tracing (Macko et al., 1982), computational morphing (Van Essen et al., 2001). But in the recent past, the identification of cortical maps by direct evidence of the coherent response of neurons to a contiguous sensorial periphery has become of primary importance, thanks to non-invasive technologies. In vision science, a probing method first introduced by Stephen Engel (1997), and widely applied and extended by Brian Wandell (1999; 2005) allows the substitution of Mountcastle's

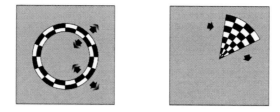

Figure 2. Sketch of the patterns used by Engel and Wandell in the search for retinotopic maps in the visual cortex. On the left, the expanding ring, on the right, the spinning wedge.

electrophysiology with neuroimaging. In this method the two concepts of cortical maps and receptive field meet: special moving patterns are presented, that span the entire retinal area, while the subject is scanned using fMRI. Patterns are high contrast checkboard sectors in a contracting ring or spinning wedges. The expanding-contracting ring measures topological organization of maps with respect to visual eccentricity, while wedges are used to assess topological organization with respect to polar angles. The two patterns are sketched in Fig. 2.

Cortical maps joined with receptive fields, helped complete the picture of neural systems as representational devices. While the notion of receptive field helps in ascribing content to the firing of a single cell, the same firing in the context of a cortical map acquires additional meaning by the spatial relationship the cell under investigation has with the cells of the same map. The most direct interpretation of this additional information is of a spatial nature itself, the concept of retinotopy, where information represented in the map concerns the topology of the stimulus in the retina. However, as Mountcastle had warned in his early studies, cortical maps should not be interpreted as modified copies of the array of receptors in the periphery. First of all, maps in the cortex are more often overlaps of several different sensorial features. In Mountcastle's experiments, he classified three different peripheral modalities: stimulations at the skin level, deep pressure stimulation, and that related with joint position. In the investigated cortical map, he found an overlap of different modalities projected by the same peripheral area, with neurons responding to skin stimulation for example, intermingling with those responding to deep pressure in a mosaic-like fashion. Even if limiting the analysis to a single modality, and the interpretation to the spatial representation of the stimuli, none of the features represented in a cortical map appear to be topographically simple. Maps often contain modular repetitions of small segments of receptor areas, within a global topography (Krubitzer, 1995; Vanduffel et al., 2002). Moreover, inside a module where topology is preserved, metrics are often distorted, with seemingly purposeful magnifications and other transformations (D. Hubel & Wiesel, 1974; Van Essen et al., 1984).

The most intriguing aspect of cortical maps, however, is that the ordering in the two dimensions of the cortical sheet might represent any feature of interest in the sensorial stimuli, without any relationship to the spatial topology of the stimulus itself. This is the case of the tonotopic organization of the auditory cortex (Verkindt et al., 1995). As in the case of submodalities of the sensorial periphery, also in respect to features it has to be expected that more than one feature will find simultaneous representation on the same cortical map. Area V1 is one where an impressive number of overlapping features have been discovered:

ocular dominance (Wiesel & Hubel, 1965; Tootell, Switkes, et al., 1988c), orientation selectivity (D. Hubel & Wiesel, 1968; Vanduffel et al., 2002), retinotopy (Tootell, Switkes,
et al., 1988b), color (Tootell, Switkes, et al., 1988a), and spatial frequency (Tootell, Silverman, et al., 1988). The suspicion is that such a complex mapping might not be unusual
in the cortex, and might very well be common to many cortical maps, just that only few
characteristic features have been discovered so far for other areas .

Questions regarding the extent to which the map architecture is ubiquitous as the representation strategy of the cortex, and how map contents should be interpreted, is a matter
of open debate, with several opinions contending for dominance. In the early discussions
on brain representation the dominant view was that topological organization might even be
detrimental or incompatible with the way the cortex functions, which was assumed to be
mainly associative (Kaas, 1997). Today, on the contrary, the widely held opinion is that
cortical maps are not incidental, but essential to the nature of brain representations. There
have been several suggestions that two dimensional topological maps are the most efficient
representation coding, given that neurons work by synaptic connections. Thus, placing connected neurons as close to each other as possible is an evolutionary strategy to save wiring
costs, and cortical maps are the resulting prevailing architecture in the brain (Swindale,
2001; Chklovskii & Koulakov, 2004). A good demonstration is retinotopy, that allows neurons to represent adjacent parts of the visual field, and to interact over short axonal and
dendritic pathways.

Other authors have argued that cortical maps are the optimal solution, but with respect to computational properties rather than anatomical constraints. For example, from
an information-theoretic point of view, ordered maps maximize the mutual information between input and output signals (Linsker, 1989), or in terms of parameter space of the stimuli,
cortical maps perform optimal dimension-reducing mappings (Durbin & Mitchison, 1990).
However, the solution of ordered maps as cortical representations is not a universal rule.
It was known since the early investigations of V1 that several rodents, like hamsters (Tiao
& Blakemore, 1976) and rabbit (Murphy & Berman, 1979) do not have orderly orientation
map in the primary visual cortex, but do have orientation-selective neurons. The lack of
orientation maps in these rodents was supposed to be related to their poor visual ability, or
their small absolute V1 size. But recently, investigations on a highly visual rodent, with a
large V1, the gray squirrel, confirmed the lack of orientation maps (Van Hooser et al., 2005).
This result of course cannot rule out that rodents may still have a system of organization of
V1 with respect to orientation, that we are not able to identify and understand.

In the effort of making progress in the interpretation of contents in higher-level maps,
where a direct relation with peripheral inputs is lost, these past few decades research has
drawn on the idea that the power of representing information in cortical circuits lies in the
combinations of activities of many columnar units. This concept is usually named "distributed coding" (Hinton et al., 1986), but also "population coding" , "vector coding" and
"state space representation", in the formulation by Paul Churchland (1989). The idea has
actually been around for some time, but mainly as intuitions without a sound relation to
neurological data, as by Pribram (1971), who suggested that brain representations are distributed in force of a supposed analogy with holograms. In the current interpretation of
population coding, a higher level map may code for a kind of object or fact, and is the concurrent level of firing of a population of cells in that map that represent a specific instance

of the kind. Since the 90's several studies have quantified how distributed the response in higher cortical areas to set of stimuli in a similar class is . In (Sakai et al., 1994), monkeys were trained to remember synthetic pictures, at least 59 cells out of 91 recorded, responded to more than one picture. Other experiments done with natural faces (E. Rolls & Tovee, 1995; Abbott, Rolls, & Tovee, 1996) confirmed that not single cells, but population of cells are necessary to discriminate single stimuli. (Pasupathy & Connor, 2002) studied the population coding by 109 cells in area V4 of macaque monkeys, of curvatures and angular positions from 49 simple patterns. The coding was demonstrated by reconstructing mathematically the 49 patterns from the population responses. A different stream of research inside distributed coding attempts to establish computationally, the reasons and advantages nature has for adopting this representational strategy in the cortex (Hinton et al., 1986; Olshausen & Field, 1996; Brunel & Nadal, 1998).

When framing questions about cortical maps in computational terms, the support for many opinions easily turns to the simulation of maps with artificial models. We will return to this topic in §4.. For now, suffice it to say that the notion of cortical maps is also very important for the possibility itself, of building computational models of complex functions like vision. In fact, one of the fundamental methodologies in the field of computation is the division of complex tasks into separate "modules". Unfortunately, the old picture of the brain as a collection of autonomous models, common in the early years of cognitive science (Fodor, 1983) has been disproved by neuroscientific and theoretic evidence (for the case of vision see P. S. Churchland et al., 1994). A modern approach used in building modular models is to appeal to the notion of cortical maps. A computational model would be fully justified, in necessarily resorting to a modular structure for simplicity, if modules are constrained to correspond to cortical maps, preserving the same hierarchy and basic connections of the cortex.

Eventually, as will be discussed later in §2.4., more insight into this theoretical discussion can be gained when considering the question of how cortical maps develop in the organism.

2.3.   The "what" and "where" Paths

Within the complex of many cortical maps in the visual system, a broad partition commonly accepted in current vision science, is that of the ventral and dorsal paths. The first experiment to investigate the existence of two visual systems were carried out by Gerard Schneider (1967) with golden hamsters (*mesocricetus auratus*), finding segregation in processing of patterns and space. This result was soon confirmed by Colwyn Trevarthen (1968), who, working on split-brain monkeys, differentiated between a system for object vision and an ambient system for guiding behavior and locomotion. Ungerleider and Mishkin (1982) went further, proposing the existence of two visual paths in terms that are currently widely held in vision science. First of all, they show that both paths are located inside the cortex, one following a dorsal path, traversing the posterior parietal region to the frontal lobe, the other following an inferior ventral route, into the temporal lobe. They also consolidated the fortunate dichotomy of "what" and "where", in that the ventral pathway is specialized for object perception whereas the dorsal pathway is specialized for spatial perception. They supported their thesis with strong evidence from careful experiments with lesioned mon-

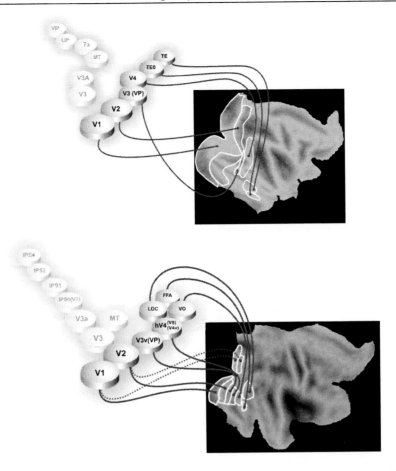

Figure 3.   Scheme of the division in ventral (darker) and dorsal (lighter) visual paths in the macaque cortex (above), and in the human cortex (below). Ventral maps are reported on flat right hemisphere cortex representations, from http://sumsdb.wustl.edu:8081/sums/, see (Van Essen, 2005).

keys. When engaged in a pattern-discrimination task severe impairment was produced by ventral but not dorsal lesions, while a landmark task was impaired in the case of damage in the dorsal path, not in the ventral path.

A few years later, a different theory for independent paths of processing in vision (D. H. Hubel & Livingstone, 1987; Livingstone & Hubel, 1987) proposed four streams, that begin in the retina, with the division into magno- and parvo-ganglion cells, that cross LGN and V1, and then proceed up to higher areas. The four paths serve the separate processing of form, color, motion and stereo information. Differently from the dorsal-ventral partition, this hypothesis, despite important evidence, has been highly controversial. The four pathways do not have the same sharp functional separation found in the dorsal-ventral case, as there is significant interaction among them (Nealey & Maunsell, 1994; Van Essen & DeYoe, 1994).

The ventral-dorsal distinction has been enormously influential in helping to interpret the functional organization of the visual cortex, and is also used in this chapter. Recently, it has been found that a similar division can be shared by other modalities, as for example in the auditory cortex, where two streams originate in the caudal and rostral parts, and target spatial and non-spatial domains of the frontal lobe (Romanski & Goldman-Rakic, 1999).

For what concerns the "what" and "where" dichotomy, while there has been large consensus on the "what" interpretation of the ventral path, the "where" has been less satisfactory, and has been subject to new proposed interpretations. One of these interpretations, considers that the dorsal system codes visual information for action organization, therefore, "where" should be read as "how", and curiously the same revision has been proposed for both the visual system (Goodale & Milner, 1992) and the auditory system (Belin & Zatorre, 2000). A possible reconciliation of the dorsal interpretation as space perception or action organization can be achieved by a further division, with a dorso-dorsal stream related to action and the ventro-dorsal stream playing a role in space perception (Rizzolatti & Matelli, 2003). We will not go too far into this debate, as this chapter will focus on areas in the ventral path only, for which the traditional division introduced by Ungerleider and Mishkin is largely agreed upon, with the view that it is the path mainly responsible for shape and object recognition.

2.4. Development of Cortical Circuits

Much of modern vision science began with the detailed analysis of neuron responses in cortical circuits, dating back to the works of D. Hubel and Wiesel. The idea is that by taking a static picture of the mapping between range of input stimuli and neural output in an organism, we can gain insight into the overall architecture of the visual system. This approach has provided a number of remarkable advances in understanding vision, and the brain as well, but as more details about cortical architecture become available, more puzzles and unanswered questions arise. The same two researchers were the first to suggest a parallel road of investigation, that being investigating how functions in visual cortical areas develop during the maturation of an organism. Their experiments demonstrated that kittens reared with one eye closed during an initial and perhaps "sensitive" period, did not develop the normal ocular dominance architecture in the primary visual cortex (D. Hubel & Wiesel, 1963; Wiesel & Hubel, 1965).

Knowledge of the role visual experience plays in the development of normal mature vision capability was not new, in fact, this was already known in psychophysiology of perception and ophthalmology. Volkmann demonstrated how the visual threshold for two-point discrimination changed with experience, finding that few hours of practice decreased the minimum detectable separation between two points by about 50%. Amblyopia is a typical visual impairment subsequent to early monocular deprivation (Vaegan & Taylor, 1979), as defined by von Gräfe (1858), it is a serious condition, without any apparent organic pathology. In an elegant experiment by Held and Hein (1962) two kittens were placed in two joint baskets, arranged so that only one basket could move, causing the movement of the other. Both kittens received much of the same visual stimulation, but the one carried passively in the basket remained effectively almost totally blind.

The novelty of (D. Hubel & Wiesel, 1963; Wiesel & Hubel, 1965) was in the attempt of tracing development back to the level of change in the cortical architecture. It met with the growing awareness on the plasticity of the mammalian cortex, and the fact that cortical circuits at their first formation have little differentiation in the computational capability they will potentially perform in the mature stage. The interaction between sensorial stimuli and basic mechanisms of development is what drives differentiation in the adult functions (Artola & Singer, 1987; L. C. Katz & Callaway, 1992; Kirkwood & Bear, 1994; Karten, 2000; Löwel & Singer, 2002; Sengpiel & Kind, 2002).

Soon after the discovery of the role of experience in modulation ocular dominance, other studies revealed a similar role in the development of orientation selectivity. The pattern of orientation preference in kitten's primary cortex shifts towards particular orientations if kittens where reared in special environments with dominant stimuli, such as striped cylinders (Blakemore & Grahame, 1970), or opaque goggles with images of lines of a single orientation (Stryker et al., 1978). One of the most impressive demonstrations of the plasticity in the cortex was a famous experiment (Roe et al., 1990) in which projections from the retina of newborn ferrets were routed to the auditory pathway through the MGN (*Medial Geniculate Nucleus*), and an orderly two-dimensional retinotopic map developed in the cortical target of MGN, that normally is called the primary "auditory cortex".

The crucial role of environmental experience in cortical development, especially in the human brain, and its interaction with genetic mechanisms, has progressed considerably in the last decades, combining advances in theoretical neurobiology (Quartz, 1993; Quartz & Sejnowski, 1997; Quartz, 2003), psychology of development and mathematical learning theory, in what is now often called "neuroconstructivism" (Westermann et al., 2007; Mareschal et al., 2007). Inside this new body of research, development of functions such as vision are often studied in the new area called "perceptual learning" (Fahle & Poggio, 2002), where, as is explicit in the name, the distinction between development and learning fades away.

For some time, a puzzle in the developmental explanation of the mammalian visual system was the presence of what seemed to be a partial organization in the brain visual area already at birth. A solution to this puzzle was discovered in the last decades, with the discovery of the existence of a kind of simulated visual environment, made possible by spontaneous retinal waves (Mastronarde, 1983; Meister, Wong, Daylor, & Shatz, 1991). While the gestation period is rich in auditory experiences, this is not true for the eyes, therefore, these semiperiodic burst of excitation, occurring spontaneously in the developing retina of most vertebrate species, may overcome the lack of experience, providing the first "practice" exercises for LGN and visual cortex (Shatz & Stryker, 1988; Shatz, 1990; L. Katz & Shatz, 1996). In the last few years progress has been made in investigating the interaction between intrinsic and environmental factors in neural circuit development, and the dynamic interplay between experience and genetic expression driving the maturation of the cortex. The overall picture appears extremely complex, and far from being fully understood. In recent studies (Majdan & Shatz, 2006; Tropea et al., 2006) the classical experiments of dark-rearing and monocular deprivation at birth are replicated on mice, applying DNA microarray and other advanced genetic methodologies in analyzing the results, finding upregulation or downregulation of specific genes subserving synaptic transmission and electrical activity.

Development has also been a key paradigm in the progress of computational modeling of the visual cortex, as will be illustrated in §4., and a valuable piece in the process of coming up with a sound answer to the basic question, on how neurons serve as representational devices, issued in §2.1.. We have already seen that a good reason for a neuron to fire could be the presence of a stimulus in its receptive field, of the topological correspondence between a feature in the current stimulus and the ordering of the map the neuron belongs to. Now it can be said that an even better reason for firing is that the actual stimulus is characterized by a feature resembling experience in a history of interesting patterns seen, and that this neuron contributes in coding. (P. S. Churchland & Churchland, 2002).

3. Inside the Ventral Visual Path

This section will provide neurophysiological details on the ventral visual path beyond V1, first with a short overview of all the maps composing this part of the cortex, followed by a broader description of two specific areas, V2 and LOC, which are also the objects of the computational models presented in §4.. Our focus is mainly on the human visual system, but several accounts on other animals, especially primates, will also be provided, considering that they are useful in understanding the human visual system.

3.1. The Hierarchy of Cortical Maps in Primate and Human Ventral Visual Paths

History has shown us how the main achievements in visual science these past 50 years, have been due to experiments done with animals rather than humans. Only recently, thanks to technologies like functional MRI (Ogawa et al., 1990; Wandell, 1999; Logothetis & Wandell, 2004) and DTI (*Diffusion Tensor Imaging*) (Hagmann et al., 2003; Dougherty et al., 2005; Wandell & Dougherty, 2006)has the direct investigation on humans rapidly progressed. It is therefore, natural to find that in the current geography of human visual cortical maps, the legacy of findings in other animals, especially primates, is still preponderant. One of the first significant difficulties in extending to human cortical maps information drawn from different species, arises from the orographic differences in the corrugations and convolutions of the cortex. This variability is exacerbated in the case of vision, because the main visual areas lie buried within deep and irregular sulci. An important step in mitigating this problem has come from advances in computerized brain mapping that allows us to move from the raw 3-D coordinate system of the brain (Talairach & Tournoux, 1988), to a surface-based geography of an artificially flattened cortex (Drury et al., 1996; Toga, 1998). Surface-based warping provided a suitable strategy for an accurate comparison between the achieved charting of visual areas in primates, especially macaque monkeys, and humans (Van Essen et al., 2001). Despite the progress made in visual cortex mapping for both primates and humans, and the now available possibility of comparing results, it should be said that the picture of maps beyond V1, is still far from being clear or universally accepted. First of all, even with extensive use of accurate invasive techniques, a complete atlas of the visual system in monkeys has never been achieved. Second, the new possibility of a detailed comparison of the visual cortex of humans and macaque monkeys has revealed that the correspondence of homologous areas beyond V1 and V2 is problematic (Kaas, 1993; Van Essen et al., 2001; M. I. Sereno & Tootell, 2005). A symptom of how controversial the situation is, is represented by the lack of an agreed upon naming criteria, apart from that of V1 and V2.

In the early study of mammalian visual cortex, the preferred names for the initially discovered maps were "V I" and "V II" (Thompson et al., 1950), if they were named at all, in fact, they often were simply referred to by their correspondence to areas 17 and 18 of the Brodmann (1909) brain topography. The use of roman numerals was deliberate, to suggest the order of importance in the processing of an area, as had been done first for the somatosensory cortex by Woolsey and Fairman (1946). But as soon as it became clear that two would have been a very small number, compared to how many cortical maps might exist in the primate visual cortex, roman numbering become unpractical, substituted by the preferred form "Vn", with "n" a digit. One digit sufficed, to our knowledge no one has yet proposed a V9 visual area. In fact, in the macaque as many as 32 visual maps have been proposed (Felleman & Van Essen, 1991), and in humans as well, the number very likely exceeds 10, but for most higher areas the form "Vn" has been abandoned in favor of specific acronyms. Sometimes the two naming conventions coexist. This is the case of the area in the dorsal stream sensitive to motion, identified in the same period by Allman and Kaas (1971) in the owl monkey, called it MT because it is located in the Middle Temporal gyrus, and Zeki (1974) in the macaque monkey, who later called it V5 Zeki (1978), because it abuts V4.

In Fig. 3 the most accepted current representations of the ventral paths in the human and the macaque monkey visual system are sketched. The first area next to V1, with the obvious name of V2, is the only area with a clear and uncontroversial definition, it will be described in detail in §3.2.. As mentioned earlier, after V2, the definition of areas becomes problematic.

3.1.1. Area V3 and Friends

One basic hypothesis was that V2 is surrounded anteriorly by a narrow strip of cortex that encompasses a single representation of the visual field, and therefore could be named "V3", following the same hierarchy from V1 to V2. However, it soon was found that the putative V3 seems to differ substantially in many respects from V1 and V2, in the symmetry between the dorsal and the ventral part (Felleman et al., 1984; Van Essen et al., 1984; Burkhalter et al., 1986). Not only is the anatomy different, the connectivity is different as well, with V1 projecting in the upper part of V3 but not in the lower part, and even functionally, with the dorsal part having a higher incidence of directionally selective neurons but less color selective neurons (Burkhalter & Van Essen, 1986). Van Essen's group, therefore, proposed that in the case of macaque monkey, the lower part of what was called V3 should not be considered as part of V3 at all, but a distinct area they called "VP" (*Ventral Posterior*). In absence of more convincing data in humans, the same naming has been inherited from the macaque monkey. However, there was one puzzling consequence of the two independent areas anterior to V2, with VP in the ventral location, this map seems to only represent the upper quadrant of the visual field. It is highly improbable that a cortical map is computing a specific processing of something happening in upper quadrants, without machinery for processing the same attribute when it occurs in lower quadrants. The idea of VP has thus been disputed (Kaas & Lyon, 2001; Zeki, 2003b), in favor of a unified map with its dorsal and ventral parts. The doubt is still there, however, evident in the addition of a ventral/dorsal suffix in the names, such as "V3v" and "V3d". Furthermore, another region located between V3 and V4, in the lunate and parieto-occipital sulci, has been proposed (Van Essen & Zeki, 1978), and labeled as "V3A". This area has full hemifield representation, and in humans has not only been confirmed, but an additional V3B, inferior and lateral to V3A, has been supposed as well (A. T. Smith, Greenlee, Kraemer, & Hennig, 1998; Press, Brewer, Dougherty, Wade, & Wandell, 2001). What all those putative maps share functionally, is selectivity in response by a consistent population of neurons to the direction of motion in the scene, and of some cells in response to stereovisual disparity, suggesting a role in the processing of motion information (Felleman et al., 1984; Gegenfurtner, Kiper, & Levitt, 1997; Press et al., 2001).

3.1.2. The Color Center

The dispute concerning V3 is in fact less vigorous, than that concerning what is next to V3. This is the point where dorsal and ventral streams clearly depart, and there is no symmetric correspondence between maps in the upper and lower areas. In the ventral stream, an area called "V4" was first identified in monkeys by Zeki (1971b), initially as two distinct areas, V4 and V4a. This area was associated to color processing. In a series of elegant experiments Zeki (1983a, 1983b) made a distinction between cells that respond selectively to "wavelengths" and those responding to "colors", where the last term refers to the astonishing perceptual property of seeing a surface as constantly colored despite the large variation in the composition of the energy and wavelength of the light that is reflected from it. Even if both color-sensitive and wavelength-sensitive cells were found in V1 as in V4, the specificity in V4 was in the strong contribution of the surroundings of a color-coding cell in its response. This is the necessary condition for assigning a constant color to a surface seen in its environment. Further support came from lesions and deficits studies, showing that in the monkey, lesions to V4 severely impair color discrimination and partially impair color constancy (Walsh, Kulikowski, Butler, & Carden, 1992; Walsh, Carden, Butler, & Kulikowski, 1993), and that achromatopsic human patients lose color perception following damage to fusiform and lingual gyri, a location that apparently includes V4 (Pearlman, Birch, & Meadows, 1979; Damasio, Yamada, Damasio, Corbett, & McKee, 1980; Verriest, 1980; Zeki, 1990).

The conscious experience of color also seems to be supported by V4, as shown in experiments using the McCollough effect (Barnes et al., 1999; Morita et al., 2004). It is an illusory effect, in which the color stimuli are constant, but their perception can be varied gradually, by alternating two orthogonally oriented grating patterns (McCollough, 1965). By inducing this effect it is possible to expose several subjects to the same color, but only part of them can consciously perceive the color. The studies demonstrated that V4 was activated only in subjects aware of the color.

Another intriguing piece of evidence was found in colored-hearing synesthesia, the phenomenon of experiencing colors in response to words heard. Synesthetes showed activations in V4 area and not in V1 or V2 (Nunn et al., 2002). Despite these results, whether or not V4 is principally processing color is still an open question. Several authors have reported on the role of V4 in shape processing (David, Hayden, & Gallant, 2006), and others have argued that most of the color processing might be accomplished just in the retina (Wade & Wandell, 2002) and in V1 (Engel, Zhang, & Wandell, 1997; Boynton, 2002).

The details of this controversy are outside the scope of this section, but it is included in a more general discussion on the relationship between visual cortical maps and computational functions, that will be addressed in §4.1..

Here we limit ourselves to listing supposed cortical maps, something that is no less controversial. Decades later than in monkeys, an equivalent to monkey's V4 was ascertained by Lueck et al. (1989); Zeki et al. (1991) in humans, in the lingual fusiform gyrus. The studies were based on PET (Positron Emission Tomography), the imaging technique already available at that period, which did not allow, however, the retinotopic identification of visual fields in a cortical map. When the method of visual field mapping (Engel, Glover, & Wandell, 1997) became available (see §2.2.), M. Sereno et al. (1995) redefined the borders of the early visual maps in humans, calling "V4v" ("v" for ventral) in the fusiform gyrus, because of it having upper visual fields only. Working on this new cortical geography, in a further study that focused on the color area only, Hadjikhani, Liu, Dale, Cavanagh, and Tootell (1998) argued that the real color center in humans is not V4v, but an anterior area with full hemifield representation. Extending the tradition of baptizing new areas with "V" followed by a digit, they called it "V8".

This thesis has been rejected by Zeki, McKeefry, Bartels, and Frackowiak (1998) who deemed V8 equivalent to the previously identified V4 in humans, and considered it a mistake to suppose a posterior quarter-field map V4v, this led to yet another vivid discussion (Tootell & Hadjikhani, 2001; Zeki, 2003b, 2003a). In the meantime, different hypotheses have come forth. In (Wade et al., 2002) it is suggested that there is a full hemifield representation adjacent to V3, that should be called hV4 ("h" for humans), even if nearby regions along the ventral pathway could also have additional retinotopic maps and color selectivity. Tyler et al. (2005) measured two distinct maps anterior to V3 in the ventral pathway, and proposed abandoning the use of digits after "V", in naming the two areas "VMO" (VentroMedial Occipital) and "VOF" (Ventral Occipital Foveal), this last naming is justified by the strong foveal representation of the area. In a series of studies Wandell's group retained the name of hV4 as the area that abuts V3, but includes as involved in color processing additional maps in the fusiform gyrus, unified as belonging to the VO (Ventral Occipital) cluster (Wandell et al., 2005; Brewer, Liu, Wade, & Wandell, 2005). The two maps next to hV4 have been named VO-1 and VO-2, but the possibility that additional areas in this cluster might be identified in the future is left open.

3.1.3. Higher Visual Maps

The investigation on the role of the temporal lobe in macaques began with Kluver and Bucy (1937), and since the beginnings of modern vision science it has been known that area IT (InferoTemporal), was involved in crucial vision tasks (Mishkin, 1966; Gross et al., 1972). The first characterization of this area was in terms of receptive fields, that always included the center of gaze and were much larger than in posterior areas, and were bilateral (Gross et al., 1969; Desimone & Gross, 1979). Later research attempted to investigate at a higher level of detail the behavior of IT, and a cytoarchitectural division into two areas was initially adopted von Bonin and Bailey (1947). In their charting of the macaque brain, von Bonin and Bailey kept the name "TE" for the anterior portion of IT from the classical human atlas of von Economo and Koskinas (1925), which is defined there as *Area temporalis propria*, and called "TEO" (as a more Occipital TE), the posterior part. It was especially TE that exhibited properties of responding to complex patterns, and even, for some cells, of responding best to specific objects, like hands or faces (Desimone et al., 1984; Tanaka et al., 1991; Kobatake & Tanaka, 1994; Tanaka, 1996).

In the meantime, research on human visual areas that respond to objects, proved unfruitful. Farah and Aguirre (1999), when reviewing ten years of attempts to isolate the neural substrates of human visual recognition with PET and fMRI studies, concluded that "The pooled results of these studies can be summarized by the following, rather anticlimactic, statement: visual recognition activates posterior brain regions". Only in the last decade, thanks to improvements in fMRI resolution, and the use of sophisticated computational processing of data, a more complete picture of human higher visual areas began to emerge. LOC was one of the first areas to be identified (Malach et al., 1995), and will be described in detail in §3.3.. Most of the investigations beyond LOC have searched for areas specialized in the recognition of specific classes of objects. The first was identified by Kanwisher, McDermott, and Chun (1997) and named FFA (Fusiform Face Area), because of its location in the fusiform gyrus and because it is more active when viewing faces, compared to other objects. How FFA could be specifically dedicated to faces is still controversial, it has been found for example, that if experts of cars or birds viewed stimuli from their domains of expertise, cars or birds respectively, the right FFA was significantly more active than for other common objects (Gauthier et al., 2000; Xu, 2005). It is in this area, nevertheless, where proof for specificity for a class of objects is more convincing (Grill-Spector, 2003; Kanwisher, 2003). There are clues for a region in the medial temporal lobe, called PPA (Parahippocampal Place Area), that responds to "places", that is, scenes where the overall layout is important (Epstein & Kanwisher, 1998). Yet another area, in the lateral occipitotemporal cortex on the lower lip of the posterior temporal sulcus, called EBA (Extrastriate Body Area), seems to respond to images of parts of the human body (Downing, Jiang, Shuman, & Kanwisher, 2001). Ongoing attempts are being made to find other regions that respond to tools, chairs, written words, animals, objects that are able to move, etc. One fundamental unanswered question, concerns how valid the entire research enterprise of trying to come up with a parcellation of the higher ventral visual cortex is, on the basis of preferences for object categories. The issue will be discussed in detail in §4.1..

3.2. Next to V1

Despite V2's being as large as V1, and its being located in the main path of the visual hierarchy, immediately anterior to V1, it is nonetheless, much less studied than the primary visual cortex, and its contribution to the task of vision, much less clear. The existence of a full visuotopic map next to the striate cortex in mammals was first accounted for by Talbot (1942) more than half a century ago, in the cat's cortex. Shortly after Thompson et al. (1950) investigated this area in more detail in the rabbit, pioneering a method different from that of single cell electrode readings. They presented stimuli with a tangent-screen projection, and recorded cortical responses with evoked potentials. They also were the first to introduce the name "V II", to indicate an area dedicated to vision, which was "secondary" in respect to the striate cortex, which was therefore dubbed "primary".

3.2.1. Retinotopic Organization

Several years later, V2 was studied in primates as well, in the squirrel monkey (*Saimiri sciureus*) by Cowey (1964), who showed that the central representation of V2 shares the projection of the visual field vertical meridian with V1. In those years, the organization of V2 was disclosed also for the macaque, in a series of studies carried out by Zeki (1969, 1971a). A major step in arriving at a better comprehension of the retinotopy in V2 was made by Allman and Kaas (1974) in the owl monkey (*Aotus trivirgatus*), with the finding that while the anterior border, abutting V1, represents the vertical meridian, the posterior border of V2, instead represents the horizontal meridian. They called this topology a second-order transformation of the visual field, in contrast with the first-order transformation taking place in V1, where adjacent loci in the visual field are always represented in adjacent cortical loci. In the macaque Van Essen and Zeki (1978) found a very similar topography, with the only difference found in the place at which the representation of the horizontal meridian bifurcates. In the new world owl monkey, it occurs several mm from the edge of striate cortex, corresponding to a visual representation approximately 6° from the fovea, in the macaque it occurs much earlier, well within the fovea. Van Essen and Zeki also measured the cortical magnification factor in V2, finding values similar to those in V1. Gattass et al. (1981) measured the size of receptive fields in the macaque's V2, that are more than twice as large as in V1, at any given eccentricity.

For reasons explained in §2.2., a characterization of V2 in humans, came only decades after that in other primates. For years the main source of information on how visual fields are represented in the human visual cortex came from lesion studies, and in particular from war wounds. Tatsuji Inouye, a Japanese ophthalmologist treated survivors of the Russo-Japan War (1904-5) (1909), and examined the locations of bullet wounds in the occiput. Of special scientific interest were the cases of quadrantanopia, which is the loss of a single quadrant from the visual field, that would allow a coarse mapping of the retinal field on the visual cortex. A decade later Holmes and Lister (1916) reported on similar cases during their years as officer surgeons in French hospitals. They spoke of visual field deficits that occurred as a consequence of penetrating wounds made by missile shell fragments and shrapnel. They confirmed Inouye's charts, concluding that the upper and lower visual quadrants are localized, respectively, in the lower and upper calcarine banks of the striate cortex. Rather unconvincing in this reconstruction, was the existence of cases with a precise homonymous quadrantanopia (loss of the same upper or lower quadrants from each hemifield), that would require a bullet to divide the striate cortex exactly along the cortical representation of the horizontal meridian along the base of the calcarine fissure (Rönne, 1919). An answer was proposed many decade later by Horton and Hoyt (1991): the lesions were not in V1 but in V2, which has the upper and the lower quadrants split into its ventral and dorsal parts. They reported two patients with homonymous quadrantanopia, with lesions due to astrocytoma in the occipital lobe, where the diagnosis was clear, but extended it as a possible explanation of the puzzling facts of the quadrantanopia caused by war wound lesions. This peculiar organization of the visual fields in V2 is sketched in Fig. 4.

Thanks to fMRI, responses to angle/eccentricity retinal stimulation (see §2.2.) M. Sereno et al. (1995) have determined with better precision the borders of V2 in humans, and found that the foveal field has a greater emphasis than in monkeys. The accuracy of these

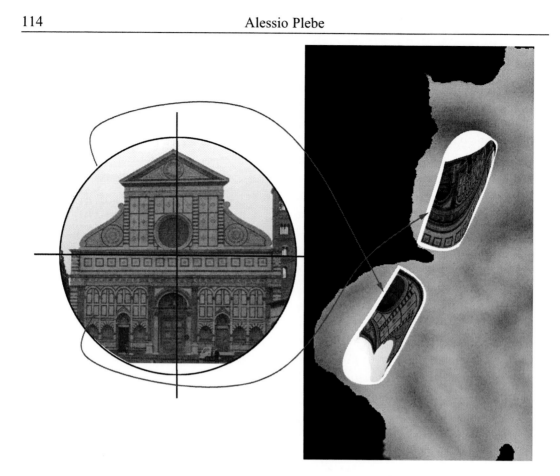

Figure 4. Schematic representation of the retinotopic organization of V2. Given the scene on the left, the left quadrants are processed in the right hemisphere V2 (right in the figure), with the upper quadrant represented in the ventral part and the lower quadrant in the dorsal part of V2. Note how for both quadrant representations the horizontal meridian lies on the anterior border, and the vertical meridian on the posterior border of V2.

measures is continuously improving, A. Smith et al. (2001) assessed the size of receptive fields in human V2, that spans from $1°$ in the fovea up to $2.5°$ at the periphery. Other details on the geometry of human V2 has been recently provided (Schira et al., 2007), showing that this map is elongated by a factor of 2 in eccentricity direction relative to V1, and has significantly more local anisotropy.

3.2.2.   What is V2 Doing for Vision

The main gap that exists in current knowledge on V2 concerns its functional role in vision. In a first attempt to investigate the specificity of V2, D. Hubel and Wiesel (1970) provided evidence of some cells in this area of the macaque cortex sensitive to binocular depth. The search for neurons supporting stereopsis progressed in the years that followed, and in nonhuman primates disparity-selective cells were identified in several visual areas other than V2, for a review see Poggio (1995). A version that returned to suggesting a special involvement of V2 in stereopsis was provided by von der Heydt et al. (2000), in their measures on monkeys with stereograms as stimuli, the well known pictures invented by Julesz (1971) where no figure is present but one appears when the view of both eyes is combined. von der Heydt et al. (2000) found that several cells in both V1 and V2 were sensitive to disparity in general, but only V2 responds to the edges of figures in stereograms. However, later fMRI studies on humans did not confirm a role of V2 in stereopsis, that seems to be more correlated with activity in V3 (Backus et al., 2001) and higher areas (Neri et al., 2004), including LOC (Chandrasekaran et al., 2007).

In a different line of research, aimed to identify neural correlates of illusory contours, it was found that V2 is a good candidate (von der Heydt & Peterhans, 1989; Peterhans & von der Heydt, 1989). When presenting the same stimuli to monkeys that had been presented to human observers, and in which the human subjects had been able to perceive contours that were not actually present (akin to the contour of the Kanizsa triangle), several cells in the monkeys' V2 responded. Some responded even better to illusory contours than to optimum oriented bars or edges, and no significant responses where measured in V1. How specific the responsiveness to illusory contours in V2 is, remains controversial. Later studies reported that monkey V1 does respond to illusory contours, as that of Ramsden et al. (2001), in which optical imaging and single unit electrophysiology were combined, or Lee and Nguyen (2001), in which conventional microelectrode recordings were used. But mostly, studies on humans with neuroimaging reported responses to illusory contours in visual maps from V1 (Maertens & Pollmann, 2005) up to LOC (Stanley & Rubin, 2003), and in almost all intermediate areas (Montaser-Kouhsari et al., 2007). Also, in another perceptual phenomena, the automatic filling-in of holes in textures, it has been proven in monkeys that V2 is, at least partially and together with V3, responsible for it (Weerd et al., 2002).

The search of a role of V2 in Gestalt mechanisms that link diverse feature signals to larger entities has expanded, inquiring aspects of figure-ground organization. The group of von der Heydt found that in monkeys V2 is coding for edges of 3-D objects, not just their 2-D appearance (von der Heydt et al., 2000), and some cells seems to discriminate the "ownership" of contours (Zhou et al., 2000; von der Heydt et al., 2003). Assigning a surface contour to a real object is a compulsory perceptual tendency of our vision, well demonstrated by Rubin's famous vase, reproduced in Fig. 5, where the bistable perception of either the flower vase or the faces depends on whether the contour in the image is interpreted as owned by the lighter or darker regions.

The discovery of the cytochrome oxidase enzyme as an endogenous metabolic marker for neural activity (Wong-Riley, 1979) has been followed by a new impetus in research on the monkey visual cortex, that involves V2 as well. DeYoe and Van Essen (1985) used the cytochrome oxidase enzyme to stain V2 tissue. Similarly to results in V1 (Livingstone & Hubel, 1982), dark staining stripes alternate with parallel stripes of lighter staining, and the dark stripes alternate between thin and thick stripes. In an oversimplification, cells in the thin stripes are supposed to code for colors, and those in the thick stripes for disparity and light for orientation (D. H. Hubel & Livingstone, 1987). A similar study of Tootell, Hamilton, and Switkes (1989) revealed in monkeys' V2, responsiveness to orientation and color, but lack of ocular dominance segregation. After these remarkable findings, this stream of research has slowed perhaps due to an increasing amount of reflection on how results obtained with this method should be interpreted (K. A. C. Martin, 1988). One of the recent

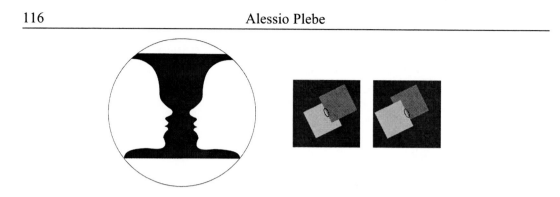

Figure 5. On the left the bistable Rubin's vase, where the black-white borders are perceived either as contours of the vase or of the faces. On the right two stimuli used by Zhou et al. (2000), in which the same V2 cell, which receptive field is shown in black, responds differently if the same contour belongs to the right or the left object.

studies done on monkeys' V2 with this method was (Gegenfurtner et al., 1996), that probed cells for orientation, color, disparity and motion, confirming previous results on the high proportion of cells responding for color and orientation, and much less for motion. Ts'o et al. (2001) combined cytochrome oxidase histochemistry with optical imaging and single unit electrophysiology, confirming again the organization of cells with responses to color, disparity and orientation, but in more granular compartments than the stripes revealed by cytochrome oxidase only. More recently, it has been found that the three systems of stripes in V2 actually receive projections from only two organizations in V1: the thin stripes in V2 from V1 cytochrome patches, and thick and light V2 stripes from V1 interpatches (Sincich & Horton, 2002).

3.2.3.   In Search of the Best Patterns

An alternative way of discovering the main tasks hidden in the layout and in the single responsiveness of cells in V2, is to search for a pattern clearly preferred by a consistent population of neurons. The difficulty here is exactly in the a priori knowledge of which stimuli to use to probe the neural preference.

In one study extended to the entire ventral visual pathway of the macaque, the problem of choosing a set of candidate stimuli was overcome with a reduction method (Kobatake & Tanaka, 1994). A complex 3-D image, to which the neuron under study responds, is progressively simplified, gradually eliminating parts of the features present in the image. The feature that cannot be reduced further without significantly decreasing the responses of the cells, is labeled as the effective stimulus for those cells. However, the process of simplifying a natural image may easily miss the basic patterns to which neurons are tuned. The main results were of an increase in feature complexity from area V2 to IT, with a few cells in V2 responding to some pattern of medium complexity, like sharp triangles. (Heider et al., 2000) searched for responses in monkey V1 and V2 to simple patterns such as end-lines and corners, finding neurons in V2 responding selectively to right corners.

A first extensive exploration of the pattern tuning in V2 was done by (Hegdé & Van Essen, 2000), on the macaque, using a large set of stimuli. It consisted of 48 varieties of gratings, and 80 shapes representative of natural contours, like three-way intersections, an-

Figure 6. Examples of patterns used by (Hegdé & Van Essen, 2000): on the left, simple gratings, in the middle, more complex gratings, on the right, some complex shapes.

gles and semicircles, examples are in Fig. 6.

Over 180 recorded cells, the large majority, 152, preferred a most complex shape over the most effective simple oriented bar. Also for gratings, more than half of the cells, 110, responded better to complex gratings than to the most effective single-orientated grating. In a subsequent analysis of cell responses at population level (Hegdé & Van Essen, 2003), a strong correlation in the overall response variation to different stimulus types was found, suggesting a sort of distributed representation of the shape information in the map. This body of results, however, proved to be still too weak an answer to the question regarding the specific role of V2, when Hegdé and Van Essen (2007) extended the exposure to the same set of stimuli to V1 and V4. Even though the analysis revealed several differences between areas in terms of the details of the responses, the data does not reveal a marked preference for complex stimuli in V2 compared with V1, nor V4 compared with V2. There was no class of stimuli that was segregated in only one of the three investigated cortical maps.

M. A. Smith et al. (2007) measured responses of V2 to Glass patterns, that are patterns of dots made by pairing a kernel of randomly placed dots with a set of partner dots shifted according to a particular geometric rule (Glass & Perez, 1973). Comparing the results with their previous observations of Glass pattern responses in V1 (M. A. Smith et al., 2002), no significant difference was found. In V2 as in V1, neurons respond to translational Glass patterns confined in their receptive fields, but did not appear to provide strong signals about global concentric or radial Glass patterns.

In a highly focused study Ito and Komatsu (2004) attempted to systematically explore selectivity to angles, with single-unit recordings from 114 neurons in macaque V2. In the above mentioned investigations, several clues had already pointed to angles as preferred patterns in V2, like selectivity to triangular shapes by Kobatake and Tanaka (1994), right-angled corners by Heider et al. (2000) and acute angles by Hegdé and Van Essen (2000). Moreover, angles are the natural next step in complexity after oriented lines, and are basic components for detecting contours in natural scenes (Geisler et al., 2001). The set of stimuli used by Ito and Komatsu (2004) was 66 angles, generated by combining two segments with orientation changed in 30 degree steps. Out of 114 recorded cells, 91 were responding selectively to angles, and 25 of the 91, with a primary peak on one angle and a secondary peak on a different angle. The data was carefully investigated, finding that neurons, in fact,

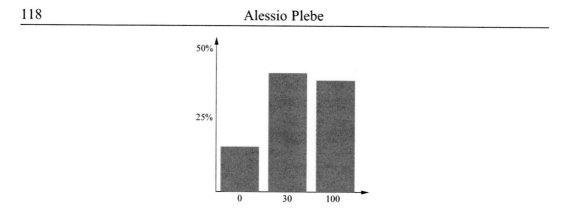

Figure 7. Distribution of selectivity to angle width in the study of Ito and Komatsu (2004). Angle size 0 corresponds to straight lines

are not coding features like angle width or angle orientation, regardless of the individual half-line components of angle stimuli. Instead, angle selectivity was closely related to the specific combination between the orientation of the two components. However, the presence of either line component alone is not sufficient to elicit a response, nor it could be explained by a simple linear summation of the responses to the individual line components. In fact, given a stimulus with a single half-line with the most preferred orientation, the response can be weakened by combining a second half-line with orientation different from the preferred angle. The specialty of some neurons in V2 to code for angles is consistent with the findings of Anzai, Peng, and Essen (2007) that about one-third of cells in V2 are selective for orientation, but also significantly change their firing rate if a second bar, with a different orientation, is within a subregion of its receptive field.

3.3. Towards Object Recognition

Object recognition, as mentioned in §1., is both one of the most crucial yet obscure capabilities of human vision. As described in §3.1.3., for the monkey it is well established that object recognition takes place mainly in area IT. It was, therefore, surprising to discover several years ago, that a different area in the geography of the human cortex is involved in object recognition.

Malach et al. (1995) first identified this region, an area located anterior to Brodmann's area 19, near the lateral occipital sulcus, extending into the posterior and mid fusiform gyrus and occipital-temporal sulcus, with an overall surface size similar to V1. They called it "lateral occipital complex", where the term "complex" denotes the uncertainty on whether this region is a single visual map or a cluster of several maps. Not many years earlier, actually, other PET studies had revealed selective activation of ventral and temporal regions associated with recognition tasks (Corbetta et al., 1991; Sergent et al., 1992), but the precise location of these activation foci remained unclear. The experiment conducted by Malach et al. (1995) was aimed to discriminate the involvement of cortical regions in object recognition, by differential measures of fMRI signals when viewing semantic rich real-like pictures, or meaningless textures. To ensure comparability of the two sets, the meaningless pictures were generated using the same spectrum of spatial frequencies of the object pictures. In addition to the object/texture comparison, further tests were performed to eliminate possible

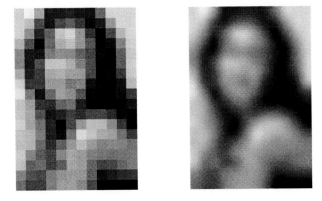

Figure 8. Example of the Lincoln effect, used in (Malach et al., 1995) to demonstrate the relationship of LOC to effective recognition. An image like that on the left will elicit weaker response than its blurred version, on the right, in which a face is recognized.

artifacts in the results, one of the strongest supports for this area being related to recognition came from the so-called "Lincoln" illusion. It is an effect in which portraits, sampled and quantized so coarsely to be unrecognizable, have increased detectability when blurred (Harmon & Julesz, 1973), an example is in Fig. 8. Responses in this cortical area were significantly larger when blurring allowed recognition.

The acronym used in (Malach et al., 1995) was "LO", here we adopt the most common abbreviation, that includes the "C" for complex: LOC. However, we should anticipate that this is another cortical area where no standard terminology has yet been established, and so has lead to a flourish in baptisms.

The discovery of LOC soon captured the interest of the vision science community, and many studies have followed in the last decade. Almost contemporary to Malach, Nancy Kanwisher found a region in a location close to that of Malach (slightly more anterior and ventral), involved in visual object recognition, first in a PET study (Kanwisher, Woods, et al., 1996), replicated with fMRI (Kanwisher, Chun, et al., 1996). The paradigm was even more rigorous, in that the comparison in stimuli was between pictures of objects, and pictures of the same object scrambled in such way that recognition was impossible, but all the low-level features were preserved. Being such a young subject of research, a clear picture of LOC characteristics and its role in vision is still lacking, however, the impetus given by its discovery has lead to an interesting and intriguing body of knowledge.

3.3.1. LOC Visual Field

A shared observation is that in LOC, retinotopy is weaker than in earlier areas in the ventral pathway, a consequence is that the standard procedure (see §2.2.) used for mapping cortical areas against the eccentric and angular dimensions of the visual field, becomes less reliable for assessing it. Initially, studies (Tootell, Hadjikhani, Mendola, Marrett, & Dale, 1998; Tootell & Hadjikhani, 2001) reported two adjacent regions with a sharp difference in eccentricity representation, with an apparent gap existing between the most central and the peripheral representations. The areas were called again LOC, but now with the "C" standing for "central", and LOP, Lateral Occipital "Peripheral". Both seem to lack angular representations. From a purely linguistic point of view, having introduced a duplicate LOC name was not the best contribution to the somewhat messy nomenclature of visual areas, this notwithstanding, the purpose was to highlight the anomaly in eccentricity representation, leaving open the question of whether or not LOC and LOP where components of a same cortical map, or instead, two distinct visual fields driven preferentially by stimuli in central or peripheral areas, respectively. Others (Levy, Hasson, Avidan, et al., 2001; Hasson et al., 2002, 2003) proposed a deeper interpretation, in which center/periphery mapping in higher areas is a strategic organization for recognizing two broad classes of scenes. There are objects, like faces, that require central scrutiny for their recognition. On the contrary, buildings or places needs peripheral analysis for the grasping of their overall layout. Malach et al. (2002) preferred to name the two parts of LOC "LO" the more dorsal part, responding to images presented foveally, and "pFs" (posterior Fusiform) the ventral part, more periphery biased. The name pFs had already been used in (Grill-Spector et al., 1999), with the alternative "LOa" (Lateral Occipital anterior).

Independently from its functional interpretation, the eccentricity anomaly and the lack of angular representations in LOC (with "C" now again for "complex") is controversial. Wandell et al. (2005) observed both eccentricity map and angular maps in LOC, and supposed that the discrepancies from the the works cited above might be due to differences in the methodologies, having used a more powerful MRI scanner, and more angular samples. Other studies (Larsson & Heeger, 2006; Larsson et al., 2006) confirmed the presence of eccentricity and angular fields, in two distinct regions, augmenting the number of different naming convention in this area, with "LO1" for a more posterior visual field, and "LO2" the abutting anterior field. A question that has come regards how reasonable it is to search for retinotopic mapping in LOC, where probably a more invariant coordinate frame, appropriate for object recognition, might be established (McKyton & Zohary, 2007).

In comparison with the geography of the monkey cortex, the LOC area continues to be enigmatic. Tootell and Hadjikhani (2001) argued that LOC could be the homologue of the dorsal part of V4 in the macaque brain, and the overlapping with surface-based warping matches (Van Essen et al., 2001). (Denys et al., 2004) made a functional comparison, mapping with fMRI the responses to object recognition tasks in both humans and nonhuman primates, using the paradigm of intact and scrambled images of objects introduced in (Kanwisher, Woods, et al., 1996), discussed on the basis of the warping anatomical mapping. They found that object recognition activates two areas in the lateral occipital complex, now re-baptized "post-ITG" (corresponding to Malach LO or Tootell LOC, possibly Larsson LO1) and "mid-FG" (corresponds to Malach pFs, Tootell LOP, Larsson LO2). They also describe a third subregion, named "LOS" (Lateral Occipital Sulcus), that is the posterior extension of post-ITG. This part is the best candidate of being anatomically correspondent to macaque V4d, although their retinotopic organization is different. From a functional point of view, responses in human LOC correspond mostly to activation found in the posterior and dorsal part of the monkey IT complex.

3.3.2. The Role of LOC

The discovery of LOC itself, was supported by the hypothesis that the identified area worked for object recognition, and most of the studies that followed insisted in ascertaining that this area was involved in visual behavior in which recognition was the main task. But to examine closely the role of LOC, requires asking more precisely what sort of processing is expected in a cortical map subserving visual recognition.

Probably the most important property to fulfill the requirement for an object-recognition area, is that its cells should exhibit several forms of invariance. Invariance in vision is the ability to recognize known objects despite large changes in their appearance on the sensory surface. It is one of the features of the biological vision system most difficult to understand, but it is also a challenging theoretical problem, because it is related with the philosophical issue of the format of mental representations (Cummins, 1989). For example, invariance has been central in the debate on whether representations in the brain are 3D object-centered or image-based ("Image-based object recognition in man, monkey, and machine", 1998; Edelman, 1999).

Invariance is actually a collection of abilities concerning several classes of changes. There are precise mathematical formulation of what invariance includes (Wood, 1996), but more informal descriptions are used in perceptual and neuroscientific vision (Hayward & Tarr, 1997). In practice, the most common changes of viewpoint that affect the appearance of the object in a two dimensional projection are size, translation, and rotation. Although the term invariance is commonly used in vision, it is not mathematically correct, in that in no cortical map the responses are absolutely invariant to transformations of the same object (Cox et al., 2005), a better term would be "degree of tolerance" with respect to classes of changes in appearance of the same object.

Grill-Spector et al. (1999) investigated invariance using fMR-A (functional Magnetic Resonance Adaptation), a methodology based on the reduction of neural activity when visual areas are presented repetitively with the same visual stimulus (A. Martin et al., 1995; Grill-Spector & Malach, 2001). It is especially useful in studying invariance, by gradually manipulating a single property in the presented image, and checking if the neural signals recover from adaptation. If the response remains adapted, it will indicate that the neurons in the area under investigation are invariant, to some degree, to that feature. They found invariance to translation and size in anterior LOC (LOa or pFs) and not in posterior LOC (LO), and no invariance to rotation, which instead is found in (Kourtzi et al., 2003) and in (Vuilleumier et al., 2002) (but only in the left hemisphere). The difference is probably due to the amount of rotation taken into account: 90° in (Grill-Spector et al., 1999) and 45° in (Kourtzi et al., 2003), suggesting invariance in LOC to a moderate amount of rotations that do not dramatically change the viewed shape of the object. Invariance to the overall level of intensity, and the contrast between the recognized object and the background was also demonstrated in LOC (Avidan et al., 2002), and related to the attention given to the object in order to segregate it from the background (Murray & He, 2001). Invariance to a special class of rotation has been found by Weigelt et al. (2007). The viewpoint rotation that LOC seems to be invariant to, is that where different views of an object are linked by apparent motion, thereby creating the illusion of a smooth rotational object motion.

Grill-Spector et al. (1998) addressed a special kind of invariance, with respect to "cues". It is the ability to respond selectively to objects, independently (at least, in part) to the way this object is represented. In the experiment several kinds of stimuli were presented, in which objects might be identified by a variety of cues: motion, luminance, and texture. Luminance is the most obvious feature in a scene for detecting objects, thanks to variations in contrast with respect to the background. In the motion stimuli, all the values of luminance used were random noise, but by coherently moving a section of the noise pattern over the stationary background, an image of drifting object silhouette was perceived. In the texture stimuli there was also no significant difference in luminance between objects and background, but the shape of the objects was derived by wrapping a texture around a three-dimensional object and filling the background with a flat texture. The results demonstrated that LOC responds to visual recognition, in a manner largely independent from the visual cue used to define objects. Other variations of cue are the representations of the same objects under photographs or as line drawings. Kourtzi and Kanwisher (2000), using also fMR-A, found that LOC responds invariantly with respect to this cue variation.

Further support of the role LOC plays in recognition, not independent from cue invariance, is the involvement of LOC in completing the shape of an object from degraded views, called "perceptual closure" or "perceptual filling-in" (Bartlett, 1916). It is not independent from cue invariance, where recognition is also obtained despite differences in visual cues, and perceptual closure is obtained despite differences in the completeness of the shape. A series of studies with ERP (Doniger et al., 2000, 2001) established a robust event-related potential component that appeared to track the neural processes subserving perceptual closure, named N_{CL}, located in the LOC cortical area. Another mechanism that concurs in recognizing complex objects is the ability to select and group elements that belong to a single entity, and Murray et al. (2004) showed, using fMRI, that LOC is involved in this task.

Despite all this evidence, a difficulty in establishing a clear role as object recognizer for LOC, is the obvious consideration that recognition requires many processing steps, including those carried by V1 and V2, and therefore, one area might be necessary for recognition, without for this reason being the main one actually responsible for this task. Kourtzi and Kanwisher (2001) addressed this issue, by contrasting contour extraction versus shape recognition, using the methodology of fMR-A. They found adaptation in the LOC when the shape perceived from the stimuli was identical but contours differed, but no adaptation when the contours were identical and the perceived shape differed. Therefore, a change in contour did not affect in LOC, the equivalence of two stimuli, while it produced large differences in responses in V1 and V2. Proving the involvement in recognition was the objective of Bar et al. (2001), using a design that allowed a gradual accomplishment of object recognition, by very brief presentations of object pictures. Playing around the threshold of presentation duration, over which participants were able to recognize picture contents, and below which they were very close to but unable to recognize, they assessed that in LOC, or at least in a anterior portion they call "OTS" (OccipitalTemporal Sulcus), there is a direct correlation of elicited response and awareness of recognition in the subjects. In (Tjan et al., 2006) stronger responses in LOC were measured, when pictures mixed with graded amounts of artificial noise became recognizable. In summary, the evidence for LOC being at the heart of what can be called recognition is abundant (Grill-Spector et al., 2001; Grill-Spector, 2003; Kanwisher, 2003). However the last word has not been said, for example Ferber et al. (2005) argue that LOC subserves figure-ground segregation, that they deem as being a low-level task in the visual processing hierarchy.

LOC seems to be somewhat human specific, at least in that it lacks a clear direct monkey homologue, as V1 or V2. We should also remember that one of the most important human specific traits is language. Object recognition is very likely to be biased by language in humans, at least for the simple fact that all objects we can visually recognize are categorized by names. The strong lateralization of language functions have therefore stimulated investigations on laterality in LOC. Evidence of hemispheric asymmetry was already found in (Vuilleumier et al., 2002) concerning larger rotation invariance in left LOC, an indication of a more semantic biased representation in the left hemisphere. Stronger evidence of a linguistic connection of the left LOC comes from studies applying categorial differentiation in test objects, and adding linguistic test conditions. For example, the adaptation of fMR signal is compared using a series of pictures of the same umbrella, or a series of different exemplars of umbrellas, or followed by an object of a different category. The left anterior LOC seems to be more invariant to exemplars of the same category than its right counterpart (Koutstaal et al., 2001). Moreover, if pictures are presented in conjunction to the sound of words, left anterior LOC is found to be more sensitive to the auditory perception of the object names as opposed to nonsense words (Simons et al., 2003). When the task is to name the recognized object, again, left LOC is more active than when the subject is just required to check the matching of two pictures in a sequence (Large et al., 2007).

The responsiveness of LOC to stimuli other than visual stimuli is intriguing, and seems to span over auditory linguistic inputs. A surprising discovery of Amedi et al. (2001) was that LOC activates when subjects recognize objects not only by sight, but also by touching, confirmed by subsequent studies (James et al., 2002; Amedi et al., 2002).

In the end, the growing effort in investigating LOC, ever since its discovery, has provided a great deal of insight, but has also raised many new questions still left to answer. For example, about its development, that as seen in §2.4. is one of the key aspects in understanding visual areas, and has revealed much concerning V1, but has yet to shed light on LOC. The only data available is that, unlike higher areas, LOC is already at a mature stage at 7 years of age (Golarai et al., 2007). In the following section, we will show how computational models can contribute to the effort in understanding the shift towards recognition in the visual pathway. TBD

4.   Computational Models of the Ventral Stream

4.1.   What Models Can Tell About the Visual System

Computational models have been a valid complement to neurophysiology and neuroimaging in the enterprise of understanding how our brain works. The qualities of rigor, precision, and power of synthesis that characterize mathematics may greatly elucidate the function of the nervous system. At the same time, the possibility to run models on a computer allows the simulation and the comparison of brain tasks under investigation. Models, in abstracting biophysical phenomena at different levels, can help bridge neurophysiology with behavior and cognition. It was actually within vision science that computational modeling was established as a helpful tool in exploring brain functions. The appeal to computation has dominated research on object recognition ever since the seminal work of David Marr (1982). The guiding principles, however, were quite different from today's computational neuroscience, and were strongly based on the epistemological value of the algorithmic design, corroborated by the philosophical view of the mind as a computing machine, that prevailed in the

80's and '90s (Fodor, 1981, 1983). In recent years, this early form of computationalism has been seriously challenged, and one of the sources of criticism was exactly due to its failure in the case of vision (P. S. Churchland et al., 1994).

In the meantime, computational neuroscience has grown, reaching solid theoretical foundations (Dayan & Abbott, 2001). Today it is possible to constrain models of vision, in order to get relatively close to real brain mechanisms, avoiding the errors made by previously unconstrained computational models. However, the adherence to the known chemical and electrical processes of the nervous system is necessarily inverse to the degree of complexity of the problem at hand. In the case of recognition, the main task of the ventral visual pathway, complexity is very high, and therefore, the replication of biology cannot be detailed. This means that the risk of solving problems in our own head and then subsequently creating specific algorithms is always at the door. A good antidote for this is to focus models on the repertoire of basic principles underlying cortical organization, and to study the ontogenesis of complex functions by implementing these principles in a simulated environment. This way of proceeding is characteristic of research done within a recent framework called neuroconstructivism (Quartz & Sejnowski, 1997; Westermann et al., 2007).

4.1.1.   What Kind of Processes Are Going on in the Ventral Pathway?

The business of understanding the ventral visual system faces its first challenge in making sense of the number of different modules, and the kinds of divisions of labor between them. On one side, this is certainly a critical issue for the design of any model that claims to reproduce the hierarchy of the visual cortex. On the other, models can help test the different theoretical options on the table, and possibly help distinguish between those that work and those that don't. Two extremes in the interpretation of the roles of maps in the ventral stream are the holistic view, that sees all areas as equally involved in all aspects of object recognition, and the opposite view that sees each area as an autonomous and independent processing module. Needless to say, both views, in the bare bones definition just given, are too simplistic and are no longer defended today by anyone. Thus, the notion of maps as modules is generally represented by the idea that each map, or at least certain maps, are specialized in one main function, although the same maps might also marginally extend to other operations, and conversely, other maps may overlap the elective function of that map as well.

Moreover, modularity might refer to the kind of process that a map is specialized to carry, or the kind of content a map is specialized to process. One prominent example of modularity in processing, is the theory of a color center area in the ventral visual stream, proposed primarily by Zeki (1983a, 1983b); Lueck et al. (1989). As discussed in §3.1.2. the same area was later revealed to be engaged in many other types of activities such as shape or motion processing. A possible compromise is to hold processing modularity as a graded feature. For example, it has been found that although both areas VO and MT respond to color as well as temporal variations, there is a large gap in the amount of responsiveness (Liu & Wandell, 2002), suggesting a relative specialization for color in VO, not too different from what Zeki originally claimed, and motion in MT. There are also modularist views of processing streams encompassing more areas, that in general attempt to segregate areas with respect to low level cues, which in turn contribute to a single aspect of perception, as in the first suggestion of a division between form, color, motion and stereo information (D. H. Hubel & Livingstone, 1987; Livingstone & Hubel, 1987). This kind of compartmentalization has also been challenged in the light of much evidence on a more holistic cooperation among the cortical areas belonging to the distinct processing streams (DeYoe & Van Essen, 1988; Van Essen & DeYoe, 1994; Schiller, 1996).

Modularity with respect to content is often proposed as an explanation of upper visual maps, as held by Kanwisher et al. (1997) for FFA (see §3.1.3.), putatively specialized in face recognition. In contrast, others (Tarr & Gauthier, 2000) propose that FFA, like other higher level areas, are still specialized in processes, just that they are the kind of processes that are appropriate for particular types of recognition. That's the reason why FFA is recruited in processing a wide range of stimuli, including faces and non-face objects. Moreover, higher level specialization can be highly dependent on subjective experience (Gauthier & Tarr, 2002). For this purpose, it is useful to note that already in the first experiments of Kanwisher et al. (1997), for 3 subjects out of 15 no stronger response for faces was recorded, in FFA or any other brain areas. On the holistic side of the debate, one prevailing idea is that of distributed representations of object categories, with a population of neurons over several upper areas contributing to the coding of various objects (Edelman, 1999). Rather impressive data leaning towards holism is the number of about two hundred million neurons in the entire visual cortex, and at least one million neurons in the anterior ventral cortex, involved in the representation of a single object image (Levy, Hasson, & Malach, 2001).

Convincing support is also provided by Haxby et al. (2001); O'Toole et al. (2005) elaborating patterns of fMRI responses to objects, excluding the maximally respondent cortical area. The pattern was still sufficient to predict the stimulus category that a subject was viewing, showing therefore that the marginally respondent areas are just as important in object representation as the maximally responsive area. Nevertheless, the debate is just at its beginning, an intermediate view that lies between modularism and holism about content is the one mentioned in 3.3.1., regarding a center/periphery organization of the higher areas.

4.2. Building Blocks for Cortical Maps

Hundreds of models of vision have been proposed in the literature, as well as many models of cortical networks. Not many neural architectures are currently available, however, that can serve as useful building blocks for the maps composing the ventral visual cortex. Most of the available artificial neural systems that simulate vision, are abstract and not specifically related to any map in the cortex (Mel, 1997; Edelman & Duvdevani-Bar, 1997; Amit & Mascaro, 2003). On the other hand, computational models of the cortex are often conceived for simulating detailed mechanisms of a single area (Bressloff & D. Cowan, 2002; Ben-Shahar & Zucker, 2004; Mariño et al., 2005), and are not suitable as blocks for composing a complex hierarchy of cortical maps. Here, without wanting to pass as an exhaustive review effort, we briefly discuss some of the most representative computational architectures, that are effective in building cortical maps to be integrated in complex systems of vision.

4.2.1. The Mathematics of Cortical Development

One of the most fruitful mathematical frameworks for simulating cortical development is the concept of *self-organization* that has been the object of several proposals for artificial neural network schemes. The first implementation in a model representing how the visual cortex can spontaneously develop its mature organization, was proposed by von der Malsburg (von der Malsburg, 1973; Willshaw & von der Malsburg, 1976), and was based exclusively on the local interaction of neurons, ruled by Hebb's principle. In the case of the development of orientation-sensitive patterns in the primary cortex, the model was based on the following system of differential equations:

$$\frac{\partial y_i}{\partial t} = -\alpha y_i + \vec{k}_i \cdot f(\vec{y}_i) + \vec{w}_i \cdot f(\vec{z}_i) + x_i, \tag{1}$$

$$\frac{\partial w_{i,j}}{\partial t} = \eta f(y_i) \left(f(z_j) - w_{i,j} \sum_{l \in \mathcal{Z}_i} f(z_l) \right), \tag{2}$$

where y and z are the activities of neurons in different layers of the same cortical area, the former in layer IV, where typically thalamocortical afferents project, the latter in other layers, where lateral intercortical interactions take place. $w_{i,j}$ is the connections strength between z_j and x_i, and the vector $\vec{w}_i$ is composed by all connections of intercortical neurons projecting to i. The vectors $\vec{y}_i$ and $\vec{z}_i$ are the activations of all neurons belonging to columns where intercortical connections with neurons i exist. Using the same convention for the corresponding scalars, $\vec{y}_i$ refers to cells in layer IV and $\vec{z}_i$ to cells in other layers. The constant kernel vector $\vec{k}$ modulates the activation of neighbors with the distance from i, typically with a Gaussian difference. The function f is the monotonic squeezing nonlinearity, typically a sigmoid. In equation (2) the first term corresponds to Hebbian growth in response to coinciding activity on the presynaptic and postsynaptic sides of the connection between i and j. The second term, where $\mathcal{Z}_i$ is the set of cells out of layer IV connected to i, performs a competitive effect, ensuring that the sum of synaptic strengths converging on position i is kept constant at 1.

4.2.2. The Simplified SOM Implementation

Kohonen has made the mechanism of self-organization popular, with his very simple but efficient SOM (*Self-Organizing Maps*) model (Kohonen, 1982, 1984, 1995).

The learning rule is on a *winner-takes-all* basis: if the input data are vectors $\vec{v} \in \mathbb{R}^N$, the SOM will be made of some M neurons, each associated with a vector $\vec{x} \in \mathbb{R}^N$ and a two dimensional (in vision applications) coordinate $\vec{r} \in \{< [0,1], [0,1] >\} \subset \mathbb{R}^2$. For an input v there will be a winner neuron w satisfying:

$$w = \arg \min_{i \in \{1,\dots,M\}} \{\|\vec{v} - \vec{x}_i\|\}. \tag{3}$$

The winner-takes-all mechanism is a mathematical substitution for the effect of lateral connections, which, as seen in §2.1., play a fundamental role in the emergence of complex response functions in the cortex. The serious limitation is that this substitution implicitly assumes that lateral connections are fixed, however, its simplicity and elegance is what has caused its increasing use in the simulation of visual cortex (Schwabe & Obermayer, 2003). In practice the (3) can be replaced by an even simpler rule adopting proper vector normalizations:

$$w = \arg \max_{i \in \{1,\dots,M\}} \{\vec{v} \cdot \vec{x}_i\}. \tag{4}$$

Once the winner is identified, neural vectors are updated during training using:

$$\Delta \vec{x}_i = \eta e^{-\frac{\|\vec{r}_w - \vec{r}_i\|^2}{2\sigma^2}} (\vec{v} - \vec{x}_i), \tag{5}$$

where η is the learning rate, σ the amplitude of the neighborhood affected by the updating. In practice, often both η and σ are decreasing functions of the training epochs.

4.2.3. The VisNet Architecture

Wallis and Rolls (1997) designed a model for a cortical map that still achieves competitive self-organization, but without the SOM winner-takes-all mechanism, introducing an explicit lateral inhibitory effect of neighbor units. The activations x of all neurons are first computed as the synaptically weighted sum of the afferent signals, and then are processed by the following steps:

$$x_j \Leftarrow (1 - \delta)x_j - \sum_{i \neq j} e^{-\frac{\|\vec{r}_i - \vec{r}_j\|^2}{2\sigma^2}} x_i \tag{6}$$

$$x_j \Leftarrow \frac{x_j^p}{\sum_{i \neq j} x_i^p}, \tag{7}$$

where $\vec{r}$ are coordinates of the nodes as above, δ and σ are parameters ruling, respectively, the amount and the extent of the lateral inhibition. Equation (7), where $p > 1$, is used to maintain the average activation of the neurons constant. Learning in the network is achieved with a special modification of Hebb's rule, in which a decaying trace of previous cell activity is kept. The synaptic weight w_i connecting a neuron x with its input v_i is updated as follows:

$$\Delta w_i = \eta \overline{x}^{(t-1)} v^{(t)} \tag{8}$$

$$\overline{x}^{(t)} = (1 - \beta)x^{(t)} + \beta \overline{x}^{(t-1)}. \tag{9}$$

The object is that of inducing invariant capability in the map. If the map is presented with sequences of changing views of the same object, the neuron will be forced to respond to different appearances of the same object. This model is in fact, the building block of VisNet, a system that simulates object recognition and that will be discussed in §4.4., it is for this reason that invariance has been treated with specific care. This architecture is closer to the reality of cortical maps than the SOM is, but still, due to the fixed modeling of inhibition, and the lack of excitatory connections, may miss the full set of functional and developmental phenomena of a real visual map.

4.2.4. The LISSOM Architecture

An attempt to implement flexible and modifiable lateral connections, while keeping the architecture relatively simple, is represented by the model developed by Sirosh and Miikkulainen (1997) called LISSOM (*Laterally Interconnected Synergetically Self-Organizing Map*). In this model, each neuron is not only connected with the afferent input vector, but

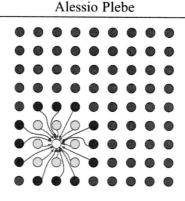

Figure 9. The LISSOM architecture with lateral connections for one neuron (in white). Excitatory links are in pale gray and inhibitory links in dark gray.

receives excitatory and inhibitory inputs from several neighbor neurons on the same map, as shown in Fig. 9

The activation level a_i of a neuron i at a certain time step k will now be given by:

$$a_i^{(k)} = f\left(\frac{\gamma_X}{1 + \gamma_N \vec{I} \cdot \vec{x}_i}\vec{x}_i \cdot \vec{v} + \gamma_E \vec{e}_i \cdot \vec{y}_i^{(k-1)} - \gamma_H \vec{h}_i \cdot \vec{z}_i^{(k-1)}\right), \qquad (10)$$

where the vectors $\vec{y}_i$ and $\vec{z}_i$ are the activations of all neurons in the map, where a lateral connection exists with neuron i of an excitatory or inhibitory type, respectively. Their fields are circular areas of radius, respectively, r_X, r_E, r_H. Vectors $\vec{e}_i$ and $\vec{h}_i$ are composed by all connection strengths of, the excitatory or inhibitory neurons projecting to i. The vectors $\vec{v}$ and $\vec{x}_i$, as before, are the input and the neural code. The scalars γ_X, γ_E, and γ_H, are constants modulating the contribution of afferents. The map is characterized by the matrices $\mathbf{X}, \mathbf{E}, \mathbf{H}$, whose columns are all vectors $\vec{x}, \vec{e}, \vec{h}$ for every neuron in the map. The scalar γ_N controls the setting of a push-pull effect in the afferent weights, allowing inhibitory effects without negative weight values. Mathematically, it represents dividing the response from the excitatory weights by the response from a uniform disc of inhibitory weights over the receptive field of neuron i. Vector $\vec{I}$ is just a vector of 1's of the same dimension of $\vec{x}_i$. The function f is any monotonic non-linear function limited between 0 and 1.

The final activation value of the neurons is assessed after a certain settling time K, typically about 10 time steps. It is easy to recognize the resemblance of (10) with the original formulation of von der Malsburg in (1). All connection strengths adapt according to the general Hebbian principle, but include a normalization mechanism that counterbalances the overall increase of connections of the pure Hebbian rule. The afferent connections to a neuron i will be modified at each training step by the following rule:

$$\Delta \vec{x}_i = \frac{\vec{x}_i + \eta a_i \vec{v}}{\|\vec{x}_i + \eta a_i \vec{v}\|} - \vec{x}_i, \qquad (11)$$

and similarly for weights $\vec{e}$ and $\vec{h}$.

LISSOM has been adapted as a model for vision (Bednar, 2002), with an organization of the components of input as receptive fields. The vector $\vec{v}$ is now made of afferent signals organized in a two-dimensional fashion, and $\vec{x}$ can be thought as a two dimensional function shaping the receptive field. Therefore, using two orthogonal indexes r and c, equation (10) may be rewritten as:

$$a_{r,c}^{(k)} = f\left(\frac{\gamma_X}{1 + \gamma_N \vec{I} \cdot \vec{x}_{r,c}} \gamma_X \vec{x}_{r,c} \cdot \vec{v}_{r,c} + \gamma_E \vec{e}_{r,c} \cdot \vec{y}_{r,c}^{(k-1)} - \gamma_H \vec{h}_{r,c} \cdot \vec{z}_{r,c}^{(k-1)}\right), \qquad (12)$$

where $\vec{v}_{r,c}$ now is a vector composed by all values in a two-dimensional array, included in the circular receptive field projected by the neural element at coordinates r, c. There is a topological correspondence between a translation of r, c on the map and the translation of the field in the input array. The input array can be the retina, as well as another LISSOM map, so that complex models can be built using this architecture. The following is a further extension of equation (12), with and additional term that takes into account backprojections from an upper LISSOM map:

$$a_{r,c}^{(k)} = f\left(\frac{\gamma_X}{1 + \gamma_N \vec{I} \cdot \vec{x}_{r,c}} \gamma_X \vec{x}_{r,c} \cdot \vec{v}_{r,c} + \gamma_E \vec{e}_{r,c} \cdot \vec{y}_{r,c}^{(k-1)} - \right.$$
$$\left. \gamma_H \vec{h}_{r,c} \cdot \vec{z}_{r,c}^{(k-1)} + \gamma_B \vec{b}_{r,c} \cdot \vec{u}_{r,c}^{(k-1)}\right). \qquad (13)$$

In the last term the vector $\vec{u}_{r,c}^{(k-1)}$ is composed by all activations in the upper map connected to the neural element at coordinates r, c, and its contribution is weighted by synaptic strengths $\vec{b}_{r,c}$. The feedback projections are learned using the same form of equation (11).

The LISSOM model has been extensively used in vision studies, for modeling several low-level visual phenomena (Miikkulainen, Bednar, Choe, & Sirosh, 1997), the simulation of aftereffects (Bednar & Miikkulainen, 2000), perceptual grouping (Choe & Miikkulainen, 2004), face detection (Bednar & Miikkulainen, 2003), color response development (Bednar, Paula, & Miikkulainen, 2005), motion direction selectivity (Bednar & Miikkulainen, 2006), and 3D object recognition (Plebe & Domenella, 2006, 2007), as shown later in §4.4.3.. A comprehensive review of LISSOM applications is in (Miikkulainen, Bednar, Choe, & Sirosh, 2005).

4.3. Models of V2

Similarly to the gap of neurophysiological studies on V2 with respect to V1, while there have been many suggested artificial models of V1, not much modeling has been performed for V2.

4.3.1. Models of Global Processes in V2

Following the number of cues recently gathered on V2, regarding its being involved in certain Gestalt perceptual phenomena, described in §3.2.2., attempts have been made to computationally model the properties of neurons in V2 responsible for non-local processes.

Some models have addressed the putative role played by V2 cells selective to edges and stereographic disparity in depth perception. Zhaoping Li (2002) gave a possible computational explanation of why some cells in V2 are able to respond to illusory contours in

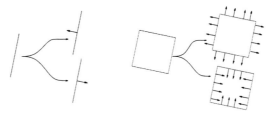

Figure 10. Correspondence between responses in V1 and V2, according to the model of Zhaoping Li (2005). On the left orientation cells in model V1 may activate two cells in V2, preferring the same orientation, but with opposite border ownership bias. In the left picture we show how a global shape in V1 may elicit two different representations in V2, where the upper response signals a squared hole in a main figure, while the lower response indicates a square in the foreground.

dot stereograms. In her model, cells respond to binocular disparity, and are also laterally interconnected, with the effect that nearby cells tuned to similar depths inhibit each other. The overall effect is that cells whose receptive fields are near the edge of the depth plane respond more vigorously in comparison to others, because they have fewer iso-disparity neighbors that actively inhibit them.

A peculiar effect contributing to depth perception and reproduced in (Assee & Qian, 2007) is the so-called Da Vinci stereopsis. The cue used by the visual system in estimating depth is now not the conventional disparity, but the differences in monocular occlusion. When a near opaque object partially occludes a far surface, there are regions on this surface that can be seen by one eye but not the other, that are used by the visual system in perceiving depth (Nakayama & Shimojo, 1990). The cells in the model's V2 are pooling from several binocular disparity sensitive V1 cells, and the detection of monocular occluded regions is given simply by the difference between the responses in disparity between V1 cells on the left or the right with respect to the center of the V2's cell receptive field. For example, a significant smaller disparity of most afferent V1 cells on the left, indicates a likely monocular left-eye location, with the farthest region on the left, and the nearer occluding surface on the right.

Zhaoping Li (2005) has modeled the inclusion of a border in one of the two alternative regions, that preludes to the organization of entities in three dimensions, as mentioned in §3.2.2.. The model includes V1 and V2, each with cells tuned to a range of orientations, but in V2 for each orientation there is a pair of cells, with opposite preferred ownership of the contour. Cells in V2 are connected with lateral excitation or inhibition, and this mechanism suffices for computing a coherent global ownership. In fact, two neighbor neurons facilitate or suppress each other's activities if the two corresponding border segments and ownership are consistent or inconsistent with being owned by a single figure surface. See example in Fig. 10.

4.3.2. Models of Angle Selectivity

A different category of models has investigated the peculiar quality V2 has of responding to specific classes of patterns, such as angles, as discussed in §3.2.3..

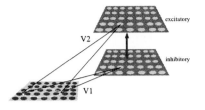

Figure 11. Connections between V1-V2 in the model of Taylor et al. (2005).

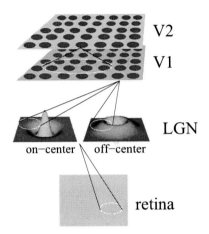

Figure 12. Scheme of the V2 model by Plebe (2007).

Boynton and Hegdé (2004) outlined what could be the simplest computational explanation of angle responsiveness in V2, suggesting that V2 neurons are summing the responses from two orientation selective V1 cells. So in a V2 cell responding vigorously to a given angle, the orientation of the two half lines of the angle are the same orientation preferred by the two V1 cells connected to this V2 cell. The authors caution, however, that the arrangement of one V2 cell summing over two V1 oriented cells is possible, and probably plays a role in V2 angle selectivity, but is unlikely to account by itself, for all aspects of angle responses in V2.

The V2 model proposed by (Taylor et al., 2005) is embedded in a computational system aimed at studying object representations, but with special attention dedicated to V2 organization with respect to angle responsiveness. V2 is designed as two layers, each composed by 28×28 leaky integrate and fire neurons, outlined in Fig. 11. The two layers act as a population of inhibitory and excitatory neurons, both are connected to V1, the output of V2 is taken as the excitatory layer. Model V1 is a fixed bank of 4 orientation filters, repeated topographically, while V2 connections are learned, from a set of 28 pictures of angles, like those used in the study of Ito and Komatsu (2004). At the end of the training most neurons have weak angle selectivity (non-preferred angles responding at least within 65% of the maximal response). Within the neurons with highly selective response the preference was distributed similarly to (Ito & Komatsu, 2004), with more neurons preferentially active for the acute angles.

In the model by Plebe (2007) the focus is shifted to the development of the computational properties making V2 able to respond to angles. The model, sketched in Fig. 12, uses two cortical maps based on the same computational architecture, the LISSOM (see §4.2.4.). The input to V1 is a simulation of on-center and off-center receptive fields, typical of ganglion cells and LNG responses, computed by differences of Gaussians. The V1 and V2 layers behave according to equations (10) and (12). The model demonstrated that, under a variety of stimuli, both V1 and V2 develop orientation and angle selectivity, but with much stronger orientation responses in V1, and angle responses in V2. The first class of stimuli used in training the system are synthetic elongated random blobs. This class mimics the ontogenesis of the biological visual system, where waves of spontaneous activity play a fundamental role in pre-natal neural development and in the first period after eyes opening (Mastronarde, 1983; Chapman et al., 1996; L. Katz & Shatz, 1996). A simple extension designed for stimulating V2 is a couple of elongated Gaussian blobs, with a coinciding end point. The class of stimuli representative of the later stage of development was the COIL-100 collection of 100 ordinary objects (Nayar & Murase, 1995). For each object there are 72 images taken at a 5 degree incremental rotation on a turntable.

Table 1 summarizes the differences in selectivity with respect to oriented bars or angles, in V1 and V2, with several combinations of stimuli. In all experiments V1 is trained first, and V2 follows, except in cases #4, #5 and #6 where the training is simultaneous. In general, at the end of the training, V1 is always more sensitive to orientation and V2 to angles, the best condition for angle selectivity in V2 is when both V1 and V2 are trained with angle patterns case #3. The worst pattern is white noise, which leads, in experiment #9, to a final selectivity in V2 of about one-third of that in case #3. In the last experiment (#10), where V2 is trained with random noise directly, bypassing V1, there is no selectivity development. Experiments #7 and #8 use natural images, in #7 the training set is a selection of sharp-edged objects, while in #8 ordinary and rounded objects are included. The first set stimulates a higher angle selectivity. From the experiments it seems that V1 and V2 develop different behaviors, although built with the same computational architecture, due mainly to their hierarchical position, with V2 taking afferents from V1.

Table 1. Selectivity developed in V1 and V2 of the model by Plebe (2007), with different exposure to training patterns: synthetic blobs, angles, natural images and white noise. The values are a measure of how much stronger the response to the preferred pattern is with respect to all the others is, with 0 if the response is the same to all patterns. The values are the average over all neurons in a cortical map. In experiments #6 V1 and V2 are trained simultaneously with patterns composed by blobs and angles together in the same retinal image. In experiment #10 V2 is directly connected with the retinal input, and trained with white noise.

#	training V1	V2	V1 bars orientation	V1 angle orientation	V1 angle amplitude	V2 bars orientation	V2 angle orientation	V2 angle amplitude
1			0.659	0.0684	0.0371	0.111	0.331	0.147
2			0.659	0.0684	0.0371	0.104	0.505	0.266
3			0.360	0.0535	0.0290	0.0815	0.701	0.341
4			0.659	0.0684	0.0371	0.102	0.342	0.154
5			0.360	0.0535	0.0290	0.121	0.472	0.221
6			0.449	0.0609	0.0330	0.119	0.472	0.234
7			0.659	0.0684	0.0371	0.145	0.376	0.179
8			0.659	0.0684	0.0371	0.165	0.314	0.136
9			0.659	0.0684	0.0371	0.085	0.260	0.107
10			-	-	-	0.00048	0.0362	0.0156

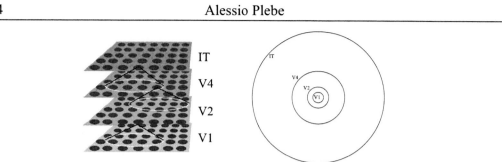

Figure 13. Scheme of the VisNet model of invariant recognition. On the right we show the relative size of receptive fields in the four maps.

A different model based on LISSOM (Sit & Miikkulainen, 2006) uses the same architecture sketched in Fig. 12, but includes backprojections from V2 to V1. Therefore the V2 layer behaves according to equation (12), while V1 is ruled by equation (13). In this experiment corners composed of two elongated Gaussian blobs, with a coinciding end point, are used as the input, like in the model by Plebe (2007). However, in this case, only right-angled corners are used, in four possible orientations ($< \wedge > \vee$). At the end of the training, V1 map stabilized to form units that were highly selective to edges. In V2 most of the units formed receptive fields that were selective to the patterns of V1 activations that corresponded to a corner, and units that preferred similar corner orientation clustered together. In the model of Plebe (2007) most neurons in V2 have robust tuning with respect to angle amplitude and orientation, but without a smoothly varying map. This difference may be an effect of the backprojections from V2 to V1.

4.4.   Cortical Models of Object Recognition

Recognition, as we have had the opportunity to mention more than once (see §1. and §3.3.), is the most ambitious target in attempts to understand the visual cortex. Today, no computational model has so far been able to account for the contributions of all maps in the ventral pathway up to recognition. However, new research endeavors are beginning to shift from the abstract models of recognition based on mathematical ideas lacking any biological correlate, that have dominated the vision science literature these past decades, to models that respect the real organization of the ventral visual cortex.

4.4.1.   The VisNet System

The architecture described in §4.2.3. has been one of the most influential building blocks for modeling the cortical visual path up to object recognition. The idea behind VisNet design was that the stumbling-block hampering recognition, was the achievement of invariance (see §3.3.2.). The solution was searched in the combination of the trace learning rule, and a hierarchy of expanding receptive fields in maps from V1 to the inferior temporal areas (E. Rolls, 1992; Wallis & Rolls, 1997). A scheme of this system, together with the hierarchy of receptive fields in the maps, is provided in Fig. 13. The system successfully produced invariance with respect to rotation, translation, and size invariance, using drawings of simple shapes like "T" and "L", and real images of faces. The invariance was learned if all views

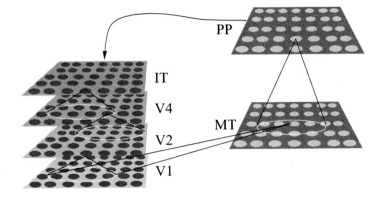

Figure 14. VisNet extended to include attentional bias, driven by the additional middle temporal (MT) and posterior parietal (PP) maps.

were presented in a time sequence during the training. More recently (Stettler et al., 2002), a certain capability of generalizing over new transformations has also been demonstrated. In this case the images were simple combinations of three bars, arranged to form 6 different stimuli, and each was available in 5 views, resulting as they were laying on a sphere, rotated in the range $-60 \div 60$ degrees. In VisNet, the first two layers were trained with the full combination of 6 stimuli and 5 views, while the upper two layers were exposed to only 4 of the 5 views, and nevertheless, was able to generalize the unseen view. Another invariance property demonstrated in this model, was the independence from the lighting source, and the consequent shading on simple shapes (E. T. Rolls & Stringer, 2006).

A significant extension of VisNet has been its integration with a model of visual attention, developed by Deco (2001), that allows a biased competition between more than one object in the field of view. The resulting system (Deco & Rolls, 2004), sketched in Fig. 14, comprises elements of the dorsal path, as MT (Middle Temporal area) and PP (Posterior Parietal cortex), performing the localization of objects and the competitive selection. The model feature two visual attentional phenomena: space-cued search and object-cued search. In the first case, module PP receives an input about the location at which to identify an object, and by backprojections drives the ventral modules in favor of the shape located in the prescribed position. In the second case, the input is the object category, that is introduced by biasing the corresponding coding pool of neurons in IT. By backprojection, lower ventral areas are biased over spatial locations where the features best match the higher level representation of the object. This in turn, will lead to increased activity in the forward pathway to PP, resulting in increased activity in the location that corresponds to where the object being searched for is located.

4.4.2. A Developmental Account of Face Detection

The model discussed in this section is relevant for epistemological and methodological reasons. Face recognition in humans, and non-humans primates as well, is often held to be somehow special (Farah, 1996; Farah et al., 1998). In particular, it seems to be the only form of innate recognition ability in humans. Although at the moment no clear information at the neuronal level is available, there are several behavioral tests showing some ability

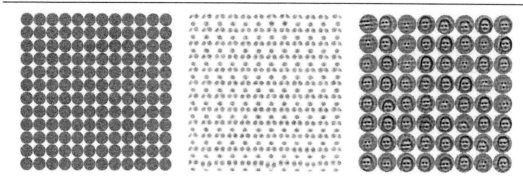

Figure 15. The FSA map in the model of face recognition. All plots show the afferent weights for every third neuron in the map. On the left the map before the training is shown, the central plot is the result of the pre-natal training with spontaneous waves, while on the right the responses after the post-natal training with natural images are visible. From Bednar (2002), with permission.

to detect faces in human newborns within hours, or even minutes after birth (Simion et al., 1998; de Haan, 2001). The studies are generally based on measuring how longer, or more often, newborns turn their eyes (or head) towards facelike stimuli, as opposed to other stimuli. Being a quite indirect and difficult measure, it has always been controversial whether a genuine recognition capability is already in place or not, however, there is good amount of agreement between most of these studies. The most common explanation is that face recognition most probably relies on functionally and anatomically distinct mechanisms from those required for other kinds of recognition, and that it is genetically determined.

Bednar (2002) proposed a computational model where face detection instead, develops spontaneously, in response to pre-natal training with spontaneous visual system activity. His model has a methodological relevance because it used the LISSOM architecture (see §4.2.4.) for the first time in a model with more than a single map: one as V1, and another called FSA (*Face Selective Area*), where face sensitivity develops. Thus, even if it is not a simulation of the detailed components in the visual ventral path, it is a significant step towards computational systems of vision, that are made up of a hierarchy of cortical maps, all built with the same architecture and that functionally differentiate by development only.

The training in the model is organized to simulate the different accounts of prenatal development, from spontaneous neural activity and postnatal neural development, based on natural scenes. The lower V1 map is trained with random blobs, that can be taken as the equivalents of the spontaneous waves in the retina, as mentioned in §3.2.3.. The main idea is that an area in the cortex, here named FSA, will develop a sensitivity to a higher level of complexity in the correlation patterns induced by the spontaneous waves, and more precisely will specialize a response to waves arranged spatially in a configuration, consisting in two blobs of activity above a third. Postnatally, the training regime represented gradual learning of specific individuals and objects seen against a variety of different backgrounds. For each postnatal iteration, one of six face images or six object images was chosen randomly, and presented in front of a randomly chosen natural background scene. The result of the two training phases on FSA is shown in Fig. 15. It is remarkable how the three dot

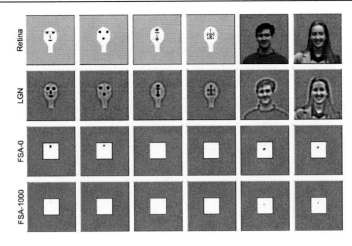

Figure 16. Results of the LISSOM face recognition model. The original stimulus is in the top row. The bottom row is the response of a FSA with complete prenatal and postnatal training (the rightmost in Fig. 15), while the third row from the top is the response of the same map at birth (the middle map in Fig. 15). The two leftmost patterns are facelike schemas typically attracting newborns in psychological experiments, while the following two central patterns are not. The rightmost two columns are natural faces. From Bednar (2002), with permission.

sensitivity acquired in prenatal time prevents the FSA area from developing responsiveness to any object except faces, unlike an untrained map would do, when exposed to the same series of natural images. Moreover, several neurons in FSA, in the postnatal experience, have refined their face responses from the rough eyes and mouth stylization, now including representations of average facial features and hair outlines.

This model is not only able to show empirically that internal spontaneous waves are in principle sufficient for evolving neural circuits capable of responding to faces before any other experience, it can also reproduce several detailed phenomena found in the development literature.

One of the most notable, is the account the model gives on the variation in response to schematic faces found in human infants, during the initial post-natal period. It has been found (Johnson & Morton, 1991) that immediately after birth schematic faces can attract equally as well as natural faces, with a certain ranking of preferences depending on the particular drawing. In a period ranging from 6 weeks to 5 months of age, however, there is a decline in response to schematic faces, in favor of natural ones. This indeed is exactly the kind of performance obtained by the LISSOM model, shown in Fig. 16: the FSA trained with prenatal spontaneous waves responds to facelike schema as well as real faces, while in the same FSA, after eye-opening and exposure to natural scenes, there is a strong prevalence of real face responses rather than to schematic drawings.

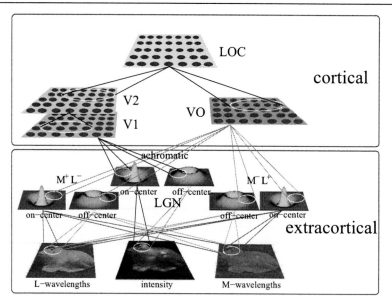

Figure 17. Overall scheme of the invariant recognition model (Plebe & Domenella, 2007).

4.4.3.   Invariant Recognition in a LISSOM-Based Model

A model proposed by Plebe (2006); Plebe and Domenella (2006, 2007) attempts to simulate the ventral visual path in performing invariant recognition of generic real objects. The overall system is shown in Fig. 17. The model uses the green and red planes of color images, which correspond to the wavelengths of peak responses of the M- and L-cones (Middle and Long wavelength sensitive) in the human retina, at 530 and 558 nm, respectively, and which are dominant in the fovea. The achromatic signal is the average luminance over the spectral components. Since the approach is focused on replicating cortical development, the subcortical process is not developed in the model, but has a fixed behavior. The profile of the receptive fields in these areas have been simulated by the difference of the two Gaussians. In the case of chromatic signals differences in the Gaussian are applied to photoreceptors with different wavelengths, with a resulting profile approximating the color-opponent cells (Valois & Jacobs, 1968).

The model's cortical ventral pathway is a hierarchy of LISSOM maps, with sizes and field parameters summarized in Tab. 2. There are two streams of processing: on the left, with reference to Fig. 17, the two spectral components are integrated and processed as intensity signals, while the right stream takes into account the chromatic information. In the approximation of the model, the elaborations performed by V1 and V2 are based on patterns of intensity on the retina, without any accounting for differences in colors. The map, which is here called VO, receives the chromatic information from the color-opponent cells, and is approximated as the only area responsible for processing color constancy. This is the tendency of the color of a surface to appear more constant than it ought to by the physical composition of the reflected light under changing luminance condition (see §3.1.2.). This property is a clear contribution to object recognition by allowing more reliable judgments of the object's surface properties regardless of ambient light. The paths from VO and V2

Table 2. Main dimensions of the layers in the model by Plebe and Domenella (2007): the linear size of the maps, and the radius for the afferent, excitatory and inhibitory fields.

layer	size	r_A	r_E	r_H
retina	148	-	-	-
LGN	112	2.6	-	-
V1	96	8.5	1.5	7
V2	30	7.5	8.5	3.5
VO	30	24.5	4	8
LOC	16	6.5	1.5	3.5

rejoin in the cortical map LOC, the highest in this model, and the seat of object recognition. The training of this system was based on a combination of pre-natal stimuli, simulated by synthetic random elongated blobs, and real images from the COIL-100 collection of 100 ordinary objects (Nayar & Murase, 1995), as in the model described in §4.3.2.. In addition, VO was stimulated with random circular blobs with variable hues.

As a consequence of the stimuli experience, functions develop in the lower maps of the model: orientation selectivity in V1, angle selectivity in V2, and color constancy in VO. The most remarkable property developed in model's LOC is invariance with respect to several dimensions of variations in the visual signals when viewing the same object. The Fig. 18 shows the compared responses of LOC to viewpoint changes, for a selection of objects with the highest difference in appearance during rotation. The response patterns are clustered into a small set of blobs, distinctive of a specific object. The variation of appearance during rotations of 30° induces a marginal modification of the activation pattern, in general with 60° the overall pattern is maintained.

The responses in the model's LOC do not represent local features of the stimuli, nor objects by themselves, but are an intermediate coding towards an abstraction of the object from its visual appearance. The activation of a neuron might not be a specific representation, but rather a member of a distributed representation. This hypothesis has been tested, in the model, measuring how populations of neurons in the model's LOC could suffice for the classification of individual objects, or classes of objects, from the set of stimuli. For each object statistics have been performed on every neuron, selecting those with a response that is significantly higher on all 72 available examples of that object than for examples of all other objects. In this way, a set of neural populations has been identified, which is associated with each object. Then the LOC is evaluated as a classifier, on the basis of how many examples of an object elicit the stronger response in the corresponding neural population. A similar procedure can be applied by taking single objects as classes categories of objects: toys, bottles, and so on, or shape classes (like spherical, cylindrical) and hue classes. For all these properties the amount of coding in model's LOC can be evaluated. Moreover, since for each object 72 different individual views are available, it is possible to evaluate the generalization ability in LOC, by exposing it to a subset of views only during the training. The resulting accuracies are shown in Tab. 3. It is out of the purpose of this model to

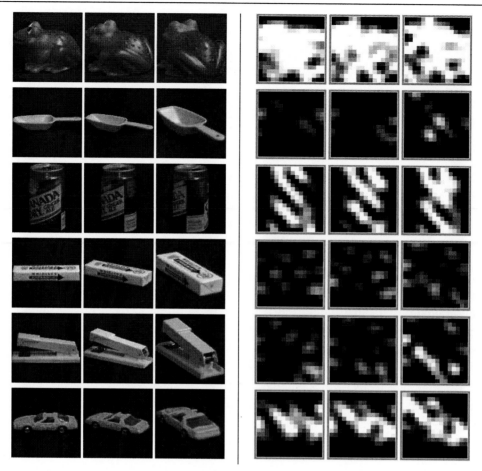

Figure 18. Invariance properties of the LOC map. The right block shows the activations of the LOC map in response to the corresponding input images in the left block. The 3 columns in the input block are different object rotation, at 30° steps.

achieve classification accuracies competitive with other image processing techniques, it is intended for simulating the process occurring in the ventral visual cortex up to LOC. Therefore the results in Tab. 3 reflect simply the neural coding in LOC, when read as a distributed representation. The same contents of LOC, if processed by other decoders, like a SOM, would give much better categorization performance (Plebe & Domenella, 2007).

4.4.4. Further Approaches to Modeling Recognition

Even if the detailed modeling of the cortex in the human visual ventral pathway is in its infancy, with just a few examples, there are indeed many other investigations that can be considered a step forward in the enterprise of computationally explaining object recognition, in a way that is compatible with the biology of the visual cortex and which are worthy of mention.

A series of models developed by Stephen Grossberg and his group in the last decades (Grossberg & Mingolla, 1987; Grossberg, 1994; Kelly & Grossberg, 2000; Grossberg &

Table 3. Classification accuracy in the model's LOC as a function of the number of views used in the training. From comparison, the accuracy achieved by classifying by chance is included.

training	object classification	category classification	hue classification	shape classification
4 views	0.60	0.46	0.39	0.32
8 views	0.62	0.47	0.40	0.32
18 views	0.63	0.44	0.41	0.35
by chance	0.01	0.03	0.10	0.08

Howe, 2003; Grossberg et al., 2007) has faced the problem of surface perception, that is indeed one of the most critical aspect of object recognition. Their approach is not aimed at simulating specific areas in the ventral visual cortex, rather at reproducing, with neural plausible computations, certain processing steps towards surface perception, which have been identified theoretically (Grossberg, 1983). According to this theory, the models are based on two main processes, called the boundary contour system, and the feature contour system (Grossberg & Mingolla, 1987). The former creates an emergent 3-D boundary segmentation of edges, texture, shading and stereo information, based on the amount and orientation of scenic contrast, but not on the direction of contrast. The feature contour system compensates for variable illumination conditions and fills-in surface properties of brightness, color, depth and form, using both the amount and the direction of scenic contrast. These two main systems interact each other, making them mutually consistent. A significant extension of this system has been its integration with a module that carry out stereopsis and solve the correspondence problem, using both monocular and binocular visual informations (Grossberg & Howe, 2003). These models succeeded in simulating challenging psychophysical data about 3-D surface perception, like figure-ground separation and amodal completion (Kelly & Grossberg, 2000), perception of golf balls, elliptical cylinders and prolate ellipsoids (Grossberg et al., 2007). While at macroscopic level there is no direct correspondence between modules of the models and areas in the visual cortex, at lower level the computations in the model reflect closely the behavior of cells in cortical areas as V1 and V2.

A computational approach to object recognition that does not account explicitly for the role of cortical maps, but that is still aimed at replicating some functional aspects of the ventral cortex, is the one pursued by Riesenhuber and Poggio (1999, 2000, 2002), based on a previous idea known as "Neocognitron" (Fukushima, 1980). The approach attempts to gradually build more complicated features from the input with a hierarchy of alternated layers of "simple"and "complex" cells. The simple cells of an intermediate layer combine signals from complex cells in the layer below, with different features but same view parameters (position, for example). The complex cells of these units, instead, pool the output of simple cells responding to the same feature, but at different view parameters (different positions), selecting the maximum value. This operation of maximum selection allows invariance. There might be a loose relationship between layers of simple and complex cells, and in the hierarchy of cortical maps, from V1 to LOC, but the main issue is the use of the mathematical operation of maximum over a pool of values, that does not seem to correspond to mechanisms found in the cortex.

A model of the ventral pathway encompassing V1, V4, IT and PP is proposed in (Kashimori, Suzuki, Fujita, Zheng, & Kambara, 2004; Suzuki, Hashimoto, Kashimori, & Kambara, 2004), with the special property of associating each cortical area with two maps, with high and low spatial resolution. The rationale is that the broad resolution maps should retrieve the memories of inferotemporal cortex, which are categorized by the outline of an object, while the fine resolution maps are used to compare the feedforward signals from the lower system with the feedback signals from the higher order visual system. Although the overlap of spatial scales within the same cortical areas is known (Born & Tootell, 1991), there is no evidence that their role is the one supposed in this model.

5. Conclusion

This chapter has given an overview of recent advancements in the understanding of the ventral visual pathway in the human cortex, deliberately biased by a personal perspective. My view is that the ability to recognize is the most valuable outcome of vision for humans, and yet the most mysterious. For this reason, recent discoveries like LOC as a recognition-specific complex of areas, are believed to be crucial for the advancement in understanding vision, and have been treated with special detail here. Moreover, for the same reason I argue that computational modeling is a necessary complement of investigation, because understanding recognition means nothing else than understanding the chain of functional processes that lead from the array of photoreceptor signals to the assignment of meaning to objects seen. A wide section has therefore been devoted to recent models of the ventral visual cortex. A third consequence of my personal view in this chapter is the emphasis given to V2. This is the first area, beyond V1, where the convergence of neurophysiological studies and computational models begin to offer a picture of what kind of functions are performed in a cortical map involved in recognition. Despite the large gap that exists between the state-of-the-art in vision science and an adequate explanation of the workings of vision, regarding complex aspects such as recognition, recent trends such as those here presented are surely encouraging. The task of explaining visual recognition not only seems more feasible in the near future, but also promises to enlighten us on other important functions of the brain as well. In fact, understanding visual recognition will be the first fruitful example of the bridging of neurophysiology to cognition.

References

Abbott, L. F., Rolls, E., & Tovee, M. J. (1996). Representational capacity of face coding in monkeys. *Cerebral Cortex*, **6**, 498–505.

Adrian, E. D., & Matthews, R. (1927a). The action of light on the eye: Part ii. the processes involved in retinal excitation. *Journal of Physiology*, **64**, 279–301.

Adrian, E. D., & Matthews, R. (1927b). The action of light on the eye: Part i. the discharge of impulses in the optic nerve and its relation to the electric changes in the retina. *Journal of Physiology*, **63**, 378–414.

Allman, J. M., & Kaas, J. H. (1971). A representation of the visual field in the caudal third of the middle temporal gyrus of the owl monkey. *Brain Research*, **31**, 85–105.

Allman, J. M., & Kaas, J. H. (1974). The organization of the second visual area (V II) in the owl monkey: a second order transformation of the visual hemifield. *Brain Research*, **76**, 247–265.

Amedi, A., Jacobson, G., Hendler, T., Malach, R., & Zohary, E. (2002). Convergence of visual and tactile shape processing in the human lateral occipital complex. *Cerebral Cortex*, **12**, 1202–1212.

Amedi, A., Malach, R., Hendler, T., Peled, S., & Zohary, E. (2001). Visuo-haptic object-related activation in the ventral visual pathway. *Nature Neuroscience*, **4**, 324–330.

Amit, Y., & Mascaro, M. (2003). An integrated network for invariant visual detection and recognition. *Vision Research*, **43**, 2073-2088.

Anzai, A., Peng, X., & Essen, D. C. V. (2007). Neurons in monkey visual area V2 encode combinations of orientations. *Nature Neuroscience*, **10**, 1313-1321.

Artola, A., & Singer, W. (1987). Long term potentiation and NMDA receptors in rat visual cortex. *Nature*, **330**, 649–652.

Assee, A., & Qian, N. (2007). Solving da vinci stereopsis with depth-edge-selective v2 cells. *Vision Research*, **47**, 2585-2602.

Avidan, G., Harel, M., Hendler, T., Ben-Bashat, D., Zohary, E., & Malach, R. (2002). Contrast sensitivity in human visual areas and its relationship to object recognition. *Journal of Neurophysiology*, **87**, 3102–3116.

Backus, B. T., Fleet, D. J., Parker, A. J., & Heeger, D. J. (2001). Human cortical activity correlates with stereoscopic depth perception. *Journal of Neurophysiology*, **86**, 2054–2068.

Bar, M., Tootell, R. B. H., Schacter, D. L., Greve, D. N., Fischl, B., Mendola, J. D., et al. (2001). Cortical mechanisms specific to explicit visual object recognition. *Neuron*, **29**, 529–535.

Barnes, J., Howard, R., Senior, C., Brammer, M., Bullmore, E., Simmons, A., et al. (1999). The functional anatomy of the mccollough contingent colour after-effect. *NeuroReport*, **10**, 195–199.

Bartlett, F. (1916). An experimental study of some problems of perceiving and imagining. *British Journal of Psychology*, **8**, 222–260.

Bednar, J. A. (2002). *Learning to see: Genetic and environmental influences on visual development*. Unpublished doctoral dissertation, University of Texas at Austin. (Tech Report AI-TR-02-294)

Bednar, J. A., & Miikkulainen, R. (2000). Tilt aftereffects in a self-organizing model of the primary visual cortex. *Neural Computation*, **12**, 1721–1740.

Bednar, J. A., & Miikkulainen, R. (2003). Learning innate face preferences. *Neural Computation*, **15**, 1525–1557.

Bednar, J. A., & Miikkulainen, R. (2006). Joint maps for orientation, eye, and direction preference in a self-organizing model of v1. *Neurocomputing*, **69**, 1272–1276.

Bednar, J. A., Paula, J. B. D., & Miikkulainen, R. (2005). Self-organization of color opponent receptive fields and laterally connected orientation maps. *Neurocomputing*, **65-66**, 69–76.

Belin, P., & Zatorre, R. J. (2000). 'what', 'where' and 'how' in auditory cortex. *Nature*

Neuroscience, **3**, 965–966.

Ben-Shahar, O., & Zucker, S. (2004). Geometrical computations explain projection patterns of long-range horizontal connections in visual cortex. *Neural Computation*, **16**, 445–476.

Blakemore, C., & Grahame, C. F. (1970). A relational model for large shared data banks. *Communications of the Association for Computing Machinery*, **13**, 377–387.

Born, R., & Tootell, R. B. (1991). Spatial frequency tuning of single units in macaque supragranular striate cortex. *Proceedings of the Natural Academy of Science USA*, **88**, 7066–7070.

Boynton, G. M. (2002). Color vision: How the cortex represents color. *Current Biology*, **12**, R838-R84.

Boynton, G. M., & Hegdé, J. (2004). Visual cortex: The continuing puzzle of area v2. *Current Biology*, **14**, R523–R524.

Bressloff, P. C., & D. Cowan, J. k. (2002). An amplitude equation approach to contextual effect s in visual cortex. *Neural Computation*, **14**, 493-525.

Brewer, A. A., Liu, J., Wade, A. R., & Wandell, B. A. (2005). Visual field maps and stimulus selectivity in human ventral occipital cortex. *Nature Neuroscience*, **8**, 1102–1109.

Brodmann, K. (1909). *Vergleichende lokalisationslehre der grosshirnrinde*. Leipzig: Barth.

Brunel, N., & Nadal, J.-P. (1998). Mutual information, fisher information, and population coding. *Neural Computation*, **10**, 1731–1757.

Burkhalter, A., Felleman, D. J., Newsome, W., & Van Essen, D. C. (1986). Anatomical and physiological asymmetries related to visual areas V3 and VP in macaque extrastriate cortex. *Vision Research*, **26**, 63–80.

Burkhalter, A., & Van Essen, D. C. (1986). Processing of color, form and disparity information in visual areas VP and V2 of ventral extrastriate cortex in the macaque monkey. *Journal of Neuroscience*, **6**, 2327–2351.

Chalupa, L., & Werner, J. (Eds.). (2003). *The visual neurosciences*. Cambridge (MA): MIT Press.

Chandrasekaran, C., Canon, V., Dahmen, J. C., Kourtzi, Z., & Welchman, A. E. (2007). Neural correlates of disparity-defined shape discrimination in the human brain. *Journal of Neurophysiology*, **97**, 1553–1565.

Chapman, B., Stryker, M. P., & Bonhoeffer, T. (1996). Development of orientation preference maps in ferret primary visual cortex. *Journal of Neuroscience*, **16**, 6443–6453.

Chklovskii, D. B., & Koulakov, A. A. (2004). Maps in the brain: what can we learn from them? *Annual Review of Neuroscience*, **27**, 369–392.

Choe, Y., & Miikkulainen, R. (2004). Contour integration and segmentation with self-organized lateral connections. *Biological Cybernetics*, **90**, 75–88.

Churchland, P. M. (1989). *A neurocomputational perspective: The nature of mind and the structure of science*. Cambridge (MA): MIT Press.

Churchland, P. S., & Churchland, P. M. (2002). Neural worlds and real worlds. *Nature Reviews Neuroscience*, **3**, 903–907.

Churchland, P. S., Ramachandran, V., & Sejnowski, T. (1994). A critique of pure vision. In C. Koch & J. Davis (Eds.), *Large-scale neuronal theories of the brain*. Cambridge (MA): MIT Press.

Churchland, P. S., & Sejnowski, T. (1994). *The computational brain*. Cambridge (MA): MIT Press.

Churchland, P. S., & Sejnowski, T. J. (1990). Neural representation and neural computation. *Philosophical Perspectives*, **4**, 343–382.

Corbetta, M., Miezin, F., Dobmeyer, S., Shulman, G., & Petersen, S. (1991). Selective and divided attention during visual discriminations of shape, color, and speed: functional anatomy by positron emission tomography. *Journal of Neuroscience*, **11**, 2383–2402.

Cowey, A. (1964). Projection of the retina on to striate and prestriate cortex in the squirrel monkey, *Saimiri sciureus*. *Journal of Neurophysiology*, **27**, 366–393.

Cox, D. D., Meier, P., Oertelt, N., & DiCarlo, J. J. (2005). 'breaking' position-invariant object recognition. *Nature Neuroscience*, **8**, 1145–1147.

Cummins, R. (1989). *Meaning and mental representation*. Cambridge (MA): MIT Press.

Damasio, A., Yamada, T., Damasio, H., Corbett, J., & McKee, J. (1980). Central achromatopsia: behavioral, anatomic, and physiologic aspects. *Neurology*, **30**, 1064–1071.

Daugman, J. G. (1980). Two-dimensional spectral analysis of cortical receptive field profiles. *Vision Research*, **20**, 847–856.

Daugman, J. G. (1985). Uncertainty relation for resolution in space, spatial frequency, and orientation optimized by two-dimensional visual cortical filters. *Journal of the Optical Society of America A*, **2**, 1160–1169.

David, S. V., Hayden, B. Y., & Gallant, J. L. (2006). Spectral receptive field properties explain shape selectivity in area v4. *Journal of Neurophysiology*, **96**, 3492–3505.

Dayan, P., & Abbott, L. F. (2001). *Theoretical neuroscience*. Cambridge (MA): MIT Press.

de Haan, M. (2001). The neuropsychology of face processing during infancy and childhood. In C. A. Nelson & M. Luciana (Eds.), *Handbook of developmental cognitive neuroscience*. Cambridge (MA): MIT Press.

deCharms, R. C., & Zador, A. (2000). Neural representation and the cortical code. *Annual Review of Neuroscience*, **23**, 613–647.

Deco, G. (2001). Biased competition mechanisms for visual attention in a multimodular neurodynamical system. In S. Wermter, J. Austin, & D. Willshaw (Eds.), *Emergent neural computational architectures based on neuroscience: towards neuroscience-inspired computing* (pp. 114–126). Berlin: Springer-Verlag.

Deco, G., & Rolls, E. (2004). A neurodynamical cortical model of visual attention and invariant object recognition. *Vision Research*, **44**, 621–642.

Denys, K., Vanduffel, W., Fize, D., Nelissen, K., Peuskens, H., Van Essen, D., et al. (2004). The processing of visual shape in the cerebral cortex of human and nonhuman primates: A functional magnetic resonance imaging study. *Journal of Neuroscience*, **24**, 2551–2565.

Desimone, R., Albright, T. D., Gross, C. D., & Bruce, C. (1984). Stimulus-selective properties of inferior temporal neurons in the macaque. *Journal of Neuroscience*, **4**, 2051–2062.

Desimone, R., & Gross, C. G. (1979). Visual areas in the temporal cortex of the macaque. *Brain*, **178**, 363–380.

DeYoe, E. A., & Van Essen, D. C. (1985). Segregation of efferent connections and receptive field properties in visual area V2 of the macaque. *Nature*, **317**, 58–61.

DeYoe, E. A., & Van Essen, D. C. (1988). Concurrent processing in the primate visual cortex. *Trends in Neuroscience*, **11**, 219–226.

Doniger, G. M., Foxe, J. J., Murray, M. M., Higgins, B. A., Schroeder, C. E., & Javitt, D. C. (2000). Activation timecourse of ventral visual stream object-recognition areas: High density electrical mapping of perceptual closure processes. *Journal of Cognitive Neuroscience*, **12**, 615–621.

Doniger, G. M., Foxe, J. J., Schroeder, C. E., Murray, M. M., Higgins, B. A., & Javitt, D. C. (2001). Visual perceptual learning in human object recognition areas: A repetition priming study using high-density electrical mapping. *NeuroImage*, **13**, 305–313.

Dougherty, R. F., Ben-Shachar, M., Bammer, R., Brewer, A. A., & Wandell, B. A. (2005). Functional organization of human occipital-callosal fiber tracts. *Proceedings of the Natural Academy of Science USA*, **20**, 7350–7355.

Downing, P. E., Jiang, Y., Shuman, M., & Kanwisher, N. (2001). A cortical area selective for visual processing of the human body. *Science*, **293**, 2470–2473.

Drury, H. A., Van Essen, D. C., Anderson, C., Lee, C., Coogan, T., & Lewis, J. W. (1996). Computerized mappings of the cerebral cortex: A multiresolution flattening method and a surface-based coordinate system. *Journal of Cognitive Neuroscience*, **8**, 1–28.

Durbin, R., & Mitchison, G. (1990). A dimension reduction framework for understanding cortical maps. *Nature*, **343**, 644–647.

Edelman, S. (1999). *Representation and recognition in vision*. Cambridge (MA): MIT Press.

Edelman, S., & Duvdevani-Bar, S. (1997). A model of visual recognition and categorization. *Philosophical transactions of the Royal Society of London*, **352**, 1191–1202.

Engel, S. A., Glover, G. H., & Wandell, B. A. (1997). Retinotopic organization in human visual cortex and the spatial precision of functional mri. *Cerebral Cortex*, **7**, 181–192.

Engel, S. A., Zhang, X., & Wandell, B. A. (1997). Colour tuning in human visual cortex measured with functional magnetic resonance imaging. *Nature*, **388**, 68–71.

Epstein, R., & Kanwisher, N. (1998). A cortical representation of the local visual environment. *Nature*, **9**, 598–601.

Fahle, M., & Poggio, T. (Eds.). (2002). *Perceptual learning*. Cambridge (MA): MIT Press.

Farah, M. J. (1996). Is face recognition 'special'? evidence from neuropsychology. *Behavioural Brain Research*, **76**, 181–189.

Farah, M. J., & Aguirre, G. K. (1999). Imaging visual recognition: PET and fMRI studies of the functional anatomy of human visual recognition. *Trends in Cognitive Sciences*, **3**, 179–186.

Farah, M. J., Wilson, K. D., Drain, M., & Tanaka, J. N. (1998). What is 'special' about face perception? *Psychological Review*, **105**, 482–498.

Felleman, D. J., Carman, G., & Van Essen, D. C. (1984). Distributed hierarchical processing in the primate cerebral cortex. *Invest. Ophthalmol. Vis. Sci.*, **25**, 278.

Felleman, D. J., & Van Essen, D. C. (1991). Distributed hierarchical processing in the primate cerebral cortex. *Cerebral Cortex*, **1**, 1–47.

Ferber, S., Humphrey, G. K., & Vilis, T. (2005). Segregation and persistence of form in the lateral occipital complex. *Neuropsychologia*, **43**, 41–45.

Fodor, J. (1981). *Representations: Philosofical essay on the foundation of cognitive science*. Cambridge (MA): MIT Press.

Fodor, J. (1983). *Modularity of mind: and essay on faculty psychology*. Cambridge (MA): MIT Press.

Fukushima, K. (1980). Neocognitron: a self-organizing neural network model for a mechanism of pattern recognition unaffected by shift in position. *Biological Cybernetics*, **36**, 193–202.

Gabor, D. (1946). Theory of communication. *Journal IEE*, **93**, 429–459.

Gattass, R., Gross, C., & Sandell, J. (1981). Visual topography of V2 in the macaque. *Journal of Comparative Neurology*, **201**, 519–539.

Gauthier, I., Skudlarski, P., Gore, J. C., & Anderson, A. W. (2000). Expertise for cars and birds recruits brain areas involved in face recognition. *Nature Neuroscience*, **3**, 191–197.

Gauthier, I., & Tarr, M. (2002). Unraveling mechanisms for expert object recognition: bridging brain activity and behavior. *Journal of experimental psychology. Human perception and performance*, **28**, 431–446.

Gegenfurtner, K. R., Kiper, D. C., & Fenstemaker, S. B. (1996). Processing of color, form, and motion in macaque area V2. *Visual Neuroscience*, **13**, 161–172.

Gegenfurtner, K. R., Kiper, D. C., & Levitt, J. B. (1997). Functional properties of neurons in macaque area V3. *Journal of Neurophysiology*, **77**, 1906–1923.

Geisler, W., Perry, J., Super, B., & Gallogly, D. (2001). Edge co-occurrence in natural images predicts contour grouping performance. *Vision Research*, **41**, 711–724.

Gennari, F. (1782). *De peculiari structura cerebri, nonnulisque ejus morbis*. Parma (Italy): Ex regio typographeo.

Gilbert, C. D., & Wiesel, T. N. (1983). Clustered intrinsic connections in cat visual cortex. *Journal of Neuroscience*, **3**, 1116–1133.

Glass, L., & Perez, R. (1973). Perception of random dot interference patterns. *Nature*, **246**, 360–362.

Golarai, G., Ghahremani, D. G., Whitfield-Gabrieli, S., Reiss, A., Eberhardt, J. L., Gabrieli, J. D., et al. (2007). Differential development of high-level visual cortex correlates with category-specific recognition memory. *Nature Neuroscience*, **10**, 512–522.

Goodale, M. A., & Milner, A. D. (1992). Separate visual pathways for perception and action. *Trends in Neuroscience*, **15**, 20–25.

Grill-Spector, K. (2003). The functional organization of the ventral visual pathway and its relationship to object recognition. In N. Kanwisher & J. Duncan (Eds.), *Attention and performance xx. functional brain imaging of visual cognition*. Oxford (UK): Oxford University Press.

Grill-Spector, K., Kourtzi, Z., & Kanwisher, N. (2001). The lateral occipital complex and its role in object recognition. *Vision Research*, **41**, 1409–1422.

Grill-Spector, K., Kushnir, T., Edelman, S., Avidan-Carmel, G., Itzchak, Y., & Malach, R. (1999). Differential processing of objects under various viewing conditions in the human lateral occipital complex. *Neuron*, **24**, 187–203.

Grill-Spector, K., Kushnir, T., Edelman, S., Itzchak, Y., & Malach, R. (1998). Cue-invariant activation in object-related areas in the human occipital lobe. *Neuron*, **21**, 191–202.

Grill-Spector, K., & Malach, R. (2001). fMR-adaptation: a tool for studying the functional properties of human cortical neurons. *Acta Psychologica*, **107**, 293–321.

Gross, C. G., Bender, D., & Rocha-Miranda, C. (1969). Visual receptive fields of neurons in inferotemporal cortex of the monkey. *Science*, **166**, 1303–1306.

Gross, C. G., Rocha-Miranda, C., & Bender, D. (1972). Visual properties of neurons in inferotemporal cortex of the macaque. *Journal of Neurophysiology*, **35**, 96–111.

Grossberg, S. (1983). The quantized geometry of visual space: The coherent computation of depth, form, and lightness. *Behavioral and Brain Science*, **6**, 625–692.

Grossberg, S. (1994). 3-d vision and figure-ground separation by visual cortex. *Perception and Psychophysics*, **55**, 48–120.

Grossberg, S., & Howe, P. D. L. (2003). A laminar cortical model of stereopsis and three-dimensional surface perception. vision research. *Vision Research*, **43**, 801–829.

Grossberg, S., Kuhlmann, L., & Mingolla, E. (2007). A neural model of 3D shape-from-texture: Multiple-scale filtering, boundary grouping, and surface filling-in. *Vision Research*, **47**, 634–672.

Grossberg, S., & Mingolla, E. (1987). Neural dynamics of surface perception: Boundary webs, illuminants, and shape-from-shading. *Computer Vision, Graphics, and Image Processing*, **37**, 116–165.

Hadjikhani, N., Liu, A. K., Dale, A. M., Cavanagh, P., & Tootell, R. B. H. (1998). Retinotopy and color sensitivity in human visual cortical area v8. *Nature Neuroscience*, **1**, 235–241.

Hagmann, P., Thiran, J.-P., Jonasson, L., Vandergheynst, P., Clarke, S., Maeder, P., et al. (2003). Dti mapping of human brain connectivity: statistical fibre tracking and virtual dissection. *NeuroImage*, **19**, 545–554.

Harmon, L. D., & Julesz, B. (1973). Masking in visual recognition: Effects of two-dimensional filtered noise. *Science*, **180**, 1194–1197.

Hartline, H. K. (1938). The response of single optic nerve fibers of the vertebrate eye to illumination of the retina. *American Journal of Physiology*, **121**, 400–415.

Hartline, H. K. (1967). Visual receptors and retinal interaction. *Science*, **164**, 270–278.

Hartline, H. K., Ratliff, F., & Miller, W. H. (1961). Inhibitory interaction in the retina and its significance in vision. In E. Florey (Ed.), *Nervous inhibition*. New York: Pergamon Press.

Hasson, U., Harel, M., Levy, I., & Malach, R. (2003). Large-scale mirror-symmetry organization of human occipito-temporal object areas. *Neuron*, **37**, 1027–1041.

Hasson, U., Levy, I., Behrmann, M., Hendler, T., & Malach, R. (2002). Eccentricity bias as an organizing principle for human high-order object areas. *Neuron*, **34**, 479–490.

Haxby, J. V., Gobbini, M. I., Furey, M. L., Ishai, A., Schouten, J. L., & Pietrini, P. (2001). Distributed and overlapping representations of objects and faces in ventral temporal cortex. *Science*, **293**, 2425–2430.

Hayward, W. G., & Tarr, M. J. (1997). Testing conditions for viewpoint invariance in object recognition. *Human Perception and Performance*, **23**, 1511–1521.

Hegdé, J., & Van Essen, D. C. (2000). Selectivity for complex shapes in primate visual area V2. *Journal of Neuroscience*, **20**, 4117–4130.

Hegdé, J., & Van Essen, D. C. (2003). Strategies of shape representation in macaque visual area V2. *Visual Neuroscience*, **20**, 313–328.

Hegdé, J., & Van Essen, D. C. (2007). A comparative study of shape representation in macaque visual areas V2 and V4. *Cerebral Cortex*, **17**, 1100–1116.

Heider, B., Meskenaite, V., & Peterhans, E. (2000). Anatomy and physiology of a neural mechanism defining depth order and contrast polarity at illusory contours. *The European Journal of Neuroscience*, **12**, 4117–4130.

Held, R., & Hein, A. (1962). Movement-produced stimulation in the development of visually guided behavior. *Journal of Comparative and Physiological Psychology*, **56**, 872–876.

Hinton, G. E., McClelland, J. L., & Rumelhart, D. E. (1986). Distributed representations. In D. E. Rumelhart & J. L. McClelland (Eds.), *Parallel distributed processing: Explorations in the microstructure of cognition* (Vol. 1, pp. 77–109). Cambridge (MA): MIT Press.

Holmes, G., & Lister, W. (1916). Disturbances of vision from cerebral lesions with special reference to the cortical representation of the macula. *Brain*, **39**, 34–73.

Horton, J. C., & Hoyt, W. F. (1991). Quadrantic visual field defects. a hallmark of lesions in extrastriate (V2/V3) cortex. *Brain*, **114**, 1703–1718.

Hubel, D., & Wiesel, T. (1959). Receptive fields of single neurones in the cat's striate cortex. *Journal of Physiology*, **148**, 574–591.

Hubel, D., & Wiesel, T. (1962). Receptive fields, binocular interaction, and functional architecture in the cat's visual cortex. *Journal of Physiology*, **160**, 106–154.

Hubel, D., & Wiesel, T. (1963). Single-cell responses in striate cortex of kittens deprived of vision in one eye. *Journal of Neurophysiology*, **26**, 1003–1017.

Hubel, D., & Wiesel, T. (1968). Receptive fields and functional architecture of mokey striate cortex. *Journal of Physiology*, **195**, 215–243.

Hubel, D., & Wiesel, T. (1970). Stereoscopic vision in macaque monkey: Cells sensitive to binocular depth in area 18 of the macaque monkey cortex. *Nature*, **225**, 41–42.

Hubel, D., & Wiesel, T. (1974). Uniformity of monkey striate cortex: a parallel relationship between field size, scatter, and magnification factor. *Journal of Comparative Neurology*, **158**, 295–305.

Hubel, D. H., & Livingstone, M. S. (1987). Segregation of form, color, and stereopsis in primate area 18. *Journal of Neuroscience*, **7**, 3378–3415.

Image-based object recognition in man, monkey, and machine. (1998). In M. J. Tarr & H. H. Bülthoff (Eds.), *Object recognition in man, monkey, and machine.* Cambridge (MA): MIT Press.

Inouye, T. (1909). *Die sehstörungen bei schussverletzungen der kortikalen sehsphäre nach beobachtungen an verwundeten der letzten japanischen kriege.* Leipzig: Wilhelm Engelmann.

Ito, M., & Komatsu, H. (2004). Representation of angles embedded within contour stimuli in area V2 of macaque monkeys. *Journal of Neuroscience*, **24**, 3313–3324.

James, T. W., & Gauthier, I. (2004). Brain areas engaged during visual judgments by involuntary access to novel semantic information. *Vision Research*, **44**, 429–439.

James, T. W., Humphrey, G. K., Gati, J. S., Servos, P., Menon, R. S., & Goodale, M. A. (2002). Haptic study of three-dimensional objects activates extrastriate visual areas. *Neuropsychologia*, **40**, 1706–1714.

Johnson, M. H., & Morton, J. (1991). *Biology and cognitive development: The case of face recognition.* Oxford (UK): Basil Blackwell.

Julesz, B. (1971). *Foundations of cyclopean vision.* Chicago (IL): Chicago University

Press.

Kaas, J. H. (1993). The organization of the visual cortex in primates: problems, conclusions and the use of comparative studies in understanding the human brain. In B. Gulyas, D. Ottoson, & P. Roland (Eds.), *The functional organization of the human visual cortex*. New York: Pergamon Press.

Kaas, J. H. (1997). Topographic maps are fundamental to sensory processing. *Brain Research Bulletin*, **44**, 107–112.

Kaas, J. H., & Lyon, D. C. (2001). Visual cortex organization in primates: theories of v3 and adjoining visual areas. *Progress in Brain Research*, **134**, 285–295.

Kanwisher, N. (2003). The ventral visual object pathway in humans: Evidence from fMRI. In L. Chalupa & J. Werner (Eds.), *The visual neurosciences*. Cambridge (MA): MIT Press.

Kanwisher, N., Chun, M., McDermott, J., & Ledden, P. J. (1996). Functional imaging of human visual recognition. *Cognitive Brain Research*, **5**, 55–67.

Kanwisher, N., McDermott, J., & Chun, M. (1997). The fusiform face area: a module in human extrastriate cortex specialized for face perception. *Journal of Neuroscience*, **17**, 4302–4311.

Kanwisher, N., Woods, R. P., Iacoboni, M., & Mazziotta, J. C. (1996). A locus in human extrastriate cortex for visual shape analysis. *Journal of Cognitive Neuroscience*, **9**, 133–142.

Karten, H. (Ed.). (2000). *Evolutionary developmental biology of the cerebral cortex*. New York: John Wiley.

Kashimori, Y., Suzuki, N., Fujita, K., Zheng, M., & Kambara, T. (2004). A functional role of multiple spatial resolution maps in form perception along the ventral visual pathway. *Neurocomputing*, **65-66**, 219–228.

Katz, L., & Shatz, C. (1996). Synaptic activity and the construction of cortical circuits. *Science*, **274**, 1133–1138.

Katz, L. C., & Callaway, E. M. (1992). Development of local circuits in mammalian visual cortex. *Annual Review of Neuroscience*, **15**, 31–56.

Kelly, F. J., & Grossberg, S. (2000). Neural dynamics of 3-D surface perception: Figure-ground separation and lightness perception. *Perception and Psychophysics*, **62**, 1596–1619.

Kirkwood, A., & Bear, M. F. (1994). Hebbian synapses in visual cortex. *Journal of Neuroscience*, **14**, 1634–1645.

Kluver, H., & Bucy, P. C. (1937). Psychic blindness and other symptomps following bilateral temporal lobectomy in rhesus monkey. *American Journal of Physiology*, **119**, 352–353.

Kobatake, E., & Tanaka, K. (1994). Neuronal selectivities to complex object features in the ventral visual pathway of the macaque cerebral cortex. *Journal of Neurophysiology*, **71**, 856–867.

Kohonen, T. (1982). Self-organizing formation of topologically correct feature maps. *Biological Cybernetics*, **43**, 59–69.

Kohonen, T. (1984). *Self-organization and associative memory*. Berlin: Springer-Verlag.

Kohonen, T. (1995). *Self-organizing maps*. Berlin: Springer-Verlag.

Kourtzi, Z., Erb, M., Grodd, W., & Bülthoff, H. H. (2003). Representation of the perceived

3-d object shape in the human lateral occipital complex. *Cerebral Cortex*, **13**, 911–920.

Kourtzi, Z., & Kanwisher, N. (2000). Cortical regions involved in perceiving object shape. *Journal of Neuroscience*, **20**, 3310–3318.

Kourtzi, Z., & Kanwisher, N. (2001). Representation of perceived object shape by the human lateral occipital complex. *Science*, **293**, 1506–1509.

Koutstaal, W., Wagner, A. D., Rotte, M., Maril, A., Buckner, R., & Schacter, D. L. (2001). Perceptual specificity in visual object priming: functional magnetic resonance imaging evidence for a laterality difference in fusiform cortex. *Neuropsychologia*, **2**, 184–199.

Krubitzer, L. (1995). The organization of neocortex in mammals: are species differences really so different? *Trends in Neuroscience*, **8**, 408–417.

Kuffler, S. W. (1953). Discharge patterns and functional organization of mammalian retina. *Journal of Neurophysiology*, **16**, 37–68.

Large, M.-E., Aldcroft, A., & Vilis, T. (2007). Task-related laterality effects in the lateral occipital complex. *Brain*, **1128**, 130–138.

Larsson, J., & Heeger, D. J. (2006). Two retinotopic visual areas in human lateral occipital cortex. *Journal of Neuroscience*, **20**, 13128–1314.

Larsson, J., Landy, M. S., & Heeger, D. J. (2006). Orientation-selective adaptation to first- and second-order patterns in human visual cortex. *Journal of Neurophysiology*, **95**, 862–881.

Lee, T. S., & Nguyen, M. (2001). Center-periphery organization of human object areas. *Nature Neuroscience*, **4**, 533–539.

Levy, I., Hasson, U., Avidan, G., Hendler, T., & Malach, R. (2001). Center-periphery organization of human object areas. *Nature Neuroscience*, **4**, 533–539.

Levy, I., Hasson, U., & Malach, R. (2001). One picture is worth at least a million neurons. *Current Biology*, **14**, 996–1001.

Linsker, R. (1989). How to generate ordered maps by maximizing the mutual information between input and output signals. *Neural Computation*, **1**, 402–411.

Liu, J., & Wandell, B. A. (2002). Specializations for chromatic and temporal signals in human visual cortex. *Journal of Neuroscience*, **35**, 3459–3468.

Livingstone, M. S., & Hubel, D. H. (1982). Thalamic inputs to cytochrome oxidase-rich regions in monkey visual cortex. *Proceedings of the Natural Academy of Science USA*, **79**, 6098–6101.

Livingstone, M. S., & Hubel, D. H. (1987). Psychophysical evidence for separate channels for the perception of form, color, movement, and depth. *Journal of Neuroscience*, **7**, 3416–3468.

Logothetis, N. K., & Wandell, B. A. (2004). Interpreting the BOLD signal. *Annual Review of Physiology*, **66**, 735–769.

Löwel, S., & Singer, W. (2002). Experience-dependent plasticity of intracortical connections. In M. Fahle & T. Poggio (Eds.), *Perceptual learning.* Cambridge (MA): MIT Press.

Lueck, C., Zeki, S., Friston, K., Deiber, M.-P., Cope, P., Cunningham, V., et al. (1989). The colour centre in the cerebral cortex of man. *Nature*, **340**, 386–389.

Macko, K., Jarvis, C., Kennedy, C., Miyaoka, M., Shinohara, M., Sololoff, L., et al. (1982).

Mapping the primate visual system with [2-14c]deoxyglucose. *Science*, **218**, 394–397.

Maertens, M., & Pollmann, S. (2005). fMRI reveals a common neural substrate of illusory and real contours in V1 after perceptual learning. *Journal of Cognitive Neuroscience*, **17**, 1553–1564.

Majdan, M., & Shatz, C. J. (2006). Effects of visual experience on activity-dependent gene regulation in cortex. *Nature Neuroscience*, **9**, 650–659.

Malach, R., Levy, I., & Hasson, U. (2002). The topography of high-order human object areas. *Trends in Cognitive Sciences*, **6**, 176–184.

Malach, R., Reppas, J. B., Benson, R. R., Kwong, K. K., Jiang, H., Kennedy, W. A., et al. (1995). Object-related activity revealed by functional magnetic resonance imaging in human occipital cortex. *Proceedings of the Natural Academy of Science USA*, **92**, 8135–8139.

Mareschal, D., Johnson, M. H., Sirois, S., Spratling, M. S., Thomas, M. S. C., & Westermann, G. (Eds.). (2007). *Neuroconstructivism: How the brain constructs cognition* (Vol. I). Oxford (UK): Oxford University Press.

Mariño, J., Schummers, J., Lyon, D. C., Schwabe, L., Beck, O., Wiesing, P., et al. (2005). Invariant computations in local cortical networks with balanced excitation and inhibition. *Nature Neuroscience*, **8**, 194–201.

Marr, D. (1982). *Vision: A computational investigation into the human representation and processing of visual information.* San Francisco (CA): W. H. Freeman.

Martin, A., Lalonde, F., Wiggs, C., Weisberg, J., Ungerleider, L., & Haxby, J. (1995). Repeated presentation of objects reduces activity in ventral occipitotemporal cortex: an fMRI study of repetition priming. *Society for Neuroscience Abstracts*, **21**, 1497.

Martin, K. A. C. (1988). From enzymes to visualperception: a bridge too far? *Trends in Neuroscience*, **11**, 380–387.

Mastronarde, D. N. (1983). Correlated firing of retinal ganglion cells: I. spontaneously active inputs in X- and Y-cells. *Journal of Neuroscience*, **14**, 409–441.

Maunsell, J., & Van Essen, D. C. (1983). The connections of the middle temporal visual area (mt) and their relation ship to a cortical hierarchy in the macaque monkey. *Journal of Neuroscience*, **3**, 2563–2586.

McCollough, C. (1965). Color adaptation of edge-detectors in the human visual system. *Science*, **149**, 1115–1116.

McKyton, A., & Zohary, E. (2007). Beyond retinotopic mapping: The spatial representation of objects in the human lateral occipital complex. *Cerebral Cortex*, **17**, 164–1172.

Meister, M., Wong, R., Daylor, D., & Shatz, C. (1991). Synchronous bursts of action potentials in ganglion cells of the developing mammalian retina. *Science*, **252**, 939–943.

Mel, B. W. (1997). SEEMORE: Combining color, shape and texture histogramming in a neurally-inspired approach to visual object recognition. *Neural Computation*, **9**, 777–804.

Miikkulainen, R., Bednar, J., Choe, Y., & Sirosh, J. (2005). *Computational maps in the visual cortex.* New York: Springer-Science.

Miikkulainen, R., Bednar, J. A., Choe, Y., & Sirosh, J. (1997). Self-organization, plasticity, and low-level visual phenomena in a laterally connected map model of the primary visual cortex. In R. L. Goldstone, P. G. Schyns, & D. L. Medin (Eds.), *Psychology of learning and motivation* (Vol. 36, pp. 257–308). New York: Academic Press.

Mishkin, M. (1966). Visual mechanisms beyond the striate cortex. In *Frontiers of physiological psychology*. New York: Academic Press.

Montaser-Kouhsari, L., Landy, M. S., Heeger, D. J., & Larsson, J. (2007). Orientation-selective adaptation to illusory contours in human visual cortex. *Journal of Neuroscience*, **27**, 2186–2195.

Morita, T., Kochiyama, T., Okada, T., Yonekura, Y., Matsumura, M., & Sadato, N. (2004). The neural substrates of conscious color perception demonstrated using fMRI. *NeuroImage*, **21**, 1665–1673.

Mountcastle, V. (1957). Modality and topographic properties of single neurons in cats somatic sensory cortex. *Journal of Neurophysiology*, **20**, 408–434.

Murphy, E. H., & Berman, N. (1979). The rabbit and the cat: A comparison of some features of response properties of single cells in the primary visual cortex. *Journal of Comparative Neurology*, **188**, 401–427.

Murray, S. O., & He, S. (2001). Contrast invariance in the human lateral occipital complex depends on attention. *Cerebral Cortex*, **16**, 606–611.

Murray, S. O., Schrater, P., & Kersten, D. (2004). Perceptual grouping and the interactions between visual cortical areas. *Neural Networks*, **17**, 695–705.

Nakayama, K., & Shimojo, S. (1990). da Vinci stereopsis: depth and subjective occluding contours from unpaired image points. *Vision Research*, **30**, 1811–1825.

Nayar, S., & Murase, H. (1995). Visual learning and recognition of 3-d object by appearence. *International Journal of Computer Vision*, **14**, 5–24.

Nealey, T. A., & Maunsell, J. H. R. (1994). Magnocellular and parvocellular contributions to the responses of neurons in macaque striate cortex. *Journal of Neuroscience*, **14**, 2069–2079.

Neri, P., Bridge, H., & Heeger, D. J. (2004). Stereoscopic processing of absolute and relative disparity in human visual cortex. *Journal of Neurophysiology*, **92**, 1880–1891.

Nunn, J. A., Gregory, L. J., Brammer, M., Williams, S. C. R., Parslow, D. M., Morgan, M. J., et al. (2002). Functional magnetic resonance imaging of synesthesia: activation of v4/v8 by spoken words. *Nature Neuroscience*, **5**, 371–375.

Ogawa, S., Lee, T., Kay, A., & Tank, D. (1990). Brain magnetic resonance imaging with contrast dependent on blood oxygenation. *Proceedings of the Natural Academy of Science USA*, **87**, 9868–9872.

Olshausen, B. A., & Field, D. J. (1996). Natural image statistics and efficient coding. *Network: Computation in Neural Systems*, **7**, 333–339.

O'Toole, A. J., Jiang, F., Abdi, H., & Haxby, J. V. (2005). Partially distributed representations of objects and faces in ventral temporal cortex. *Journal of Cognitive Neuroscience*, **17**, 580–590.

Pasupathy, A., & Connor, C. E. (2002). Population coding of shape in area v4. *Nature Neuroscience*, **5**, 1332–1338.

Pearlman, A., Birch, J., & Meadows, J. (1979). Cerebral color blindness: An acquired defect in hue discrimination. *Ann. Neurol.*, **5**, 253–261.

Peterhans, E., & von der Heydt, R. (1989). Mechanisms of contour perception in monkey visual cortex. II. contours bridging gaps. *Journal of Neuroscience*, **9**, 1749–1763.

Plebe, A. (2006). Learning visual invariance. In M. Verleysen (Ed.), *Esann 2006 – 14th european symposium on artificial neural networks* (pp. 71–76). Evere (BE): d-side Publications.

Plebe, A. (2007). A model of angle selectivity development in visual area v2. *Neurocomputing*, **70**, 2060–2066.

Plebe, A., & Domenella, R. G. (2006). Early development of visual recognition. *BioSystems*, **86**, 63–74.

Plebe, A., & Domenella, R. G. (2007). Object recognition by artificial cortical maps. *Neural Networks*, **20**, 763–780.

Poggio, G. F. (1995). Stereoscopic processing in monkey visual cortex: a review. In T. V. Papathomas (Ed.), *Early vision and beyond.* Cambridge (MA): MIT Press.

Press, W. A., Brewer, A. A., Dougherty, R. F., Wade, A. R., & Wandell, B. A. (2001). Visual areas and spatial summation in human visual cortex. *Vision Research*, **41**, 1321–1332.

Pribram, K. H. (1971). *Languages of the brain: Experimental paradoxes and principles in neuropsychology.* Englewood Cliffs (NJ): Prentice Hall.

Quartz, S. R. (1993). Neural networks, nativism and the plausibility of constructivism. *Cognition*, **48**, 223–242.

Quartz, S. R. (2003). Innateness and the brain. *Biology and Philosophy*, **18**, 13–40.

Quartz, S. R., & Sejnowski, T. J. (1997). The neural basis of cognitive development: a constructivist manifesto. *Behavioral and Brain Science*, **20**, 537–596.

Ramsden, B. M., Hung, C. P., & Roe, A. W. (2001). Real and illusory contour processing in area V1 of the primate: a cortical balancing act. *Cerebral Cortex*, **11**, 648–665.

Riesenhuber, M., & Poggio, T. (1999). Hierarchical models of object recognition in cortex. *Nature Neuroscience*, **2**, 1019–1025.

Riesenhuber, M., & Poggio, T. (2000). Models of object recognition. *Nature Neuroscience*, **3**, 1199–1204.

Riesenhuber, M., & Poggio, T. (2002). Neural mechanisms of object recognition. *Current Opinion in Neurobiology*, **12**, 162–168.

Rizzolatti, G., & Matelli, M. (2003). Two different streams form the dorsal visual system: anatomy and functions. *Experimental Brain Research*, **153**, 146–157.

Rodieck, R. W. (1965). Quantitative analysis of cat retinal ganglion cell response to visual stimuli. *Vision Research*, **5**, 583–601.

Roe, A. W., Garraghty, P., Esguerra, M., & Sur, M. (1990). A map of visual space induced in primary auditory cortex. *Science*, **250**, 818–820.

Rolls, E. (1992). Neurophysiological mechanisms underlying face processing within and beyond the temporal cortical visual areas. *Philosophical transactions of the Royal Society B*, **335**, 11–21.

Rolls, E., & Tovee, M. J. (1995). Sparseness of the neuronal representation of stimuli in the primate temporal visual cortex. *Journal of Neurophysiology*, **73**, 713–726.

Rolls, E. T., & Stringer, S. M. (2006). Invariant visual object recognition: A model, with lighting invariance. *Journal of Physiology – Paris*, **100**, 43–62.

Romanski, L. M., & Goldman-Rakic, P. S. (1999). Dual streams of auditory afferents target multiple domains in the primate prefrontal cortex. *Nature Neuroscience*, **2**, 1131–1136.

Rönne, H. (1919). Über quadranthemianopsie und die lage der makulafasern in der okzipitalen sehbahn. *Klinische Monatsblätter für Augenheilkunde*, **63**, 358–374.

Rose, D. (1979). Mechanisms underlying the receptive field properties of neurons in cat visual cortex. *Vision Research*, **19**, 533–544.

Sakai, K., Naya, Y., & Miyashita, Y. (1994). Neuronal tuning and associative mechanisms in form representation. *Learning and Menory*, **1**, 83–105.

Schiller, P. H. (1996). On the specificity of neurons and visual areas. *Behavioural Brain Research*, **76**, 21–35.

Schira, M. M., Wade, A. R., & Tyler, C. W. (2007). Two-dimensional mapping of the central and parafoveal visual field to human visual cortex. *Journal of Neurophysiology*, **97**, 4284–4295.

Schneider, G. E. (1967). Visual receptors and retinal interaction. *Science*, **164**, 270–278.

Schwabe, L., & Obermayer, K. (2003). Modeling the adaptive visual system: a survey of principled approaches. *Neural Networks*, **16**, 1353–1371.

Sengpiel, F., & Kind, P. C. (2002). The role of activity in development of the visual system. *Current Biology*, **12**, 818–826.

Sereno, M., Dale, A., Reppas, J., Kwong, K., Belliveau, J., Brady, T., et al. (1995). Borders of multiple visual areas in human revealed by functional magnetic resonance imaging. *Science*, **268**, 889–893.

Sereno, M. I., & Tootell, R. B. (2005). From monkeys to humans: what do we now know about brain homologies? *Current Opinion in Neurobiology*, **15**, 135–144.

Sergent, J., Ohta, S., & MacDonald, B. (1992). Functional neuroanatomy of face and object processing. a positron emission tomography study. *Brain*, **115**, 15–36.

Shatz, C. (1990). Impulse activity and the patterning of connections durimg CNS development. *Neuron*, **5**, 1–10.

Shatz, C., & Stryker, M. (1988). Prenatal tetrodotoxin infusion blocks segregation of retinogeniculate afferents. *Science*, **242**, 87–89.

Simion, F., Valenza, E., & Umiltà, C. (1998). Mechanisms underlying face preference at birth. In F. Simion & G. Butterworth (Eds.), *The development of sensory, motor and cognitive capacities in early infancy: From perception to cognition*. East Sussex (UK): Psychology Press.

Simons, J. S., Koutstaal, W., Prince, S., Wagner, A. D., & Schacter, D. L. (2003). Neural mechanisms of visual object priming: evidence for perceptual and semantic distinctions in fusiform cortex. *NeuroImage*, **19**, 613–626.

Sincich, L. C., & Horton, J. C. (2002). Divided by cytochrome oxidase: A map of the projections from V1 to V2 in macaques. *Science*, **295**, 1734–1737.

Sirosh, J., & Miikkulainen, R. (1997). Topographic receptive fields and patterned lateral interaction in a self-organizing model of the primary visual cortex. *Neural Computation*, **9**, 577–594.

Sirosh, J., Miikkulainen, R., & Choe, Y. (Eds.). (1996). *Lateral interactions in the cortex: Structure and function*. Austin, (TX): The UTCS Neural Networks Research Group.

Sit, Y. F., & Miikkulainen, R. (2006). Self-organization of hierarchical visual maps with feedback connections. *Neurocomputing*, **69**, 1309–1312.

Smith, A., Singh, K., Williams, A., & Greenlee, M. (2001). Estimating receptive field size from fMRI data in human striate and extrastriate visual cortex. *Cerebral Cortex*, **11**, 1182–1190.

Smith, A. T., Greenlee, M. W., Kraemer, K. D. S. F. M., & Hennig, J. (1998). The processing of first- and second-order motion in human visual cortex assessed by functional magnetic resonance imaging (fMRI). *Journal of Neuroscience*, **18**, 3816–3830.

Smith, M. A., Kohn, A., & Movshon, J. A. (2002). Signals in macaque V1 that support the perception of Glass patterns. *Journal of Neuroscience*, **22**, 8334–8345.

Smith, M. A., Kohn, A., & Movshon, J. A. (2007). Glass pattern responses in macaque V2 neurons. *Journal of Neurophysiology*, **97**, 4284–4295.

Stanley, D. A., & Rubin, N. (2003). fMRI activation in response to illusory contours and salient regions in the human lateral occipital complex. *Neuron*, **37**, 323-331.

Stettler, D. D., Das, A., Bennett, J., & Gilbert, C. D. (2002). Lateral connectivity and contextual interactions in macaque primary visual cortex. *Neuron*, **36**, 739–750.

Stryker, M. P., Sherk, H., Leventhal, A. G., & Hirsch, H. V. (1978). Physiological consequences for the cat's visual cortex of effectively restricting early visual experience with oriented contours. *Journal of Neurophysiology*, **41**, 896–909.

Suzuki, N., Hashimoto, N., Kashimori, Y., & Kambara, M. Z. T. (2004). A neural model of predictive recognition in form pathway of visual cortex. *BioSystems*, **76**, 33–42.

Swindale, N. V. (2001). Keeping the wires short: a singularly difficult problem. *Neuron*, **29**, 316–317.

Talairach, J., & Tournoux, P. (1988). *Co-planar stereotaxic atlas of the human brain*. New York: Thieme Medical Publishers.

Talbot, S. A. (1942). A lateral localization in the cat's visual cortex. *Federation Proceeding*, **1**, 84.

Tanaka, K. (1996). Inferotemporal cortex and object vision. *Annual Review of Neuroscience*, **19**, 109–139.

Tanaka, K., Saito, H., Fukada, Y., & Moriya, M. (1991). Coding visual images of objects in the inferotemporal cortex of the macaque monkey. *Journal of Neurophysiology*, **66**, 170–189.

Tarr, M., & Gauthier, I. (2000). FFA: a flexible fusiform area for subordinate-level visual processing automatized by expertise. *Nature Neuroscience*, **3**, 764–769.

Taylor, N. R., Hartley, M., & Taylor, J. G. (2005). Coding of objects in low-level visual cortical areas. In W. Duch, J. Kacprzyk, E. Oja, & S. Zadrony (Eds.), *Artificial neural networks – icann '05. 15th international conference proceedings* (pp. 57–63). Berlin: Springer-Verlag.

Thompson, J. M., Woolsey, C. N., & Talbot, S. A. (1950). Visual areas I and II of cerebral cortex of rabbit. *Journal of Neurophysiology*, **13**, 277–288.

Tiao, Y., & Blakemore, C. (1976). Functional organization in the visual cortex of the golden hamster. *Journal of Comparative Neurology*, **168**, 459–481.

Tjan, B. S., Lestou, V., & Kourtzi, Z. (2006). Uncertainty and invariance in the human visual cortex. *Journal of Neurophysiology*, **96**, 1556–1568.

Toga, A. (Ed.). (1998). *Brain warping*. Amsterdam: Elsevier.

Tootell, R. B., & Hadjikhani, N. (2001). Where is 'dorsal v4' in human visual cortex? retinotopic, topographic and functional evidence. *Cerebral Cortex*, **1**, 39–55.

Tootell, R. B., Hadjikhani, N., Mendola, J. D., Marrett, S., & Dale, A. M. (1998). From retinotopy to recognition: fMRI in human visual cortex. *Trends in Cognitive Sciences*, **2**, 174–183.

Tootell, R. B., Hamilton, S. L., & Switkes, E. (1989). Functional anatomy of the macaque striate cortex. IV. contrast and magno–parvo streams. *Journal of Neuroscience*, **8**, 1610–1624.

Tootell, R. B., Silverman, M. S., Hamilton, S. L., Switkes, E., & De Valois, R. (1988). Functional anatomy of the macaque striate cortex. V. spatial frequency. *Journal of Neuroscience*, **8**, 1610–1624.

Tootell, R. B., Switkes, E., Silverman, M. S., & Hamilton, S. L. (1988a). Functional anatomy of the macaque striate cortex. III. color. *Journal of Neuroscience*, **8**, 1531–1568.

Tootell, R. B., Switkes, E., Silverman, M. S., & Hamilton, S. L. (1988b). Functional anatomy of the macaque striate cortex. II. retinotopic organization. *Journal of Neuroscience*, **8**, 1531–1568.

Tootell, R. B., Switkes, E., Silverman, M. S., & Hamilton, S. L. (1988c). Functional anatomy of the macaque striate cortex. I. ocular dominance, binocular interactions, and baseline conditions. *Journal of Neuroscience*, **8**, 1531–1568.

Trevarthen, C., & Sperry, R. W. (1968). Two mechanisms of vision in primates. *Psychological Research*, **31**, 299–337.

Tropea, D., Kreiman, G., Lyckman, A., Mukherjee, S., Yu, H., Horngl, S., et al. (2006). Gene expression changes and molecular pathways mediating activity-dependent plasticity in visual cortex. *Nature Neuroscience*, **9**, 660–668.

Ts'o, D. Y., Roe, A. W., & Gilbert, C. D. (2001). A hierarchy of the functional organization for color, form and disparity in primate visual area V2. *Vision Research*, **41**, 1333–1349.

Tyler, C. W., Likova, L. T., Chen, C.-C., Kontsevich, L. L., Schira, M. M., & Wade, A. R. (2005). Extended concepts of occipital retinotopy. *Current Medical Imaging Reviews*, **1**, 319–329.

Ungerleider, L., & Mishkin, M. (1982). Two cortical visual systems. In D. J. Ingle, M. A. Goodale, & R. J. W. Mansfield (Eds.), *Analysis of visual behavior* (pp. 549–586). Cambridge (MA): MIT Press.

Vaegan, & Taylor, D. (1979). Critical period for deprivation amblyopia in children. *Transactions of the Ophthalmological Societies of the UK*, **99**, 432–439.

Valois, R. L. D., & Jacobs, G. H. (1968). Primate color vision. *Science*, **162**, 533–540.

Van Essen, D. C. (2005). A population-average, landmark- and surface-based (PALS) atlas of human cerebral cortex. *NeuroImage*, **28**, 635–662.

Van Essen, D. C., & DeYoe, E. A. (1994). Concurrent processing in the primate visual cortex. In M. S. Gazzaniga (Ed.), *The cognitive neurosciences*. Cambridge (MA): MIT Press.

Van Essen, D. C., Lewis, J. W., Drury, H. A., Hadjikhani, N., Tootell, R. B., Bakircioglu, M., et al. (2001). Mapping visual cortex in monkeys and humans using surface-based atlases. *Vision Research*, **41**, 1359–1378.

Van Essen, D. C., Newsome, W., & Maunsell, J. (1984). The visual field representation in striate cortex of the macaque monkey: asymmetries, anisotropies, and individual variability. *Vision Research*, **24**, 429–448.

Van Essen, D. C., & Zeki, S. (1978). The topographic organization of rhesus monkey prestriate cortex. *Journal of Physiology*, **277**, 193–226.

Van Hooser, S. D., Heimel, J. A. F., Chung, S., Nelson, S. B., , & Toth, L. J. (2005). Orientation selectivity without orientation maps in visual cortex of a highly visual mammal. *Journal of Neuroscience*, **25**, 19–28.

Vanduffel, W., Tootell, R. B., Schoups, A. A., & Orban, G. A. (2002). The organization of orientation selectivity throughout the macaque visual cortex. *Cerebral Cortex*, **12**, 647–662.

Verkindt, C., Bertrand, O., Echallier, F., & Pernier, J. (1995). Tonotopic organization of the human auditory cortex: N100 topography and multiple dipole model analysis. *Electroencephalography and Clinical Neurophisiology*, **96**, 143–156.

Verriest, G. (Ed.). (1980). *Color vision deficiencies*. Bristol: Hilger.

Volkmann, A. W. (1858). Über den einfluss der Übung auf das erkennen räumlicher distanzen. *Berichte über die Verhandlungen der Sächsischen Leibzig, mathematische und physische Abtheilung*, **10**, 38–69.

von Bonin, G., & Bailey, P. (1947). *The neocortex of macaca mulatta*. Urbana (IL): University of Illinois Press.

von der Heydt, R., & Peterhans, E. (1989). Mechanisms of contour perception in monkey visual cortex. I. lines of pattern discontinuity. *Journal of Neuroscience*, **9**, 1731–1748.

von der Heydt, R., Zhou, H., & Friedman, H. S. (2000). Representation of stereoscopic edges in monkey visual cortex. *Vision Research*, **40**, 1955–1967.

von der Heydt, R., Zhou, H., & Friedman, H. S. (2003). Neural coding of border ownership: Implications for the theory of figure-ground perception. In M. Behrmann, R. Kimchi, & C. R. Olson (Eds.), *Perceptual organization in vision: Behavioral and neural perspectives* (pp. 281–304). Mahwah (NJ): Lawrence Erlbaum Associates.

von der Malsburg, C. (1973). Self-organization of orientation sensitive cells in the striate cortex. *Kibernetic*, **14**, 85–100.

von Economo, C., & Koskinas, G. N. (1925). *Die cytoarchitektonik der hirnrinde des erwachsenen menschen*. Berlin: Springer-Verlag.

von Gräfe, F. W. E. A. (1858). Über das gesichtsfeld bei amblyopie. *Archiv für Ophthalmologie*, **4**.

Vuilleumier, P., Henson, R. N., Driver, J., & Dolan, R. J. (2002). Multiple levels of visual object constancy revealed by event-related fmri of repetition priming. *Nature Neuroscience*, **5**, 491–499.

Wade, A. R., Brewer, A. A., Rieger, J. W., & Wandell, B. A. (2002). Functional measurements of human ventral occipital cortex: retinotopy and colour. *Philosophical transactions of the Royal Society B*, **357**, 963–973.

Wade, A. R., & Wandell, B. A. (2002). Chromatic light adaptation measured using functional magnetic resonance imaging. *Journal of Neuroscience*, **22**, 8148–8157.

Wallis, G., & Rolls, E. (1997). Invariant face and object recognition in the visual system. *Progress in Neurobiology*, **51**, 167–194.

Walsh, V., Carden, D., Butler, S., & Kulikowski, J. (1993). The effects of lesions of area V4 on the visual abilities of macaques: hue discriminatino and color constancy. *Behavioral and Brain Science*, **53**, 51–62.

Walsh, V., Kulikowski, S. R., Butler, S. R., & Carden, D. (1992). The effects of lesions of area V4 on the visual abilities of macaques: color categorization. *Behavioral and Brain Science*, **52**, 82–89.

Wandell, B. A. (1999). Computational neuroimaging of human visual cortex. *Annual Review of Neuroscience*, **10**, 145–173.

Wandell, B. A., Brewer, A. A., & Dougher, R. F. (2005). Visual field map clusters in human cortex. *Philosophical transactions of the Royal Society of London*, **360**, 693–707.

Wandell, B. A., & Dougherty, R. F. (2006). Computational neuroimaging: maps and tracts in the human brain. *Proceedings of SPIE*, **6057**, 1–12.

Weerd, P. D., Gattass, R., Desimone, R., & Ungerleider, L. G. (2002). Responses of cells in monkey visual cortex during perceptual filling-in of an artificial scotoma. *Neural Networks*, **15**, 603–616.

Weigelt, S., Kourtzi, Z., Kohler, A., Singer, W., & Muckli, L. (2007). The cortical representation of objects rotating in depth. *Journal of Neuroscience*, **27**, 3864–3874.

Westermann, G., Mareschal, D., Johnson, M. H., Sirois, S., Spratling, M. S., & Thomas, M. S. C. (2007). Neuroconstructivism. *Developmental Science*, **10**, 75–83.

Wiesel, T., & Hubel, D. (1965). Binocular interaction in striate cortex of kittens reared with artificial squint. *Journal of Neurophysiology*, **28**, 1041–1059.

Willshaw, D. J., & von der Malsburg, C. (1976). How patterned neural connections can be set up by self-organization. *Proceedings of the Royal Society of London*, **B194**, 431–445.

Wong-Riley, M. (1979). Changes in the visual system of monocularly sutured or enucleated cats demonstrable with cytochrome oxidase histochemistry. *Brain*, **171**, 11–28.

Wood, J. (1996). Invariant pattern recognition: a review. *Pattern Recognition*, **29**, 1–17.

Woolsey, C. N., & Fairman, D. (1946). Contralateral, ipsilateral and bilateral representation of cutaneous receptors in somatic area I and II of the cerebral cortex of pig, sheep and other mammals. *Surgery*, **19**, 684–702.

Xu, Y. (2005). Revisiting the role of the fusiform face area in visual expertise. *Cerebral Cortex*, **15**, 1234–1242.

Zeki, S. (1969). Representation of central visual fields in prestriate cortex of monkey. *Brain*, **28**, 338–340.

Zeki, S. (1971a). Cortical projections from two prestriate areas in the monkey. *Brain*, **34**, 19–35.

Zeki, S. (1971b). Functional organization of a visual area in the posterior bank of the superior temporal sulcus of the rhesus monkey. *Journal of Physiology*, **236**, 549–573.

Zeki, S. (1974). Functional organization of a visual area in the posterior bank of the superior temporal sulcus of the rhesus monkey. *Journal of Physiology*, **236**, 549–573.

Zeki, S. (1978). Functional specialisation in the visual cortex of the rhesus monkey. *Nature*, **274**, 423–428.

Zeki, S. (1983a). Colour coding in the cerebral cortex: The reaction of cells in monkey visual cortex to wavelenghts and colours. *Neuroscience*, **9**, 741–765.

Zeki, S. (1983b). Colour coding in the cerebral cortex: the responses of wavelength-selective and colour-coded cells in monkey visual cortex to changes in wavelength composition. *Neuroscience*, **9**, 767–781.

Zeki, S. (1990). A century of cerebral achromatopsia. *Brain*, **113**, 1721–1777.

Zeki, S. (2003a). Improbable areas in color vision. In L. Chalupa & J. Werner (Eds.), *The visual neurosciences.* Cambridge (MA): MIT Press.

Zeki, S. (2003b). Improbable areas in the visual brain. *Trends in Neuroscience, 26,* 23–26.

Zeki, S., McKeefry, D., Bartels, A., & Frackowiak, R. (1998). Has a new color area been discovered? *Nature Neuroscience, 1,* 335–336.

Zeki, S., Watson, J., Lueck, C., Friston, K., Kennard, C., & Frackowiak, R. (1991). A direct demonstration of functional specialization in human visual cortex. *Journal of Neuroscience, 11,* 641–649.

Zhaoping, L. (2002). Pre-attentive segmentation and correspondence in stereo. *Proceedings of the Natural Academy of Science USA, 357,* 1877–1883.

Zhaoping, L. (2005). Border ownership from intracortical interactions in visual area V2. *Neuron, 47,* 143–153.

Zhou, H., Friedman, H. S., & von der Heydt, R. (2000). Coding of border ownership in monkey visual cortex. *Journal of Neuroscience, 20,* 6594–6611.

In: Visual Cortex: New Research
Editors: T. A. Portocello and R. B. Velloti

ISBN 978-1-60456-530-0
© 2008 Nova Science Publishers, Inc.

Chapter 3

THE "HORIZONTAL EFFECT": A PERCEPTUAL ANISOTROPY IN VISUAL PROCESSING OF NATURALISTIC BROADBAND STIMULI

Bruce C. Hansen[*1], *Andrew M. Haun*[2] *and Edward A. Essock*[2,3]

[1]Department of Psychology, Colgate University, Hamilton, NY USA
[2]Department of Psychological and Brain Sciences,
University of Louisville, Louisville, KY USA
[3]Department of Ophthalmology and Visual Science,
University of Louisville, Louisville, KY USA

Keywords: horizontal effect, oblique effect, natural scenes, broadband noise, 1/f noise, orientation, spatial frequency.

1.0. General Overview

The fundamental components that make up the content of the natural visual world at any given point in time consist of a complex amalgamation of variations in luminance and color contrast. These variations in contrast across space in scenes are expressed at different spatial scales and orientations which are perceptually grouped by advanced visual processes into edges and regions defined by luminance, color and texture, and into surfaces, objects, and shadows to name a few. In the current chapter we will focus on how human primary visual cortex (i.e., area V1) processes the variations in luminance contrast in real-world natural scene imagery for structures of different sizes (i.e., spatial frequency) and different orientations. The complex luminance contrast relationships that make up the objects within natural scenes have been repeatedly shown to obey two primary relationships. The first is that the magnitude of the amplitude across different spatial frequencies, f, is biased toward the lower frequencies (i.e., gradual changes in luminance contrast across an image) and decreases with increasing spatial frequency (i.e., smaller structural details within an image) in

_____
[*] Correspondence should be addressed to BCH: bchansen@mail.colgate.edu.

accordance with a $1/f^\alpha$ relationship, with an average $\alpha \approx 1.0$. The second regularity observed in natural scene imagery is a bias in amplitude at the horizontal and vertical orientations (i.e., the cardinal axes) relative to the oblique orientations (i.e., oblique axes). Interestingly, it has been repeatedly demonstrated that some encoding mechanisms of visual cortex are "hard-wired" to match such naturalistic regularities. This has lead to recent efforts to better understand how neural encoding biases relate to the structural biases which exist in our everyday, natural environment. Recently, we have shown that with naturalistic stimuli, performance for detecting oriented content is worst at horizontal, best at oblique orientations, and intermediate at vertical orientations – a bias that we termed the "horizontal effect". This finding was unique as it challenged the long-standing dogma that the human visual system is most sensitive to horizontal and vertical orientations, and least sensitive to oblique orientations (i.e., the "oblique effect"), when viewing any type of scene content. We've shown that the long-established oblique-effect anisotropy is apparent when processing simple, un-naturalistic narrow-band stimuli (e.g., a sinusoidal luminance grating), whereas the horizontal effect is present when viewing naturalistic (broadband) stimuli. Here, we discuss the specific spatial attributes (e.g., spatial frequency distribution, structural sparseness, spatial frequency and orientation bandwidths) of naturalistic stimuli which can lead to a horizontal effect and discuss how those characteristics may be encoded in a cortical contrast normalization model of visual cortex that is both local (over orientation and spatial frequency) and anisotropic (due to a numerical bias of neurons with different preferred orientations) and thus provides efficient coding of natural stimuli. In addition, we provide empirical evidence in support of how such an anisotropic contrast normalization might function at the level of visual cortex.

In the following sections we provide brief reviews of the types of structural regularities observed in natural scene imagery with respect to luminance contrast. We then consider how such structural regularities have been related to human visual processing of natural scene imagery and how some of the theories drawn by multiple laboratories about those relationships do not hold when tested empirically. We will then present our findings over the past 5 years in support of the horizontal effect perceptual anisotropy obtained when viewing naturalistic images and the variations of this effect as a function of different physical properties of the naturalistic stimuli (e.g., spatial frequency distribution, structural sparseness, spatial frequency and orientation bandwidths). Finally, we present a contrast normalization model that can account for the behavioral data as well as the result of recent experiments that directly test this model.

2.0. Regularities of Luminance Contrast in Natural Scenes

2.1. Luminance Contrast Regularities with Respect to Spatial Frequency

Consider the two images shown in Figure 1. While there is a significant difference between the types of semantic structures contained in each, the fall-off of the averaged amplitude across spatial frequency for both images is identical. Specifically, the amplitude spectra of both images obey the same $1/f^\alpha$ relationship mentioned in *Section 1.0*. In fact, within the past 20 years there have been numerous studies that have documented the $1/f^\alpha$ relationship for all varieties of natural scene imagery ranging in semantic content from purely carpentered structures (e.g., buildings, highways, automobiles, houses, etc.) to purely naturalistic structures (e.g., woodlands, meadows, general shrubbery, etc.). One particular measurement that has been used to demonstrate the $1/f^{\alpha}$ relationship in natural scene imagery is the global 2-D Discrete Fourier Transform (DFT). Any complex waveform (in this case, an image is treated as a complex 2-D luminance waveform) can be represented as the sum of sinusoidal waveforms of different amplitudes, frequencies, orientations, and phases. The amplitude plotted as a function of spatial frequency and orientation is often referred to as the amplitude spectrum and the phase of the waveforms as a function of orientation and spatial frequency is called the phase spectrum (Shapley and Lennie, 1985; Bracewell, 2000) – both the amplitude and phase spectrum are referenced in the Fourier (or frequency) domain. The amplitude (or power/energy) spectra of different natural scene images have been measured in a number of studies (e.g., Kretzmer, 1952; Field, 1987; Tolhurst, Tadmor, and Chao, 1992; Ruderman and Bialek, 1994; van der Schaaf and van Hateren, 1996; Field and Brady, 1997; Billock, 2000; Oliva and Torralba, 2001; Torralba and Oliva, 2003; Hansen and Essock, 2005).

Figure 1. Two examples of natural scene images. Notice that while both images possess dramatically different types of structures (e.g., the image on the left consists of general shrubbery, while the image on the right consists of landscape structures including a skyline and clouds), the falloff of the orientation averaged amplitude across spatial frequency for both images is identical.

A typical method of analysis involves examining global spectral properties as a function of spatial frequency. This involves averaging the amplitudes across orientation at each spatial frequency and plotting the results on logarithmic axes.

The typical plot peaks at the lowest spatial frequencies and falls with increasing frequency with a slope of -1 when plotted in logarithmic coordinates as in Figure 2a. In order to provide a more intuitive understanding of how a given image's amplitude spectrum fall-off, or slope, (as defined by α) relates to the image contents, consider Figure 3. The example image patches (sampled from natural scene imagery) are arranged from top to bottom from relatively shallow αs (i.e., α less than 1.0) to relatively steep αs (i.e., greater than 1.0). Notice that the shallow-α image patches in the upper portion of the set of image patches are dominated by sharp edges and few broad changes in luminance. The lack of broad luminance changes and preponderance of sharp edges translates to relatively large amplitudes in the higher spatial frequency range of their amplitude spectra. Accordingly, the image patches in the lower portion of the set are dominated by gradual luminance transitions and relatively few sharp edges. These large luminance transitions translate to relatively larger amplitudes in the low spatial frequency range of their amplitude spectra.

The exact exponent, α, or slope of the log amplitude spectrum falloff, which characterizes most natural scenes has been the subject of much debate, but the general consensus that has emerged is that α typically falls in the range from 0.6 to 1.6 (Field and Brady, 1997), with the peak of the α distribution typically falling between 0.9 and 1.2 (Burton and Moorhead, 1987; Tolhurst et al., 1992; Dong and Atick, 1995; Field, 1993; Ruderman and Bialek, 1994; van der Schaaf and van Hateren, 1996; Thomson and Foster, 1997; Hansen and Essock, 2005;) and a typical average of 1.08 (Billock, 2000), suggesting a reasonable degree of scale invariance across the majority of natural scenes. The issue of determining the exact exponent is far from trivial.

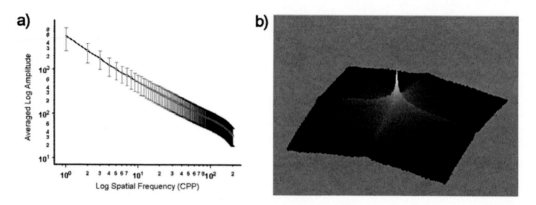

Figure 2. a) Plot of the typical $1/f^{\alpha}$ falloff of amplitude (averaged across orientation) as a function of spatial scale (cycles per picture). This particular example is the average of over 1000 natural scene images; error bars are ±1 SD. b) Two-dimensional representation of an amplitude spectrum (spatial frequency increases with radius, orientation changes with theta) obtained by averaging the same spectra used in (a); note the concentration of amplitude is along the horizontal and vertical axes. Such a plot is organized in polar coordinates, with the lowest spatial frequencies near the center and as one moves out radially, the frequencies increase (brighter coordinates correspond to higher amplitude). Orientation is represented along the theta dimension.

Specifically, different exponents of the amplitude falloff have been shown to (1) shift the peak of the human contrast sensitivity function (Webster and Miyahara, 1997), (2) determine the ability of humans to discriminate between different α values (Knill, Field, and Kersten, 1990; Tadmor and Tolhurst, 1994; Tolhurst and Tadmor, 1997a, 1997b; Párraga and Tolhurst, 2000; Hansen and Hess, 2006), and (3) modulate the ability of humans to discriminate between changes in the content (or objects) of natural scenes (Párraga, Troscianko, and Tolhurst, 2000, 2005; Tolhurst and Tadmor, 2000).

Figure 3. Set of natural scene image patches arranged in increasing α steepness from top-to-bottom (image patches at the top possess shallow αs, while image patches at the bottom possess steep αs). Notice that the structure in the shallow α images is dominated by few gradual luminance changes and contain many fine detail structures while the steep α image patches are dominated by gradual changes in luminance.

2.2. Luminance Contrast Regularities with Respect to Orientation

The first type of regularity discussed in the preceding section involved analyses of the orientation-averaged amplitude spectra of real-world imagery. However, such an account ignores the variation of amplitude as a function of orientation. As mentioned in the introduction, there have been numerous studies that set out to measure the distribution of content in real-world imagery, with many of those investigations focusing on the distribution of content with respect to orientation. A number of methods have been utilized to measure oriented content biases, including: Fourier analysis (Switkes, Mayer, and Sloan, 1978; van der Schaaf and van Hateren, 1996; Keil and Cristóbal, 2000; Oliva and Torralba, 2001; Torralba and Oliva, 2003; Hansen and Essock, 2004), second and higher-order autocorrelation analyses (Baddeley, 1997; Thomson, 1999; 2001a; 2001b), principle components analysis (Baddeley and Hancock, 1991; Hancock, Baddeley, and Smith, 1992), and a variety of convolution kernels (Craven, 1993; Coppola, Purves, McCoy, and Purves, 1998). As mentioned earlier, typical natural scenes are found to be anisotropic with relatively less content near the oblique axes and the most content at orientations near the cardinal axes (see Figure 2b). The first study to address this, Switkes, Mayer, and Sloan (1978), used optical Fourier analysis and found a prominent power bias at the cardinal axes, and also observed the anisotropy regardless of whether the scene content was purely natural outdoor scenery or scenes of carpentered content. Studies of magnitude and direction of gradients in imagery (Coppola, Purves, McCoy, and Purves, 1998) and of Fourier energy/amplitude examined as a function of orientation within weighted or sectored regions of images (Van der Schaaf and van Hateren, 1996; Keil and Cristóbal, 2000; Oliva and Torralba, 2001; Torralba and Oliva, 2003; Hansen and Essock, 2004) support the finding of an anisotropic distribution of image content.

An important issue that arose more recently was whether or not there is, on average, more horizontal content relative to vertical content in natural scenes. Unfortunately the answer has not been clear. The primary reason for this lies in the fact that of the studies that do report magnitudes for the different orientations, the image sample size was very limited, or the method in which measurements were made likely suffer from sampling errors induced by the digital structure of the amplitude spectrum. On the other hand, some studies (e.g., Baddeley and Hancock, 1991; Hancock, Baddeley, and Smith, 1992) report a greater bias for horizontal relative to vertical content. Of course, a definitive answer for all natural scenes cannot be determined as natural scene composition varies and the extent to which horizontal and vertical content differs within any given sample will depend on the specific environments in which the imagery is gathered. However, in a recent study by Hansen and Essock (2004), support was given to the argument that a larger bias of horizontal content relative to vertical content for typical or modal outdoor scenes exists (see Figure 4). Specifically they found that: (1) horizontal physical content indeed dominates horizon-containing images, (2) horizontal content is dominant even in non-horizon-containing scenes composed of ground surfaces, hillsides, or other regions consisting of similar vegetation or structure, (3) horizontal content is dominant in a *sample* of scenes that contain neither a horizon nor ground plane (such as close-ups of bushes, brush or general foliage), (4) horizontal structure persists in dominating the analysis even when *all* imagery containing a receding ground plane or predominant horizon line were removed from the image sample, and (5) a horizontal content bias was also found in an alternative set of "standardized" calibrated imagery frequently used in natural scene analysis (van Hateren and van der Schaaf, 1998). These findings provided support for prior published reports on the horizontal bias (Baddeley and Hancock, 1991; Hancock, Baddeley, and Smith, 1992) assessed with smaller sets of natural imagery.

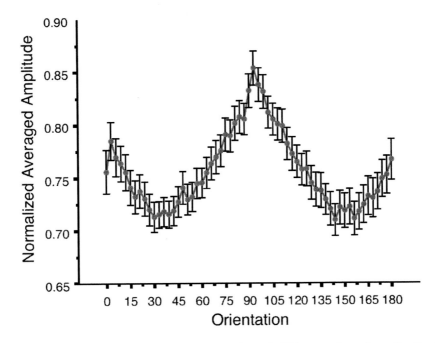

Figure 4. Average normalized amplitude for a number of different orientations for the image set gathered by Hansen and Essock (2004). On the ordinate is the normalized average of amplitude across all spatial frequencies for specific orientations, error bars are ±1 SE. On the abscissa is the specific orientation at which amplitude was assessed (90° corresponds to horizontal). The bias in amplitude at horizontal and vertical was shown to persist across almost the entire range of spatial frequencies (Hansen and Essock, 2004).

3.0. The Relationship between Luminance Contrast Regularities and Human Perception of Natural Scenes

3.1. Human Discrimination between Natural Images Possessing Different Spectral Slopes

As mentioned earlier in this chapter, the usual α for any typical natural scene is approximately 1.0. Thus, the visual world that we have experienced through development has exhibited relatively stable regularities with respect to luminance contrast at different spatial frequencies. Given that, it has been suggested that during early development (ontogeny) or long-term development on an evolutionary time scale (phylogeny), such image statistics would have likely been present and thus, over time, our visual systems became "wired" in a manner best suited to process visual scenes that possessed an amplitude distribution with a slope of ~ 1.0. Knill, Field, and Kersten (1990) first set out to examine whether or not our visual systems might be optimally suited to process complex imagery at a particular α. In their study, Knill et al. used visual noise stimuli with varying αs where observers were engaged in a 2AFC task in which they were to detect a change in spectral slope. The results revealed that observers were best at detecting a change in α when the standard noise pattern was in the range of 1.4 to 1.8. It was concluded that the human visual system is "tuned" to better process images with these α values. However, these findings were questioned by Tadmor and Tolhurst (1994) since the range that was proposed to be best in terms of visual processing was well outside the typical range one might encounter; they also pointed out that while the noise patterns had spectral properties similar to natural scenes, they were still not representative in their content (i.e., random phase spectra). Tadmor and Tolhurst (1994) sought to determine whether or not the human visual system was best suited to process information in the form of the typical $1/f^{\alpha}$ relationship when actual natural scene imagery was used for stimuli. The results were quite similar to the results obtained from the Knill et al. study; lower thresholds were found for steeper αs, with the highest thresholds obtained for reference αs near 1.0. The authors interpreted this finding as supporting the fact that the human visual system is optimally suited to process images exhibiting αs in the range of 0.8 to 1.0. Tadmor and Tolhurst (1994) argued that such a high discrimination threshold for reference images in the typical α range suggests a high degree of "tolerance" for changes in α that might occur within this range (but see Hansen and Hess, 2006). They reasoned that since we typically encounter scenes with αs near 1.0, slight deviations from this value that might occur as a result of, for example, shifting our gaze from one area to another within a given environment, or slight accommodative errors due to fixating objects at different distances, and it would be beneficial if this had little impact on our ability to effectively process visual information. Such a tolerance allows us to view the visual system as being set up to "expect" small deviations from the typical α and therefore not waste valuable processing time and resources by signaling to the observer that such changes have occurred. It is in this sense that higher thresholds for images with typical α values can be considered optimal. Other studies have shown that the ability of human observers to discriminate between structural changes of specific objects within different images is best when the slope of the amplitude spectra of those images is near 1.0 (Párraga, Troscianko, and Tolhurst, 2000, 2005; Tolhurst and Tadmor, 2000).

3.2. A Relationship between Human Perception of Oriented Stimuli and the Orientation Biases in Natural Scenes?

It is well established that visual sensitivity varies as a function of stimulus orientation. There is a long history of research devoted to examining how human (e.g., Jastrow, 1893) and animal (e.g., Lashley, 1938) performance on a variety of tasks varies with stimulus orientation. The typical finding is that performance is superior for cardinal orientations, relative to oblique orientations. This general perceptual bias in visual processing has been labeled the oblique effect (Appelle, 1972). However, it is important to realize that there are two different sources of anisotropic "oblique effect" behavioral performance: an orientation bias in the basic functioning of the visual system (e.g., contrast sensitivity and acuity), and a bias of later visual processing (presumably beyond initial image filtering in V1) obtained on more-cognitive tasks such as the naming, encoding, and memory of orientation, in which oblique orientations are more confused with each other than are stimuli of cardinal orientations. To help avoid confusing these two oblique effects in the literature, they have been termed *class 1* and *class 2* oblique effects, respectively, distinguishing them on the basis of the type of task on which they occur (Essock, 1980). That the two types of oblique effect are fundamentally different is readily apparent by considering that the bias of contrast sensitivity is fixed to retinal coordinates if the viewer's head or body is rotated, but that the oblique effect of orientation memory/recall is often labile, dependent upon the observer's sense of "up". Furthermore, the memory anisotropy is readily obtained with somatosensory stimuli, whereas the class 1 oblique effect is closely tied to a physiological bias in the early visual cortical area. For the remainder of this review, any mention of the oblique effect will be in reference to the first class; specifically, in terms of overall orientation sensitivity to simple stimuli such as lines or high spatial frequency gratings, its neurophysiological basis, its evolution, and its relation to the visual anisotropy demonstrated to exist in the context of visual processing of natural scenes.

Several authors (Annis and Frost, 1973; Timney and Muir, 1976; Switkes et al., 1978; Ross and Woodhouse, 1979; Coppola et al., 1998; Keil and Cristóbal, 2000) have presumed a possible phylogenic or ontogenetic relationship between the physical anisotropy in natural scene content and the oblique effect. In essence, this conjecture is that since, in the natural environment, there is less information aligned with oblique axes, the relative number of cortical units devoted to processing such information should be less when compared to the other, more prominent orientations. As evidence, these authors point to the numerous reports from neurophysiological studies utilizing single-unit recording, visual evoked potentials, optical imaging of intrinsic signals, and functional magnetic resonance imaging that show a bias in cortical processing of orientation favoring the cardinal axes (Maffei and Campbell, 1970; Mansfield, 1974; Mansfield and Ronner, 1978; Orban and Kennedy, 1980; De Valois, Yund, and Hepler, 1982; Zemon, Gutowski, and Horton, 1983; Sokol, Moskowitz, and Hansen, 1989; Chapman, Stryker, and Bonhoeffer, 1996; Coppola, White, Fitzpatrick, and Purves, 1998; Furmanski and Engel, 2000; Yu, and Shou, 2000; Li, Peterson, and Freeman, 2003). While there is indeed a high degree of overlap between the observed orientation biases in natural scenes and in neurophysiological processing, when human performance is measured empirically in the context of natural scenes, this parallel takes on a different interpretation.

4.0. The "Horizontal Effect"

4.1. A Perceptual Anisotropy in Perceiving Orientation in "Naturalistic" Stimuli

In a series of psychophysical studies, Essock et al. (2003) sought to determine whether or not the oblique effect would be present with stimuli that possessed broadband structure such as contained in natural scenes (natural scenes possess amplitude across all spatial frequencies and orientations and are thus referred to as broadband). The fundamental goal of these experiments was to examine the ability of human observers to accurately perceive or detect the presence of oriented content in the context of broadband structure representative of natural scenes. One primary issue that had to be overcome concerned how to generate stimuli that resembled natural scenes, while at the same time did not confound scene meaning or content within test conditions. Another issue had to do with how to add oriented content to the patterns at specific orientations, while at the same time assuring that the distribution of the added oriented content also resembled that typically found in natural scenes. The first issue was resolved with the use of broadband visual noise patterns (i.e., random phase) like what had been used in previous studies designed to investigate human processing with respect to changes made to α (Knill et al., 1990; Tadmor and Tolhurst, 1994; Webster and Miyahara, 1997; Thomson and Foster, 1997). The use of such patterns allowed the authors to construct broadband patterns in the Fourier domain that could be made to have any desired α, while being absent of any meaningful semantic content that might result in potentially misleading results. The second issue was addressed by constructing a broadband triangle increment filter in the Fourier domain. This filter allowed Essock et al. (2003) to make increments to the amplitude spectra of different noise patterns in a way that resembled how amplitude biases are typically observed to occur in natural scenes (i.e., the biases are typically peaked at whatever orientation possesses the bias) while preserving the relative magnitude of the amplitude coefficients at other non-incremented orientations. Thus, oriented biases of amplitude could be added to a given noise pattern with the peak centered on the orientation at which sensitivity would be tested. Perceptually (and physically), an increment in amplitude in the Fourier domain along a given orientation essentially results in increasing the contrast of spatial content within a limited range of orientations relative to the other orientations present in the imagery. In this particular study, Essock et al. (2003) utilized three psychophysical paradigms to examine human visual processing of broadband oriented content embedded in

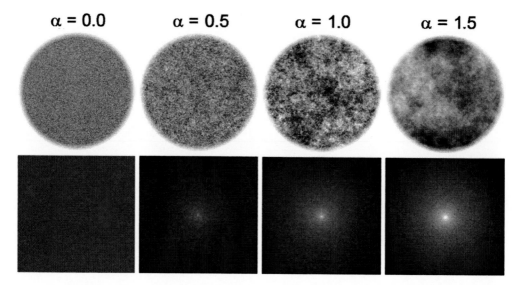

Figure 5. Top row: Examples of broadband visual noise patterns that have random phase spectra and different amplitude spectrum slopes. Bottom row: Examples of the amplitude spectra used to form the spatial noise patterns shown in the top row.

broadband visual noise patterns. The paradigms involved measuring three levels of human sensitivity including a suprathreshold matching paradigm, a temporal two-alternative forced-choice (2AFC) threshold paradigm, and a near-threshold single interval Yes/No Signal Detection Theory (SDT) paradigm. Since the results for all three of the paradigms were similar, we will focus on the suprathreshold paradigm since we will revisit that paradigm later in this chapter. The suprathreshold paradigm utilized by Essock et al. (2003) employed several sets of visual noise stimuli that were constructed to have amplitude spectra with α values of 0.0, 0.5, 1.0, and 1.5 (see Figure 5 for examples of these patterns).

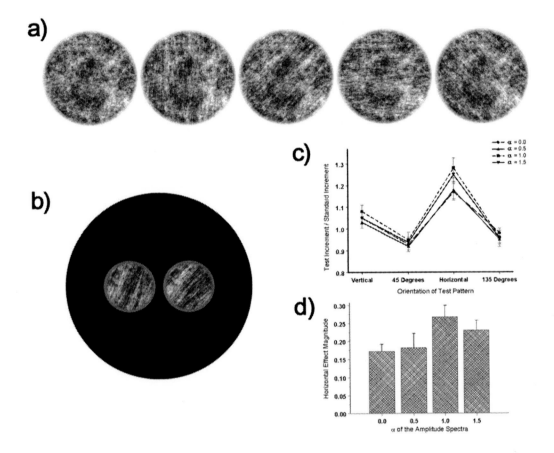

Figure 6. a) Examples of a visual noise pattern containing an oriented increment in amplitude at one of the four test orientations mentioned in the text. From left to right, isotropic visual noise pattern with no oriented increment (for comparison); vertical increment of amplitude; 45° increment of amplitude; horizontal increment of amplitude; and 135° increment of amplitude. b) Illustration of the mask used in the matching experiments of Essock at el. (2003). c) Data re-plotted from Essock et al. (2003) showing a horizontal effect. On the ordinate is the averaged ratio of the standard increment to the test increment observers judged as being perceptually equivalent, error bars are ± 1 SE – *note that larger values indicate poor perceptual salience (i.e., less sensitivity)*, values close to 1 indicate accurate perceptual matches. On the abscissa is the orientation of each of the test increment orientation conditions. d) Histogram created using the matching data from Essock et al. (2003) showing the change in the magnitude (ordinate, error bars are ± 1 SE) of the horizontal effect for the different amplitude spectrum slopes (abscissa).

All noise stimuli were made to contain biased orientation structure by multiplying their amplitude spectra with a triangle weighting function (with an orientation bandwidth of 45°) that was centered at one of four different orientations: vertical, 45° oblique, horizontal, and 135° oblique (refer to Figure 6a for examples). Participants were seated in front of a monitor covered by a large circular mask with two circular, laterally-displaced windows in which two noise patterns were presented (see Figure 6b). On the left was a comparison pattern that contained a fixed suprathreshold oriented increment of amplitude (at either 22.5° or 112.5°), and on the right was a test pattern (with an oriented increment of amplitude at one of the four nominal orientations) in which observers were instructed to adjust (via key-press) the size of the physical increment in the pattern until the *magnitude* of the oriented content in the test pattern appeared to match that contained in the comparison pattern. The results (depicted in Figure 6c) clearly demonstrate that matches were most accurate for oblique stimuli, least accurate for horizontal, and intermediate for vertical; an effect the authors termed the "horizontal effect". Specifically, to match the appearance (strength) of the oriented content in an arbitrary comparison stimulus, less *physical* contrast was needed in the oblique test stimuli and the most physical contrast was needed in the horizontal test orientation – in broadband patterns, oblique content is most salient and horizontal content is least salient. This effect was found to occur in all α conditions. Furthermore, the magnitude of the effect was maximal in the condition where α was equal to1.0 (Figure 6d). Possible explanations for this effect are discussed in *Section 6.0*.

4.2. A Perceptual Anisotropy in Perceiving Orientation in Natural Scene Stimuli

Based on the results reported by Essock et al. (2003), an argument could be made that the results were specific to stimuli consisting of broadband visual noise, and that such an effect may not have been present if the stimuli had consisted of actual real-world scenes. Essentially, this argument reduces to whether or not the nature of the phase spectra would interact with the detection of oriented structure defined as broadband increments of amplitude. That is, since it is the phase spectrum that specifies how the different sinusoidal components of an image sum to form a given scene, the amount and localization of the lines and edges that form the meaningful content are determined by each scene's phase spectrum. In order to address this issue, Hansen et al. (2003) and Hansen and Essock (2004) gathered a set of images obtained from the natural environment (devoid of any carpentered structures) that possessed an approximately equivalent amount of amplitude across all orientations (i.e., the images were "naturally isotropic"), all possessing αs equal to 1.0. The natural scene stimuli were made to contain biased orientation structure by multiplying their amplitude spectra with the same triangle weighting function used by Essock et al. (2003), see Figure 7a for examples. Performance for detecting the amplitude increments was evaluated with a near-threshold signal-detection single-interval yes/no task in which observers responded by key-press to indicate whether or not the presented stimulus contained an oriented increment. The results were consistent with those reported by Essock et al. (2003) in that all participants were less sensitive to horizontal increments than for the oblique orientations, with vertical orientations being intermediate (see Figure 7b). Thus, when considered alongside the results reported by Essock et al. (2003), the horizontal effect can be demonstrated in broadband visual noise patterns which do not possess any semantically meaningful structure (i.e., they possess random phase spectra) as well as with natural scene imagery (which possess highly systematic phase spectra) with an equal amount of semantically meaningful structure at all orientations. Again, the implications of this finding are discussed in *Section 6.0*.

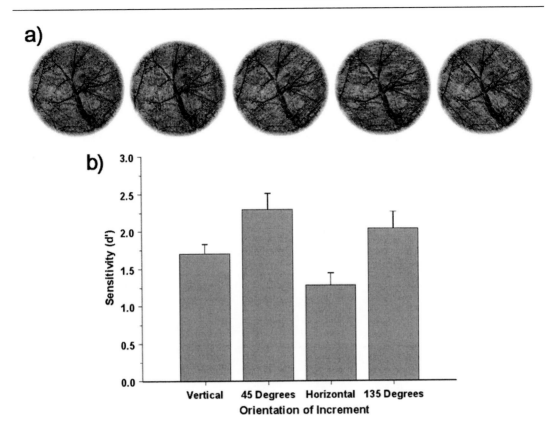

Figure 7. a) Examples of a "naturally isotropic" natural scene image containing an oriented increment in amplitude at one of the four test orientations mentioned in the text. From left to right, isotropic image with no oriented increment (for comparison); vertical increment of amplitude; 45° increment of amplitude; horizontal increment of amplitude; and 135° increment of amplitude. b) Data re-plotted from Hansen and Essock (2004) showing a horizontal effect. On the ordinate is averaged sensitivity (d'), error bars are ± 1 SE – *note that smaller values indicate poor perceptual sensitivity*. On the abscissa is the orientation of each of the test increment orientation conditions.

5.0. The Horizontal Effect in Natural Scene Stimuli with Variable Structural Biases

In *Sub-sections 2.1* and *2.2* we described two fundamental structural regularities that are *typically* observed in the natural environment. It is worth noting that, while such regularities are the norm with respect to natural scene imagery, there are certainly exceptions. Consider Figure 8a which plots the distribution of α for over 1000 natural scene images possessing content ranging from purely natural to purely carpentered. Notice that while the distribution peaks in the range of α = 0.9 to α = 1.1, there are a number of image possessing αs outside this range.

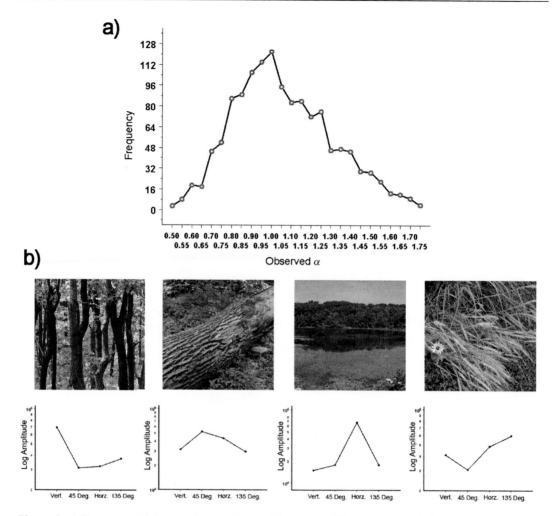

Figure 8. a) Frequency histogram for αs observed in a natural image set consisting of more that 1000 images. b) Top Row: example natural scene images possessing biases in image structure (e.g., tree trunks, skyline, grass, leaves, etc.) at one of four different orientations. Bottom Row: plots of the averaged amplitude within a 45° band of orientations centered at one of the nominal orientations – from left-to-right: vertical, 45° oblique, horizontal, and 135° oblique. On the ordinate is averaged log amplitude over a range of orientations and across all spatial frequencies. On the abscissa is nominal orientation for each image. Note that in each of the plots, there is a specific bias in amplitude for one specific orientation.

Likewise, while the typical bias in amplitude for natural images consists of more amplitude near the cardinal axes (relative to the oblique axes), it is possible to find images with biases that do not follow such an orientation bias (see Figure 8b). In the following sub-sections we will review the results from a number of psychophysical experiments that examined how the horizontal effect anisotropy is influenced when the stimuli consisted of natural scenes that possessed structural biases other than those typically observed (i.e., the cardinal bias).

5.1. Perceptual Anisotropies in Natural Scene Imagery Possessing Different Spectral Slopes

In *Sub-section 4.1* experiments were reviewed where human perception of orientation in the context of broadband visual noise stimuli with amplitude spectra αs that ranged from 0.0 to 1.5 (in steps of 0.5) was found to exhibit a horizontal effect, with the magnitude of the effect being highest when α = 1.0. However, as mentioned earlier, those stimuli were visual noise patterns possessing naturalistic amplitude spectra, but not the semantic structure inherent in natural scenes (i.e., possessed random phase spectra). Thus, the question of whether or not the ability to detect oriented increments of amplitude for real-world stimuli possessing naturalistic structures would depend on α was not addressed. Hansen and Essock (2005) addressed this issue in a set of experiments that utilized sets of natural scene imagery that possessed a broad range of amplitude spectrum α values, but without any predominant 'natural' structural biases (i.e., the imagery was naturally isotropic). Specifically, the authors sought to determine if the magnitude of the horizontal effect changed as a function of the α value of natural scenes as it did with the noise patterns used by Essock et al. (2003). Hansen and Essock (2005) thus gathered sets of images that contained approximately equal content (amplitude) at all orientations, with each set containing images that had amplitude spectra α values within one of several narrow ranges (see Figure 9 for example imagery). Oriented increments of amplitude were applied in the same manner as with the noise patterns utilized by Essock et al. (2003). The psychophysical paradigm was identical to the signal-detection task mentioned in *Sub-section 4.2*.

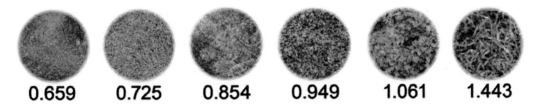

0.659   0.725   0.854   0.949   1.061   1.443

Figure 9. Stimulus examples from each α image set used in Hansen and Essock (2005); the numbers at the bottom indicate the respective α value from which the examples were selected. The images have had their amplitude spectra made isotropic in order to eliminate any subtle biases in amplitude, but do not contain an oriented increment of amplitude.

The results showed a horizontal effect that was observed in all α conditions, with the magnitude of the horizontal effect being highest for imagery that had α values closest to 1.0. However, an important distinction is that, while the magnitude of the horizontal effect was dependent on the slope of natural scene stimuli, sensitivity for detecting horizontal increments was relatively independent of α, with relative sensitivity to the other three orientations tested demonstrating the change in sensitivity with α (being best when α was approximately equal to 1.0.

5.2. Perceptual Anisotropies in Natural Scene Imagery Possessing Orientation Biases: Global Amplitude

It was discussed in *Sub-section 4.2* that the horizontal-effect perceptual anisotropy was observed with natural scene imagery that possessed equal amounts of amplitude at all orientations. The fundamental difference between those stimuli and those discussed in *Sub-section 4.1* was that the content in the natural scene stimuli possessed semantically meaningful structure compared to visual noise patterns. Specifically, the stimuli discussed in *Sub-section 4.2* possessed structures (tree branches, grass, general shrubbery) at all orientations. This raises the question of whether or not the presence of naturally occurring oriented structure (carried by the phase spectra) in natural scenes at *specific* orientations might have any impact on the sensitivity of the human visual system for oriented content in natural scenes. This issue was addressed by Hansen et al. (2003) and Hansen and Essock (2004). In those studies, sets of imagery were gathered that contained naturalistic content biases at one of each of the four nominal orientations (vertical, 45° oblique, horizontal, or 135° oblique) -- all imagery had amplitude spectra αs approximately equal to 1.0. The natural scene imagery was comparable to that shown in Figure 8b. These images were made to be globally isotropic (thus equating with respect to amplitude, but not phase – i.e., the only differences between the stimuli would be carried by the phase spectra), then oriented increments of amplitude were applied in the same manner as with the noise patterns utilized by Essock et al. (2003). The same psychophysical paradigm was used (measuring sensitivity, d'), as mentioned in *Sub-section 4.2*. The results show the presence of two performance biases. First, regardless of the structural bias present in the natural stimulus images, performance for detecting horizontal increments of amplitude was always poor. Second, performance for detecting an oriented increment of amplitude was reduced when the oriented increment was at the same orientation as the natural structural bias of the stimuli. For example, if the natural scene stimulus image contained a bias of structure at 135° oblique (as in the example image shown at the far right of Figure 8b), the ability of human observers to detect an amplitude increment at that same orientation was reduced (i.e., a "content-dependent" or "structure-dependent effect"). Since the global amplitude spectrum of the natural scene stimuli was made isotropic, the structure dependent effect cannot be explained by masking with respect to global amplitude at the test orientation.

Since the lines/edges that make up the structures in natural scenes are carried by the images phase spectrum, the structure-dependent effect can be explained by a masking effect associated with the phase-alignments in the structurally-biased imagery. Hansen et al. (2003) provided support for this by demonstrating that when the values of the phase spectrum corresponding to the biased structure in the spatial image (at any one of the four orientations tested) was scrambled (thereby eliminating the presence of the content biases at any of those orientations), performance for detecting increments of amplitude at the previously content-biased orientations improved considerably. A similar effect has also been demonstrated by Bex and colleagues for discriminating narrow-band (1-octave) contrast increments made to natural scene images (Bex, Mareschal, and Dakin, 2007).

5.3. Perceptual Anisotropies in Natural Scene Imagery Possessing Orientation Biases: Local Structure

As mentioned in *Sub-section 2.2*, the orientation bias typically observed in natural scene imagery has, for the most part, been assessed through measuring biases in amplitude at different orientations globally in the image. One potential problem with such an approach is that it does not reflect the total number of edges/lines (i.e., multi-scale phase correspondences) that make up the oriented structures of the imagery. Consider the two images shown in Figure 10a along with their corresponding plots of averaged amplitude at four different orientations (Figure 10b). Both images show a large global bias at horizontal, yet differ significantly with respect to the total number of edges and lines that make up the local horizontal structures in both images. One method that can quantify this difference was reported by Hansen and Hess (2007), where standard local filtering with spatial filters similar to those believed to be employed in human primary visual cortex are applied to natural scene images. By summing filter responses at a given spatial scale and taking the ratio of summed responses to total image area, a metric which quantifies the difference in number of edges/lines in images at different orientations for a given spatial scale is achieved. Notice that in Figure 10c that the filter responses are limited to two main regions in the filter response image for the target image on the right, whereas there are many more filter responses distributed across the entire filter response image for the target image on the left. Thus the image on the right can be referred to as being more sparse with respect to horizontal structures relative to the image on the left. The fact that natural scene images vary with respect to their "structural sparseness" at different orientations may have a different effect on the sensitivity to detecting increments of amplitude at different orientations than previously discussed in *Sub-section 5.2*. Hansen and Essock (2005) sought to examine this issue by measuring human visual sensitivity with natural scene imagery containing variable amounts of structural sparseness at each of the four nominal orientations to determine if sensitivity for detecting amplitude increments at those orientations depended on structural sparseness at a given orientation for a given image. While the structural sparseness of content at four different orientations was considered, the focus was on structural sparseness of natural scene content at horizontal orientations.

The idea here is that if the visual system is optimized to process orientation in the presence of the typical orientation bias found to occur in natural scenes (i.e., the horizontal bias mentioned in *Sub-section 2.2*), overall orientation performance should follow the magnitude of the horizontal bias (i.e., high overall performance with imagery containing large amounts of horizontal content and low overall performance with imagery containing relatively small amounts of horizontal content), and not biases at other orientations.

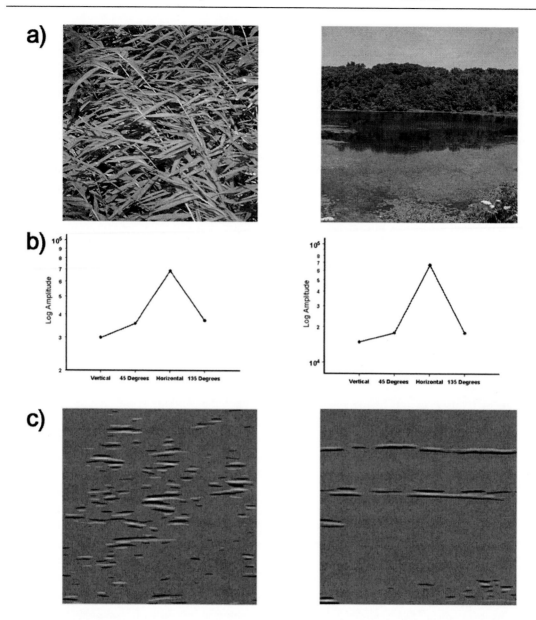

Figure 10. a) Two natural scene images dominated by horizontal amplitude, but differing with respect to structural sparseness at horizontal (refer to text for details). b) Plots of averaged log amplitude at the four nominal orientations for each image (each graph corresponds to the image directly above it). The graphs are constructed in an identical manner as those shown the bottom row of Figure 8b. Notice that both images possess a similar bias in amplitude as a function of orientation. c) Filter response images resulting from filtering each of the corresponding images with filters resembling those believed to be employed by the human visual system at a particular spatial frequency oriented along the horizontal dimension. The filter responses were further filtered to pass only those responses significantly above or below the mean luminance of the corresponding natural scene image. Notice that for the filter response image on the left, there are many horizontal responses distributed across the entire image (i.e., low horizontal structural sparseness), whereas the filter response image in the right has relatively few horizontal responses primarily restricted to two regions in the image (i.e., high horizontal structural sparseness).

In order to test this, Hansen and Essock (2005) compiled a set of natural scene imagery to serve as experimental stimuli in which the amount of horizontal structural sparseness varied from high sparseness (i.e., limited number of structures at horizontal – see Figure 10a, right) to low sparseness (i.e., many distributed structures at horizontal – see Figure 10a, left). Additional control image sets were also obtained that contained variable levels of structural sparseness at the other nominal orientations (i.e., vertical, 45° and 135°oblique). Oriented increments of amplitude were applied in the same manner as with the noise patterns utilized by Essock et al. (2003). The psychophysical paradigm was identical to that mentioned in *Subsection 4.2* (i.e., signal detection). The ability of human observers to detect horizontal increments of amplitude was poor across all conditions, thereby providing further support for a horizontal effect anisotropy when perceiving orientation in natural scenes. However, and more interestingly, performance for detecting increments of amplitude at all tested orientations was significantly positively related to the amount of horizontal structural sparseness present in the horizontal content-biased image set, with no significant relationship to the amount of content-bias contained in the control image sets. Thus, the ability of human observers to detect increments at different orientations depends on the structural sparseness of horizontal content. Specifically, the more the structural sparseness of natural scenes resembles that typically observed in the environment (i.e., structural bias in favor of the cardinal axes, with more horizontal structures relative to vertical), the better humans are at detecting additional increments of amplitude at all orientations, while still exhibiting the horizontal effect.

6.0. The Horizontal Effect: An Inherent Orientation Processing Anisotropy

In *Section 4.0* and *Section 5.0* the horizontal effect perceptual anisotropy in human observers for perceiving orientation in broadband stimuli (either broadband visual noise or natural scenes) was described. In those sections the effect was shown to be very robust with respect to the many types of structural biases (either typical or atypical) known to exist in natural scenes. However, when those biases were consistent with the typical structural regularities observed in natural scenes (e.g., amplitude spectrum slope equal to 1.0), the horizontal effect appears to be at its strongest, but was always significant regardless of the structural biases (either in the form of variable α or variable orientation biases) present in the stimuli. That is, despite the fact that specific "structure-dependent" effects were observed with "atypical" natural scene stimuli (e.g., poor perceptual performance for detecting amplitude increments oriented at 45° when the stimuli contained phase-aligned structure at that same orientation), such effects were dependent on the specific structural biases present in the imagery (i.e., dependent on the phase spectra), whereas poor perceptual ability associated with horizontal orientations persisted across all stimulus image types. It is therefore clear that the horizontal effect results from an inherent processing anisotropy within the human visual system.

We now return to the numerous reports from neurophysiological studies that indicate a bias in cortical processing of orientation at the cardinal axes (Maffei and Campbell, 1970; Mansfield, 1974; Mansfield and Ronner, 1978; Orban and Kennedy, 1980; De Valois, Yund, and Hepler, 1982; Zemon, Gutowski, and Horton, 1983; Sokol, Moskowitz, and Hansen,

1989; Chapman, Stryker, and Bonhoeffer, 1996; Coppola, White, Fitzpatrick, and Purves, 1998; Furmanski and Engel, 2000; Yu, and Shou, 2000; Li, Peterson, and Freeman, 2003) and, indeed, when horizontal and vertical are carefully compared, a bias favoring horizontal over vertical is seen as well as a bias of vertical over oblique (Li, Peterson, and Freeman, 2003; Zemen, Gutowski, and Horton, 1983; Furmanski and Engel, 2000; Mansfield and Ronner, 1978). If visual cortex is equipped with a larger number of neurons devoted to processing horizontal and vertical orientations, one might expect to find superior perceptual performance with any type of stimulus configuration (not just narrow-band sinusoidal gratings) where the task of the observer was to detect or judge the saliency of oriented structures. Indeed, it was the fact that the natural environment contains biases at the cardinal orientations that led many to propose that the human visual system acquired a bias in the number of neurons at those same orientations in order to better represent the typical structures in our natural environments. While there is indeed a high degree of overlap between the observed orientation biases in natural scenes and the visual phenomenon known as the oblique effect, we've shown that when perception of stimuli at different orientations is assessed with broadband (i.e., naturalistic) stimuli, a horizontal effect is observed. Thus, the association between the orientation biases in natural scenes and behavioral performance for perceiving orientation is actually an inverse relation -- while typical natural scenes contain a large bias in content at horizontal orientations, least amount at oblique orientations and an intermediate amount of content at vertical orientations, human perceptual performance is worst for horizontal orientations, best for oblique orientations and intermediate for vertical orientations.

The association between the behavioral performance horizontal effect observed with broadband natural stimuli and the prevalence of content at the nominal orientations in natural scenes was investigated by Hansen and Essock (2004). That the content contained in typical scenes exhibit a horizontal bias is an important finding as those authors have proposed that the behavioral horizontal effect would have evolutionary utility in such environments (Essock et al., 2003; Hansen et al., 2003). Specifically, such a hypothesis predicts the existence of a cortical mechanism (presumably at the level of primary visual cortex) that acts to reduce the perceptual saliency of the most prevalent content (i.e., horizontally oriented structures) in a scene, thereby relatively enhancing the less often occurring content of natural scenes. That is, a mechanism that turns down sensitivity for the 'expected' content in a typical scene would serve to relatively enhance the salience of 'unexpected', or novel, content at off-horizontal orientations. The nature of such a mechanism is explored in the subsequent sections of this review.

7.0. Anisotropic Contrast Normalization Model for Orientation Processing in Broadband Stimuli

The pattern of sensitivity adjustment described in *Section 6.0* could readily be accounted for by a cortical contrast-gain-control mechanism. However, the change in the orientation sensitivity obtained with broadband stimuli would not be predicted by standard models of contrast gain control (e.g., Bonds, 1989; Heeger, 1992, Geisler and Albrecht 1992; Wilson and Humanski, 1993, Carandini and Heeger, 1994). Specifically, most contrast normalization models provide response normalization by dividing the activity of a given cortical unit by the pooled activity of striate neurons tuned to a broad range of spatial frequencies and *all* orientations. One implication of such an "untuned" model of gain control is that the response of each neuron is altered equally (i.e., divided by the same pooled response). While such a mechanism would work well for adjusting neural responses to overall local image contrast, it would ignore large orientation- or spatial-frequency-specific differences in the spatial make-up of the structures from one image region to the next. A more specialized normalization mechanism could adjust a unit's gain, not on the basis of general (broad-spectrum) total content in the scene driving all neurons, but rather on the basis of content that is similar to the tuning preference (orientation and spatial frequency) of the unit under consideration. A few models do propose that contrast normalization is tuned in these dimensions – i.e., local in the Fourier domain. One model (Wainwright, Schwartz and Simoncelli, 2001; Schwartz and Simoncelli, 2001) achieves this by making the weights of the neural filters dynamic, with the weight dependent upon the extent to which a neighboring filter and the filter under consideration are jointly stimulated by a natural scene (considered with respect to spatial frequency and orientation). Specifically, the amount of normalization signal is a function of the likelihood that one filter is stimulated relative to another filter when stimulated by a natural scene, and is represented in a weighting component, w_{ij}, proposed by Wainwright et al. (2001) (see model equation below). Thus, if two filters are tuned to similar orientations, spatial frequencies and locations, their response will be highly correlated. Implementing this weight achieves two things: (1) it provides a localized (in the Fourier domain) gain-control pool where more-similar filters contribute more to contrast gain control, and (2) it serves to further "whiten" the neural representation of the image with respect to typical natural scene content.

We've noted previously that a numerical bias in the filters across a dimension, here orientation, could create a bias in the strength of the pooled normalization response so that activity at certain stimulus values would produce more profound sensitivity adjustment for equal stimulus magnitudes. That is, given that there is strong evidence in the neurophysiological literature that there are relatively fewer neurons tuned to oblique orientations and most at horizontal, with an intermediate number at vertical, otherwise-identical image content at different orientations would produce a different amount of contribution to the normalization pool (specifically, most at horizontal, least at the obliques) unless compensated for by another mechanism. This inherent anisotropy of filter number has been incorporated into a gain control model that added an anisotropic weighting factor, termed o_j (Hansen et al., 2003; Hansen and Essock, 2004) and is described below. This neurophysiological numerical bias (a horizontal effect of orientation preferences) was most clearly documented by Li et al. (2003) in a survey of about 4400 cat neurons, but is also apparent in the data of several other reports (Chapman et al., 1996; Chapman and Bonhoeffer, 1998; Coppola et al., 1998; Mansfield, 1974; Mansfield and Ronner, 1978; Tiao and Blakemore, 1976; Yu and Shou, 2000). Thus, in addition to the w_{ij} weighting component, we have proposed a second weighting component, o_j, that represents an anisotropy of the gain pool as suggested by the neurophysiological literature. The model can be expressed as:

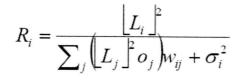

$$R_i = \frac{\lfloor L_i \rfloor^2}{\sum_j \left(\lfloor L_j \rfloor^2 o_j\right) w_{ij} + \sigma_i^2}$$

where the response of the output channel linear filter i (L_i), is half-wave rectified and then squared; the result is then divided by a weighted (o_j) sum of the rectified and then squared responses of the other linear filters, L_j, which represents the total neural output at the jth orientation/spatial frequency in its respective 'neural neighborhood' (w_{ij}) plus an offset term σ_i^2 (the "structure-dependent" effects described in *Sub-sections 5.2* and *5.3* are represented by the w_{ij} component). Therefore, R_i represents the adjusted response of the output channel corresponding to i. Essentially, the main dynamic gain control (normalization) comes from the division of L_i, by the activity of filters within its local striate neighborhood constrained in Fourier response space by weighting the effect of other filters by w_{ij} which serves to make the gain pool for a given neuron local in the Fourier plane. The "inherent" neural population anisotropy (believed to underpin the behavioral horizontal effect), is represented by o_j.

Due to the inverting nature of the gain-control mechanism described above (e.g., a divisive adjustment), human vision shows a horizontal effect anisotropy for seeing content in broadband images. On the other hand, when human vision is tested, for example, with un-naturalistic narrowband stimuli of few components (such as a single sine-wave or square-wave grating), an oblique effect anisotropic pattern of performance is observed, with poorest contrast sensitivity or acuity at oblique orientations and best sensitivity at cardinal orientations (including suprathreshold performance; Essock, 1982). This oblique effect anisotropy is presumed to be determined by the greater number of neurons available to detect horizontal/vertical narrowband patterns (Essock, Krebs, and Prather, 1997). In short, when there is significant activity in neighboring neurons (i.e., due to a broadband stimulus), the effect of a gain control process localized in the orientation dimension would be significant, resulting in a horizontal-effect anisotropy (Essock et al., 2003; Hansen et al., 2003; Hansen and Essock, 2004; Hansen and Essock, 2005). When viewing a narrowband pattern, the pooled response of neighboring filters would be small, resulting in an insignificant gain adjustment, thereby leading to an oblique-effect anisotropy. While it may seem odd that the visual system would be equipped with a bias in the number of neurons preferring cardinal orientations only to use normalization to reduce the sensitivity or the perceived magnitude of those orientations, we have argued that such a mechanism would have considerable utility, serving to make novel content (e.g., textures, objects, etc.) segment from background content (e.g., Li, 1999) as well as make novel content stand out from a typical background. Finally, this "whitening" would be an efficient neural representation.

8.0. Psychophysical Investigation of The Anisotropic Contrast Normalization Model

In *Section 4.0* and *Section 5.0*, the ability of human observers to perceive different orientations was assessed by incrementing the amplitude coefficients across all spatial frequencies within a relatively broad (45°) range of orientations. With respect to the anisotropic contrast normalization model described above, an increase in the saliency of oriented structure in a given stimulus image would therefore be equivalent to an increase in response of the L_j channel in the model. Given that the contrast gain model described in the previous section is based on local operations (local in the Fourier domain), questions remain regarding the L_j channel output for increments of different ranges of spatial frequencies and orientations – that is, just *how* local is the local pooling.

In a recent study conducted by Hansen and Essock (2006), the changes in the magnitude of the L_j channel, were measured by assessing how broad the spatial content (with respect to orientation and spatial frequency) needed to be in order to produce psychophysical responses indicative of the activation of that component. As in Essock et al. (2003), the stimuli consisted of broadband visual noise patterns all possessing an amplitude spectrum slope equal to 1.0. However, instead of applying a single fixed broadband orientation increment, Hansen and Essock (2006) employed increment filters that varied in bandwidth with respect to orientation and spatial frequency and ranged from incrementing a single orientation and spatial frequency to incrementing all spatial frequencies and a 45° band of orientations centered at one of the four nominal orientations (resulting in a total of 16 levels of spatial frequency/orientation increment bandwidth for each of the nominal orientations). The psychophysical paradigm was identical to the suprathreshold matching task employed by Essock et al. (2003) described in *Sub-section 4.1.*

In general, the results observed by Hansen and Essock (2006) showed an oblique effect perceptual anisotropy when a fairly small range of orientations and high spatial frequencies were incremented and the horizontal effect was observed for orientation band increments that were equal to or greater than 20° and 1 octave (or greater) in frequency. At intermediate spatial frequency and orientation increment bandwidths, a blend of the two anisotropies was observed (see Figure 11 for stimulus examples and data exerts). This finding provides strong support for the inherent anisotropy in contrast normalization pooling mentioned above by demonstrating a strong horizontal effect when activity in the normalization pool is large, and no horizontal effect when the pooled contribution is minimal. Specifically, when stimuli possessed very narrowband increments, the greater numbers of horizontal and vertical tuned neurons that exist yield an oblique effect, reflecting the greater output across filters tuned to horizontal and vertical. In addition, when the background content is minimal, contrast gain control is therefore not significantly involved and the slightly greater number of horizontal neurons compared to vertical would be expected to result in visual performance that is best at horizontal, nearly as good at vertical, and lowest for obliques (rather than a strict oblique effect where vertical performance equals horizontal performance). We suggest that the greater response at horizontal compared to vertical is very small and thus is not typically noted in measurement of grating contrast sensitivity and resolution acuity. However, when this small bias for each of many spatial frequencies is accumulated across a broadband target, the horizontal/vertical difference becomes apparent.

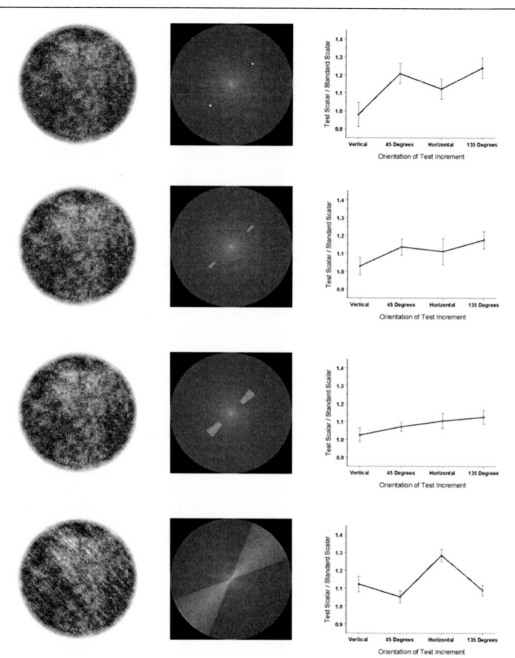

Figure 11. Left Column: example noise stimuli containing an increment in amplitude along the 135° oblique orientation – from top-to-bottom, the bandwidth of the increment increases from a single frequency and orientation, ½ octave frequency band and 5° orientation band, 1 octave frequency band and 20° orientation band, all frequencies and a 45° band of orientations. Note that the increment has been adjusted so that the increment can be seen by the reader and are thus not physically equivalent. Middle Column: amplitude spectra containing the amplitude increment shown in the images in the spatial domain directly to the left of each spectrum. Right Column: data re-plotted from Hansen and Essock (2006) showing the gradual transition from an oblique effect (top graph) to the horizontal effect (bottom graph). All graphs are a constructed in an identical manner as the data graph shown in Figure 6c, with larger values indicating poor perceptual salience.

The results reported by Hansen and Essock (2006) demonstrate that the transition from human anisotropic performance being an oblique effect (where there are very few or only one Fourier component incremented in the stimulus), to the anisotropy being a horizontal effect, is gradual. As either more image components of different orientations or different spatial frequencies are added, the horizontal effect becomes more pronounced and the oblique effect becomes less apparent.

8.1. Narrowband Contrast Sensitivity and Anisotropic Contrast Gain Control

The evidence presented thus far is consistent with the contrast normalization hypothesis described in *Section 7.0*. Greater suppression of horizontal (or vertical) contrast structure relative to oblique structure may indeed result in poorer sensitivity to broadband increments (as in Essock et al., 2003) or less perceived intensity at horizontal (as in Hansen and Essock, 2006). However, to this point, our hypothesis has relied on theories of contrast gain control which are grounded in physiological neuroscience. A great deal of work has been done in recent decades to establish that contrast gain control operates in a manner that can be characterized through more traditional 'grating-based' psychophysical paradigms (e.g., Foley, 1994; Huang and Dobkins, 2005; Meese and Holmes, 2002). Whereas the prior 'standard model' of contrast transduction assumed an intrinsically compressive transformation of contrast into channel response (normally thought to be the cause of the increasing portion of the typical threshold-versus-contrast, or "dipper" function; Legge and Foley, 1980), Foley (1994) showed convincingly that this compression should be attributed to a divisive inhibitory mechanism operating across spatial channels -- channels previously thought to be functionally independent, a formulation essentially identical with that given above in *Section 7.0*. It is now commonly accepted that two test stimuli which are *detected* by separate mechanisms serve to mask one another, raising detection thresholds as in the phenomenon of cross-orientation suppression (e.g., Meese and Holmes, 2007). However, this work has been carried out using narrowband gratings as stimuli, thereby leaving the orientation domain largely unexplored and precluding a prior description of anisotropic factors such as those which may underlie the horizontal effect. That is, there has been a gap between the established 'channel-by-channel' contrast sensitivity literature and our more recent experiments using broadband stimuli. Recently, Essock, Haun and Kim, (2008) have worked to close this gap by using gratings as test stimuli while using a broadband noise mask to probe the properties of the apparently anisotropic suppressive mechanism (operating from the gain pool) upon the tested channel. That is, the effect of varying the content available to the gain pool (i.e., denominator of the model specified in *Section 7.0*) on the L_j channel for narrowband signals was investigated (discussed later in the current sub-section).

As discussed previously, it is well known that in the high frequency range, above the peak of the contrast sensitivity function, an oblique effect of contrast sensitivity becomes apparent, increasing in magnitude with increasing frequency (Campbell and Kulikowski, 1967). Having hypothesized that the horizontal effect in broadband contrast perception arises from a physiological basis common with this oblique effect, we reasoned that the first place to look for a horizontal effect in narrowband contrast sensitivity (masked by broadband noise at different orientations) would be in this high-frequency range. If simultaneous stimulation of many spatial channels by a broadband noise image tends to evoke a horizontal effect in a sensitivity task (Essock et al., 2003), we reasoned that during such broadband stimulation, it would be possible to 'probe' the sensitivity of a single channel (represented above as L_j) by using a sinewave grating as a contrast sensitivity target. This turns out to be a conventional masking paradigm, but with oriented broadband noise used to mask a grating. By the conventional wisdom of 'higher thresholds mean more gain control', if the broadband horizontal effect is indeed due to anisotropic contrast gain control, a corresponding anisotropy in sensitivity to a simple grating should be seen while a broad range of filters are loaded with $1/f^\alpha$ noise.

Since it has also been noted that the gain control pool must be local with respect to orientation in the Fourier domain and centered on the detecting mechanism in order to obtain certain of the effects described here (i.e. the sensitivity horizontal effect, Essock et al., 2003), it was convenient to simultaneously look for a horizontal effect in masking and to establish the spectral localization of the masking process. To this end, Essock et al. (2008) used narrow spectral wedges of $1/f^\alpha$ noise (oriented symmetrically about the test orientation in order to eliminate the possibility of off-channel looking; Henning and Wichmann, 2007; Blake and Holopigian, 1986), as masks in a contrast sensitivity masking experiment with an 8cpd grating (oriented at vertical, 45°, horizontal, or 135°) as a sensitivity test. The masks were placed at ±5°, 15°, 25°, 35°, or 45° from the test orientation. Given prior results using broad frequency-band, narrow orientation-band stimuli (Hansen and Essock, 2006), a horizontal effect would be predicted using such stimuli. Indeed, a horizontal effect was obtained using the ±5° mask, in that threshold for the horizontal test reliably exceeded thresholds for the other orientations. As shown in Figure 12, the masking is clearly orientation-tuned, with bandwidths tending to be Gaussian and just narrower than 40° width-at-half-height, confirming that the gain control mechanism is indeed local with respect to orientation in the Fourier domain. In fact, some form of the effect appears to be present at all mask positions; even the least effective mask (±45° from the test orientation) is enough to produce a horizontal effect or inverse oblique effect in most subjects.

Other spatiotemporal conditions have also been tested under this noise masking paradigm (Essock et al., 2008). We find that even for very brief stimulus presentations, the $1/f^\alpha$ noise masking pattern follows a horizontal effect, particularly interesting because other labs (e.g. Wilson and Phillips, 1984; Petrov, Carandini and McKee, 2005) have provided evidence that under such "high-speed" test conditions (see Meese, et al., 2007), orientation tuning of masking processes is very broad. It is unknown, however, whether very brief duration stimuli would yield a horizontal effect with broadband stimuli. A narrowly tuned gain control pool is necessary to produce the broadband detection horizontal effect first shown in Essock et al (2003), but not, strictly speaking, these grating detection effects. If gain pool tuning truly is much broader for very brief stimuli, the horizontal effect we see here may be a more fundamental precursor to the broadband effects discussed above, and is consistent with anisotropic contrast gain control. Using such brief presentations of gratings, we have been able to show that the effect of a broadband mask on contrast sensitivity is closely linked with its temporal proximity with the target. By varying stimulus onset asynchrony (SOA) between the grating and the broadband mask, we have found that a very fast (<200ms) process is responsible for the presence of the horizontal effect (Figure 12). Various authors have described low-level gain-control as having extremely short latency (e.g. Bonds 1991;

Albrecht and Geisler, 1992; Wilson and Humanski, 1993), and so this finding is also consistent with our anisotropic contrast gain control hypothesis.

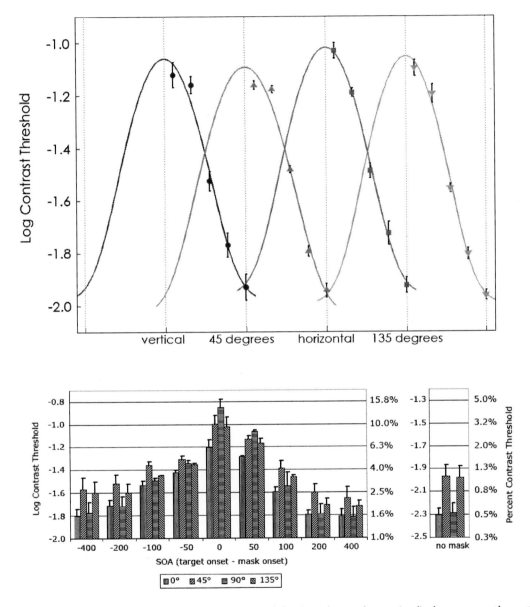

Figure 12. Top: Detection thresholds were measured for 8 cycle per degree (cpd) sinewave gratings at each of the four orientations indicated by the ordinate labels. For each orientation five oriented $1/f^{\alpha}$ noise images, at ±5, 15, 25, 35, and 45° from the test orientation, were used to mask the target grating in separate experimental blocks. Masks oriented nearer to the target orientation raised thresholds the most, with elevation declining with increasing difference between mask and target orientation. At the ±5° mask orientation, a horizontal effect is clearly seen (data are replotted in Figure 13), with indications of a similar effect at other mask orientations. Data are averaged across four subjects; error bars are the standard error of the subject mean. Bottom: A small SOA is necessary for the horizontal effect to emerge in a measure of narrowband contrast sensitivity; longer SOAs result in an oblique effect pattern similar to the baseline measurement, shown at right.

Interestingly, we also find that a horizontal effect can be obtained at *low* spatial frequencies. We find that 1 cpd gratings masked with $1/f^{\alpha}$ noise (spanning frequencies from 1 to 16 cpd in a 15° orientation band) show worst contrast sensitivity for the horizontal grating (Figure 13). This is unexpected, as the oblique effect in human contrast sensitivity is normally seen at frequencies above the peak of the CSF. It may be that anisotropic suppression from higher frequencies is what results in this horizontal effect; such an effect of 'downward' cross-channel suppression has been characterized previously (Meese and Hess, 2004), and would be consistent with cross-channel 'overlay masking'. Furthermore, we find that at both 1 and 8 cpd, above and below the peak of the CSF, a horizontal effect is obtained whether the temporal waveform of the stimuli is static (with a 500 ms stimulus duration) or rapidly flickered at 16 Hz. These recent findings suggest that the horizontal effect may be ubiquitous, found across spatial and temporal frequency when an observer views $1/f^{\alpha}$ spatial structure.

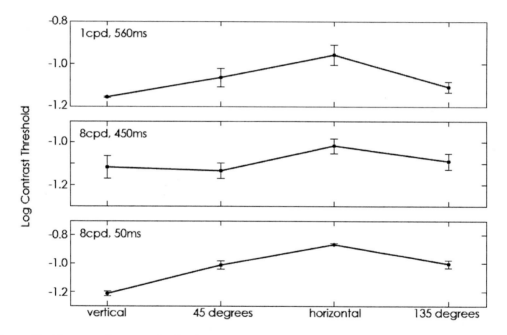

Figure 13. Three spatiotemporal stimulus conditions each show a horizontal effect. Top: A 1 cpd grating masked by oriented $1/f^{\alpha}$ noise spanning frequencies from 1 to 16 cpd is most difficult to detect when the orientation of noise and target is horizontal. Data are the average of two subjects, with standard error of the subject mean shown. Middle: A similar effect is seen at 8cpd; data are replotted from Figure 12. Bottom: A very brief simultaneous presentation (50 ms) of oriented $1/f^{\alpha}$ noise and grating follows a horizontal effect pattern. Data are averaged across three subjects, with error plotted as above.

9.0. Conclusions

In sum, research reviewed in the current chapter indicates that in the context of broadband content such as in natural scenes, oblique content is most salient and most visible to human observers, while horizontal content is least so. This "horizontal effect" anisotropy was shown to persist when tested with stimuli containing many different types of natural structural biases, clearly demonstrating that the effect itself must be an inherent property of the visual system. Our work suggests that this orientation bias stems from a contrast gain control process such as demonstrated to occur in neurons in early visual cortex. However, the modeling of this anisotropy in a gain-control context suggests that the gain control pooling must be local and anisotropic, emphasizing activity in similarly-tuned units and within the same part of the visual field (as within a hypercolumn). This horizontal effect of visual performance matches, inversely, the bias of oriented content in typical natural scenes (i.e., most content near horizontal and the least at oblique orientations), We propose that the anisotropy of gain control serves the ecological role of discounting the structure typically prevalent in the 'background' and thereby making novel content in a scene relatively more salient. We also note the efficiency of such a neural whitening of the natural visual world for brain encoding.

Acknowledgement

This research was supported by grants #N00014-99-1-0516 and #N00014-03-1-0224 from the Office of Naval Research, and by grants from the Kentucky Space Grant Consortium – NASA EPSCOR.

References

Annis, R.C. and Frost, B. (1973). Human visual ecology and orientation anisotropies in acuity. *Science*, 182, 729-731.

Appelle, S. (1972). Perception and discrimination as a function of stimulus orientation: The oblique effect in man and animals. *Psychological Bulletin*, 78, 266-278.

Baddeley, R.J. and Hancock, P.J.B. (1991). A statistical analysis of natural images matches psychophysically derived orientation tuning curves. *Proceedings of the Royal Society of London B*, 246, 219-223.

Baddeley, R.J. (1997). The correlational structure of natural images and the calibration of spatial representations. *Cognitive Science*, 21, 351-372.

Bex, P. J., Mareschal, I., and Dakin, S. C. (2007). Contrast gain control in natural scenes. *Journal of Vision*, 7, 1-12.

Billock, V.A. (2000). Neural acclimation to 1/f spatial frequency spectra in natural images transduced by the human visual system. *Physica D*, 137, 379–391.

Blake, R. and Holopigian, K. (1985). Orientation selectivity in cats and humans assessed by masking. *Vision Research*, 25, 1459-1468.

Bonds, A.B. (1989). Role of inhibition in the specification of orientation selectivity of cells in the cat striate cortex. *Visual Neuroscience*, 2, 41-55.

Bonds, A.B. (1991). Temporal dynamics of contrast gain in single cells of the cat striate cortex. *Visual Neuroscience*, 6, 239-255.

Bracewell, R.N. (2000). The fourier transform and its applications. McGraw-Hill Companies, Boston.

Burton, G.J. and Moorhead, I.R. (1987). Color and spatial structure in natural scenes. *Applied Optics*, 26, 157-170.

Campbell, F.W., Kulikowski, J.J., and Levinson, J.Z. (1967). The effect of orientation on the visual resolution of gratings. *Journal of Physiology*, 187, 427-436.

Carandini, M. and Heeger, D.J. (1994). Summation and division in primate visual cortex. *Science*, 264, 1333-1336.

Chapman, B., Stryker, M.P., and Bonhoeffer, T. (1996). Development of orientation preference maps in ferret primary visual cortex. *The Journal of Neuroscience*, 16, 6443-6453.

Chapman, B., and Bonhoeffer, T. (1998). Overrepresentation of horizontal and vertical orientation preferences in developing ferret area 17. *Neurobiology*, 95, 2609-2614.

Coppola, D.M., Purves, H.R., McCoy, A.N., and Purves, D. (1998). The distribution of oriented contours in the real world. *Proceedings of the National Academy of Sciences USA*, 95, 4002-4006.

Coppola, D.M., White, L.E., Fitzpatrick, D., and Purves, D. (1998). Unequal representation of cardinal and oblique contours in ferret visual cortex. *Proceedings of the National Academy of Sciences USA*, 95, 2621-2623.

Craven, B.J. (1993). Orientation dependence of human line-length judgments matches statistical structure in real-world scenes. *Proceedings of the Royal Society of London*, 253, 101-106.

De Valois, R.L., Yund, E.W., and Hepler, N. (1982). The orientation and direction selectivity of cells in macaque visual cortex. *Vision Research*, 22, 531-544.

Dong, D.W.,and Atick, J. J. (1995). Statistics of time-varying images. *Network: Computation in Neural Systems*, 6, 345–358.

Essock, E.A. (1980). The oblique effect of stimulus identification considered with respect to two classes of oblique effects. *Perception*, 9, 37-46.

Essock, E. A. (1982). Anisotropies of perceived contrast and detection speed. *Vision Research*, 22, 1185–1191.

Essock, E. A., Krebs, W. K., and Prather, J. R. (1997). Superior sensitivity for tactile stimuli oriented proximal-distally on the finger: Implications of mixed Class 1 and Class 2 anisotropies. *Journal of Experimental Psychology: Human Perception and Performance*, 23, 515–527.

Essock, E.A., DeFord, J.K., Hansen, B.C., and Sinai, M.J. (2003). Oblique stimuli are seen best (not worst!) in naturalistic broad-band stimuli: A horizontal effect. *Vision Research*, 43, 1329-1335.

Essock, E.A., Haun, A.M., and Kim, Y-J. (2008). An Anisotropy of orientation-tuned suppression that matches the anisotropy of typical natural scenes. (under review).

Field, D.J. (1987). Relations between the statistics of natural images and the response properties of cortical cells. *Journal of the Optical Society of America A*, 4, 2379-2394.

Field, D. J. (1993). Scale-invariance and self-similar 'wavelet' transforms: An analysis of natural scenes and mammalian visual systems. In M. Farge, J. C. R. Hunt, and J. C. Vassilicos (Eds.), *Wavelets, Fractals and Fourier Transforms: New Developments and New Applications*. Oxford University Press.

Field, D.J. and Brady, N. (1997). Visual sensitivity, blur and the sources of variability in the amplitude spectra of natural scenes. *Vision Research*, 37, 3367-3383.

Foley, J.M. (1994). Human luminance pattern-vision mechanisms – masking experiments require a new model. *Journal of the Optical Society of America A*, 11, 1710-1719.

Furmanski, C.S. and Engel, S.A. (2000). An oblique effect in human primary visual cortex. *Nature Neuroscience*, 3, 535-536.

Geisler, W.S. and Albrecht, D.G. (1992). Cortical-neurons-isolation of contrast gain control. *Vision Research*, 32, 1409-1410.

Hancock, P.J.B., Baddeley, R.J., and Smith, L.S. (1992). The principle components of natural images. *Network: Computation in Neural Systems*, 3, 61-70.

Hansen, B.C., Essock, E.A., Zheng, Y., and DeFord, J.K. (2003). Perceptual anisotropies in visual processing and their relation to natural image statistics. *Network: Computation in Neural Systems*, 14, 501-526.

Hansen, B.C. and Essock, E.A. (2004). A horizontal bias in human visual processing of orientation and its correspondence to the structural components of natural scenes. *Journal of Vision*, 4, 1044-1060.

Hansen, B.C. and Essock, E.A. (2005). Influence of scale and orientation on the visual perception of natural scenes. *Visual Cognition*, 12, 1199-1234.

Hansen, B.C. and Essock, E.A. (2006). Anisotropic local contrast normalization: The role of stimulus orientation and spatial frequency bandwidths in the oblique and horizontal effect perceptual anisotropies. *Vision Research*, 46, 4398-4415.

Hansen, B.C. and Hess, R.F. (2006). Discrimination of amplitude spectrum slope in the fovea and parafovea and the local amplitude distributions of natural scene imagery. *Journal of Vision*, 6, 696-711.

Hansen, B.C. and Hess, R.F. (2007). Structural sparseness and spatial phase alignment in natural scenes. *Journal of the Optical Society of America A*, 24, 1873-1885.

Heeger, D.J. (1992). Normalization of cell responses in cat striate cortex. *Visual Neuroscience*, 9, 181-197.

Henning, G.B. and Wichmann, F.A. (2007). Some observations on the pedestal effect. *Journal of Vision*, 7, 1-15.

Huang, L.Q. and Dobkins, K.R. (2005). Attentional effects on contrast discrimination in humans: evidence for both contrast gain and response gain. *Vision Research*, 45, 1201-1212.

Keil, M.S. and Cristóbal, G. (2000). Separating the chaff from the wheat: Possible origins of the oblique effect. *Journal of the Optical Society of America A*, 17, 697-710.

Knill, D.C., Field, D.J., and Kersten, D. (1990). Human discrimination of fractal images. *Journal of the Optical Society of America*, 7, 1113-1123.

Kretzmer, E. R. (1952). The statistics of television signals. *Bell System Technical Journal*, 31, 751–763.

Lashley, K.S. (1938). The mechanisms of vision: Xv. preliminary studies of the rat's capacity for detail vision. *Journal of General Psychology*, 18, 123-193.

Legge, G.E. and Foley, J.M. (1980). Contrast masking in human vision. *Journal of the Optical Society of America A*, 70, 1458-1471.

Li, B., Peterson, M. R., and Freeman, R. D. (2003). Oblique effect: A neural bias in the visual cortex. *Journal of Neurophysiology*, 90, 204-217.

Li, Z. (1999). Visual segmentation by contextual influences via intra-cortical interactions in the primary visual cortex. *Network: Computation and Neural Systems*, 10, 187-212.

Maffei, L. and Campbell, F.W. (1970). Neurophysiological localization of the vertical and horizontal visual coordinates in man. *Science*, 187, 386-387.

Mansfield, R.J.W. (1974). Neural basis of orientation perception in primate vision. *Science*, 186, 1133-1135.

Mansfield, R.J.W. and Ronner, S.P. (1978). Orientation anisotropy in monkey visual cortex. *Brian Research*, 149, 229-234.

Meese, T.S. and Holmes, D.J. (2002). Adaptation and gain pool summation: alternative models and masking data. *Vision Research*, 42, 1113-1125.

Meese, T.S. and Hess, R.F. (2004). Low spatial frequencies are suppressively masked across spatial scale, orientation, field position, and eye of origin. *Journal of Vision*, 4, 843-859.

Meese, T.S. and Holmes, D.J. (2007). Spatial and temporal dependencies of cross-orientation suppression in human vision. *Proceedings of the Royal Society B: Biological Sciences*, 274, 127-136.

Meese, T.S., Summers, R.J., Holmes, D.J., and Wallis, S.A. (2007). Contextual modulation involves suppression and facilitation from the center and the surround. *Journal of Vision*, 7, 1-21.

Oliva, A. and Torralba, A. (2001). Modeling the shape of the scene: A holistic representation of the spatial envelope. *International Journal of Computer Vision*, 42, 145-175.

Orban, G.A. and Kennedy, H. (1980). Evidence for meridional anisotropies in orientation selectivity of visual cortical neurons. Archives Internationales de Physiologie et de Biochimie, 88, 13-14.

Párraga, C.A. and Tolhurst, D.J. (2000). The effect of contrast randomization on the discrimination of changes in the slopes of the amplitude spectra of natural scenes. *Perception*, 29, 1101-1116.

Párraga, C.A., Troscianko, T., and Tolhurst, D. J. (2000). The human visual system is optimized for processing the spatial information in natural visual images. *Current Biology*, 10, 35–38.

Párraga, C.A., Troscianko, T., and Tolhurst, D. J. (2005). The effects of amplitude–spectrum statistics on foveal and peripheral discrimination of changes in natural images and a multi-resolution model. *Vision Research*, 45, 3145–3168.

Petrov, Y., Carandini, M., and McKee, S. (2005). Two distinct mechanisms of suppression in human vision. *Journal of Neuroscience*, 25, 8704-8707.

Phillips, G.C. and Wilson, H.R . (1984). Orientation bandwidths of spatial mechanisms measured by masking. *Journal of the Optical Society of America A*, 1, 226-232.

Ross, H.E., and Woodhouse, J.M. (1979). Genetic and environmental factors in orientation anisotropy-field-study in the british-isles. *Perception*, 8, 507-521.

Ruderman, D.L., and Bialek, W. (1994). Statistics of natural images: Scaling in the woods. *Physical Review Letters*, 73, 814–817.

Schwartz, O. and Simoncelli, E.P. (2001). Natural signal statistics and sensory gain control. *Nature Neuroscience*, 4, 819–825.

Shapley, R. and Lennie, P. (1985). Spatial frequency analysis in the visual system. *Annual Review of Neuroscience*, 8, 547-583.

Sokol, S., Moskowitz, A., and Hansen, V. (1989). Evoked potential and preferential looking correlates of the oblique effect in 3-month-old infants. *Documenta Opthalmologica*, 71, 321-328.

Switkes, E., Mayer, M.J., and Sloan, J.A. (1978). Spatial frequency analysis of the visual environment: Anisotropy and the carpentered environment hypothesis. *Vision Research*, 18, 1393-1399.

Tadmor, Y. and Tolhurst, D.J. (1994). Discrimination of changes in the second-order statistics of natural and synthetic images. *Vision Research*, 34, 541-554.

Thomson, M.G.A. and Foster, D.H. (1997). Role of second- and third-order statistics in the discriminability of natural images. *Journal of the Optical Society of America A*, 14, 2081-2090.

Thomson, M.G.A. (1999). Higher-order structure in natural scenes. *Journal of the Optical Society of America A*, 16, 1549-1553.

Thomson, M.G.A. (2001a). Sensory coding and the second spectra of natural signals. *Physical Review Letters*, 86, 2901-2904.

Thomson, M.G.A. (2001b). Beats, kurtosis and visual coding. *Network: Computation in Neural Systems*, 12, 271-287.

Tiao, Y-C. and Blakemore, C. (1976). Functional organization in the visual cortex of the golden hamster. *Journal of Comparative Neurology*, 168, 459-482.

Timney, B.N., and Muir, D.W. (1976). Orientation anisotropy: Incidence and magnitude in caucasian and chinese subjects. *Science, 193*, 699-701.

Tolhurst, D.J., Tadmor, Y., and Chao, T. (1992). Amplitude spectra of natural images. *Ophthalmic and Physiological Optics*, 12, 229-232.

Tolhurst, D.J., and Tadmor, Y. (1997a). Band-limited contrast in natural images explains the detectability of changes in the amplitude spectra. *Vision Research*, 37, 3203–3215.

Tolhurst, D.J., and Tadmor, Y. (1997b). Discrimination of changes in the slopes of the amplitude spectra of natural images: Band-limited contrast and psychometric functions. *Perception*, 26, 1011–1025.

Tolhurst, D.J. and Tadmor, Y. (2000). Discrimination of spectrally blended natural images: Optimization of the human visual system for encoding natural images. *Perception*, 29, 1087-1100.

Torralba, A. and Oliva, A. (2003). Statistics of natural image categories. *Network: Computation in Neural Systems*, 14, 391-412.

van der Schaaf, A. and van Hateren, J.H. (1996). Modeling the power spectra of natural images: Statistics and Information. *Vision Research*, 36, 2759-2770.

van Hateren, J.H. and van der Schaaf, A. (1998). Independent component filters of natural images compared with simple cells in primary visual cortex. *Proceedings of the Royal society of London: B*, 265, 359-366.

Wainwright, M.J., Schwartz, O. and Simoncelli, E.P. (2001). Natural image statistics and divisive normalization: modeling nonlinearities and adaptation in cortical neurons In R. Rao, B. Olshausen and M. Lewicki (Eds.) *Probabilistic Models of the Brain: Perception and Neural Function*, Cambridge, MA: MIT Press.

Webster, M.A. and Miyahara, E. (1997). Contrast adaptation on the spatial structure of natural images. *Journal of the Optical Society of America A*, 14, 2355-2366.

Wilson, H.R. and Humanski, R. (1993). Spatial frequency adaptation and contrast gain control. *Vision Research*, 33, 1133-1149.

Yu, H-B. and Shou, T-D. (2000). The oblique effect revealed by optical imaging in primary visual cortex of cats. *Acta Physiologica Sinica*, 52, 431-434.

Zemon, V., Gutowski, W., and Horton, T. (1983). Orientational anisotropy in the human visual system: An evoked potential and psychophysical study. *International Journal of Neuroscience*, 19, 259-286.

In: Visual Cortex: New Research
Editors: T. A. Portocello and R. B. Velloti

ISBN 978-1-60456-530-0
© 2008 Nova Science Publishers, Inc.

Chapter 4

LARGE- AND SMALL-SCALE FUNCTIONAL ORGANIZATION OF VISUAL FIELD REPRESENTATION IN THE HUMAN VISUAL CORTEX

Hiroki Yamamoto[1], Hiroshi Ban[1,2], Masaki Fukunaga[3], Chuzo Tanaka[4], Masahiro Umeda[3] and Yoshimichi Ejima[5]*

[1]Department of Human Coexistence, Graduate School of Human and Environmental Studies, Kyoto University, Kyoto, Japan
[2]KOKORO Research Center, Kyoto University, Kyoto, Japan
[3]Department of Medical Informatics,
Meiji University of Oriental Medicine, Kyoto, Japan
[4]Department of Neurosurgery, Meiji University of Oriental Medicine, Kyoto, Japan
[5]Kyoto Institute of Technology, Kyoto, Japan

Abstract

A fundamental characteristic of the human visual cortex is its retinotopic organization. Taking advantage of the systematic association between cortical position and visual field position, many important aspects of visual processing have been revealed by functional brain imaging. We have investigated, visualized, and characterized retinotopic organization using fMRI, in conjunction with several novel methods of analysis. In this chapter, we describe the methodology used and present findings on the basic functional organization of the visual cortex from two interlocking large- and small-scale perspectives. By larger-scale analyses of retinotopic organization, we have been able to delineate hierarchically organized visual areas (V1, V2, V3, V3A, V3B, V4v, V8, LOc, and MT+) for ten hemispheres and investigated their individual variability in size and location using a probabilistic approach, in which probability maps of the visual areas were created. With smaller-scale analyses of retinotopy, we obtained two basic factors of visual field representation within each area (cortical magnification factor and average receptive field size), and with these factors estimated the cortical point spread of fMRI activity. We found that point spread is nearly constant across eccentricities and

* Correspondence to: Dr. Hiroki Yamamoto. Department of Human Coexistence, Graduate School of Human and Environmental Studies, Kyoto University, Yoshida Nihonmatsu-cho, Sakyo-ku, Kyoto 606-8501, Japan, E-mail: yamamoto@cv.jinkan.kyoto-u.ac.jp, Tel: +81-75-753-2978; Fax: +81-75-753-6574

increases as one ascends the visual cortical hierarchy. Knowledge of retinotopic organization is important not only in itself; it also provides essential information for analysis and interpretation of functional activity in visual cortex. As representative examples, we present our recent findings on visual functions involving contextual effects. The present findings on the large- and small-scale functional organization of the human visual cortex shed new light on the relationship between functional segregation and cortical processing hierarchy in the visual system.

Keywords: retinotopy, probabilistic atlas, magnification factor, point spread, contextual effects, fMRI.

1. Introduction

Functional brain imaging, including positron emission tomography (PET) and functional magnetic resonance imaging (fMRI), provides strong clues to understanding the functional organization of the human visual cortex. Although this understanding is far from complete, recent advances in imaging technology have enabled investigation of brain functional activity at mm-order resolution across the cortical surface [1] and thereby yielded detailed maps of the functions of its many zones [2, 3].

Over the last decade or two, brain mapping studies of human visual cortex have revealed two major principles of its functional organization. The first is organization with respect to visual categories. Following the discovery of the color center, exhibiting high selectivity for color [4], multiple zones, seemingly specialized for representing different visual attributes such as color, shape, face, and motion, have been found within occipito-temporal cortex [3, 5-7]. The demonstration of such functional specialization has been one major criterion for defining high-level visual areas dedicated to the processing of specific visual categories.

The second principle is organization with respect to the retinal and visual field positions being represented. Visual neurons respond only to stimuli located in a finite region of the visual field known as the classical receptive field (RF). In many parts of the visual cortex, the RF centers of neurons all point to the same location in visual space with some scatter if they reside at the same cortical location, and RF center position gradually shifts over the cortex [8, 9]. This systematic association between cortical position and visual field position is termed retinotopy. Like functional specialization, evidence for a single complete retinotopic representation of the entire visual field has been an important criterion for defining a visual area [10, 11].

The present paper focuses on the second organizational principle of retinotopy in the human visual cortex. We describe our findings on retinotopic organization along with two interlocking large- and small-scale perspectives, placing special emphasis on experimental techniques and analysis. By larger- scale analyses of retinotopic organization, we have delineated multiple visual areas and investigated their individual variability in size and location using a probabilistic approach. With smaller-scale analyses of retinotopy, we have obtained two basic factors of visual field representation (cortical magnification factor and average receptive field size), and from these factors estimated the cortical point spread of fMRI activity. Knowledge of retinotopic organization is important not only in itself; it also provides essential information for analysis and interpretation of functional activity in visual cortex. As representative examples, we present our recent findings on visual functions involving visual contextual effects. Unless mentioned otherwise, the analyses described in this chapter were performed and visualized using in-house software [12, 13] written in VTK (Kitware, Clifton Park, NY) and MATLAB (Mathworks, Natick, MA).

2. Retinotopic Organization of Human Visual Cortex

Polar Coordinate Representation of the Visual Field

We have measured retinotopic organization with fMRI [14-18] using a phase-encoding technique in which receptive field centers are temporally coded using polar coordinates [19]. An overview of the method and results for the region that surrounds the right calcarine sulcus are presented in Figure 1. Eccentricity and polar angle were measured by performance of fMRI while the subject viewed a checkered annulus that expanded from the fovea to 16° peripherally (Figure 1A) or a wedge-shaped checkered pattern rotated around the fixation point (Figure 1B), respectively. Each stimulus was presented repeatedly with a 60s period, evoking a periodic response at a given point on retinotopic cortex, whose corresponding position in the visual field was encoded in the phase of its 60s periodic component and thus could be estimated using Fourier analysis (Figure 1C, D). Comparison of Figure 1C and D

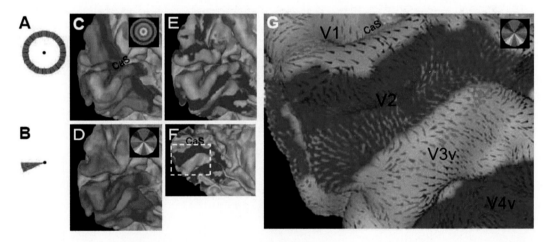

Figure 1. Phase-encoding method for measurements of retinotopy. (A) The thin (2 °) annulus expanded from the fovea to 16° periphery repeatedly with a 60s period in the eccentricity mapping experiment. (B) The wedge (24°) rotated around the fixation point repeatedly with a 60s period. (C) The eccentricity map around the calcarine sulcus. The color overlay on the cortex indicates the preferred stimulus eccentricity at each cortical point, in accordance with the color code in the upper right. (D) The polar angle map, presented in the same format as C. (E) Field sign map. The yellow region indicates the mirror image representation, while the blue indicates the non-mirror image. (F) Field sign map for the region ventral to the calcarine sulcus. (G) Zoom-in of F. Each triangular glyph represents the direction of the gradient at the point in the polar angle map, the colors of which code polar angle as in D. Note that the directions of the gradients reverse at the border of the mirror/non-mirror representation.

shows that the eccentricity and polar angle of the visual field are represented systematically in orthogonal maps around the calcarine sulcus. Figure 1C shows that the posterior part represents central vision and the more anterior part peripheral vision. Figure 1D shows that the regions dorsal and ventral to the calcarine sulcus, respectively, represent the lower and upper contralateral quadrants of the visual field. Notably, the quarter-field representation is duplicated along the dorsal-ventral axis and adjacent pairs mirror each other. Mirror-imageduplication can be assessed using the visual field sign [20], defined as the sign of the cross-product of the gradients of the polar angle and eccentricity maps (Figure 1E-G). For details of the procedure, see Appendix A for the imaging method and Appendix B for the phase-encoding technique.

Layout of Areas

Figure 2 displays the retinotopic organization measured with the phase-encoding method for the entire visual cortex in inflated format. Based on the global pattern of retinotopy, we identified multiple retinotopic areas as possessing at least eccentricity maps. The polar angle map (Figure 2A, C) allowed us to reliably identify the borders V1v(d)/V2v(d), V2v(d)/V3v(d), V3d/V3A, and V3A/V7 as reversals in the polar angle and field sign map (Figure 2I, L). The foveal representations of V3A and V7 were displaced superiorly with the confluent foveal representation of areas V1, V2, and V3 (Figure 2E, G) [21]. As in other studies [22], the borders of other visual areas were placed with less certainty, since their angle maps were not clear. We designated the region just anterior to V3d as V3B [23], whose peripheral representation appeared to be located just inferior to the V3A foveal representation. We identified the region within the dorsal posterior limb of the inferior temporal sulcus as MT+, which featured a crude eccentricity map with a predominance of foveal representation inferiorly and peripheral representation superiorly [24]. We confirmed that this region mostly overlapped the middle temporal region, exhibiting a strong response to motion stimuli (Figure 2K, N). We refer to the large fan-shaped region between areas V3B and MT+ as LOc [25], which had a relatively clear eccentricity representation in the superior anterior direction from the confluent foveal representation [26, 27].

An enduring dispute exists regarding subdivision of the ventral occipital cortex anterior to V3v [10, 11, 22, 28, 29]. Here, we identified two areas, V4v and V8, after Hadjikhani et al. (1998)[30], stressing consistency not in the angle but in the eccentricity map of our data. Firstly, area V8 was determined as the small posterior region of the fusiform gyrus, which featured an eccentricity map with foveal representation anteriorly and peripheral representation posteriorly (Figure 2F, H), which roughly corresponds to the anterior part of hV4 (human V4) and the posterior part of VO (ventral occipital) [22, 31, 32]. Then, area V4v was determined as the region from the V3v/V4v border to the anterior limit of V8 (Figure 2B, D), which exhibited mirror-image representation (Figure 2I, L) and roughly corresponded to the posterior half of hV4 [31, 33, 34]. Notably, the entire region enclosing areas V4v and V8 has a simple angular map spanning the entire hemifield (Figure 2B, D), suggesting a single area instead of the two separated areas delineated here. However, if the hemifield region was defined as proposed in the definition of hV4, the region would have dual representations of eccentricity dimension (Figure 2F, H), resulting in loss of consistency in the eccentricity map.

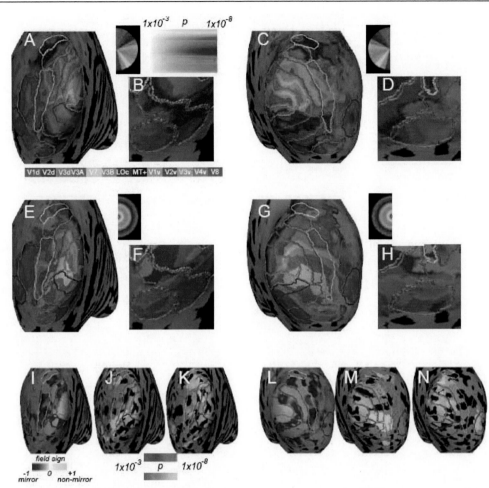

Figure 2. Locations of retinotopic areas, V1d/v, V2d/v, V3d/v, V3A, V3B, V7, V4v, V8, LOc, and MT+, in one subject's (S1) hemispheres and their relation to visual field representation (up to 16□ eccentricities) and motion-responsive regions of visual cortex. Information for the left and right hemispheres is shown in the left- and right-half regions of the figure, respectively. The colored lines on the inflated cortices indicate each area's border in accordance with the color code below A and B. (A, B, C, and D) Angular visual field representation measured by the phase-encoding retinotopy experiment. A and C display all data for visual cortex, while B and D zoom in on the posterior ventral region to better visualize the angular representation near areas V4v and V8. The color overlay on the cortex indicates the preferred stimulus angle at each cortical point, in accordance with the color code to the right of A or C. The more saturated the color, the higher the statistical significance of retinotopic activity, as shown in the rainbow-like color bar. (E, F, G, and H) Eccentricity visual field representation measured by the phase-encoding retinotopy experiment. Data are presented in the same format as in A, B, C, and D. (I and L) Field sign map computed from the angular and eccentricity maps. The blue code indicates mirror-image representation, while the yellow code indicates non-mirror-image representation. The greater the saturation of color, the stronger the degree of the mirror- or non-mirror-image (see the color bar on the bottom). (J and M) Foveal or peripheral representation measured by the experiment using the standard block paradigm. The yellow region indicates fMRI activity evoked by foveal stimulation, while the blue region indicates activity evoked by peripheral (16 °) stimulation (see the color bar on the bottom). (K and N). Motion-sensitive regions. The yellow region indicates fMRI activity evoked by expanding motion of a low-contrast concentric grating (see the color bar on the bottom).

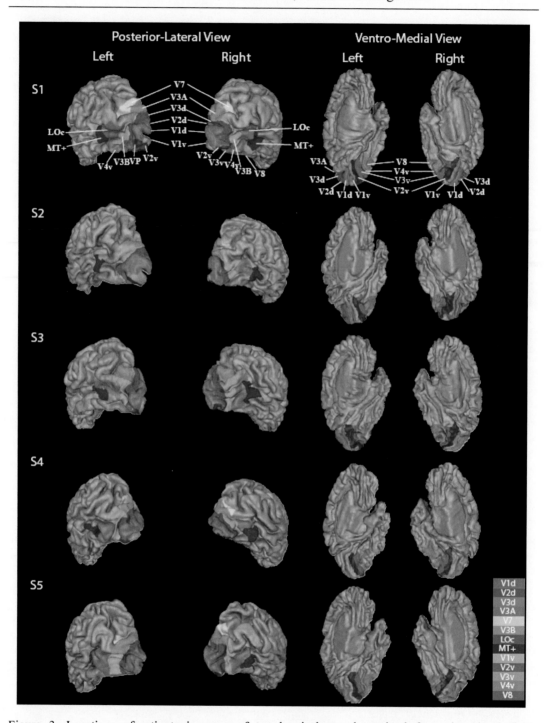

Figure 3. Locations of retinotopic areas of ten hemispheres determined from the visual field representation (e.g., Fig. 2). The five different rows show the layout of the areas from the five different subjects. The left two panels show the layout in the left and right visual cortex from a posterior lateral view (left), while the right two panels show them from a ventro-medial view. The icon on the bottom right indicates the relationship between color and visual areas.

Table 1. Talairach coordinates of visual areas

	Center of mass		
	X	Y	Z
V1d	8(2)	-91(4)	8(5)
V2d	13(4)	-95(3)	12(4)
V3d	18(4)	-92(3)	14(3)
V3A	17(5)	-87(3)	26(4)
V7	23(5)	-80(3)	28(5)
V3B	29(3)	-89(3)	9(4)
LOc	39(4)	-81(4)	7(4)
MT+	45(3)	-70(4)	4(4)
V1v	7(2)	-83(4)	3(4)
V2v	12(3)	-81(4)	-2(4)
V3v	19(3)	-78(4)	-4(3)
V4v	25(2)	-74(3)	-6(2)
V8	33(3)	-69(5)	-10(2)

Talairach coordinates specifying the center of mass of each area are listed. The columns labeled "Center of mass" show mean values (±SD) of the coordinates for ten hemispheres from five subjects.

Notably, along with localized areas, human visual cortex should contain retinotopic areas. For example, areas LOc and MT+ have been further subdivided (24, 26). New retinotopic areas have been reported just outside the zone defined here [31, 35-37].

Locations of Visual Areas in Talairach Space

We evaluated interindividual variability in Talairach space with respect to the position of a particular visual area, based on its center of mass (CM) [14]. Specifically, we began with the reconstruction of 10 cortical surfaces of both hemispheres from five subjects' anatomical scans (for details, see Appendix C). Next, we localized visual areas on each surface by the procedure described above. Figure 3 displays the locations of the areas on each of the ten reconstructed surfaces. Finally, the surface representation of each area was converted to a volumetric representation assuming that the cortical gray matter was 3 mm thick, and normalized into Talairach space by means of linear transformation (translation, rotation, and scaling) (for details, see Appendix D).

For each visual area, we computed the CM of its volumetric representations for 10 hemispheres in Talairach space. There was high intersubject variability in the CM for all visual areas (Table 1). The standard deviations of the X, Y, and Z coordinates of the CM ranged from 2 to 5 mm (mean, 3 mm), 3 to 5 mm (mean, 4 mm), and 2 to 5 mm (mean, 4 mm), respectively. These values were comparable to or greater than the thickness of the cortical gray matter, implying small overlaps between volumetric area representations from different hemispheres and thus the possibility of large inconsistencies between hemispheres in Talairach space.

The finding of ~4mm SD agrees well with previously reported values measured using various methods. In a positron emission tomography study (38), the average SD across areas other than V7, LOc, and V8 was 5 mm. In a cytoarchitectonic study [39], the average SD across V1 and V2 was 4 mm. In an fMRI study [40], in which the representative point was not the CM but the cortical point representing 12° eccentricity along the horizontal meridian, the average SD across V1 and the V2/V3 border was 6 mm.

Maximum Probability Maps

Although CM analysis suggests large positional inconsistency of visual areas in Talairach space, this analysis is limited in that evaluation is conducted using only one reference point of the volumetric area representation.

To examine potential inconsistency more directly and thoroughly, we created a 3D probability map of the visual areas, in which each voxel was associated with probabilities of occurrence for each of the areas [14, 15, 41-43]. The probability that a particular area was located there was determined for each voxel (1-mm cube) in Talairach space by assessing the frequency with which the volumetric representation of that area resided at each voxel across the ten hemispheres (for details, see Appendix D.).

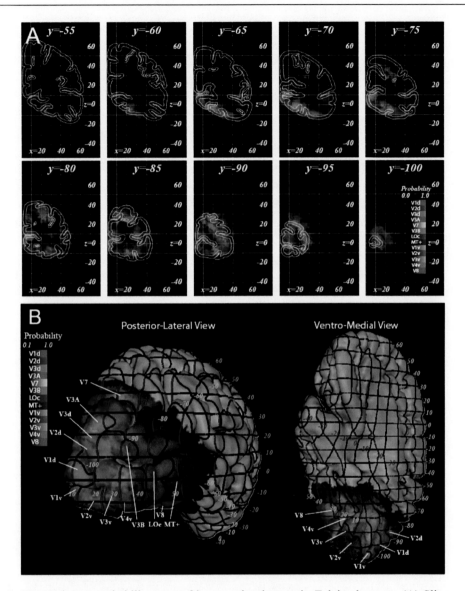

Figure 4. 3D maximum probability map of human visual areas in Talairach space. (A) Slice maps of visual areas V1d/v, V2d/v, V3d/v, V3A, V3B, V7, V4v, V8, LOc, and MT+ in Talairach space on serial coronal sections. The visual area with the most occurrences and its probability of occurrence (i.e., maximum probability) for each voxel are color-coded using 13 different colors and 10 brightness levels, respectively (see the color bar in the lower right-most panel), and are superimposed on the outline drawing of the Talairach brain showing the cortical gray matter. The probability of occurrence of a given area was calculated by dividing the number of overlapping hemispheres by the total number (n = 10) of samples, all of which were aligned into Talairach space using global linear transformations (translation, scaling, and rotation). The maximum value of the probability obtained across all voxels was 0.8. (B) Surface representation of the 3D maximum probability map of the areas from two different views. The visual area with the most occurrences and the maximum probability at the nearest neighbor voxel in Talairach space are color-coded on the Talairach brain surface running midway between the outlines of the cortical gray matter depicted in A. The color codes (see the color bar on the upper left) are the same as in A. The red, green, and blue lines on the surface indicate X, Y, and Z Talairach coordinates, respectively.

Since it is difficult to display all such multivariate volume data in only two dimensions, only essential data are graphically presented in Figure 4A and 4B in the form of a maximum probability map, in which each point has been color-coded according to the visual area that resided there with the greatest frequency (the maximum probability area) and brightness represents the probability that that area resides at that voxel. Regions of maximal consistency are shown with maximal brightness, while regions with minimal consistency are shown with minimal brightness. Figure 4A displays this information using the same coronal serial slices as the 1988 atlas of Talairach and Tournoux (1988), overlaid on the Talairach brain, the gray matter of which is outlined using white lines. The maximum probability area changes within the slices in the same hierarchical order as in individual hemispheres. This topographic pattern is clearly illustrated in Figure 4B, which shows the maximum probability map overlaid on the surface representation of the Talairach brain. Topographic preservation can be confirmed, except for the island-like V3 regions within V3B, by comparing the probabilistic map with the individual maps (Figure 3).

In contrast to the almost complete preservation of the topographic relations of the maximum probability areas, the probability maps of corresponding areas revealed substantial inconsistency. As can be seen to some extent in Figure 4A, the probabilistic volume for a corresponding area is rarefied and blurred so strongly that its extent is much wider than the thickness of the cortical gray matter. The strength of this tendency appears to vary among the visual areas, being strongest for area V7.

3. Retinotopic Organization within Visual Areas

As noted above, visual signal from the retina is locally processed in the visual areas with preservation of retinotopy. The basic question regarding such topographic processing concerns the possibility of its anisotropy across the retinotopic cortex, especially as regards the retinal eccentricity dimension. Since the central retina features a one- to two-thousand-fold higher density of retinal cones and ganglion cells than peripheral retina [44] and thus contains much fine-grained visual information, foveal and parafoveal signals are undoubtedly analyzed extensively in higher resolution. Indeed, such center-weighted analysis has been demonstrated physiologically in monkey visual cortex. The area of V1 devoted to representation of the central retina is much larger than that to peripheral retinal [8, 45, 46]; this is referred to as cortical magnification of central vision [47]. In addition, V1 neurons contributing to central vision have smaller receptive fields (RFs) than do those contributing to peripheral vision [48].

We investigated the cortical magnification and receptive field size of human lower areas across the cortex along the eccentricity dimension, by reanalyzing fMRI time series in the expanding annulus experiments. The analysis was performed not with the response phase mapping method but with a more elaborate method which took account of possible variations in waveform along the eccentricity dimension. This is illustrated with V3 as an example in Figure 5.

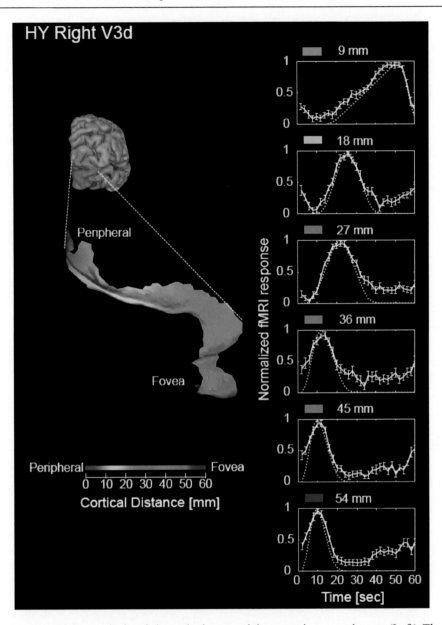

Figure 5. Isoeccentricity analysis of the retinal eccentricity mapping experiment. (Left) The cortical surface of V3 isolated from the right hemisphere of one subject. The color overlay on the cortex indicates the cortical distance measured from the superior edge representing 16°, in accordance with the color code at the bottom of the surface. Cortical bands of identical colors thus represent the same eccentricities. (Right) Each panel show one cycle of fMRI time-series (average of repeats) at each isoeccentricity band, when a checkered annulus expanded repeatedly from the central to peripheral visual field with a period of 60 s. Retinal eccentricity increases from bottom to top panels. Error bars denote SE across 5 subjects. The dotted smooth lines are the best fits obtained with a two-stage linear model (see the text).

Using a method we term isoeccentricity analysis (Appendix E) [49], we first divided the areal cortical surface into isoeccentricity bands based on the cortical distance from the peripheral 16° contour in the superior region of the area as shown in Figure 5 on the left, and then separately pooled the fMRI responses evoked from different isoeccentricity bands. The right panels of Figure 5 compare the pooled fMRI time-series across the bands. As expected, fMRI activity progressed from inferior to superior as the stimulus ring moved from foveal to peripheral vision. Two important points should be noted concerning this finding. First, the peak of the waveform progressed more slowly across the fovea and parafoveal regions than the peripheral region, indicating that the RF centers of neurons representing the central visual field shift slowly, indicating higher cortical magnification for central vision. Second, the shape of the waveform changed markedly from peaked to broad with increasing eccentricity, indicating larger RF size for peripheral vision.

To obtain quantitative estimates of these RF characteristics, we constructed a two-stage linear model of the fMRI response, in which neuronal activation was first determined by spatial summation of the stimulus within a RF model, and it was then mapped onto the fMRI response via convolution with a hemodynamic impulse response [50]. The RF model has two parameters, RF center and size, and its sensitivity profile is approximately linear. The appropriate model parameters were then determined by a grid search technique. This procedure yielded good fit for the data, as shown in the right panels of Figure 5 (solid lines), and two reliable parameters, RF center eccentricity and size, could be extracted for areas V1, V2, V3, V3A, VP, and V4v from ten hemispheres.

Cortical Magnification Factor

Figure 6A plots the estimated RF center eccentricity for each of the lower areas as a function of cortical distance relative to the 8° point for ten hemispheres from five subjects. Although the data are somewhat scattered, the plots clearly show cortical magnification and suggest an exponential or logarithmic mapping between cortical position x and RF eccentricity E, which is a standard model for primate retino-striate mapping [51, 52]. We therefore fitted the data with an exponential function

$$E(x) = -(8 + \sigma)\exp(x/A) - \sigma \tag{1}$$

where A and σ are constants. The data were fit well by the retino-cortical mapping function (smooth curves; least-squares fit, $R^2 = 0.77 \sim 0.85$). Table 2 shows the parameter values and their confidence intervals from the curve fits. No significant differences were found in two parameters among the areas. Superimposition of the mapping function also reveals no clear differences in the mapping functions among the areas, although small deviations from the others were demonstrated for V3A and V3v in the opposite directions (Figure 6B). The mean values of the parameters A and σ among the six areas were 22.9 (SD = 4.2) and 2.4 (SD = 1.2), respectively. A larger variance was obtained for σ mainly because we could not measure eccentricities near the fovea.

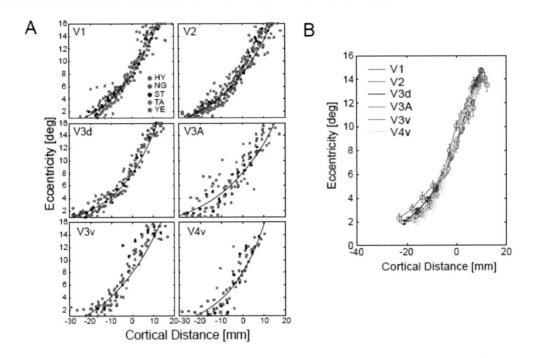

Figure 6. Retino-cortical mapping functions of human visual areas V1, V2, V3, V3A, VP, and V4v. (A) Each panel shows the visual field eccentricity of RF center in each area as a function of cortical position. The position is specified by the cortical distance from the point representing 8° eccentricity; negative and positive values indicate respectively more central and peripheral positions with respect to the origin. For each area, the mapping functions from 10 hemispheres were shifted to match at the origin. The smooth curves are the exponential functions (Eq. 1. in the text) that best fit the data. (B) Superposition of the mapping functions of different visual areas. Each symbol type represents the function for each visual area. Error bars denote SE across 5 subjects. For the data for A, cortical distances were grouped into bins and the average eccentricity within each bin was computed.

Based on the curve fits, a principal measure of retino-cortical mapping, called the cortical magnification factor and introduced by Daniel and Whitteridge (1961), can be computed. The magnification factor M is defined as the distance in cortex (in millimeters) dx devoted to representation of a step of 1° in visual field eccentricity dE and thus corresponds to the derivative of the inverse function of Eq. (1)

$$M(E) = \frac{dx}{dE} = \frac{A}{E + \sigma} \text{ [mm / deg]}. \tag{2}$$

Consequently, the cortical magnification factor M can be obtained using Eq. (2) from the two estimated parameters σ [deg] and A [mm]. Notice from Eq. (2) that foveal M is given by A/σ and thereby the parameter σ represents the visual field eccentricity at which M becomes half of the foveal value. The significance of the parameter A is made clear by rearranging Eq. (2) to

$$dx = A \frac{dE}{E + \sigma}. \qquad\qquad (3)$$

The quantity A is thus the cortical distance moved per percent change in eccentricity when the eccentricity E is much larger than the value of σ.

Table 2. Parameter estimates of retino-cortical mapping function

	A	σ
V1	22.6 (18.0, 27.2)	2.9 (0.9, 5.0)
V2	25.6 (21.6, 29.7)	3.0 (1.5, 4.5)
V3d	18.7 (16.3, 21.1)	0.9 (-0.1, 1.9)
V3A	26.0 (17.0, 35.0)	1.9 (-1.0, 4.9)
V3v	27.2 (18.0, 36.4)	4.3 (0.5, 8.2)
V4v	17.0 (10.6, 23.5)	1.5 (-1.5, 4.5)

The best fitted constants of Eq.1 and Eq. 2 and 95% confidence interval (in parentheses) are listed for each area.

By substituting the parameter estimates (Table 2) into Eq. (2), we could obtain the cortical magnification factor M and its reciprocal M^{-1} as a function of visual field eccentricity. Figures 7A and 7B show the relationship between M and M^{-1} and eccentricity for each of the six areas, respectively. The values for the fovea and 16° peripherally are given in Table 2. The value of M was ~1 mm/deg with M^{-1} of 40 - 60 min/mm in peripheral cortex, and increased by a factor of 5 - 20 to 6 - 21 mm/deg in foveal cortex, with M^{-1} of ~ 3 min/mm. In calculating foveal M using the average A and σ among the areas, we obtained a value of 9.5 mm/deg.

The cortical magnification factor of monkey visual cortex has been extensively studied by electrophysiological recording [8, 9, 45, 46]. For humans, several studies have estimated it using fMRI [17, 40, 53, 54], visual evoked potential recording [55], subdural electrode recording [56], lesion imaging [57], and psychophysical methods [58, 59]. Figure 7C and 7D compare our V1 data with those obtained by some of these studies. The cortical magnification factor M we measured is in the range obtained for monkeys and humans obtained with the various methods noted above. Among other studies, the present findings (Table 2) agree remarkably well with the fMRI study by Dougherty et al (2003)[40], who have, for example, estimated M = ~4 mm/deg at 3° in V1 and the parameters A and σ of the M function (Eq. 2) to be A ~= 20 – 30 mm and σ ~= 2.5 – 3.5 for areas V1, V2, and V3.

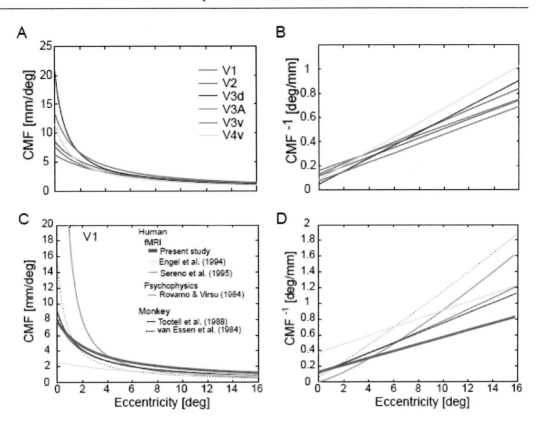

Figure 7. The relationship between cortical magnification factor M or its reciprocal M^{-1} and retinal eccentricity. (A) M in human V1, V2, V3, V3A, VP, and V4v as a function of eccentricity. This function is obtained by substituting the parameter estimates (Table 2) of the retino-cortical mapping model (Figure 5) into Eq. (2). Each symbol type represents the function of each visual area. (B) Similar plots for M^{-1} as in A. (C) Comparison of M in human and monkey V1 across studies. The red thick line displays the data from this study, compared with results for humans from fMRI studies of Engel et al. (1994) (19)and Sereno et al. (1995) (53)and from psychophysical experiments of Rovamo and Virsu (1984), as well as results for monkeys, including a C14-2 deoxy-D-glucose (2DG) uptake study by Tootell et al. (1988) (46)and the single-unit recording study by Van Essen et al. (1984)(45). The function of Engel et al. (1994) is based on the estimate by Beard et al. (1997)(58) using Engel et al.'s data. (D) Similar plots for M^{-1} as in C.

Receptive Field Size

Figure 8 plots estimated RF sizes for each of the six areas as a function of visual eccentricity, and highlights two important points. The first concerns the relation between RF size and eccentricity. For all of the areas, RF size monotonically increased by a factor of about 3 or more from 2° central to 14° peripheral visual field. The rate of increase was higher for areas V3A, VP, and V4v than for V1, V2, and V3. The second important point concerns the difference in absolute size between areas. In contrast to cortical magnification factor, there was a clear areal difference in RF size over the range of eccentricities. Importantly, RF became progressively larger with ascension of the visual cortical hierarchy from V1 to V4v.

The differences among V1, V2, and V3 were relatively small, and their RF sizes at 4° and 10° eccentricity were ~2° and ~6° in radius, respectively. The RF size of VP was larger by a factor of 1.5 – 2 than those of V1/V2/V3. The RF sizes of V3A and V4v were substantially larger than those of the lower areas, and approached 7° or more in radius at 4° in the paracentral visual field.

The enlargement of RF size with increase both in visual eccentricity and in the hierarchical level of visual areas is in line with the data reported for monkey visual areas [48]. For humans, there are two fMRI studies reporting such enlargement [60, 61], though these studies did not measure the absolute RF size. More recently, Yoshor et al. (2007) directly measured RF size by subdural recording and found that the RF width of a cortical point in V1/2 located 10 – 20 mm (eccentricity ~2° - ~6° from Figure 6) from the occipital pole is ~2°. This value is, at most, half that we measured (Figure 7), suggesting that the RF size estimated by fMRI does not directly reflect the size of classical receptive fields. This point will be considered in the next subsection.

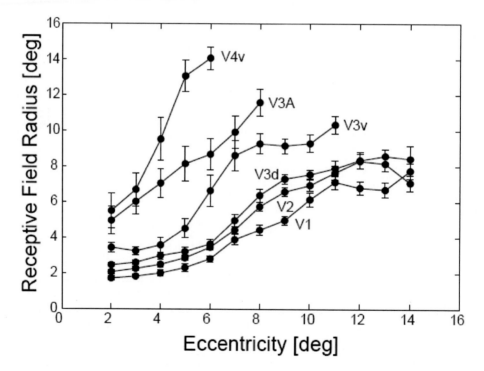

Figure 8. Relationships between receptive field size and retinal eccentricity for human V1, V2, V3, V3A, VP, and V4v. Error bars denote SE across 5 subjects.

Point Spread

We have thus seen that both the reciprocal of cortical magnification factor M^{-1} (the distance moved through the visual field corresponding to a 1 mm distance along cortex) and RF size increased with eccentricity. The relationship between M^{-1} and RF size is of fundamental significance in understanding the functional organization of the retinotopic areas. Hubel and

Wiesel (1974) first investigated this relationship in monkey V1. They found that M^{-1} increased with eccentricity in strikingly parallel fashion with RF size and scatter, and that, independent of eccentricity, a movement about 2-3 mm along the cortex was needed to get out of one region of visual field to enter an entirely new one. To put it another way, the point image or point spread, defined as the cortical region activated by a point stimulus, is constant at 2-3 mm across cortex. They argued that point spread can be considered indicative of the machinery required for analysis of the corresponding visual space, since its size is comparable to an ocular hypercolumn or an orientation hypercolumn, and that the machinery may be roughly uniform over the striate cortex. In this fashion, point spread provides information on the functional unit of local analysis of a finite region of the visual field.

To test whether a functional organization similar to that in monkeys exists in humans, we performed an analogous analysis for the retinotopic areas, based on estimated cortical magnification factor and RF size. Point spread could be calculated by multiplying RF size by the cortical magnification factor, since it corresponds to the image of RF on the cortex (Figure 9A) [62]. Figure 9B shows the relationship between point spread and visual field eccentricity. There appears to be an eccentricity-dependent variation in point spread, indicating deviation from exact parallelism between RF size and M^{-1}, since M^{-1} is modeled to increase in linear fashion (Figure 7B), whereas RF size increases in nonlinear fashion with eccentricity (Figure 8). However, because the variation was not large and no clearly defined trends could be established, the point spread may be constant along cortex, independent of eccentricity. Importantly, point spread became larger along the cortical hierarchy, as does RF size. The point spread radius averaged across eccentricities was 8.9 (SD=1.7) mm for V1, 11.8 (2.0) mm for V2, 12.2 (1.6) mm for V3, 15.5 (3.8) mm for VP, 22.6 (7.9) mm for V4v, and 26.8 (4.8) mm for V3A, in ascending order.

The near constancy of point spread suggests that, as for monkey striate cortex, human retinotopic cortex may be organized uniformly into an array of functional units, each of which analyzes visual information for a certain portion of visual space. Regarding the size of functional units, the estimated point spread of V1 was about 9 mm, and larger by a factor of ~10 than that of monkey V1 (8). We note, however, that this comparison is made difficult by methodological differences between our fMRI study and monkey single-unit electrophysiological recoding studies. Although fMRI signals reflect metabolic and vascular responses to neural activity, in particular changes in blood oxygenation and flow, their relationship to electrophysiological activity remains poorly understood [63]. Interestingly, the results of our measurement were comparable to those obtained by optical imaging based on intrinsic signals (IOS) [64], which detect blood-related signals, as fMRI does [65]. As suggested by the IOS study of Grinvald et al (1994), the large point spread of V1 detected by functional imaging may reflect long-range lateral interactions between the distinct functional units over the classical RF [66].

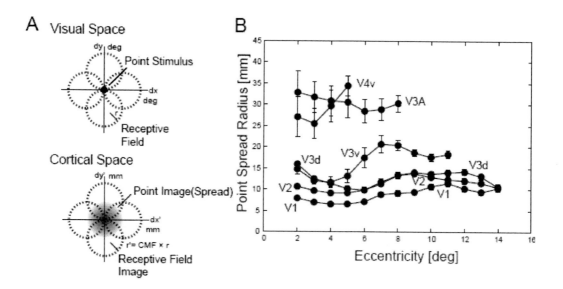

Figure 9. The concept of cortical point spread and its relationship to eccentricity (A) The left panel shows examples of the most remote receptive fields (dotted circles) of neurons activated by a given point stimulus. The right panel shows images of receptive fields (RF) on cortex (dotted circles) whose size can be computed by multiplying RF size (deg) by cortical magnification factor (mm/deg) at a given cortical point. The gray zone forms inside the center of the RF images and thus contains the neurons activated by the point stimulus. The gray zone is thus exactly the point spread, which is defined as the total area of cortex activated by a point stimulus. Consequently, the size of point spread corresponds to that of the RF image. (B) The point spread radii of human V1, V2, V3, V3A, VP, and V4v as a function of retinal eccentricity. Error bars denote SE across 5 subjects.

It is unclear what produces the enlargement of point spread with hierarchy level in extrastriate visual areas. Two factors relevant to their functional organization can be suggested. The first is the possibility of enlargement of their functional units themselves, which are comprised of multiple modules representing different functional domains such as the orientation hypercolumns of V1. The functional unit may become larger because the modules contained may increase in number to represent more functional domains. The second factor is the possibility of growth of the long-range lateral network between units, as found between V1 and the inferior temporal (TE) cortex of monkeys [67].

4. Retinotopy-Based Analyses of Visual Cortical Processing

Knowledge of retinotopic organization is important not only in itself, it also provides essential information for analysis and interpretation of functional activity in retinotopic cortex. In the previous section, we have already seen that findings from retino-cortical mapping enable employment of isoeccentricity analysis of phase-encoded activity to assess cortical point spread. In this section, we will summarize some of our studies that have employed similar retinotopy-based analyses.

Analysis of Visual Contextual Effects

Surround suppression: Retinotopy-based analysis is useful for investigating the neural substrates of visual contextual effects. Visual contextual effects refer to the change in perception of a visual stimulus caused by remote stimuli. One of the most representative of these phenomena is surround suppression, in which the perceived contrast of a test grating is reduced when similarly oriented and spaced surrounding gratings are presented nearby it [68, 69]. Neural correlates of surround suppression can be explored utilizing retinotopy, by first localizing the cortical regions that represent the test grating and then testing whether fMRI activities in the regions are correlated with perception. Isoeccentricity analysis does this in rigorous fashion using eccentricity-cortical mapping (Figure 5) when the stimulus can be specified by the eccentricity dimension alone. Based on this, we have investigated the neural correlate of surround suppression and found strong evidence for it in V1 and V2 [70, 71]. We also found an antagonistic pattern of response modulations between the test and surround region, suggesting that lateral interaction could be antagonistic between them. These findings confirm those of studies that have shown suppressive interaction among nearby stimuli in human early visual areas [72-74].

Bilateral contextual modulation: The existence of surround suppression in V1 suggests that some global feature integration begins at the earliest stage of the visual cortical hierarchy. However, it remains unclear how much remote space can be integrated. It is generally assumed that, in a bottom-up visual hierarchy, dissociated representations of an object located across the visual vertical meridian are combined only in higher visual areas in which the receptive fields of neurons are large enough to cover ipsilateral as well as contralateral visual hemifields. However, given the existence of massive feedback connections from higher areas targeting early visual cortex and reports of their contribution to contextual modulation [75, 76], it might be expected that early visual areas contribute to more global feature integration than previously thought, even beyond dissociated representations of visual hemifields.

To test this intriguing hypothesis, we performed block-design human fMRI experiments in which circular visual patterns aligned with various configurations were used (77-79). Each pattern consisted of centrally foveated quarter arcs, each of which was located in one quadrant of the visual field (Figure 10A), which permitted precise localization and anatomical separation of an early cortical representation of an arc from others. Using isoeccentricity analysis, we investigated whether the retinotopic neural responses corresponding to a target arc were modulated by other arcs presented in nonassociated visual fields when such elements were perceptually linked into a whole structure. Figure 10B shows spatiotemporal fMRI activity in right V1d for localize, target arc alone, and target plus context conditions. The spatiotemporal plot clearly shows that retinotopic responses to the target arc were significantly enhanced when another arc was simultaneously presented at the point-symmetrical position in the nonassociated visual field quadrant. This finding is convincing evidence that contextual effects involve feedback from higher areas, since there are no direct callosal connections that permit such interhemispheric contextual modulation. Early visual areas as well as higher ones may thus play more essential roles in perceiving the unity of the real world than previously thought.

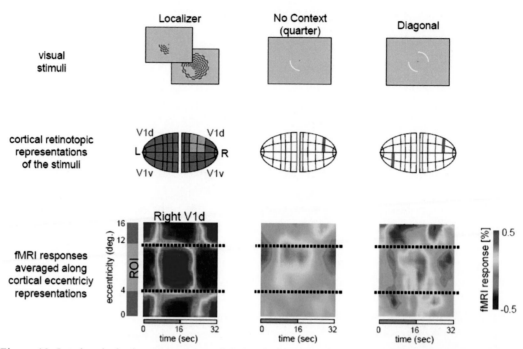

Figure 10. Interhemispheric contextual modulation in V1. [Top Row] Visual stimuli. (Left) Localizer. We localized the cortical sub-regions representing a portion of the visual field where the target stimulus was presented in the subsequent main experiments (4-12 deg in eccentricity in the lower-left visual quadrant). This localization was performed for V1d, V2d, and V3 on the right cerebral hemisphere of each participant using a checkerboard pattern spanning the target zone. (Middle) No context stimulus. In the No Context condition, we presented the target quarter arc alone within the pre-defined lower-left visual field quadrant. (Right) Context stimulus. In the Context condition, we presented the target arc with another arc in the non-associated visual field quadrant so that the two arcs were globally completed into a complete annulus. Note that although these annular stimuli (middle and right panels) differed in global configuration, their lower-left portions were completely identical, and were represented retinotopically within the pre-defined regions in early visual cortex. [Middle Row] Each icon shows the cortical retinotopic representation for the corresponding stimulus in the top row panels. [Bottom Row] Representative spatiotemporal fMRI activation patterns for different eccentricities in the right V1d of one representative participant are shown as images with an interpolated pseudo-color format indicating the magnitude of fMRI responses. In these spatiotemporal plots, the vertical axis represents eccentricity (top-peripheral and bottom-foveal) and the horizontal axis represents time per period of stimulus presentation (16 sec stimulus presentation and 16 sec rest). Each horizontal trace of the 2D plot shows the averaged fMRI time course within a given isoeccentricity region. (Left) fMRI response patterns evoked by the localizer. (Middle) fMRI response patterns evoked by a quarter arc presented alone within the lower-left visual field quadrant (No Context). (Right) fMRI responses evoked by the target stimulus with the context leading to completion of the entire annulus.

Inverse Mapping: Representation of Brain Activities in the Visual Field

In isoeccentricity analysis, fMRI activity is collapsed across the polar dimension to improve signal-to-noise ratio. However, it is also possible not to perform such pooling and to analyze and represent fMRI activity in both the eccentricity and polar angle dimensions, that is, in the visual field as is. We have produced software that can map fMRI activity from the retinotopic cortex to the visual field [80]. Using this inverse mapping, we can create movies of fMRI activity in the visual field for a given retinotopic area while subjects view a stimulus movie. Figure 11A displays shots from such activity movies for the phase-encoding experiments. As illustrated in Figure 11A, this technique permits direct comparison of brain activity with visual stimuli in a common reference frame. Their topographic relation can thus be captured intuitively and easily analyzed, in evaluating hypotheses linking brain activities and visual perception [81, 82].

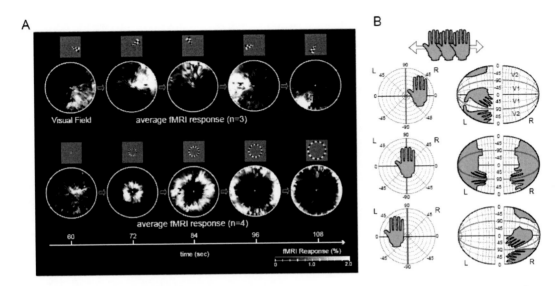

Figure 11. Inverse mapping: representation of brain activities in the visual field. (A) Snapshots from fMRI activity movies for the phase-encoded stimuli in V1 represented in the visual field coordinate (time for stimulus presentation shifts from left to right). [Above] fMRI activities for the rotating wedge stimulus. The wedge rotated along the central fixation point counter-clockwise from slightly below the right horizontal meridian. The circular image snapshots represent the corresponding fMRI response patterns obtained at each stimulus presentation period inversely mapped in visual field coordinates and averaged among three subjects. Interpolated pseudo-colors represent the magnitude of fMRI responses as shown in the indicator below. [Below] fMRI activities associated with the expanding annulus stimulus. The annulus expanded from central fixation to the peripheral visual field. The circular image snapshots represent the corresponding fMRI response patterns obtained at each stimulus presentation period and averaged among four subjects. (B) Cortical retinotopic representations of the right hand. [Left Panels] The position of the right hand in the visual field. [Right Panels] The cortical retinotopic representations of the right hand corresponding to the position shown in the left panels. When the right hand is entirely located within the right (or left) visual hemifield, it is represented only within the left (or right) cerebral cortex (top or bottom row). Yet, when the right hand is located across the vertical visual field meridian, it is represented separately in each cerebral hemisphere, forming fragmented imprints (middle row). As demonstrated in these panels, imprints formed by objects on the cerebral cortex change remarkably from the way that they appear, depending on subtle changes in spatial position in the visual field.

It should be noted that such comparison is not easy with standard forward mapping, since the topology of activation on retinotopic cortex is often quite different from that of stimuli due to singularities in retinotopy (split between left/right hemispheres and dorsal/ventral cortices, mirror-image duplication between areas, nonlinear scaling for different eccentricities), even if the stimulus configuration is simple [79, 83]. This is nicely illustrated in Figure 11B, which shows the retinotopic representation of a hand in V1 and V2.

Another advantage of inverse mapping is that it can be applied to comparison or integration of functional data among individuals. As shown in the first section, linear Talairach registration cannot actually normalize individual differences in locations of visual areas. Nonlinear or surface-based methods based on anatomical structures exhibit significantly better performance in this regard [2], though they have the inherent limit that no clear structure-function relationships are found in most visual areas. Inverse mapping provides an ideal method of normalization of individual differences not only in the layout of visual areas but also retino-cortical mapping within each area.

Conclusion

Measurement of retinotopy has significantly advanced our understanding of the functional organization of the human visual cortex. Not only has it revealed how multiple visual areas are distributed over the cortex for repeated analysis of the entire visual field, it has uncovered how populations of neurons form an array of functional units, each of which analyzes a finite region of the visual field. The human visual cortex appears to analyze a visual scene with functional units having common machinery within a given area, but with more elaborate machinery as the visual hierarchy is ascended. Furthermore, measurement of retinotopy has provided strong clues to elucidation of the interaction between the functional units that underlie visual contextual effects.

While much of visual cortex is composed of visual field maps, there is also emerging evidence for visual category or feature-specific maps. How do these two types of organization coexist on the cortex and cooperate in visual function? Although the answer to this question is far from certain, as only a few studies have explored the relationship between them (84, 85), the findings described here provide basic data of use in obtaining it.

Acknowledgements

Sections 2 and 3 of this chapter are based on parts of H. Yamamoto's doctoral dissertation [86]. A portion of section 4 is based on parts of H. Ban's doctoral dissertation [87]. This work was supported by the 21st Century COE Program (D-2, Kyoto University) and Global COE Program (D07, Kyoto University), a Grant-in-Aid for Young Scientists (B) of the Ministry of Education, Culture, Sports, Science, and Technology of Japan, and the Strategic Information and Communications RandD Promotion Programme (SCOPE) of the Ministry of Internal Affairs and Communications of Japan.

Appendix A. Imaging Methods

Structural and functional MR measurements were carried out using a standard clinical 1.5 Tesla scanner (General Electric Signa NV/i, Milwaukee, WI). Before the experimental scans, high-contrast structural images of the whole brain were recorded as a standard brain once for each subject using a T1-weighted three-dimensional (3D) SPGR [echo time (TE) = 3.0 ms, repetition time (TR) = 56 ms, flip angle (FA) = 55°; excitations (NEX) = 1, voxel size (VS) = 0.781 × 0.781 × 1.4 or 0.938 × 0.938 × 1.4 mm]. A standard quadrature head coil was used for radiofrequency transmission and reception. This standard structural volume was used for reconstructing the brain surface (Appendix C).

For each subject, three types of images were obtained on each scan day, with a standard flexible surface coil placed at the occipital pole. First, structural images for anatomical registration were acquired using a T1-weighted Inversion Recovery 3D Fast SPGR [TE = 2.7 ms, TR = 6.0 ms, inversion time (TI) = 600 ms, FA = 15°; NEX = 1, VS = 0.781 × 0.781 × 1.4 mm]. Second, a set of 16 or 17 adjacent high-resolution anatomical slices was obtained using a T1-weighted spin echo [TE = 9 ms, TR = 420 ms, NEX = 2, VS = 0.781 × 0.781 × 4 mm]. These slices included the occipital, posterior parietal, and temporal lobes, oriented roughly parallel with or perpendicular to the calcarine sulcus. Finally, multiple functional scans were obtained in the same slices as these oblique anatomical slices while the subject viewed visual stimuli, using T2*-weighted two-dimensional gradient echo, echo planar imaging [TE = 50 ms, TR = 2000 ms, FA = 90°, VS = 1.563 × 1.563 × 4 mm]. For each scan, 180 functional images depicting blood-oxygen-level-dependent (BOLD) contrast (Ogawa, et al. 1992) were collected for each of the slices. Head movement was minimized using a custom-made head fixation device, which is best described as a screw-operated clamp that holds the temporal region of the head.

Appendix B. Localization of Retinotopic Areas Using fMRI

The locations of retinotopic visual areas on each individual's cortical surfaces were identified with fMRI, using standard techniques for measurement and analysis of retinotopic organization [53, 88, 89]. The retinotopic map was constructed using a phase-encoding technique in which receptive field centers are temporally coded using polar coordinates [19]. The eccentricity component was measured while the subject viewed a checkered annulus (2° width; Figure 1A) that expanded from the fovea to 16° peripherally over 50 s and then disappeared for 10 s. The polar angle component of the map was measured by carrying out fMRI while the subject viewed a wedge-shaped checkered pattern (24° center angle; Figure 1B) rotated counter-clockwise around the fixation point, making one rotation in 60 s. Each stimulus underwent color (black/white, red/green, blue/yellow) pattern reversal (1 Hz) and was presented in six cycles, evoking a periodic response at a given point on the retinotopy map, whose corresponding position in the visual field was encoded in the phase of the response. The response phase for each of the eccentricity and polar angle components was computed by Fourier analysis and mapped onto the cortical surface after correction for hemodynamic delay (Figure 1C, D; Figure 2). The statistical significance of retinotopic activity was determined by Fourier F-test [90]. We further calculated the visual field sign [20] from the polar angle and eccentricity maps. After the gradient vectors of the angular and eccentricity representation were computed at each cortical point, the field sign was determined as the sign of the cross-product of the two gradients and mapped onto the cortical surface (Figure 1E-G).

Two other series of fMRI experiments were conducted to help determine localization. First, foveal and peripheral representations were localized (Figure 2J, M) using a block design in which foveal and peripheral (16°) dot stimuli were presented in alternating blocks of 16 s each, interleaved with blank periods or not interleaved. Second, motion-sensitive regions were localized (Figure 2K, N) using a block design in which expanding motion of a low-contrast concentric grating was presented in blocks of 16 s interleaved with blank periods. The statistical significance of these activities was determined by the Fourier F-test.

Appendix C. Cortical Surface Reconstruction

Individuals' cortical surfaces (Figure 3) were reconstructed using the standard structural volume for each hemisphere. We generated a surface lying approximately in the middle of the gray matter using a method that was a hybrid of volume segmentation [91] and surface deformation [92]. First, the voxels that belonged to the cortical gray matter were segmented from the rest of the volume using mrGray software (93). mrGray enabled us to identify the white matter, cerebrospinal fluid (CSF), and three layers of gray matter. The segmented gray matter was approximately 3 mm thick and the first, second, and third layers were positioned in that order relative to the white matter. From the output, we constructed a segmented volume whose voxels were numerically labeled as white matter (label = 200), CSF (0), or the first (150), second (100), or third (50) layer of gray matter. The segmented volume was then slightly smoothed using a 3D Gaussian filter with a SD of 1 voxel. The resultant volume was smooth and noiseless enough that we were able to minimize any non-biological irregularities that might have arisen in subsequent processing. Next, a surface representation was created for the gray-white matter boundary. At this point, we did not create the surface for the middle of the gray matter, in order to minimize topological defects, in particular bridges between cortical sulci. We then computed a concrete average voxel value for the first gray matter layer in the smoothed segmented volume and inputted it into the marching cube algorithm [94], which extracted an isosurface tessellated with ~300000 triangles. The number of triangles was then reduced to 200000 using the decimation algorithm [95]. Finally, the triangulated surface was deformed such that it lay in the middle of the gray matter by relaxing it against the smoothed segmented volume. We used the deformable template algorithm [92] for deformation. Finally, the resultant surface was visually inspected for positional accuracy and topological errors by overlapping it on the structural MR volume?. Extensive smoothing of the surface, which highlighted defects as sharp edges, was also performed to detect topological defects. If the surface was inaccurate or had defects, corrections were made in mrGray and subsequent processing was repeated. Reconstructed cortical surfaces were used to map or sample functional data. In addition, inflated, that is, hyper-smoothed versions of the reconstructed surface (Figure 2), were created for analysis of retinotopic organization. We used an inflation algorithm that was quite similar to that proposed by Fischl et al. (1999a)[96].

Appendix D. Generation of Probability Maps

Construction of volumetric models of retinotopic areas. The localized retinotopic areas were separated from one another and from other portions of the cortical surface. The isolated surfaces had no thickness, whereas the real cerebral cortex is about 2.5 mm thick on average, but exhibits regional variation (standard deviation) of 0.7 mm [97]. Here, we simplified cortical thickness to a constant 3 mm and incorporated this into the models of retinotopic areas by converting the surface models into volumetric ones with 3-mm thickness. The first step of this conversion was to compute the distance from the surface of each area to the points of an output volume. In the second step, the distance data were thresholded at half the distance of the assumed thickness to produce a draft version of the volumetric model for each area. In the final step, the draft models of different areas in one hemisphere were brought into a common space to detect where dilation caused overlap among them, and the overlapping voxels detected were removed from the models, producing a final volumetric model for each area. The volumetric model is a 3D binary array of voxels with each voxel having a label indicating the presence or absence of the area. We confirmed by visual inspection of 3D volume and surface-rendered models that each model did not overlap with the other models and lacked topological defects such as discontinuities and holes.

Talairach transformation. The volumetric models of retinotopic areas in each hemisphere were transformed into Talairach space using a single homogeneous transformation consisting of nine parameters, three translations, three rotations, and three scalings with respect to the axes of a cartesian frame. The Talairach coordinate system [98] has its origin at the superior edge of the anterior commissure (AC). In this system, a brain is scaled along X, Y, and Z axes. The X-axis (right to left) is defined by a line that runs through the origin and is orthogonal to the midline plane defined by the interhemispheric fissure. The Y-axis (anterior to posterior) is defined by a line that passes through the origin and the inferior edge of the posterior commissure (PC). The Z-axis (superior to inferior) is defined as a line that is orthogonal to the X- and Y-axes. We computed the homogeneous transformation matrix that converted each point in the volumetric models into a point in the Talairach system using a standard method [99]. First, the translation and rotation components of the matrix were computed from the locations of anatomical landmarks (AC, PC, and mid-sagittal plane) identified via visual inspection of the standard structural volume. The alignment was checked and corrected by graphically comparing the X, Y, and Z axes with three orthogonal slices of the standard volume and the reconstructed surface. Next, the scale components were determined by measuring the size of the brain along each of the three axes as the bounding box dimensions of the surface and then computing scaling factors to match the size to that of the 1988 Talairach atlas brain (X dimension: 136 mm; Y: 172 mm; Z: 118 mm). The scaling factor was determined separately for the left and right hemispheres. Since the Talairach atlas contains only a right hemisphere, the volumetric models for the left hemispheres were mirrored around the Y-axis and treated as though they were in right hemispheres.

Generation of the probability map. The probability of occurrence of each area in Talairach space was computed by counting the number of overlaps of the area's volumetric models in different hemispheres and dividing this by the total number of hemispheres (N = 10). This computation was repeated every 1 mm in Talairach space covering the visual cortex, and thus yielded a 3D probability map for each retinotopic area. Furthermore, the probability maps for all the retinotopic areas were integrated into a maximum probability map, in which each voxel was assigned a label indicating which area had the greatest probability of being present there and was given the maximum value.

We visualized the 3D probability data in two ways, by mapping the data on orthogonal slices (Figure 4A) and on the surface (Figure 4B) of the Talairach brain. The slice representation was created for the same coronal, horizontal, and sagittal sections in the occipital region as those contained in the Talairach atlas. The surface representation was created by sampling the data at each node of the surface mesh, using a nearest neighbor algorithm within a radius of 2 mm. In both representations, probabilistic information was color-coded by assigning different colors to different areas, and by altering the brightness of colors such that increasing brightness corresponded to increasing probability.

The surface of the Talairach brain was reconstructed from a series of color tracings contained in the 1988 Talairach atlas in the form of coronal, horizontal, and sagittal sections. Each section was digitized using a flatbed scanner with a resolution of 150 dpi and segmented into three cortical structures, white matter, gray matter, and CSF, with decreasing integer labels in that order, using Photoshop software (Adobe Inc. San Jose, CA). The labels were the same as those used for the subjects' brains, as described above. All the segmented images for the orthogonal sections were resampled to volume data with 1 mm^3-resolution. We regarded this volume as the segmented volume of the Talairach brain, and reconstructed the Talairach surface in the same fashion as the subjects' brains, as described above.

Appendix E. Isoeccentricity Analysis

The fMRI signal was first sampled independently from each visual area delineated on the cortical surface reconstructed as a triangular mesh. For each node within a visual area, fMRI voxels were sampled from the cortical gray matter, except for the voxels located near the area boundary, and converted from raw intensity units to contrast, followed by omission of outliers.

The fMRI contrast responses from the phase encoding experiment for retinal eccentricities were analyzed spatially within each visual area, as a function of cortical geodesic distance along which retinotopic representation of visual field eccentricity shifted from the fovea to the periphery. First, for each node within the cortical mesh of a visual area, the shortest geodesic distance from the peripheral 16° contour was computed using Dijkstra's algorithm (Figure 5) [1, 100]. Second, using the distance information, the cortical mesh was divided into "iso-eccentricity bands" (3 mm width, 50% overlap) from posterior to anterior cortex, so that the eccentricity representation changed from fovea to periphery. Third, the fMRI responses were averaged within each iso-eccentricity band. Finally, the responses for different eccentricities were further averaged across repeated scanning sessions and stimulus cycles.

References

[1] Wandell BA, Chial S, Backus BT. Visualization and measurement of the cortical surface. *J. Cogn. Neurosci.* 2000 Sep;12(5):739-52.

[2] Van Essen DC, Dierker DL. Surface-Based and Probabilistic Atlases of Primate Cerebral Cortex. *Neuron.* 2007;56(2):209-25.

[3] Van Essen DC, Drury HA. Structural and functional analyses of human cerebral cortex using a surface-based atlas. *J. Neurosci.* 1997;17(18):7079.

[4] Lueck CJ, Zeki S, Friston KJ, Deiber MP, Cope P, Cunningham VJ, et al. The colour centre in the cerebral cortex of man. *Nature.* 1989;340(6232):386-9.

[5] Gulyás B. Functional organization of human visual cortical areas. In: Peters A, Jones EG, editors. *Cerebral Cortex Plenum Press*; 1997. p. 743-75.

[6] Courtney SM, Ungerleider LG. What fMRI has taught us about human vision. *Current Opinion in Neurobiology.* 1997;7(4):554-61.

[7] Grill-Spector K, Malach R. THE HUMAN VISUAL CORTEX. *Annual Review of Neuroscience.* 2004;27(1):649-77.

[8] Hubel DH, Wiesel TN. Uniformity of monkey striate cortex: a parallel relationship between field size, scatter, and magnification factor. *J. Comp. Neurol.* 1974 Dec 1;158(3):295-305.

[9] Dow BM, Snyder AZ, Vautin RG, Bauer R. Magnification factor and receptive field size in foveal striate cortex of the monkey. *Exp. Brain Res.* 1981;44(2):213-28.

[10] Wandell BA, Dumoulin SO, Brewer AA. Visual field maps in human cortex. *Neuron.* 2007 Oct 25;56(2):366-83.

[11] Sereno MI, Tootell RBH. From monkeys to humans: what do we now know about brain homologies? *Current Opinion in Neurobiology.* 2005;15(2):135-44.

[12] Yamamoto H, Fukunaga M, Takahashi S, Tanaka C, Ebisu T, Umeda M, et al., editors. BrainFactory: an integrated software system for surface-based analysis of fMRI data. *Human Brain Mapping 2002*; Sendai, Japan.

[13] Yamamoto H, Azukawa T, Takahashi S, Ejima Y. Software for surface-based analysis of fMRI. *IEICE Technical Report*, MBE2000-64. 2000;100(330):79-86.

[14] Yamamoto H, Fukunaga M, Tanaka C, Ebisu T, Umeda M, Ejima Y. Inconsistency and Uncertainty in the Locations of Human Visual Areas in Talairach Space: *Probability and Entropy Maps.* (in preparation).

[15] Yamamoto H, Ohtani Y. *Functional Brain Imaging and Visual Psychophysics.* Kougaku. 2004;33(2):80-8.

[16] Ejima Y, Takahashi S. Positioning of retinotopic areas and patterning of cerebral cortex layout. *Neuroreport.* 2005 Jan 19;16(1):9-12.

[17] Ejima Y, Takahashi S, Yamamoto H, Fukunaga M, Tanaka C, Ebisu T, et al. Interindividual and interspecies variations of the extrastriate visual cortex. *Neuroreport.* 2003 Aug 26;14(12):1579-83.

[18] Yamamoto H, Fukunaga M, Takahashi S, Azukawa T, Tanaka C, Ebisu T, et al. Anatomical and retinotopic organization of functional areas in the human visual cortex. *IEICE Technical Report*, MBE2000-65. 2000;100(330):87-94.

[19] Engel SA, Rumelhart DE, Wandell BA, Lee AT, Glover GH, Chichilnisky EJ, et al. fMRI of human visual cortex. *Nature.* 1994 Jun 16;369(6481):525.

[20] Sereno MI, McDonald CT, Allman JM. Analysis of retinotopic maps in extrastriate cortex. *Cereb. Cortex.* 1994 Nov-Dec;4(6):601-20.

[21] Tootell RB, Mendola JD, Hadjikhani NK, Ledden PJ, Liu AK, Reppas JB, et al. Functional analysis of V3A and related areas in human visual cortex. *J. Neurosci.* 1997 Sep 15;17(18):7060-78.

[22] Wandell BA, Brewer AA, Dougherty RF. Visual field map clusters in human cortex. *Philos. Trans R. Soc. Lond B Biol. Sci.* 2005 Apr 29;360(1456):693-707.

[23] Smith AT, Greenlee MW, Singh KD, Kraemer FM, Hennig J. The processing of first- and second-order motion in human visual cortex assessed by functional magnetic resonance imaging (fMRI). *J. Neurosci.* 1998 May 15;18(10):3816-30.

[24] Huk AC, Dougherty RF, Heeger DJ. Retinotopy and functional subdivision of human areas MT and MST. *J. Neurosci.* 2002 Aug 15;22(16):7195-205.

[25] Malach R, Reppas JB, Benson RR, Kwong KK, Jiang H, Kennedy WA, et al. Object-related activity revealed by functional magnetic resonance imaging in human occipital cortex. *Proc. Natl. Acad. Sci. USA.* 1995 Aug 29;92(18):8135-9.

[26] Larsson J, Heeger DJ. Two retinotopic visual areas in human lateral occipital cortex. *J. Neurosci.* 2006 Dec 20;26(51):13128-42.

[27] Levy I, Hasson U, Avidan G, Hendler T, Malach R. Center-periphery organization of human object areas. *Nat. Neurosci.* 2001 May;4(5):533-9.

[28] Zeki S. Improbable areas in the visual brain. *Trends in Neurosciences.* 2003;26(1):23-6.

[29] Hansen KA, Kay KN, Gallant JL. Topographic Organization in and near Human Visual Area V4. *J. Neurosci.* 2007 October 31, 2007;27(44):11896-911.

[30] Hadjikhani N, Liu AK, Dale AM, Cavanagh P, Tootell RB. Retinotopy and color sensitivity in human visual cortical area V8. *Nat. Neurosci.* 1998 Jul;1(3):235-41.

[31] Brewer AA, Liu J, Wade AR, Wandell BA. Visual field maps and stimulus selectivity in human ventral occipital cortex. *Nat. Neurosci.* 2005 Aug;8(8):1102-9.

[32] Wade AR, Brewer AA, Rieger JW, Wandell BA. Functional measurements of human ventral occipital cortex: retinotopy and colour. *Philos. Trans R. Soc. Lond B. Biol. Sci.* 2002 Aug 29;357(1424):963-73.

[33] Zeki S, Watson JD, Lueck CJ, Friston KJ, Kennard C, Frackowiak RS. A direct demonstration of functional specialization in human visual cortex. *J. Neurosci.* 1991 Mar;11(3):641-9.

[34] Bartels A, Zeki S. The architecture of the colour centre in the human visual brain: new results and a review. *Eur. J. Neurosci.* 2000 Jan;12(1):172-93.

[35] Pitzalis S, Galletti C, Huang RS, Patria F, Committeri G, Galati G, et al. Wide-field retinotopy defines human cortical visual area v6. *J. Neurosci.* 2006 Jul 26;26(30):7962-73.

[36] Sereno MI, Pitzalis S, Martinez A. Mapping of contralateral space in retinotopic coordinates by a parietal cortical area in humans. *Science.* 2001 Nov 9;294(5545):1350-4.

[37] Swisher JD, Halko MA, Merabet LB, McMains SA, Somers DC. Visual topography of human intraparietal sulcus. *J. Neurosci.* 2007 May 16;27(20):5326-37.

[38] Hasnain MK, Fox PT, Woldorff MG. Intersubject variability of functional areas in the human visual cortex. *Hum. Brain Mapp.* 1998;6(4):301-15.

[39] Amunts K, Malikovic A, Mohlberg H, Schormann T, Zilles K. Brodmann's areas 17 and 18 brought into stereotaxic space-where and how variable? *Neuroimage.* 2000 Jan;11(1):66-84.

[40] Dougherty RF, Koch VM, Brewer AA, Fischer B, Modersitzki J, Wandell BA. Visual field representations and locations of visual areas V1/2/3 in human visual cortex. *J. Vis.* 2003;3(10):586-98.

[41] Yamamoto H, Fukunaga M, Tanaka C, Umeda M, Ejima Y, editors. Inconsistency and Uncertainty in the Locations of Human Visual Areas in Talairach Space. *The 30th Annual Meeting of the Japan Neuroscience Society*; 2007; Yokohama, Japan. Elsevier.

[42] Yamamoto H, Fukunaga M, Tanaka C, Ebisu T, Umeda M, Ejima Y, editors. *A New Method for Quantifying Brain Structure-Function Relationships Based on Simultaneous Probability Map and Information Theory.* Society for Neuroscience 33rd Annual Meeting; 2003; New Orleans.

[43] Fukunaga M, Yamamoto H, Takahashi S, Tanaka C, Ebisu T, Umeda M, et al., editors. Functional and anatomical probabilistic maps of the human visual cortex [abstract]. *Human Brain Mapping*; 2002; Sendai.

[44] Wassle H, Grunert U, Rohrenbeck J, Boycott BB. Cortical magnification factor and the ganglion cell density of the primate retina. *Nature.* 1989;341(6243):643-6.

[45] Van Essen DC, Newsome WT, Maunsell JH. The visual field representation in striate cortex of the macaque monkey: asymmetries, anisotropies, and individual variability. *Vision Res.* 1984;24(5):429-48.

[46] Tootell RB, Switkes E, Silverman MS, Hamilton SL. Functional anatomy of macaque striate cortex. II. Retinotopic organization. *J. Neurosci.* 1988 May;8(5):1531-68.

[47] Daniel PM, Whitteridge D. The representation of the visual field on the cerebral cortex in monkeys. *J. Physiol.* 1961 Dec;159:203-21.

[48] Rosa MGP. Visuotopic organization of primate extrastriate cortex. In: Rockland KS, Kaas JH, Peters A, editors. *Cerebral Cortex.* New York, NY: Plenum; 1997.

[49] Maeda K, Fukunaga M, Nakagoshi A, Yamamoto H, Matsuno T, Tanaka C, et al. Isoeccentricity averaging: a new analytical technique for fMRI studies on human visual processing [ABSTRACT]. *Neuroscience Research.* 2003;46(Supplement 1):S57.

[50] Boynton GM, Engel SA, Glover GH, Heeger DJ. Linear systems analysis of functional magnetic resonance imaging in human V1. *J. Neurosci.* 1996 Jul 1;16(13):4207-21.

[51] Schwartz EL. Computational anatomy and functional architecture of striate cortex: a spatial mapping approach to perceptual coding. *Vision Res.* 1980;20(8):645-69.

[52] Schwartz EL. Topographic Mapping in Primate Visual Cortex: History, Anatomy, and Computation. In: Kelly DH, editor. *Visual science and engineering: models and applications.* New York: M. Dekker; 1994. p. 293-359.

[53] Sereno MI, Dale AM, Reppas JB, Kwong KK, Belliveau JW, Brady TJ, et al. Borders of multiple visual areas in humans revealed by functional magnetic resonance imaging. *Science.* 1995 May 12;268(5212):889-93.

[54] Schira MM, Wade AR, Tyler CW. Two-dimensional mapping of the central and parafoveal visual field to human visual cortex. *J. Neurophysiol.* 2007 Jun;97(6):4284-95.

[55] Slotnick SD, Klein SA, Carney T, Sutter EE. Electrophysiological estimate of human cortical magnification. *Clin. Neurophysiol.* 2001 Jul;112(7):1349-56.

[56] Yoshor D, Bosking WH, Ghose GM, Maunsell JHR. Receptive Fields in Human Visual Cortex Mapped with Surface Electrodes. *Cereb Cortex.* 2007 October 1, 2007;17(10):2293-302.

[57] Horton JC, Hoyt WF. The representation of the visual field in human striate cortex. A revision of the classic Holmes map. *Arch. Ophthalmol.* 1991 Jun;109(6):816-24.

[58] Beard BL, Levi DM, Klein SA. Vernier acuity with non-simultaneous targets: the cortical magnification factor estimated by psychophysics. *Vision Res.* 1997 Feb;37(3):325-46.

[59] Rovamo J, Virsu V. Isotropy of cortical magnification and topography of striate cortex. *Vision Res.* 1984;24(3):283-6.

[60] Kastner S, De Weerd P, Pinsk MA, Elizondo MI, Desimone R, Ungerleider LG. Modulation of sensory suppression: implications for receptive field sizes in the human visual cortex. *J. Neurophysiol.* 2001 Sep;86(3):1398-411.

[61] Smith AT, Singh KD, Williams AL, Greenlee MW. Estimating Receptive Field Size from fMRI Data in Human Striate and Extrastriate Visual Cortex. *Cereb Cortex.* 2001 December 1, 2001;11(12):1182-90.

[62] McLlwain JT. Point images in the visual system: new interest in an old idea. *Trends in Neurosciences.* 1986;9:354-8.

[63] Heeger DJ, Ress D. What does fMRI tell us about neuronal activity? *Nat. Rev. Neurosci.* 2002;3(2):142-51.

[64] Grinvald A, Lieke EE, Frostig RD, Hildesheim R. Cortical point-spread function and long-range lateral interactions revealed by real-time optical imaging of macaque monkey primary visual cortex. *J. Neurosci.* 1994 May;14(5 Pt 1):2545-68.

[65] Bonhoeffer T, Grinvald A. Optical imaging based on intrinsic signals: the methodology. In: Toga AW, Mazziotta JC, editors. *Brain Mapping: the Methods.* San Diego Academic Press; 1996. p. 55–97.

[66] Gilbert CD, Das A, Ito M, Kapadia M, Westheimer G. Spatial integration and cortical dynamics. *Proceedings of the National Academy of Sciences.* 1996 January 23, 1996;93(2):615-22.

[67] Tanigawa H, Wang Q, Fujita I. Organization of Horizontal Axons in the Inferior Temporal Cortex and Primary Visual Cortex of the Macaque Monkey. *Cereb Cortex.* 2005 December 1, 2005;15(12):1887-99.

[68] Cannon MW, Fullenkamp SC. Spatial interactions in apparent contrast: inhibitory effects among grating patterns of different spatial frequencies, spatial positions and orientations. *Vision Res.* 1991;31(11):1985-98.

[69] Ejima Y, Takahashi S. Apparent contrast of a sinusoidal grating in the simultaneous presence of peripheral gratings. *Vision Res.* 1985;25(9):1223-32.

[70] Goda N, Fukunaga M, Yamamoto H, Tanaka C, Ebisu T, Umeda M, et al., editors. Orientation-dependent lateral interactions in human visual areas: an fMRI study. *The 24th Annual Meeting of the Japan Neuroscience Society*; 2001; Kyoto, Japan. Elsevier.

[71] Ejima Y, Takahashi S, Yamamoto H, Goda N. Visual Perception of Contextual Effect and Its Neural Correlates In: Funahashi S, editor. *Representation and Brain.* Tokyo: Springer Verlag; 2007. p. 3-20.

[72] Williams AL, Singh KD, Smith AT. Surround Modulation Measured With Functional MRI in the Human Visual Cortex. *J. Neurophysiol.* 2003 January 1, 2003;89(1):525-33.

[73] Ohtani Y, Okamura S, Yoshida Y, Toyama K, Ejima Y. Surround suppression in the human visual cortex: an analysis using magnetoencephalography. *Vision Res.* 2002 Jul;42(15):1825-35.

[74] Zenger-Landolt B, Heeger DJ. Response suppression in v1 agrees with psychophysics of surround masking. *J. Neurosci.* 2003 Jul 30;23(17):6884-93.

[75]   Lamme VA, Roelfsema PR. The distinct modes of vision offered by feedforward and recurrent processing. *Trends Neurosci.* 2000 Nov;23(11):571-9.

[76]   Super H, Spekreijse H, Lamme VA. Two distinct modes of sensory processing observed in monkey primary visual cortex (V1). *Nat. Neurosci.* 2001 Mar;4(3):304-10.

[77]   Ban H, Fukunaga M, Nakagoshi A, Yamamoto H, Tanaka C, Ebisu T, et al. Relations between retinotopic organization of human low-level visual regions and position-invariance object perception – an fMRI study –. *IEICE Technical Report*, HIP2003-127. 2004 Aug 23;103(743):5-10.

[78]   Ban H, Yamamoto H, Fukunaga M, Nakagoshi A, Tanaka C, Ebisu T, et al. Global shape processing in human early visual cortex. *VISION.* 2005 Aug 23;17(3):191-4.

[79]   Ban H, Yamamoto H, Fukunaga M, Nakagoshi A, Umeda M, Tanaka C, et al. Toward a common circle: interhemispheric contextual modulation in human early visual areas. *J. Neurosci.* 2006 Aug 23;26(34):8804-9.

[80]   Ban H, Yamamoto H, Saiki J, editors. Retinotopy-based morphing of brain activity. *The 29th Annual Meeting of the Japan Neuroscience Society*; 2006; Kyoto, Japan. Elsevier.

[81]   Goldstein EB. Cross-Talk Between Psychophysics and Physiology in the Study of Perception In: Goldstein EB, editor. *Blackwell handbook of perception*. Oxford, UK ; Malden, Mass.: Blackwell; 2001. p. 1-23.

[82]   Teller DY. Linking propositions. *Vision Res.* 1984;24(10):1233-46.

[83]   Schiller PH. *Past and Present Ideas About How the Visual Scene is Analyzed by the Brain.* In: Peters A, Jones EG, editors. Cerebral Cortex Plenum Press; 1997. p. 59-90.

[84]   Hasson U, Harel M, Levy I, Malach R. Large-scale mirror-symmetry organization of human occipito-temporal object areas. *Neuron.* 2003;37(6):1027.

[85]   Hasson U, Levy I, Behrmann M, Hendler T, Malach R. Eccentricity bias as an organizing principle for human high-order object areas. *Neuron.* 2002;34(3):479.

[86]   Yamamoto H. *The development of a software system for computational neuroimaging and its applications to visual sicience* [Doctoral thesis]. Kyoto, Japan: Kyoto University; 2001.

[87]   Ban H. *Neural processing of Spatiotemporal Visual Contexts in Human Retinotopic Early Visual Areas: fMRI studies* [Doctoral thesis]. Kyoto, Japan: Kyoto University; 2007.

[88]   DeYoe EA, Bandettini P, Neitz J, Miller D, Winans P. Functional magnetic resonance imaging (FMRI) of the human brain. *J. Neurosci. Methods.* 1994 Oct;54(2):171-87.

[89]   Engel SA, Glover GH, Wandell BA. Retinotopic organization in human visual cortex and the spatial precision of functional MRI. *Cereb Cortex.* 1997 Mar;7(2):181-92.

[90]   Brockwell PJ, Davis RA. *Time series: theory and methods.* 2nd ed. New York: Springer-Verlag; 1991.

[91]   Drury HA, Van Essen DC, Corbetta M, Snyder AZ. *Surface-based analyses of the human cerebral cortex.* In: Toga AW, editor. Brain Warping San Diego: Academic Press; 1999. p. 337-63.

[92]   Dale AM, Sereno MI. Improved localization of cortical activity by combining EEG and MEG with MRI cortical surface reconstruction: A linear approach. *J. Cogn. Neurosci.* 1993;5(2):162-76.

[93]   Teo PC, Sapiro G, Wandell BA. Creating connected representations of cortical gray matter for functional MRI visualization. *IEEE Transactions on Medical Imaging.* 1997;16(6):852-63.

[94] Lorensen W, E. , Cline H, E. . Marching cubes: A high resolution 3D surface construction algorithm. *Proceedings of the 14th annual conference on Computer graphics and interactive techniques*; 1987. ACM Press; 1987.

[95] Schroeder W, J. , Zarge J, A., Lorensen W, E. . Decimation of triangle meshes. *Proceedings of the 19th annual conference on Computer graphics and interactive techniques*; 1992. ACM Press; 1992.

[96] Fischl B, Sereno MI, Dale AM. Cortical surface-based analysis. II: Inflation, flattening, and a surface-based coordinate system. *Neuroimage.* 1999 Feb;9(2):195-207.

[97] Fischl B, Dale AM. Measuring the thickness of the human cerebral cortex from magnetic resonance images. *Proc. Natl. Acad. Sci. USA.* 2000 Sep 26;97(20):11050-5.

[98] Talairach J, Tournoux P. *Co-Planar Stereotactic Atlas of the Human Brain.* Stuttgart/New York: Thieme; 1988.

[99] Desmond JE, Lim KO. On- and offline Talairach registration for structural and functional MRI studies. *Human Brain Mapping.* 1997;5(1):58-73.

[100] Dijkstra EW. A note on two problems in connexion with graphs. *Numerische Mathematik.* 1959;1(1): 269 - 71.

In: Visual Cortex: New Research
Editors: T. A. Portocello and R. B. Velloti

ISBN 978-1-60456-530-0
© 2008 Nova Science Publishers, Inc.

Chapter 5

THE INFEROTEMPORAL CORTEX: AN INTEGRATION MODULE FOR COMPLEX VISUAL ANALYSIS

Maria C. Romero[1], Maria A. Bermudez[1], Ana F. Vicente[1], Rogelio Perez[1,2] and Francisco Gonzalez[1,2]

[1]Laboratories of Visual Neurophysiology, Department of Physiology,
School of Medicine, University of Santiago de Compostela, Spain
[2]Service of Ophthalmology, Hospital de Monforte, Monforte, Spain
[3]Service of Ophthalmology, University Hospital of Santiago de Compostela, Spain

Abstract

The inferotemporal cortex (IT) is a visual integration area. Here, the information arriving from lower visual areas is combined in such a way that the resulting cell activity encodes complex features of the visual stimuli. Furthermore, the output originating in the IT cortex activates many of the cortical and subcortical structures involved in higher brain functions, such as recognition, remembering or emotional and visuomotor associations. For these reasons, the IT cortex has been an appealing area for many investigators during the last decades, who have devoted much of their work to this structure by using a large variety of techniques and approaches. In this review, we attempt to summarize the main findings obtained from these studies, outlining the functional characterization of IT neurons. Each section has been illustrated with data obtained in our laboratory after recording the activity of IT cells in behaving monkeys, trained to perform a visual discrimination task.

Introduction

The interest in the visual functions of the temporal lobe started in the 19th century when clinicians began to analyse the functional deficits observed in patients with localised lesions in this region. The first anatomical report was published as early as in 1937, when H. Spatz, found that the orbitofrontal atrophy normally coexisted with temporal atrophy in the Pick's disease, affecting high visual processing. Then, the neurological findings observed in the

Klüver-Bucy syndrome (Klüver and Bucy, 1939) together with the behavioural studies performed in monkeys suggested that bilateral temporal lesions induced visual discrimination deficits and hyper-reactivity to visual stimuli, together with other behavioural symptoms. Based on these classical studies, the temporal lobe has been mostly related to sensory memories, representing one of the most prolific fields for behavioural neurophysiologists. With the new techniques and models developed it has been confirmed that IT neurons are highly selective for complex visual processing, in such a way that, in humans, bilateral lesions in this region, can lead to visual agnosia (Damasio et al., 1985; Shelton et al., 1994; Sparr et al., 1991).

The visual system is often described as a hierarchy of processing modules, each specialised in a particular attribute of the visual scene. Thus, object recognition is organised as a set of hierarchically connected cortical regions consisting of V1, V2, V4, and the inferotemporal cortex (IT). These structures belong to the ventral visual stream (Seltzer and Pandya, 1978; Baizer et al., 1991; Maunsell and Newsome, 1987). As the last stage of the ventral visual stream (Ungerleider and Mishkin, 1982; Livingstone and Hubel, 1988; Webster et al., 1993), IT combines the information of earlier visual areas relative to shape, color and texture (Gross et al., 1972; Schwartz et al., 1983; Desimone et al., 1984; Tanaka et al., 1991).

The IT cortex represents a large portion of the temporal lobe. The dorsal and posterior border of the IT cortex is located next to area V4 and reaches the inferior occipital sulcus (IOS) whereas its ventral and anterior border reaches the perirhinal cortex and is a few millimetres ventral to the anterior middle temporal sulcus (AMTS). Early clinical and physiological studies in this area have shown that the IT cortex is essential for visual perception, recognition and retention of complex stimuli, such as chromatic and contrast bars, patterns, objects or scenes (Mishkin, 1966; Gross et al., 1972; Ridley and Ettlinger, 1973; Jarvis and Mishkin, 1977; Ridley et al., 1977; Rolls et al., 1977; Gross et al., 1979; Mikami and Kubota, 1980; Fuster and Jervey, 1982; Richmond et al., 1983; Gross, 1994). However, considerable specialisation of function was found in this area (Baylis et al., 1987). In human and non-human primates, IT can be subdivided into two principal regions, the temporal-occipital area (TEO), and the temporal area (TE) (Boussaoud et al., 1991). Whereas TEO receives direct projections from V4, the major source of area TE is TEO (Webster et al., 1991). According to their functional specificity, TE more than TEO has been traditionally involved in visual memory and response to critical visual features (Gross et al., 1972; Mishkin, 1982; Tanaka et al., 1991; Ungerleider and Mishkin, 1982; Miyashita, 1993), whereas TEO has been related to the attentional filtering of the stimulus (Buffalo et al., 2005).

IT Responses to Visual Stimuli

As mentioned above, IT neurons respond to visual features (Desimone et al., 1984; Tanaka et al., 1991; Kobatake and Tanaka, 1994) that combine shape, color, luminance, contrast, and texture. These features are more complex than those optimal for cells from earlier visual areas, but are still less complex than natural objects. However, although complex stimuli are usually necessary to evoke responses in the IT cortex (Gross et al., 1972; Gross, 1973; Ridley and Ettlinger, 1973), simple shapes such as bars can also be effective (Schwarz et al., 1983; Gross et al., 1985; Tanaka et al., 1990). Neurons codifying similar response properties tend to group together and are organized in columns (Gross et al., 1972; Perrett et al., 1984; Gochin et al., 1991; Tanaka et al., 1991; Fujita et al., 1992; Tanaka, 1996; Wang et al., 1996), in such a way that different objects are represented in this area, not by simple summing up the activity of different columns, but rather by combining the activation and inhibition of the whole columnar system (Tsunoda et al., 2001). This procedure increases the number of available activation patterns and thus, it can increase the amount of objects that can be represented by the same neuronal populations. The columnar organisation in the IT cortex is atypical, showing a simultaneous distribution in two different dimensions, vertical and horizontal (Fujita et al., 1992; Wang et al., 1996, 1998; Tsunoda et al, 2001). However, these columns neither extend along the whole IT cortex nor are they organised according to a strict criterion (Fujita et al. 1992). Thus, even though most IT neurons are topographically organised (Fujita et al., 1992; Tanaka, 1993, 2003), some cells show different responsiveness, as it happens in the primary visual cortex (Maldonado et al., 1997).

IT neurons are maximally activated by objects, as long as these objects contain critical features for them (Logothetis and Sheinberg, 1996; Tanaka, 1996). However, they are not exclusively tuned to object images. In fact, it has been found that up to 20% of IT cells are devoted to face recognition (Rolls, 2007), and there are also smaller populations responding to hands, and other body parts (Gross et al., 1969, 1985; Desimone and Gross, 1979; Bruce et al., 1981; Perrett et al., 1982; Desimone et al., 1984; Rolls, 1984, 1991, 1992, 2000; Desimone, 1991; Wachsmuth et al., 1994). This idea is coherent with results from previous anatomical studies suggesting that the human Face Fusiform Area (FFA) in which face neurons are common (Haxby et al., 2002; Spiridon and Kanwisher, 2002; Grill-Spector and Malach, 2004; O'Toole et al., 2005; Spiridon et al., 2006) could correspond to some specific parts of the IT cortex of the monkey -specially the lateral and ventral convexity- (Gross et al., 1972; Bruce et al., 1981; Perrett et al., 1982; Desimone et al., 1984; Baylis et al., 1987; Yamane et al., 1988; Hasselmo et al., 1989a). One particular finding in the IT sensitivity for faces is that IT neurons tuned to these stimuli also respond to isolate parts of the same images (Bruce et al., 1981; Desimone et al., 1984; Tanaka et al., 1991). Responses to facial images in the IT cortex is particular in the sense that it shows similar but graded activity to different stimuli (Gross et al., 1972; Richmond et al., 1983; Desimone et al., 1984; Baylis et al., 1985; Yamane et al., 1988; Young and Yamane, 1992). Two main populations of face-selective cells have been described in the temporal cortex (Rolls, 2007). The first population, more numerous (Gross et al., 1985; Tovee et al., 1994) is tuned to the identity. The second population is located in the STS and encodes other aspects of the face such as face expression, eye gaze, or head movement. Figure 1 shows the mean rate responses (spikes/sec) of an IT cell recorded in an awake monkey while performing a visual discrimination task. This cell responds differentially to both stimuli, which represent two different faces with different features. Some IT neurons detect facial features to build up useful schemas for recognition, therefore changes or removal of these features cause changes in the cell responses. Figure 2 shows this feature-dependence observed in an IT cell. The response rate of the cell decreases when the main facial features are replaced by a flat surface.

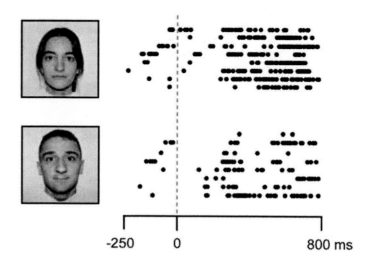

Figure 1. Response of an IT cell to two different facial images. Responses are significantly different (ANOVA, p<0.05). The red dashed line represents the stimulus onset. Cell responses are plotted as rasters where each dot corresponds to a cell discharge.

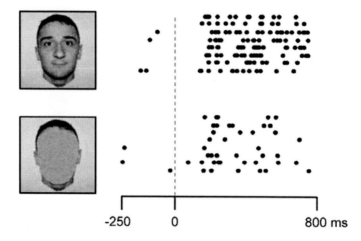

Figure 2. Response of an IT cell to the same facial image when the facial area is removed. Responses to each image are significantly different (ANOVA, p<0.05). The red dashed line represents the stimulus onset. Cell responses are represented as in Figure 1.

Response Invariance in IT

The visual experience might guide facial cell responses in the IT cortex to provide an economical and ensemble-encoded representation of those items normally found in the natural world. IT cells respond to familiar stimuli by shaping their selectivity (Miyashita, 1988; Miyashita and Chang, 1988; Sakai and Miyashita, 1991; Logothetis et al., 1995; Kobatake et al., 1998; Baker et al., 2002; Sigala et al., 2002; Freedman et al., 2006; Haushofer and Kanwisher, 2007) over the few first presentations (Rolls et al., 1989).

At this high stage of the visual processing, neurons should be able to extract the physical characteristics of the stimulus showing invariance to different representations of the same image (Tompa et al., 2002). Some authors have demonstrated that attention modulates the activity of neurons in the ventral visual pathway (Kastner et al., 1998; Wocjiulik et al., 1998). Thus, attention could work as a selective mechanism, by enhancing some areas of the visual stimulus presented on the visual scene which are more relevant (Richmond et al., 1983; Moran and Desimone, 1985; Desimone and Duncan, 1995; Avidan et al., 2003).

Size and color invariance have been reported in the IT cortex. Results from different studies suggested that large stimuli would be optimal for IT neurons because of the large size of their receptive fields (RFs) (Gross et al., 1969; 1972; Kobatake and Tanaka, 1994; Op De Beeck and Vogels, 2000). However, compared with earlier visual areas, IT cells show response invariance to changes in the stimulus size (Schwartz et al., 1983; Rolls and Baylis, 1986; Ito et al, 1995). Several authors have showed the involvement of posterior IT cortex in color processing for both human (Zeki and Marini, 1998) and non-human primates (Gross et al. 1972; Dean, 1979; Komatsu et al., 1992; Komatsu and Ideura, 1993; Horel, 1994; Heywood et al., 1995; Takechi et al., 1997). Nevertheless, the role that color plays for visual processing in the IT cortex is not clear from the literature, and whereas some studies find that color can reduce the latency and increase the accuracy of object recognition (Price and Humphreys, 1989; Wurm et al., 1993; Humphrey et al., 1994; Lee and Perrett, 1997; Delorme et al., 2000), other studies suggest that color is highly accessory for object recognition (Ostergaard and Davidoff, 1985; Biederman and Ju, 1988, Davidoff and Ostergaard, 1988). Despite of the controversy, it is clear that some face-selective IT neurons but specially those cells driven by simple shapes (Gross et al., 1972; Perrett et al., 1982; Tanaka et al., 1991; Komatsu et al., 1992; Heywood et al., 1995; Tovee et al., 1996) are color-invariant, in such a way that shape and color seem to be separately analyzed in this area (Komatsu and Ideura, 1993; Horel, 1994; Tootell et al., 2004), and organized in different columns (Tanaka, 2003; Tootell et al., 2004). In agreement with this idea, several studies found that shape sensitivity is also strongly maintained in many IT cells when luminance, texture or contrast are modified (Sáry et al., 1993; Ito et al., 1994; Tanaka et al., 2001; Koida and Komatsu, 2005), suggesting that the cell may be sensitive to some critical features of the image. Figure 3 shows an example of color-invariance response in an IT cell. Both images represent the same face maintaining all the parameters constant except color.

Another characteristic observed in the IT responses is the feature-independent response. It is believed that sensitivity of IT neurons to image features is based on their input from from area V4 (Pasupathy and Connor, 1999; Hanazawa and Komatsu, 2001) and their columnar organization (Fujita and Fujita, 1996; Tanigawa et al., 1998; Tanifuji et al., 2001).

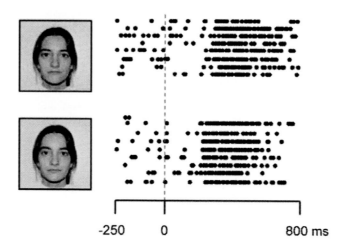

-250   0   800 ms

Figure 3. Example of one IT cell that shows response invariance to color. The color do not induce significant changes in the cell response (ANOVA, p<0.05). The red dashed line represents the stimulus onset.

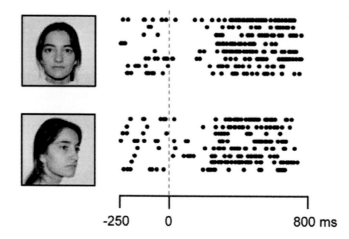

-250   0   800 ms

Figure 4. View-invariance. Responses of an IT cell to two images of the same person taken from a different point of view. Despite the images are different, the cell response does not show significant different responses to both images (ANOVA, p<0.05). The red dashed line represents the stimulus onset.

However, the number of features that can be efficiently represented in the IT cortex is limited (Wang et al., 1998; Tsunoda et al., 2001), and therefore the information about the spatial arrangement of these features is also necessary to obtain an optimal representation of objects (Elliffe et al., 2002; Yamane et al., 2006). In supporting this idea there are several studies showing that some IT neurons respond equally to object images with different colors, textures, or local shapes, as long as they maintain a specific spatial disposition or point of view (Desimone et al., 1984; Hasselmo et al., 1989a; Perrett et al., 1991; Booth and Rolls, 1998). This response constancy does not depend on the presence or absence of critical features (Perrett et al., 1982; Tanaka, 1993, 1996; Mikami et al., 1994). View-invariant cells receive direct excitatory projections from view-dependent cells (Perrett et al., 1987; Booth and Rolls, 1998; Hasselmo et al., 1989b) to guarantee an efficient storage of all the views associated to the same stimulus (Koenderink and Van Doorn, 1979; Poggio and Edelman, 1990; Logothetis et al., 1994; Ullman, 1996). Figure 4 shows a view-invariant IT cell. The image of the same person induces the same response regardless the point of view.

Sensitivity to Spatial Frequency

A relevant component in visual stimuli is the spatial frequency. The IT cortex has been proved to extract regularities from the visual scene, showing sensitivity to the spatial frequency of the images (Robson, 1975; Rolls, 1992, 2000; Wallis and Rolls, 1997; Rolls and Deco, 2002). This spatial sensitivity can be useful to extract the critical features that define shapes and objects, and therefore it can contribute to the categorisation process. Several studies have shown that frequencies between 8 and 16 cycles are crucial information for face recognition (Fiorentini et al., 1983; Costen et al., 1994, 1996; Grabowska and Nowicka, 1996; Näsänen, 1999; Morrison and Schyns, 2001; Collin et al., 2004).

Sensitivity to spatial frequency has been largely studied in the visual system since many years ago, when the idea that visual neurons, particularly at the first stages of visual processing, could work as spatial filters was proposed (Enroth-Cugell and Robson, 1966; Campbell and Robson, 1968; Cooper and Robson, 1968; Campbell et al., 1969; Blakemore and Campbell, 1969; Pollen et al., 1971; Maffei and Fiorentini, 1973; Glezer et al., 1973; Robson, 1975; Graham, 1977; Glezer and Cooperman, 1977; Movshon et al., 1978; Maffei et al., 1979; De Valois and De Valois, 1980; Robson, 1980; Braddick, 1981; Tolhurst and Thompson, 1981; De Valois et al., 1982; Kulikowski et al., 1982; Pollen and Ronner, 1983; Kelly and Burbeck, 1984; Westheimer, 1984). This had been previously described in the auditory system (Campbell, 1974, Robson, 1975; De Valois and De Valois, 1980). Thus, although the neural mechanisms involved in the spatial filtering do not perfectly fit to a Fourier analysis (Yang and Blake, 1991), it has been assumed that the visual system must perform some kind of analogous operations to allow the spatial decoding. Moreover, since this property is commonly observed in several ventral visual areas, the filtering can be considered as a continuous mechanism (Rodieck, 1965; Enroth-Cugell and Robson, 1966; Cleland et al., 1979; So and Shapley, 1979, Lisenmeier et al., 1982; Kelly and Burbeck, 1984; Westheimer, 1984; Turk and Pentland, 1991; Pessoa and Leitao, 1999), and therefore the frequency sensitivity observed in the IT cortex might result from the input this area receive from other lower visual areas (Enroth-Cugell and Robson, 1966; Victor and Shapley, 1979; De Valois et al., 1982; Foster et al., 1985; Tootell et al., 1988; Kilavic et al., 2007). The LGN could also be a relevant source of the spatial frequency sensitivity observed in the IT cortex. It has been reported that direct projections from the parvocellular dorsal LGN (Hernández-González et al. 1994; Webster et al., 1995) probably involved in the processing of high spatial frequencies (Parker et al., 1992; Delorme et al., 2000), reach the posterior ipsilateral IT cortex. Since both high and low spatial frequencies are necessary for optimal object recognition (Kulikowski and Vidyasagar, 1986) additional information related to low spatial frequencies must reach the IT cortex.

Sensitivity to Retinal Disparity

Sensitivity to retinal disparity is the most relevant cue for stereopsis. It is believed that retinal disparity information is mainly processed in the dorsal pathway. However, recent studies have provided evidence that retinal disparity is also processed in the IT cortex (Janssen et al., 1999; 2000a, 2000b, 2001; Uka et al., 2000; Tanaka et al., 2001). The extent in which disparity influences the IT activity remains unclear but some authors have proposed that up to 60% of IT neurons could be sensitive to horizontal disparity (Uka et al., 2000), suggesting that disparity sensitivity in the IT cortex could provide a reliable cue for shape perception, and therefore for object recognition.

Categorization in the IT Cortex

Different authors have related the activity of the IT cortex to the categorization process (Thorpe and Fabre-Thorpe, 2001; Matsumoto et al., 2005; Afraz et al., 2006; Kiani et al., 2007). This may indicate that the activity observed in some IT neurons could reflect a probabilistic mechanism for category associations. Since images of the same category have more features in common, by codifying those critical features defining each category, the IT cortex could reach a reliable image categorization (Thorpe and Fabre-Thorpe, 2001; Matsumoto et al., 2005; Afraz et al., 2006; Kiani et al., 2007). Figure 5 shows a cell that displays significantly different responses for two images whowing obects of different category.

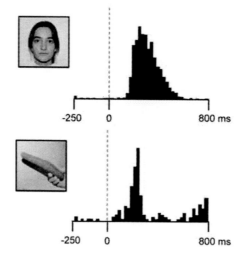

Figure 5. Example of the differential response to facial and non-facial stimuli in IT cells. The mean response rate was significantly different for both images. The red dashed line represents the stimulus onset. Cell responses are represented as peri-stimulus histograms.

Temporal Characteristics of Responses in the IT Cortex

The time required for processing the visual information across the visual system is commonly assessed by measuring the response latency of the cells (Gawne et al., 1996; Gawne, 2000; Reich et al., 2001; Tamura and Tanaka, 2001; Oram et al., 2002). The visual processing gains functional complexity along the progressive stages of the visual pathway (Carpenter and Grossberg, 1987; Schyns and Oliva, 1994; Ullman, 1995; Nowak and Bullier, 1997), and therefore the response latency should necessarily vary from stage to stage, depending on its location within the pathway (Felleman and Van Essen, 1991; Van Essen et al., 1992; Nowak et al., 1995; Hilgetag et al., 1996; Nowak and Bullier, 1997; Schmolesky et al., 1998; Azzopardi et al., 2003) and on the specific nature of its connections. Cells located in dorsal visual areas (related to the magnocellular system) show shorter latencies than cells in the ventral areas (parvocellular system) (Merigan and Maunsell, 1993; Nowak and Bullier, 1997; Schmolesky et al., 1998; Schroeder et al., 1998). Latency values are strongly dependent on both, the visual and the cognitive properties of the stimulus. Latency is influenced by contrast and luminance (Maunsell and Gibson, 1992; Gawne et al., 1996; Gawne, 2000; Reich et al., 2001; Oram et al., 2002) or the spatial arrangement among features (Perrett et al., 1982; Desimone et al., 1984; Logothetis and Sheinberg, 1996; Tanaka, 1996), but it is also influenced by familiarity (Pascalis and Bachevalier, 1998) or the category evoked by the stimulus (McCarthy et al., 1999; Carmel and Bentin, 2002; Kiani et al., 2005).

The reported latencies in the IT cortex range from 70 to 220 ms (Rolls et al., 1977; Perrett et al., 1982; Richmond et al., 1983; Hasselmo et al., 1989a; Jeffreys, 1989; Tanaka et al., 2001; Thorpe and Fabre-Thorpe, 2001; Eger et al., 2003). These data show high variability, which may be useful as a brain cognitive mechanism for attentional filtering. In this sense, some authors have suggested that the visual system can modulate their spike timing to highlight or suppress some particular information, (Eckhorn and Pöpel, 1974; Richmond et al., 1987; Rieke et al., 1997; Thorpe, 1990), and therefore to codify the relevance of the stimulus. Furthermore, it has been suggested that temporal response profile in high visual areas may be related to different aspects of the visual processing. Thus, whereas the earliest part of IT responses can be related to coarse information about the stimulus category, a later component has been more oriented to a detailed processing, including those shades involved in the emotional analysis of images (Sugase et al., 1999).

Superior Temporal Sulcus

Many authors have reported responses with similar characteritics in the IT cortex and the Superior Temporal Sulcus (STS). For this reason, in some aspects it is difficult to define the functional limits existing between these two regions. The STS is the cortical associative area, which corresponds to the anatomical border between IT and other temporal structures.

Anatomically, the STS can be divided in three different subregions: superior bank, inferior bank, and the fundus. All three are functionally different. The cells of the superior bank, known as Superior Temporal Polisensory area (STP) (Bruce et al., 1981), respond to visual (Desimone and Gross, 1979; Perrett et al., 1985 b; Baylis et al., 1987; Oram and Perrett, 1994, 1996) auditory and somatosensory stimuli (Desimone and Gross, 1979; Bruce et al., 1981; Baylis et al., 1987; Iwai et al., 1987; Mistlin and Perrett, 1990; Gibson and

Maunsell, 1997), whereas the cells in the inferior bank are exclusively visual (Seltzer and Pandya, 1978, 1991, 1994; Desimone and Gross, 1979; Baylis et al., 1987; Baizer et al., 1991; Barnes and Pandya, 1992). The fundus of the STS (FST) shows responses to those found in STP (Seltzer and Pandya, 1978, 1991, 1994; Baizer et al., 1991; Barnes and Pandya, 1992), though the percentage of polisensory cells in this region is smaller. Studies in human and non-human primates have found neurons selective to faces in both banks and the fundus of the anterior STS (Gross et al., 1972; Bruce et al., 1981; Perrett et al., 1982; Desimone et al., 1984; Baylis et al., 1987; Yamane et al., 1988; Tanaka et al., 1991; DeRenzi et al., 1994; Puce et al., 1996; Kanwisher et al., 1997; Vermeire et al., 1998; Logothetis et al., 1999; McCarthy et al., 1999; Tsao et al., 2003; Pinsk et al. 2005). Moreover, there are also some cells responding to body parts, hands, and complete bodies in these subregions (Gross et al., 1969; Desimone et al., 1984; Logothetis et al., 1999; Tsao et al., 2003; Pinsk et al., 2005). It has been suggested that neurons from the STP are sensitive to corporal movements (Bruce et al., 1981; Perrett et al., 1985a, 1989; Oram and Perrett, 1994, 1996; Anderson and Siegel, 1999; Haxby et al., 2000), as it occurs in the human Extrastriate Body Area (EBA). Cells from the FST are related to the analysis of the entire human body (Wachsmuth et al., 1994). Neurons from the inferior bank are tuned to stationary stimuli (Janssen et al., 1999), with the only exception of some specific populations which are activated with hand movements (Perrett et al., 1989).

These observations suggest that the STS and the IT cortices are both involved in the processing of visual complex stimuli. Indeed, identical firing patterns have been found in IT and STS (Perrett et al., 1982). As it occurrs with IT cells, neurons in the STS show graded responses to the visual stimuli (Baylis et al., 1985). Moreover, these responses are also sensitive to experience (Baylis and Rolls, 1987; Rolls et al., 1989), and distributed in columns according to their selectivity (Perrett et al., 1984; Wang et al., 1996, 1998; Fujita, 2002). In both, IT cortex and STS there is response invariance, although this characteristic shows some differences between both areas. Neurons from the STS show invariance to size and color changes (Perrett et al., 1982, Rolls, 1984), but still maintain some kind of view-dependent responses (Perrett et al., 1985b; Hasselmo et al., 1989b). These differences between the response patterns of IT and STS suggest subtle differences in the role played by these two areas. When using facial stimuli, it has been observed that whereas IT cells seem to be more involved in processing the identity, neurons in the STS are preferentially activated by facial expressions and gestures (Perrett et al., 1985a; Hasselmo et al., 1989a).

Neurons in the STS are also sensitive to spatial frequency (Rolls et al., 1985, 1987), showing a peculiar pattern of activity. While the optimal stimulus for a particular cell tuned to a specific band of frequencies evokes excitatory responses, a more heterogeneous stimulus generates inhibitory responses (Rolls et al., 1985). Thus, is possible that for complex images, responses will depend on the degree of interaction between facilitation and inhibition (Rolls et al., 1987).

Conclusion

The published data suggest the involvement of the IT cortex in complex visual analysis. IT cells may combine their sensitivity for specific visual cues, becoming specially tuned to natural objects such as faces or body parts. Sets of neurons that are broadly tuned to individual cues may represent the neural substrate for object recognition. The discharge rate of many IT neurons to visual stimuli is graded. Some neurons exhibit size, color or view invariance that might be the result of the convergence of simple image properties extracted at earlier stages in the visual system. Some sort of spatial frequency filtering could be involved in this processing.

References

Afraz, SR; Kiani, R; Esteky, H. Microstimulation of inferotemporal cortex influences face categorization. *Nature*, 2006 442, 692-695.

Anderson, KC; Siegel, RM. Optic flow selectivity in the anterior superior temporal polysensory area, STPa, of the behaving monkey. *The Journal of Neuroscience*, 1999 19, 2681-2692.

Avidan, G; Levy, I; Hendler, T; Zohary, E; Malach R. Spatial vs object specific attention in high-order visual areas. *Neuroimage*, 2003 19, 308-318.

Azzopardi, P; Fallah, M; Gross, CG; Rodman, HR. Response latencies of neurons in visual areas MT and MST of monkeys with striate cortex lesions. *Neurophyschologia*, 2003 41, 1738-1756.

Baizer, JS; Ungerleider, LG; Desimone R. Organization of visual inputs to the inferior temporal and posterior parietal cortex in macaques. *The Journal of Neuroscience*, 1991 11, 168-190.

Baker, IC; Behrmann, M; Olson, CR. Impact learning on representation of parts and wholes in monkey inferotemporal cortex. *Nature Neuroscience*, 2002 5, 1210-1216.

Barnes, CL; Pandya DN. Efferent cortical connections of multimodal cortex of the superior temporal sulcus in the rhesus monkey. *The Journal of Comparative Neurology*, 1992 318, 222-244.

Baylis, GC; Rolls, ET ; Leonard, CM. Functional subdivisions of the temporal lobe neocortex. *The Journal of Neuroscience*, 1987 7, 330-342.

Baylis, GC; Rolls, ET. Responses of neurons in the inferior temporal cortex in short term and serial recognition memory tasks. *Experimental Brain Research*, 1987 65, 614-622.

Baylis, GC; Rolls, ET; Leonard, CM. Selectivity between faces in the responses of a population of neurons in the cortex in the superior temporal sulcus of the monkey. *Brain Research*, 1985 342, 91-102.

Biederman, I; Ju, G. Surface versus edge-based determinants of visual recognition. *Cognitive Psychology*, 1988 20, 38-64.

Blakemore, C; Campbell, FW. Adaptation to spatial stimuli. *The Journal of Physiology*, 1969 200, 11-13.

Booth, MCA; Rolls, ET. View-invariant representations of familiar objects by neurons in the inferior temporal visual cortex. *Cerebral Cortex*, 1998 8, 510-523.

Boussaoud, D; Desimone, R; Ungerleider, LG. Visual topography of area TEO in the macaque. *The Journal of Comparative Neurology*, 1991 306, 554-575.

Braddick, O. Spatial frequency analysis in vision. *Nature*, 1981 291, 9-11.

Bruce, C; Desimone, R; Gross, CG. Visual properties of neurons in a polysensory area in superior temporal sulcus of the macaque. *Journal of Neurophysiology*, 1981 46, 369-384.

Buffalo, EA; Bertini G; Ungerleider, LG; Desimone, R. Impaired filtering of distracter stimuli by TE neurons following V4 and TEO lesions in macaques. *Cerebral Cortex*, 2005 15, 141-151.

Campbell, FW. The transmission of spatial information through the visual system. In Schmitt, O; Worden, FG, editors. *The Neurosciences: Third Study Program*. Cambridge: MIT Press; 1974.

Campbell, FW; Cooper, GF; Robson, JG; Sachs, MB. The spatial selectivity of visual cells of the cat and the squirrel monkey. *The Journal of Physiology*, 1969 204, 120-121.

Campbell, FW; Robson, JG. Application of Fourier analysis to the visibility of gratings. *The Journal of Physiology*, 1968 197, 551-566.

Carmel, D; Bentin, S. Domain specificity versus expertise: factors influencing distinct processing of faces. *Cognition*, 2002 83, 1-29.

Carpenter, GA; Grossberg, S. A massively parallel architecture for a self-organizing neural pattern recognition machine. *Computer Vision, Graphics and Image Processing*, 1987 37, 54-115.

Cleland, BG; Harding, TH; Tulunay-Keesey, U. Visual resolution and receptive field size: examination of two kinds of cat retinal ganglion cell. *Science*, 1979 205, 1015-1017.

Collin, CA; Liu, CH; Troje, NF; McMullen, PA; Chaudhuri, A. Face recognition is affected by similarity in spatial frequency range to a greater degree than within-category object recognition. *Journal of Experimental Psychology. Human Perception and Performance*, 2004 30, 975-987.

Cooper, GF; Robson, JG. Successive transformations of spatial information in the visual system. *Conference on Pattern Recognition IEE/NPL*, 1968 47, 134-143.

Costen, NP; Parker, DM; Craw, I. Effects of high-pass and low-pass spatial filtering on face identification. *Perception and Psychophysics*, 1996, 58, 602-612.

Costen, NP; Parker, DM; Craw, I. Spatial content and spatial quantisation effects in face recognition. *Perception*, 1994 23, 129-146.

Damasio, AR. Disorders of complex visual processing: agnosias, achromatopsia. Balint's syndrome and related difficulties of orientation and construction. In: Mesulam, MM, editor. *Principles of behavioural neurology*. Philadelphia: Davis, FA; 1985; 259-288.

Davidoff, JB; Ostergaard, AL. The role of color in categorical judgements. *The Quarterly Journal of Experimental Psychology*, 1988 40, 533-544.

De Valois, RL, De Valois, KK. Spatial vision. *Annual Review of Psychology*, 1980 31, 309-341.

De Valois, RL; Albrecht, DG; Thorell, LG. Spatial frequency selectivity of cells in macaque visual cortex. *Vision Research*, 1982 22, 545-559.

Dean, P. Visual cortex ablation and thresholds for successively presented stimuli in rhesus monkeys. II. Hue. *Experimental Brain Research*, 1979 35, 69-83.

Delorme, A; Richard, G; Fabre-Thorpe, M. Ultra-rapid categorisation of natural scenes does not rely on color cues: a study in monkeys and humans. *Vision Research*, 2000 40, 2187-2200.

DeRenzi, E; Perani, D; Carlesimo, GA; Silveri, MC; Fazio, F. Prosopagnosia can be associated with damage confined to the right hemisphere -an MRI and PET a study in a review of the literature-. *Neuropsychologia*, 1994 32, 893-902.

Desimone, R. Face-selective cells in the temporal cortex of monkeys. *Journal of Cognitive Neuroscience*, 1991 3, 1-8.

Desimone, R; Albright, TD, Gross, CG; Bruce, C. Stimulus-selective properties of inferior temporal neurons in the macaque. *The Journal of Neuroscience*, 1984 4, 2051-2062.

Desimone, R; Duncan, J. Neural mechanisms of selective visual attention. *Annual Review of Neuroscience*, 1995 18, 193-222.

Desimone, R; Gross, CG. Visual areas in the temporal cortex of the macaque. *Brain Research*, 1979 178, 363-380.

Eckhorn, R; Pöpel B; Rigorous and extended application of information theory to the afferent visual system of the cat. I. Basic concepts. *Kybernetik*, 1974 16, 191-200.

Eger, E; Jedynak, A; Iwaki, T; Skrandies, W. Rapid extraction of emotional expression: evidence from evoked potential fields during brief presentation of face stimuli. *Neuropsychologia*, 2003 41, 808-817.

Elliffe, MCM; Rolls, ET; Stringer, SM. Invariant recognition of feature combinations in the visual system. *Biological Cybernetics*, 2002 86, 59-71.

Enroth-Cugell, C; Robson, JG. The contrast sensitivity of retinal ganglion cells of the cat. *The Journal of Physiology*, 1966 187, 517-552.

Felleman, DJ; Van Essen, DC. Distributed hierarchical processing in the primate cerebral cortex. *Cerebral Cortex*, 1991 1, 1-47.

Fiorentini, A; Pirchio, M; Spinelli, D. Electrophysiological evidence for spatial frequency selective mechanisms in adults and infants. *Vision Research*, 1983 23, 119-127.

Foster, KH; Gaska, JP; Nagler, M; Pollen, DA. Spatial and temporal frequency selectivity of neurones in visual cortical areas V1 and V2 of the macaque monkey. *The Journal of Physiology*, 1985 365, 331-63.

Freedman, DJ; Riesenhuber, M; Poggio, T; Miller, EK. Experience-dependent sharpening of visual shape selectivity in inferior temporal cortex. *Cerebral Cortex*, 2006 16: 1631-1644.

Fujita, I. The inferior temporal cortex: architecture, computation, and representation. *Journal of Neurocytology*, 2002 31, 359-371.

Fujita, I; Fujita, T. Intrinsic connections in the macaque inferior temporal cortex. *The Journal of Comparative Neurology*, 1996 368, 467-486.

Fujita, I; Tanaka, K; Ito, M; Cheng, K. Columns for visual features of objects in monkey inferotemporal cortex. *Nature*, 1992 360, 343-346.

Fuster, JM; Jervey, JP. Neuronal firing in the inferotemporal cortex of the monkey in a visual memory task. *The Journal of Neuroscience*, 1982 2, 361-75.

Gawne, TJ. The simultaneous coding of orientation and contrast in the responses of V1 complex cells. *Experimental Brain Research*, 2000 133, 293-302.

Gawne, TJ; Kjaer, TW; Richmond, BJ. Latency: another potential code for feature binding in striate cortex. *Journal of Neurophysiology*, 1996 76, 1356-1360.

Gibson, JR; Maunsell, JH. Sensory modality specificity of neural activity related to memory in visual cortex. *Journal of Neurophysiology*, 1997 78, 1263-1275.

Glezer, VD; Cooperman, AM. Local spectral analysis in the visual cortex. *Biological Cybernetics*, 1977 28, 101-108.

Glezer, VD; Ivanoff, VA; Tscherbach, TA. Investigation of complex and hypercomplex receptive fields of visual cortex of the cat as spatial frequency filters. *Vision Research*, 1973 13, 1875-1904.

Gochin, PM; Miller, EK; Gross, CG; Gerstein, GL. Functional interactions among neurons in inferior temporal cortex of the awake macaque. *Experimental Brain Research*, 1991 84, 505-516.

Grabowska, A; Nowicka, A. Visual-spatial-frequency model of cerebral asymmetry: a critical survey of behavioural and electrophysiological studies. *Psychological Bulletin*, 1996 120, 434-449.

Graham, N. Visual detection of aperiodic spatial stimuli by probability summation among narrowband channels. *Vision Research*, 1977 17, 637-652.

Grill-Spector, K; Malach R. The human visual cortex. *Annual Review of Neuroscience*, 2004 27, 649-677.

Gross, C.G. Inferotemporal cortex and vision. *Progress in Physiological Psychology*, 1973 5, 77-123.

Gross, CG. How inferior temporal cortex became a visual area. *Cerebral Cortex*, 1994 5, 455-469.

Gross, CG; Bender, DB; Gerstein, GL. Activity of inferior temporal neurons in behaving monkeys. *Neuropsychology*, 1979 17, 215-229.

Gross, CG; Bender, DB; Rocha-Miranda, CE. Visual receptive fields of neurons in inferotemporal cortex of the monkey. *Science*, 1969 166, 1303-1306.

Gross, CG; Desimone, R; Albright, TD; Schwartz, EL. Inferior temporal cortex and pattern recognition. *Experimental Brain Research*, 1985 11, 179-201.

Gross, CG; Rocha-Miranda, CE; Bender DB. Visual properties of neurons in inferotemporal cortex of the macaque. *Journal of Neurophysiology*, 1972 35, 96-111.

Hanazawa, A; Komatsu, H. Influence of the direction of elemental luminance gradients on the responses of V4 cells to textured surfaces. *The Journal of Neuroscience*, 2001 21, 4490-4497.

Hasselmo, ME, Rolls, ET; Baylis, GC; Nalwa, V. Object-centred encoding by face-selective neurons in the cortex in the superior temporal sulcus of the monkey. *Experimental Brain Research*, 1989b 75, 417-429.

Hasselmo, ME; Rolls, ET; Baylis, GC. The role of expression and identity in the face-selective responses of neurons in the temporal visual-cortex of the monkey. *Behavioural Brain Research*, 1989a 32, 203-218.

Haushofer, J; Kanwisher, N. In the eye of the beholder: visual experience and categories in the human brain. *Neuron*, 2007 53, 773-775.

Haxby, JV; Hoffman, EA; Gobbini, MI. Human neural systems for face recognition and social communication. *Biological Psychiatry*, 2002 51, 59-67.

Haxby, JV; Hoffman, EA; Gobbini, MI. The distributed human neural system for face perception. *Trends in Cognitive Sciences*, 2000 4, 223-233.

Hernández-González, A; Cavada, C; Reinoso-Suárez, F. The lateral geniculate nucleus projects to the inferior temporal cortex in the macaque monkey. *Neuroreport*, 1994 20, 2693-2696.

Heywood, CA; Gaffan, D; Cowey, A. Cerebral achromatopsia in monkeys. *The European Journal of Neuroscience*, 1995 7, 1064-1073.

Hilgetag, CC; O'Neill, MA; Young, MP. Indeterminate organization of the visual system. *Science*, 1996 271, 776-777.

Horel, JA. Retrieval of color and form during suppression of temporal cortex with cold. *Behavioural Brain Research*, 1994 65, 165-172.

Humphrey, GK; Goodale, MA; Jakobson, LS; Servos, P. The role of surface information in object recognition: studies of a visual form agnosic and normal subjects. *Perception*, 1994 23, 1457-1481.

Ito, M; Fujita, I; Tamura, H; Tanaka, K. Processing of contrast polarity of visual images in inferotemporal cortex of the macaque monkey. *Cerebral Cortex*, 1994 4, 499-508.

Ito, M; Tamura, H; Fujita, I; Tanaka K. Size and position invariance of neuronal responses in monkey inferotemporal cortex. *Journal of Neurophysiology*, 1995 73, 218-226.

Iwai, E; Aihara, T; Hikosaka, K. Inferotemporal neurons of the monkey responsive to auditory signal. *Brain Research*, 1987 410, 121-124.

Janssen, P; Vogels, R; Liu, Y; Orban, GA. Macaque inferior temporal neurons are selective for three-dimensional boundaries and surfaces. *The Journal of Neuroscience*, 2001 21, 9419-9429.

Janssen, P; Vogels, R; Orban, GA. Macaque inferior temporal neurons are selective for disparity-defined three-dimensional shapes. *Proceedings of the National Academy of Sciences of the United States of America*, 1999 96, 8217-8222.

Janssen, P; Vogels, R; Orban, GA. Selectivity for 3D shape that reveals distinct areas within macaque inferior temporal cortex. *Science*, 2000b 288, 2054-2056.

Janssen, P; Vogels, R; Orban, GA. Three-dimensional shape coding in inferior temporal cortex. *Neuron*, 2000a 27, 385-397.

Jarvis, CD; Mishkin, M. Responses of cells in the inferior temporal cortex of monkeys during visual discrimination reversal. *Social Neuroscience*, 1977 3, 564.

Jeffreys, DA. A face-responsive potential recorded from the human scalp. *Experimental Brain Research*, 1989 78, 193-202.

Kanwisher, N; McDermott, J; Chun, MM. The fusiform face area: A module in human extrastriate cortex specialized for face perception. *The Journal of Neuroscience*, 1997 17, 4302-4311.

Kastner, S; De Weerd, P; Desimone, R; Ungerleider, LG. Mechanisms of directed attention in the human extrastriate cortex as revealed by functional MRI. *Science*, 1998 282, 108-111.

Kelly, DH; Burbeck, CA. Critical problems in spatial vision. *Critical Reviews in Biomedical Engineering*, 1984 10, 125-177.

Kiani, R; Esteky, H; Mirpour, K; Tanaka, K. Object category structure in response patterns of neuronal population in monkey inferior temporal cortex. *Journal of Neurophysiology*, 2007 97, 4296-4309.

Kiani, R; Esteky, H; Tanaka, K. Differences in onset latency of macaque inferotemporal neural responses to primate and non-primate faces. *Journal of Neurophysiology*, 2005 94, 1587-1596.

Kilavic, BE; Silveira, LC; Kremers, J. Spatial receptive field properties of lateral geniculate cells in the owl monkey (Aotus azarae) at different contrasts: a comparative study. *The European Journal of Neuroscience*, 2007 26, 992-1006.

Klüver, H; Bucy, PC. Preliminary analysis of functions of the temporal lobe in monkeys. *Archives of Neurology and Psychiatry*, 1939 42, 979-1000.

Kobatake, E; Tanaka K. Neuronal selectivities to complex object features in the ventral visual pathway of the macaque cerebral cortex. *Journal of Neurophysiology*, 1994 71, 856-67.

Kobatake, E; Wang, G; Tanaka, K. Effects of shape-discrimination training on the selectivity of inferotemporal cells in adult monkeys. *Journal of Neurophysiology*, 1998 80, 324-330.

Koenderink, JJ; Van Doorn, AJ. The internal representation of solid shape with respect to vision. *Biological Cybernetics*, 1979 32, 211-217.

Koida, K; Komatsu, H. Effect of task-demand on the response of color selective TE neurons of the monkey. *Abstracts- Society for Neuroscience*, 2005 31, 743.6.

Komatsu, H; Ideura, Y; Kaki, S; Yamane, S. Color selectivity of neurons in the inferior temporal cortex of the awake macaque monkey. *The Journal of Neuroscience*, 1992 12, 408-424.

Komatsu. H; Ideura, Y. Relationships between color, shape, and pattern selectivities of neurons in the inferior temporal cortex of the monkey. *Journal of Neurophysiology*, 1993 70, 677-694.

Kulikowski, J; Marcelja, S; Bishop, PO. Theory of spatial position and spatial frequency relations in the receptive fields of simple cells in the visual cortex. *Biological Cybernetics*, 1982 43, 187-198.

Kulikowski, JJ; Vidyasagar, TR. Space and spatial frequency: analysis and representation in the macaque striate cortex. *Experimental Brain Research*, 1986 64, 5-18.

Lee, KJ; Perrett, DI. Presentation-time measures of the effects of manipulations in color space on discrimination of famous faces. *Perception*, 1997 26, 733-752.

Lisenmeier, RA; Frishman, LJ; Jakiela, HG; Enroth-Cugell, C. Receptive field properties of x and y cells in the cat retina derived from contrast sensitivity measurements. *Vision Research*, 1982 22, 1173-1183.

Livingstone, M; Hubel, D. Segregation of form, color, movement, and depth: anatomy, physiology, and perception. *Science*, 1988 240, 740-749.

Logothetis, NK, Sheinberg, DL. Visual object recognition. *Annual Review Neuroscience*, 1996 19, 577-621.

Logothetis, NK; Guggenberger, H; Peled, S; Pauls, J. Functional imaging of the monkey brain. *Nature Neuroscience*, 1999 2, 555-562.

Logothetis, NK; Pauls, J; Bülthoff, HH; Poggio, T. View-dependent object recognition by monkeys. *Current Biology*, 1994 4, 401-414.

Logothetis, NK; Pauls, J; Poggio, T. Shape representation in the inferior temporal cortex of monkeys. *Current Biology*, 1995 5, 552-563.

Maffei, L; Fiorentini, A. The visual cortex as a spatial frequency analyser. *Vision Research*, 1973 13, 1255-1267.

Maffei, L; Morrone, C; Pirchio, M; Sandini, G. Response of visual cortical cells to periodic and non-periodic stimuli. *The Journal of Physiology*, 1979 296: 27-47.

Maldonado, PE; Godecke, I; Gray, C.M; Bonhoeffer T. Orientation selectivity in pinwheel centers in cat striate cortex. *Science*, 1997 276, 1551- 1555.

Matsumoto, N; Sugase-Miyamoto, Y; Okada, M. Categorical signals in a single-trial neuron activity of the inferotemporal cortex. *Neuroreport*, 2005 16, 1707-1710.

Maunsell, JH; Gibson, JR. Visual response latencies in striate cortex of the macaque monkey. *Journal of Neurophysiology*, 2002 68, 1332-1344.

Maunsell, JH; Newsome WT. Visual processing in monkey extrastriate cortex. *Annual Review of Neuroscience*, 1987 10, 363-401.

McCarthy, G; Puce, A; Belger, A; Allison, T. Electrophysiological studies of human face perception. II: Response properties of face-specific potentials generated in occipitotemporal cortex. *Cerebral Cortex*, 1999 9, 431-444.

Merigan, WH; Maunsell, JHR. How parallel are the primate visual pathways? *Annual Review of Neuroscience*, 1993 16, 369-402.

Mikami, A; Kubota, K. Inferotemporal neuron activities and color discrimination with delay. *Brain Research*, 1980 182, 65-78.

Mikami, A; Nakamura, K; Kubota, K. Neuronal responsas to photographs in the superior temporal sulcus of the rhesus monkeys. *Behavioural Brain Research*, 1994 60, 1-13.

Mishkin, M. A memory system in the monkey. *Philosophical Transactions of the Royal Society of London*, 1982 298, 83-95.

Mishkin, M. Visual mechanisms beyond the striate cortex. In Russell, RW, editor. *Frontiers in Physiological Psychology*. New York: Academic Press; 1966; 93-119.

Mistlin, AJ; Perrett, DI. Visual and somatosensory processing in the macaque temporal cortex: the role of 'expectatio'. *Experimental Brain Research*, 1990 82, 437-450.

Miyashita, Y. Inferior temporal cortex: where visual perception meets memory". *Annual Review of Neuroscience*, 1993 16, 245-63.

Miyashita, Y. Neuronal correlate of visual associative long-term memory in the primate temporal cortex. *Nature*, 1988 335, 817-820.

Miyashita, Y; Chang, HS. Neuronal correlate of pictorial short-term memory in the primate temporal cortex. *Nature*, 1988 331, 68-70.

Moran, J; Desimone, R. Selective attention gates visual processing in the extrastriate cortex. *Science*, 1985 229, 782-784.

Morrison, DJ; Schyns, PG. Usage of spatial scales for the categorization of faces, objects, and scenes. *Psychonomic Bulletin and Review*, 2001 8, 454-469.

Movshon, JA; Thompson, ID; Tolhurst, DJ. Spatial and temporal contrast sensitivity of neurones in areas 17 and 18 of the cat's visual cortex. *The Journal of Physiology*, 1978 283, 101-120.

Näsänen, R. Spatial frequency bandwidth used in the recognition of facial images. *Vision Research*, 1999 39, 3824-3833.

Nowak, LG; Bullier, J. The timing of information transfer in the visual system. In Kaas, JH, Rockland, K; Peters, A, editors. *Cerebral Cortex*. New York: Plenum; 1997; 205-241.

Nowak, LG; Munk, MH; Girard, P; Bullier, J. Visual latencies in areas V1 and V2 of the macaque monkey. *Visual Neuroscience*, 1995 12, 371-384.

Op De Beeck, H; Vogels, R. Spatial sensitivity of macaque inferior temporal neurons. *The Journal of Comparative Neurology*, 2000 426, 505-518.

Oram, MW; Perrett, DI. Integration of form and motion in the anterior superior temporal polysensory area (STPa) of the macaque monkey. *Journal of Neurophysiology*, 1996 76, 109-129.

Oram, MW; Perrett, DI. Responses of anterior superior temporal polysensory (STPa) neurons to 'biological motion' stimuli. *Journal of Cognitive Neuroscience*, 1994 6, 99-116.

Oram, MW; Xiao, D; Dritschel, B; Payne, KR. The temporal resolution of neural codes: does response latency have a unique role? *Philosophical Transactions of the Royal Society of London*, 2002 57, 987-1001.

Ostergaard, AL; Davidoff, JB. Some effects of color on naming and recognition of objects. *Journal of Experimental Psychology. Learning, Memory and Cognition*, 1985 11, 579-587.

O'Toole, AJ; Jiang, F; Abdi, H; Haxby, JV. Partially distributed representations of objects and faces in ventral temporal cortex. *Journal of Cognitive Neuroscience*, 2005 17, 580-590.

Parker, DM; Lishman, JR; Hughes, J. Temporal integration of spatially filtered visual images. *Perception*, 1992 21, 147- 160.

Pascalis, O; Bachevalier, J. Face recognition in Primates: a cross-species study. *Behavioural Processes*, 1998 43, 87-96.

Pasupathy, A; Connor, CE. Responses to contour features in macaque area V4. *Journal of Neurophysiology*, 1999 82, 2490-2502.

Perrett, D; Mistlin, A; Chitty, A. Visual neurons responsive to faces. *Trends in Neurosciences*, 1987 10, 358-364.

Perrett, DI; Harries, MH; Bevan, R; Thomas, S; Benson PJ; Mistlin, AJ; Chitty, AJ; Hietanen, JK; Ortega, JE. Frameworks of analysis for the neural representation of animate objects and actions. *The Journal of Experimental Biology*, 1989 146, 87-113.

Perrett, DI; Oram, MW; Harries, MH; Bevan, R; Hietanen, JK; Benson, PJ; Thomas, S. Viewer-centred and object-centred coding of heads in the macaque temporal cortex. *Science*, 1991 86, 159-173.

Perrett, DI; Rolls, ET; Caan W. Visual neurons responsive to faces in monkey temporal cortex. *Experimental Brain Research*, 1982 47, 329-342.

Perrett, DI; Smith, PA; Mistlin, AJ; Chitty, AJ; Head, AS; Potter, DD; Broennimann, R; Milner, AD; Jeeves, MA. Visual analysis of body movements by neurones in the temporal cortex of the macaque monkey: a preliminary report. *Behavioural Brain Research*, 1985a 16, 153-170.

Perrett, DI; Smith, PA; Potter, DD; Mistlin, AJ; Head, AS; Milner, AD; Jeeves, MA. Neurones responsive to faces in the temporal cortex: studies of functional organization, sensitivity to identity and relation to perception. *Human Neurobiology*, 1984 3, 197-208.

Perrett, DI; Smith, PA; Potter, DD; Mistlin, AJ; Head, AS; Milner, AD; Jeeves, MA. Visual cells in the temporal cortex sensitive to face view and gaze direction. *Proceedings of the Royal Society of London*, 1985b 223, 293-317.

Pessoa, L; Leitao, A. Complex cell prototype representation for face recognition. *IEEE Transactions on Neural Networks*, 1999 10, 1528-1531.

Pinsk, MA; DeSimone, K; Moore, T; Gross, CG; Kastner, S. Representations of faces and body parts in macaque temporal cortex: An fMRI study. *Proceedings of the National Academy of Sciences of the United States of America*, 2005 102, 6996-7001.

Poggio, T; Edelman S. A network that learns to recognize three-dimensional objects. *Nature*, 1990 343, 263-266.

Pollen, DA, Ronner, S. Visual cortical neurons as localized spatial frequency filters. *IEEE Transactions on Systems, Man, and Cybernetics*, 1983 13, 907-916.

Pollen, DA; Lee, JR; Taylor, JH. How does the striate cortex begin the reconstruction of the visual world? *Science*, 1971 173, 74-77.

Price, CJ; Humphreys, GW. The effects of surface detail on object categorization and naming. *The Quarterly Journal of Experimental Psychology*, 1989 41, 797-828.

Puce, A; Allison, T; Asgari, M; Gore, JC; McCarthy G. Differential sensitivity of human visual cortex to faces, letterstrings, and textures: A functional magnetic resonance imaging study. *The Journal of Neuroscience*, 1996 16, 5205-5215.

Reich, DS; Mechler, F; Victor, JD. Temporal coding of contrast in primary visual cortex: when, what, and why. *Journal of Neurophysiology*, 2001 85, 1039-1050.

Richmond, BJ; Optican, LM; Podell, M; Spitzer, H. Temporal encoding of two-dimensional patterns by single units in primate inferior-temporal cortex: I. Response characteristics. *Journal of Neurophysiology*, 1987 57, 132-146.

Richmond, BJ; Wurtz, RH; Sato, T. Visual responses of inferior temporal neurons in awake rhesus monkey. *Journal of Neurophysiology*, 1983 50, 1415-1432.

Ridley, RM; Ettlinger, G. Visual discrimination performance in the monkey: the activity of single cells in infero-termporal cortex. *Brain Research*, 1973 55, 179-182.

Ridley, RM; Hester, NS; Ettlinger G. Stimulus- and response-dependent units from the occipital and temporal lobes of the unaesthetized monkey performing learnt visual tasks. *Experimental Brain Research*, 1977 27, 539-52.

Rieke, F; Warland, D; Bialek, W; de Ruyter van Steveninck, RR. *Spikes: exploring the neural code*. New York: MIT Press; 1997.

Robson, JG. Neural images: the physiological basis of spatial vision. In Harris, CS, editor. *Visual Coding and Adaptability*. Hillsdale: Lawrence Erlbaum Associates; 1980; 177-214.

Robson, JG. Receptive field: Neural representation of the spatial and intensive attributes of the visual image. In Carterette, editor. *Handbook of perception*. New York: Academic Press; 1975; 8l-l16.

Rodieck, RW. Quantitative analysis of cat retinal ganglion cell response to visual stimuli. *Vision Research*, 1965 5, 583-601.

Rolls, E.T. The representation of information about faces in the temporal and frontal lobes. *Neuropsychologia*, 2007 45, 124-143.

Rolls, ET. Functions of the primate temporal lobe cortical visual areas in invariant visual object and face recognition. *Neuron*, 2000 27, 205-218.

Rolls, ET. Neural organisation of higher visual functions. *Current Opinion in Neurobiology*, 1991 1, 274-278.

Rolls, ET. Neurons in the cortex of the temporal lobe and in the amygdala of the monkey with responses selective for faces. *Human Neurobiology*, 1984 3, 209-222.

Rolls, ET. Neurophysiological mechanisms underlying face processing within and beyond the temporal cortical visual areas. *Philosophical Transactions of the Royal Society of London*, 1992 335, 11-21.

Rolls, ET; Baylis, GC. Size and contrast and contrast have only small effects on the responses to faces of neurons in the cortex of the superior temporal sulcus of the monkey. *Experimental Brain Research*, 1986 65, 38-48.

Rolls, ET; Baylis, GC; Hasselmo, ME. The responses of neurons in the cortex in the superior temporal sulcus of the monkey to band-pass spatial frequency filtered faces. *Vision Research*, 1987 27, 311-326.

Rolls, ET; Baylis, GC; Hasselmo, ME; Nalwa, V. The effect of learning on the face selective responses of neurons in the cortex in the superior temporal sulcus of the monkey. *Experimental Brain Research*, 1989 76, 153-164.

Rolls, ET; Baylis, GC; Leonard, CM. Role of low and high spatial frequencies in the face-selective responses of neurons in the cortex in the superior temporal sulcus in the monkey. *Vision Research*, 1985 25, 1021-1035.

Rolls, ET; Deco, G. Computational neuroscience of vision. Oxford: Oxford University Press; 2002.

Rolls, ET; Judge, SJ; Sanghera, MK. Activity of neurones in the inferotemporal cortex of the alert monkey. *Brain Research*, 1977 130, 229-238.

Sakai, K; Miyashita, Y. Neural organization for the long-term memory of paired associates. *Nature*, 1991 354, 152-155.

Sáry, G; Vogels, R; Orban, GA. Cue-invariant shape selectivity of macaque inferior temporal neurons. *Science*, 1993 260, 995-997.

Schmolesky, MT; Wang, Y; Hanes, DP; Thompson, KG; Leutgeb, S; Schall, JD; Leventhal, AG. Signal timing across the macaque visual system. *Journal of Neurophysiology*, 1998 79, 3272-3278.

Schroeder, CE; Mehta, AD; Givre, SJ. A spatiotemporal profile of visual system activation revealed by current source density analysis in the awake macaque. *Cerebral Cortex*, 1998 8, 575-592.

Schwartz, EL; Desimone, R; Albright, TD; Gross CG. Shape recognition and inferior temporal neurons. *Proceedings of the National Academy of Sciences of the United States of America*, 1983 80, 5776-5778.

Schyns, PG; Oliva, A. From blobs to boundaries edges: evidence for time and scale dependent scene recognition. *Psychological Science*, 1994 5, 195-200.

Seltzer, B; Pandya, DN. Afferent cortical connections and architectonics of the superior temporal sulcus and surrounding cortex in the rhesus monkey. *Brain Research*, 1978 149, 1-24.

Seltzer, B; Pandya, DN. Parietal, temporal, and occipital projections to cortex of the superior temporal sulcus in the rhesus monkey: a retrograde tracer study. *The Journal of Comparative Neurology*, 1994 343, 445-463.

Seltzer, B; Pandya, DN. Post-rolandic cortical projections of the superior temporal sulcus in the rhesus monkey. *The Journal of Comparative Neurology*, 1991 312, 625-640.

Shelton, PA; Bowers, D; Duara, R; Heilman, KM. Apperceptive visual agnosia: a case study. *Brain Cognition*, 1994 25, 1-23.

Sigala, N; Gabbiani, F; Logothetis, NK. Visual categorization and object representation in monkeys and humans. *Journal of Cognitive Neuroscience*, 2002 14, 187-198.

So, YT; Shapley, R. Spatial properties of X and Y cells in the lateral geniculate nucleus of the cat and conduction veolcities of their inputs. *Experimental Brain Research*, 1979 36, 533-550.

Sparr, SA; Jay, M; Drislane, FW; Venna N. A historic case of visual agnosia revisited after 40 years. *Brain*, 1991 114, 789-800.

Spatz, H. Uber die Bedeutung der Basalen Rinde.auf Grund von Beobachtungen bei Pickscher Krankheit und bei Gedeckten Hirnverletzungen. *Zeitschrift für die gesamte Neurologie und Psychiatrie* ,1937 158, 208-232.

Spiridon, M; Fischl, B; Kanwisher, N. Location and spatial profile of category-specific regions in human extrastriate cortex. *Human Brain Mapping*, 2006 27, 77-89.

Spiridon, M; Kanwisher, N. How distributed is visual category information in human occipito-temporal cortex? An fMRI study. *Neuron*, 2002 35, 1157-1165.

Sugase, Y; Yamane, S; Ueno, S; Kawano, K. Global and fine information coded by single neurons in the temporal visual cortex. *Nature*, 1999 400, 869-873.

Takechi, H; Onoe, H; Shizune, H; Yoshikawa, E; Sadato, N; Tsukada, H; Watanabe, Y. Mapping of cortical areas involved in color vision in non-human primates. *Neuroscience Letters*, 1997 230, 17-20.

Tamura, H; Tanaka, K. Visual response properties of cells in the ventral and dorsal parts of the macaque inferotemporal cortex. *Cerebral Cortex*, 2001 11, 384-399.

Tanaka K. Columns for complex visual object features in the inferotemporal cortex: clustering of cells with similar but slightly different stimulus selectivities. *Cerebral Cortex*, 2003 13, 90-99.

Tanaka K. Inferotemporal cortex and object vision. *Annual Review Neuroscience*, 1996 19, 109-139.

Tanaka K. Neuronal mechanisms of object rescognition. *Science*, 1993 262, 685-688.

Tanaka, H; Uka, T; Yoshiyama, K; Kato, M; Fujita, I. Processing of shape defined by disparity in monkey inferior temporal cortex. *Journal of Neurophysiology*, 2001 85, 735-744.

Tanaka, K, Saito, H; Fukada, Y; Moriya, M. Coding visual images of objects in the inferotemporal cortex of the macaque monkey. *Journal of Neurophysiology*,1991 66, 170-189.

Tanaka, K; Saito, C; Fukada, Y; Moriya M. Integration of form, texture and color information in the inferotemporal cortex of the macaque. In Iwai, E; Mishkin M., editor. *Vision, memory and the temporal lobe*. New York: Elsevier; 1990; 101-109.

Tanifuji, M; Li, H; Yamane, Y; Rockland, KS. Horizontal intrinsic connections as the anatomical basis for the functional columns in macaque inferior temporal cortex. *Abstract-Society for Neuroscience*, 2001 27, 620.7.

Tanigawa, H; Fujita, I; Kato, M; Ojima, H. Distribution, morphology, and gamma-aminobutyric acid inmunoreactivity of horizontally projecting neurons in the macaque inferior temporal cortex. *The Journal of Comparative Neurology*, 1998 401, 129-143.

Thorpe, SJ. Spike arrival times: a highly efficient coding scheme for neural networks. In Eckmiller, R; Hartman, G; Hauske, G, editors. *Parallel processing in neural systems*. Amsterdam: Elsevier; 1990; 91-94.

Thorpe, SJ; Fabre-Thorpe, M. Seeking categories in the brain. *Science*, 2001 291, 260-263.

Tolhurst, DJ; Thompson, ID. On the variety of spatial frequency selectivities shown by neurons in area 17 of the cat. *Proceedings of the Royal Society of London*, 1981 213, 183-199.

Tompa, T; Chadadide, Z; Lenti, L; Csifcsák, G; Kovacs, G; Benedek, G. Invariances of shape-processing for reduced surface cues: how IT neurons and psychophysics correlate in the macaque. *In Proceedings of ICCS 2001*. Beijin: Press of USTC; 2002; 40-44.

Tootell, RB; Nelissen, K; Vandufell, W; Orban, G. Search for color 'center(s)' in macaque visual cortex. *Cerebral Cortex*, 2004 14, 353-363.

Tootell, RB; Silverman, MS; Hamilton, SL; Switkes, E; De Valois, RL. Functional anatomy of macaque striate cortex. V. Spatial frequency. *The Journal of Neuroscience*, 1988 8, 1610-1624.

Tovee, MJ; Rolls, ET; Azzopardi, P. Translation invariance in the responses to faces of single neurons in the temporal visual cortical areas of the alert monkey. *Visual Cognition*, 1994 2, 35-58.

Tovee, MJ; Rolls, ET; Ramachandran, VS. Rapid visual learning in neurones of the primate temporal visual cortex. *Neuroreport*, 1996 7, 2757-2760.

Tsao, DY; Freiwald, WA; Knutsen, TA; Mandeville, JB; Tootell, RB. Faces and objects in macaque cerebral cortex. *Nature Neuroscience*, 2003 6, 989-995.

Tsunoda, K; Yamane, Y; Nishikazi, M; Tanifuji M. Complex objects are represented in macaque inferotemporal cortex by the combination of feature columns. *Nature Neuroscience*, 2001 4, 832-838.

Turk, M; Pentland, A. Eigenfaces for recognition. *Journal of Cognitive Neuroscience*, 1991 3, 71-86.

Uka, T; Tanaka, H; Yoshiyama, K; Kato, M; Fujita, I. Disparity selectivity of neurons in monkey inferior temporal cortex. *Journal of Neurophysiology*, 2000 84, 120-132.

Ullman, S. High-level vision: Object recognition and visual cognition. Cambridge: Bradford/MIT Press; 1996.

Ullman, S. Sequence seeking and counter streams -a computational model for bi-directional information flow in the visual-cortex. *Cerebral Cortex*, 1995 5, 1-11.

Ungerleider, LG; Mishkin, M. Two cortical visual systems. Ingle, DJ; Goodale, MA; Mansfield, RJW, editors. Cambridge: MIT Press; 1982.

Van Essen, DC; Anderson, CH; Felleman, DJ, Information processing in the primate visual system: an integrated systems perspective. *Science*, 1992 255, 419-423.

Vermeire, BA; Hamilton, CR; Erdmann, AL. Right-hemispheric superiority in split-brain monkeys for learning and remembering facial discriminations. *Behavioural Neuroscience*, 1998 112, 1048-1061.

Victor, JD; Shapley, RM. Receptive field mechanisms of cat X and Y retinal ganglion cells. *The Journal of General Physiology*, 1979 74, 275-298.

Wachsmuth, E; Oram, MW; Perrett, DI. Recognition of objects and their component parts: responses of single units in the temporal cortex of the macaque. *Cerebral Cortex*, 1994 4, 509-522.

Wallis, G, Rolls, ET. Invariant face and object recognition in the visual system. *Progress in Neurobiology*, 1997 51, 167-194.

Wang, G, Tanifuji, M.; Tanaka, K. Functional architecture in monkey inferotemporal cortex revealed by in vivo optical imaging. *Neuroscience Research*, 1998 32, 33-46.

Wang, G; Tanaka, K; Tanifuji, M. Optical imaging of functional organization in the monkey inferotemporal cortex. *Science*, 1996 272, 1665-1668.

Webster, MJ; Bachevalier, J; Ungerleider, LG. Subcortical connections of inferior temporal areas TE and TEO in macaque monkeys. *The Journal of Comparative Neurology*, 1993 335, 73-91.

Webster, MJ; Bachevalier, J; Ungerleider, LG. Transient subcortical connections of inferior temporal areas TE and TEO in infant macaque monkeys. *The Journal of Comparative Neurology*, 1995 352, 213-226.

Webster, MJ; Ungerleider, LG; Bachevalier, J. Connections of inferior temporal areas TE and TEO with medial temporal-lobe structures in infant and adult monkeys. *The Journal of Neuroscience*, 1991 11: 1095-1116.

Westheimer, G. Spatial vision. *Annual Review of Psychology*, 1984 35, 201-226.

Wocjiulik, E; Kanwisher, N; Driver, J. Modulation of activity in the fusiform face area by covert attention: an fMRI study. *Journal of Neurophysiology*, 1998 79, 1574-1578.

Wurm, LH; Legge, GE; Isenberg, LM; Luebker, A. Color improves object recognition in normal and low vision. Journal of Experimental Psychology. *Human Perception and Performance*, 1993 19, 899-911.

Yamane, S; Kaji, S; Kawano, K. What facial features activate face neurons in the inferotemporal cortex of the monkey? *Experimental Brain Research*, 1998 73, 209-214.

Yamane, Y; Tsunoda, K; Matsumoto, M; Phillips, NA; Tanifuji; M. Representation of the spatial relationship among object parts by neurons in macaque inferotemporal cortex. *Journal of Neurophysiology*, 2006 96, 3147-3156.

Yang, Y; Blake R. Spatial frequency tuning of human stereopsis. *Vision Research*, 1991 31, 1177-1189.

Young, MP; Yamane, S. Sparse population coding of faces in the inferotemporal cortex. *Science*, 1992 256, 1327-1331.

Zeki, S; Marini, L. Three cortical stages of color processing in the human brain. *Brain*, 1998 121, 1669-1685.

In: Visual Cortex: New Research
Editors: T. A. Portocello and R. B. Velloti

ISBN 978-1-60456-530-0
© 2008 Nova Science Publishers, Inc.

Chapter 6

INVESTIGATION OF THE ACTIVATED HUMAN PRIMARY VISUAL CORTEX (V1) BY FUNCTIONAL MRS

*Silvia Mangia[*1], Ivan Tkáč[1] and Kâmil Uğurbil[1,2]*

[1]Center for Magnetic Resonance Research, Department of Radiology,
University of Minnesota, Minneapolis (MN), USA
[2]Max Planck Institute for Biological Cybernetics, Tubingen, Germany

Abstract

The activation of the human primary visual cortex (V1) is often utilized as a gold standard to test the performances of newly developed methodologies for in vivo functional studies. Recent progresses in magnet technology, gradient system performance, RF coil and pulse sequence design have allowed the implementation of magnetic resonance spectroscopy (MRS) and imaging (MRI) in humans at magnetic fields up to 7T, which resulted in increased sensitivity, reliability and specificity of functional measurements compared to lower fields. Here we revise MRS applications which investigated brain metabolism during visual activation. The majority of these studies have used 1H MRS, and few of them implemented 13C and 31P MRS. The experimental findings obtained by these methodologies have provided new insights into the metabolic events occurring during increased neuronal activity, and the interpretation of some of these findings have generated intense scientific debates.

Functional magnetic resonance imaging (fMRI) and spectroscopy (fMRS) are powerful and complimentary tools for the non-invasive investigation of brain function in humans. The primary visual cortex (V1) has been the first cortical area to be investigated with both fMRI and fMRS. The very first fMRI application reported in literature is dated 1991, when Bellievau et al. utilized an external contrast agent to map regional changes in cerebral blood volume associated with visual stimulations. In the same year, Prichard et al. (1991) measured variations in metabolite concentrations (specifically lactate) during prolonged visual

---
[*] Corresponding author: Silvia Mangia, Ph.D. Center for Magnetic Resonance Research, University of Minnesota, 2021 6th St. S.E. Minneapolis, MN, 55455 (USA); E-mail: mangia@cmrr.umn.edu; Tel: +1 612-626-2001; Fax: +1 612-626-2004

stimulations. Later on, the usage of an external contrast agent for functional mapping has been replaced by a technique which utilizes deoxyhemoglobin as an endogenous contrast agent (Bandettini et al., 1992; Kwong et al., 1992; Ogawa et al., 1992), through the so-called blood oxygenation level-dependent (BOLD) contrast mechanism (Ogawa et al., 1990). Initial human applications of the BOLD effect were employed in V1. Since then, the number of fMRI investigations has literally exploded, whereas fMRS applications have remained restricted to a limited number of studies, which will be reviewed in the following sections. As we shall see, these findings have been often inconsistent and their interpretation rather controversial.

1. Technical Considerations about MRS during Functional Studies

^{1}H MRS allows the non-invasive quantification of brain metabolites (Figure 1), along with their changes associated with brain activity. However, the reliable quantification of these changes during functional studies is a very demanding task and, probably, some of the discrepancies in reported results can be ascribed to this limitation (Table 1). Challenges for quantification of NMR spectra arise from 1) the low signal-to-noise ration (SNR) originating from much lower concentration of metabolites relative to water (at least 4 orders of magnitude), which is used for MRI; and 2) the limited chemical shift range of the proton spectra (~5 ppm), which causes a significant overlap of metabolite resonances. Optimized methodology of MRS with an increased detection sensitivity and accuracy is especially critical for fMRS, because *changes* in metabolite concentrations during physiological stimulations are relatively very small. In this context, fMRS studies performed at high magnetic fields have the potential for improved accuracy and reliability. At high magnetic fields, ^{1}H MRS not only benefits from the gain in SNR (Gruetter et al., 1998; Vaughan et al., 2001), but also from the increased chemical shift dispersion (Tkac et al., 2001), which emphasizes the characteristic spectral pattern of each metabolite and decreases the spectral overlap. These features enable more accurate and reliable quantification of an increased number of metabolites, with concentration above 0.5 µmol/g. ^{1}H MRS of the human brain at ultra-high magnetic field is challenged by several factors (reviewed in Tkac and Gruetter, 2005), related to inhomogeneities in the static magnetic field B_0 and non-uniformity of transmit field B_1 of the RF coil. In order to maintain high spectral resolution, inhomogeneities in B_0 must be minimized as much as possible, which requires highly efficient B_0 field mapping method (shimming) and a suitable hardware to compensate for these inhomogeneities.

Table 1. Functional ¹H MRS in V1 - Healthy conditions

Reference	Stimulation	Stimulation length	Eyes during rest	Number of subjects	MRS parameters	Temporal resolution	Δ[Lac]	Δ[Glc]	Δ[NAA]	Δ[Glu]	Δ[Asp]
Prichard et al. 1991	16Hz flashing 5x6 grids of red light emitting diodes	12 min	open	5	2T, ISIS, 128 scans, TR=2.8s, VOI: 13ml	6-8 min	54%, transient				
Sappey Mariner et al. 1992	2Hz flashing black-white checkerboard	38.4 min	closed	6	2T, ISIS, 256 scans, TE/TR=270/1500ms, VOI: 32ml	6.4 min	150%, transient				
Merboldt et al. 1992	4-16Hz flashing red light	19.5 min	open	48	2T, STEAM, TE/TR=20-270/2000ms, VOI : 8-64ml	6.5 min	no reproducible time-courses	-50%			
Chen et al., 1993	8Hz emitting grids of red-light diodes	25 min	closed (presumably)	3	2.1T, 64 scans, TE/TR=16/2800ms, VOI: 12ml	3.3 min		-40%			
Frahm et al., 1996; 1997	10Hz flickering pattern	4÷6 min	n.a.	25	2T, STEAM, 5 scans plus group averaging, TE/TR=20/6000 ms, VOI: 11ml, LCModel	nominal: 30s	68%, transient	-40%			
Mangia et al., 2003	Achromatic square grid of high frequency black-white strips	1 s	open	5	1.5T, PRESS, TE=270ms, TR=7.5-15s, 128 scans, VOI: 12ml	2s	-50%				
Boucard et al. 2005	8Hz flickering high contrast dartboard pattern	14 min	n.a.	4	1.5T, PRESS 2D-CSI, TE/TR=135/1500 ms	7 min	no reproducible time-courses				

Table 1. (Continued)

Reference	Stimulation	Stimulation length	Eyes during rest	Number of subjects	MRS parameters	Temporal resolution	Δ [Lac]	Δ [Glc]	Δ [NAA]	Δ [Glu]	Δ [Aspl]
Katz-Brull et al., 2006	8Hz alternating black-white checkerboard	32s ON + 32s OFF, repeated 10 times	subjects free to keep their eyes closed or open (blue light during rest)	9	3T, PRESS, TE/TR=35/2000ms 160 scans (interleaved), VOI: 5.6 ml, LCModel	30s	no changes				
Tunnanen et al., 2006	8Hz contrast reversing black-white checkerboard	4.3min, alternating 16s ON an 8s OFF	open	4, normoxia and mild hypoxia	1.5T, double spin-echo, TE/TR=136/2000ms, VOI: 27ml, 128 scans, JMRUI	4 min	no changes				
Maddock et al. 2006	8Hz flickering black-white radial checkerboard	4 min repeated twice	closed	6, fasting and hyperglycemic conditions	1.5T, PRESS, TE/TR=288/1500ms, 160 scans, VOI: 30ml, JMRUI	4-5 min	~10%, steady-state				
Mangia et al., 2007a	8Hz flickering black-red radial checkerboard	5-min ON and 5 OFF repeated twice; 10-min ON 10 min OFF	open	12	7T, STEAM, TE/TR=6/5000ms, 48 scans in group averaging, VOI=8.8ml, LCModel	20s	23%, steady-state	indication of decrease (-12%)		3%	-15%
Mangia et al., 2007b	8Hz flickering black-red radial checkerboard	2-min ON, 2-min OFF, repeated 8 times	open	12	7T, STEAM, TE/Tr=6/5000ms, 48 scans in group averaging, VOI=8.8ml, LCModel	20s	~20% down to ~10%				
Baslow et al., 2007	8Hz flickering black-white radial checkerboard	10 min	closed	6	3T, PRESS, TE/TR=135/2000ms, 15 scans, VOI: 8 ml	30s			-13%		

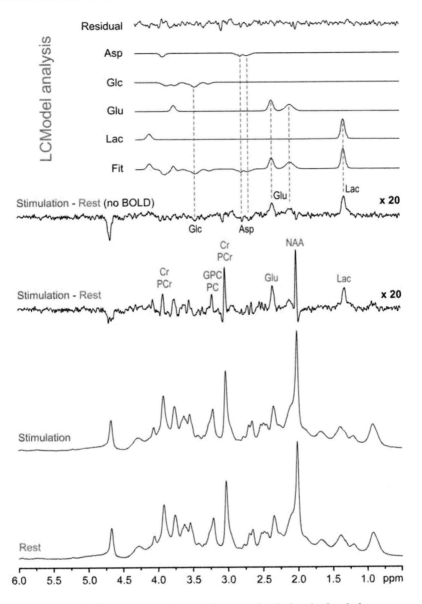

Figure 1. Changes of metabolite concentrations during sustained visual stimulation, as revealed by the analysis of the difference (C and D) between spectra acquired with ¹H MRS during rest (A) and stimulation (B). D same as C, but the spectrum acquired during stimulation was line-broadened by 0.4 Hz in order to match the linewidth of the spectrum acquired at rest (elimination of the BOLD effect on metabolites). (E-L): LCModel fit of the difference spectrum D. Spectra were summed from different subjects (N = 12). Minute but significant changes in metabolite concentrations (~0.2 μmol/g) were observed for lactate, aspartate and glutamate. In particular, [Lac] increased by 23% ± 5% (p < 0.0005), [Glu] increased by 3% ± 1% (p < 0.01), whereas [Asp] decreased by 15% ± 6% (p < 0.05). Finally, [Glc] showed a tendency to decrease during activation periods. Adapted from Mangia et al., (2007a).

The design of pulse sequences must take into account increased off-resonance effects causing chemical shift displacement errors, and the intrinsic shortening of the T_2 of metabolites at high magnetic fields. Despite increased chemical shift dispersion, sophisticated processing software is necessary to extract quantitative neurochemical information from acquired spectra. Only the combination of appropriate hardware, localization pulse sequence and processing software enabled reliable quantification up to 17 brain metabolites (neurochemical profile) at 7 T (Tkac et al., 2005). Specific to functional applications, additional challenges are introduced by the BOLD effect (Ogawa et al., 1990), which is known to alter the T_2^* of water and all metabolite signals during stimulation. This phenomenon results in a small narrowing mainly discernible on the strong singlets of the spectrum (Mangia et al., 2006; Zhu and Chen, 2001); these signal changes might be erroneously interpreted as concentration changes.

^{13}C MRS offers the capability to quantify metabolic fluxes by measuring incorporation of the ^{13}C label from ^{13}C-labelled substrate into different carbon positions of various brain metabolites. In other words, ^{13}C MRS provides complementary information to ^{1}H MRS, which provides information about steady-state concentrations of metabolites. On the basis of metabolic models, estimates of metabolic fluxes (as neurotransmitter recycling and TCA cycle rates) can be obtained by fitting the time-courses of ^{13}C incorporation from ^{13}C-labelled compounds, as [1-^{13}C]glucose or [1-^{13}C]acetate, in the resonances of metabolites as glutamate, glutamine, lactate or aspartate (for review, see de Graaf et al., 2003; Henry et al., 2006; for a figure, refer to Figure 2).

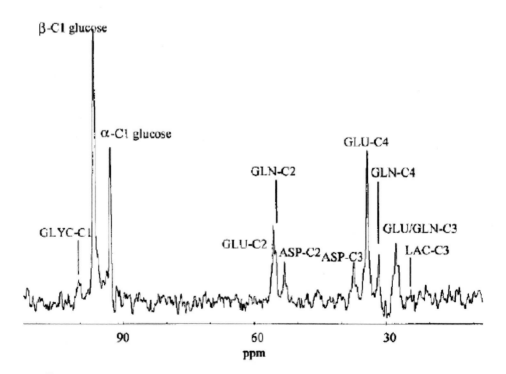

Figure 2. [13]C MR spectrum acquired from V1 at 3T during [1-^{13}C]glucose infusion (40 min of acquisition). When a highly enriched 13C-labeled substrate is administrated, ^{13}C MRS can detect the progressive incorporation of ^{13}C label into different carbon positions of various brain metabolites, as glutamate, glutamine, lactate or aspartate. From these time-courses, metabolite fluxes (e.g. TCA cycle rates) can be extracted using metabolic models. The TCA cycle rate was estimated to increase during prolonged visual stimuli, with an upper limit of 30-60% (Chen et al., 2001; Chiina et al., 2001). Figure from Chiina et al., (2001), with permission of Wiley-Liss, Inc..

Compared to ^{1}H MRS, ^{13}C MRS is less affected by resonance overlap due to the wider chemical shift range (~100ppm), but suffers from intrinsic lower sensitivity of detection. Improved sensitivity can be attained at high magnetic fields, thus resulting in more reliable estimates of metabolic fluxes.

^{31}P MRS detects high-energy phosphate (HEP) metabolites as adenosine triphosphate (ATP), phosphocreatine (PCr) and their hydrolysis product inorganic compounds (P_i). In addition, ^{31}P MRS allows the acquisition of information on the turnover of HEP. The creatine kinase (CK) reaction is involved in the HEP turnover, and its unidirectional rates in the direction of ATP synthesis and hydrolysis can be assessed through magnetization (MT) transfer approaches in ^{31}P MRS. Similarly, unidirectional rates in the ATP synthesis from or hydrolysis to ADP and P_i can be directly quantified with MT. Given the relatively low concentration of P_i in normal intact tissue, and the low intrinsic detection sensitivity of *in vivo* ^{31}P MRS, the MT methodology has been used generally in excised perfused organ models or in small animals. Thanks to the improved sensitivity and larger chemical shift dispersion offered by high magnetic field, the noninvasive investigation of the ATP synthesis rate and the CK reaction rate can now be obtained also in the human brain (Chen et al., 1997; Du *et al.*, 2007; Lei et al., 2003a; Lei et al., 2003b). Refer to Figure 3 for an example of ^{31}P MRS application in the human V1.

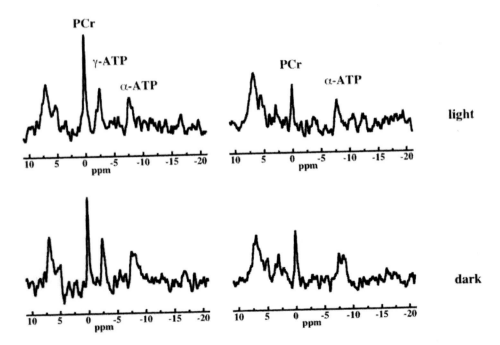

Figure 3. ^{31}P spectra acquired from V1 with (right) and without (left) magnetization transfer (MT) of the γ-ATP resonance, during rest (bottom) and visual stimuli (bottom). From the ratio of the intensities of the PCr peak acquired with and without MT, information about the unidirectional flux of PCr in ATP can be obtained. This unidirectional flux was found to increase by 34% during prolonged visual stimuli. Figure from Chen et al., 1997, with permission of Wiley-Liss, Inc..

2. The Choice of V1 as Targeted Region of Interest for Functional MRS

V1 has been the preferred targeted region of interest in most studies which utilized MRS in humans during functional protocols. This is due to several reasons. First of all, it is straightforward to generate and present visual stimuli to human subjects during functional sessions in the magnet. Second, V1 represents an ideal choice for optimizing the contrast-to-noise of the metabolic changes to be detected because visual stimuli can be designed to robustly activate the majority of V1, one of the largest cortical areas of the human brain. Third, the sensitivity of MR measurements can be improved by using surface coils, because the occipital lobe is relatively close to the surface of the head. Finally, V1 is conveniently located in a cortical region that does not suffer from major susceptibility artifacts, which otherwise would compromise the quality of the data.

3. Visual Stimulation and ^{1}H MRS

3a. Main Findings

In the first fMRS application, the evolution of lactate concentration ([Lac]) was measured in 5 subjects exposed to 12-min of red light emitting diodes flashing at 16Hz (Prichard et al., 1991). The goal of the study was to evaluate the contribution of non-oxidative processes during increased neuronal activity; this issue was raised by the observation obtained with positron emission tomography (PET) regarding a focal mismatch between the variations of oxygen consumption (5%), glucose consumption (30-50%) and cerebral blood flow (30-50%) during prolonged stimulation (Fox and Raichle, 1986; Fox et al., 1988). A ~60% increase in [Lac] was observed in V1 during the first minutes of visual stimulation (Prichard et al., 1991). In several subjects the maximum increase of [Lac] was observed in the first minutes of stimulation, followed by a slow decline toward the baseline during and after the stimulation. Similar transient changes in [Lac] were later reported by Sappey–Marinier et al. (1992), who observed 150% [Lac] increase in six subjects during the first 6.4 min of 38.4-min visual stimulations consisting of 2Hz flashing black-white checkerboard. Frahm et al. (1996) subsequently performed a study which implemented an inter-subject spectra summing from 25 volunteers and a moving average approach to increase the nominal temporal resolution up to 30s. Their results confirmed an increases of [Lac] by 68% that was restricted to the first half of 6-min presentation of patterns flickering at 10 Hz, while during the second half [Lac] decreased to basal level.

A previous study from the same group, however, reported un-reproducible time-courses of [Lac] in 48 subjects during paradigms employing 20-min visual stimulations and a wide range of experimental settings (Merboldt et al., 1992); a high variability of the basal [Lac] was also noted. Later, Boucard et al. (2005) did not observe any significant alteration of the spectra of 4 subjects during 14-min presentations of high contrast dartboard flickering at 8Hz; in their setup, the region of the spectrum around 1.33 ppm was indeed affected by unstable signals presumably coming from lipids of the scalp. No increases in [Lac] were observed either in the intersubject analysis of 9 subjects undergoing repeated 32-s presentations of 8Hz alternating black-white checkerboard (Katz-Brull et al., 2006). Similarly, no significant changes of [Lac] were found in 4 subjects under conditions of either normoxia or mild hypoxia (Tunnanen et al., 2006) during 4.3 min presentations of 8Hz contrast reversing black-white checkerboard. Comparable visual stimuli were instead reported to produce ~10% [Lac] increases in 6 subjects without any significant effect introduced by different glycemic conditions (Maddock et al., 2006); in addition, an indication of [Lac] reduction (even if not significant) was observed during the first minute of visual stimulation. By means of an event-related fMRS study, a significant decrease of [Lac] was previously reported in 5 subjects during the first seconds following impulsive achromatic stimulations (Mangia et al., 2003).

High temporal resolution and significantly higher sensitivity have been later attained at 7T (Mangia et al., 2006; 2007a; 2007b) during prolonged visual stimulations of 8Hz flickering red-black radial checkerboard (Figure 1). The authors found that, averaged over 12 subjects, [Lac] increased in the first minute of visual activation by ~0.2 μmol/g (corresponding to almost 20% [Lac] elevation), reached a new steady state during the on-going stimulation period, and came back to baseline after the end of the stimulus (Mangia et al., 2007a). The average amplitude of [Lac] increases was found to be reduced over time during stimulation protocols implementing repeated 2-min long visual stimuli (Mangia et al., 2007b). Among the 17 quantified metabolites, minute (< 0.2 μmol/g) but significant concentration changes were observed also for glutamate (Glu) and aspartate (Asp); in addition, glucose concentration ([Glc]) manifested a tendency to decrease during activation periods (Mangia et al., 2007a). Significant [Glc] decreases were previously reported by two of the afore-discussed studies (Frahm et al., 1996; Merboldt et al., 1992). A biphasic time course of [Glc] during about 30 min of presentation of red-light diodes emitting at 8Hz was further reported by Chen et al. (1993), who observed an initial decrease of [Glc] followed by a slow increase towards the baseline. Decrease in concentration of N-acetylaspartate (NAA) by 13% on average has been reported in a group of 6 healthy subjects during the presentation of 10-min long visual stimuli consisting of white-black radial checkerboard flickering at 8Hz (Baslow et al., 2007). This last observation was never reported in any of the previous fMRS studies performed in healthy subjects in physiological conditions. A summary of the above mentioned studies is reported in Table 1.

Activation of V1 has been preferentially utilized also in studies aiming at investigating alterations of metabolite concentrations during stimulation in pathological conditions (Table 2). Higher [Lac] levels were observed in patients with mitochondrial encephalomyopathy compared to healthy subjects; however, during photic stimulations [Lac] did not further increase significantly, as opposed to controls (Kuwabara et al., 1994). Similar findings applied for patients with photosensitive epilepsy (Chiappa et al., 1999). Increases of [Lac] during photic stimulation were instead observed in a subgroup of migraine patients with visual aura but not in healthy subejcts (Sandor et al. 2005). Also in this case, patients had resting [Lac] higher than controls, likely due to the involvement of a mitochondrial dysfunction. The main finding of another visual stimulation study involving migraine patients with and without aura was a decrease of [NAA], without significant alterations of [Lac] (Sarchielli et al., 2005). A reduced level of NAA/water and Cho/water ratios were also reported during sleep deprivation (Urrila et al., 2006).

Table 2. Functional ^{1}H MRS in V1 - Pathological conditions

Reference	Disease	Subjects	Metabolite concentrations
Kuwabara et al. 1994	Mitochondrial encephalomyopathy	7 controls, 4 patients	Resting [Lac] higher in patients, no further changes during stimuli (unlike controls)
Chiappa et al. 1999	Photosensitive epilepsy	12 controls, 9 patients	Resting [Lac] higher in patients, no further changes during stimuli
Sandor et al. 2005	Migraine with aura	11 controls, 10 patients (divided in two subgroups)	Increases of [Lac] during stimuli only in a subgroup of patients
Sarchielli et al. 2005	Migraine with and without aura	10 controls, 22 patients with aura, 22 patients without aura	Decreases of [NAA] during photic stimuli more significant in migraine patients with aura
Urrila et al. 2004	Sleep deprivation	8, healthy	Resting [NAA] and [Cho] lower after sleep deprivation

Table 3. Functional ^{31}P MRS in V1 - Healthy and pathological conditions

Reference	Stimulation	Stimulation length	Subjects	$([PCr]/[Pi])_{stim}$	K_f of $(PCr \rightarrow ATP)_{stim}$
Sappey Mariner et al. 1992	2Hz flashing black-white checkerboard	38.4 min	6, healthy	- 39%	
Kato et al., 1996	White light flashing at 10Hz	12 min	9, healthy	- 12%	
Chen et al., 1997	flashing light at 8Hz using goggles	12 min	7, healthy	no changes	+ 34%
Rango et al. 1997	8Hz flahing pattern	3.5 s	11, healthy	Decrease with a rate = 7.24%/s	
Murashita et al., 1999	10 Hz flashing white light	12 min	25, healthy, different ages	slight decreases only in older subjects	
Murashita et al., 2000	White light flashing at 10Hz	12 min	25 controls, 19 patients with bipolar disorder	Significant decrease only in un-treated bipolar subjects	

3b. Interpretation of the Results

The interest in investigating changes in metabolite concentrations relies on the fact that they imply changes in the metabolic patterns, such as preferential use of different pathways or alteration of fluxes. For instance, by utilizing a Michaelis–Menten kinetics for glucose transporter, both Chen et al. (1993) and Frahm et al. (1996) estimated an increase by 22% of glucose consumption during stimulation based on the observed decreases of [Glc]; similarly, the changes of [Glu] and [Asp] reported during visual stimulation (Mangia et al., 2007a) have been explained on the basis of an increased flux of the malate-aspartate shuttle (MAS), the mechanism that transfers reducing equivalents from the cytosol to the mitochondria, thus guaranteeing the continuation of aerobic glycolysis. Regarding the functional role of NAA, reduced [NAA] during visual stimulation have been interpreted as evidence that NAA functions like a "molecular water pump" during increased neuronal activity (Baslow et al., 2007), and the reduction of the NAA/water and Cho/water ratios during sleep deprivation lead to the hypothesis that NAA and Cho might be involved in the state of alertness.

The interpretation of the findings regarding [Lac] is especially controversial. Lactate is an intermediate of glucose metabolism. Although increases in [Lac] are frequently interpreted in terms of increased anaerobic glycolysis, it is important to keep in mind that lactate is a marker of metabolic activity in either aerobic or anaerobic conditions (Siesjö, 1978). Moreover, the role of lactate during brain activation has become the center of an intense debate (Chih et al., 2001; Dienel and Cruz, 2004; Pellerin and Magistretti, 2004; Schurr, 2006; Shulman et al., 2001) after the introduction of the astrocyte-neuron lactate shuttle hypothesis (ANLSH) by Pellerin and Magistretti (1994). The ANLSH suggests a metabolic coupling between glutamatergic neurons and astrocytes, and considers lactate glycolitically produced by astrocytes as the preferential metabolic substrate of neurons for the energy expenses of neurotransmission. Whereas this idea has been supported by several *in vitro* evidence (reviewed for example in Pellerin and Magistretti, 2004), solid *in vivo* evidence are still lacking. Challenges arise from the fact that *in vivo* ^{1}H MRS to measure [Lac] does not provide suitable temporal and spatial resolution to distinguish the evolution of lactate content (as for any other metabolite) in different cell types. Therefore, interpreting average tissue [Lac] in terms of compartmentalized metabolism requires the formulation of mathematical models, which generally rely on a number of assumptions often difficult to test. The situation is further challenged by the fact that a change in [Lac] depends on several factors, including the glycolytic rate (conversion of glucose to pyruvate) relative to the MAS rate, the pyruvate dehydrogenase complex and tricarboxylic acid (TCA) cycle, the cytoplasmic pH and oxidation–reduction state, the rate of glycogenolysis in astrocytes, and the rate of lactate efflux from tissue. The small increases of [Lac] observed during activation were interpreted as a consequence of the rise of oxidative metabolism to a new steady-state (Mangia et al., 2007a), and the reduction of [Lac] increases during repeated identical stimuli was suggested to indicate lower energy demands related to the adaptation of cortical output of the visual cortex. Those interpretations did not involve cellular compartmentalization of metabolism.

4. Visual Stimulation and ^{13}C MRS

^{13}C MRS has been used for investigating the energy cost of neuronal activity mostly in animal models, while only a couple of applications (one of them is shown in Figure 2) have been published in humans (Chen et al., 2001; Chhina et al., 2001). The conclusions of both studies were limited to the definition of upper limits for functional changes of the TCA cycle rate, which were in reasonable agreement with previous results obtained with other methodologies (for review see Giove et al., 2003; Shulman et al., 2001). In addition, ^{13}C MRS has been implemented to investigate the effect of prolonged visual stimuli on the turnover of glycogen in the human brain (Oz et al., 2007). Glycogen is a glucose storage molecule primarily localized in astrocytes; based on the results reported by Oz et al. (2007), glycogen does not provide fuel during increased neurotransmission following physiological stimuli, as opposed to pathological conditions involving glucose deprivation.

5. Visual Stimulation and ^{31}P MRS

^{31}P MRS has been utilized in several human studies during functional paradigms; all of them involved the implementation of visual stimulation (Table 3). Prolonged photic stimuli have been reported to produce either significant decreases of the [PCr]/[Pi] ratios (Kato et al., 1996; Sappey-Marinier et al., 1992), or non significant effects on the concentrations and ratios of HEP (Chen et al., 1997), or significant effects on pH and PCr in middle-aged subjects but not in younger subjects (Murashita et al, 1999). One study further investigated the effect of very short visual stimulations (3.5s), and a PCr decrease with a mean rate = 7.24%/s (Rango et al. 1997) was reported. The inconsistent results of the afore-mentioned studies suggest that the measurement of steady-state level of HEP might be not sensitive enough to reliably detect metabolic changes under physiological stimulations. Decreases in PCr signal during photic stimulation instead appeared more pronounced in pathological conditions with putative mitochondrial impairment, as in patients with bipolar disorders (Murashita et al., 2000) or MELAS - mitochondrial myopathy, encephalopathy, lactic acidosis, and stroke-like episodes (Kato et al., 1998). By using MT approaches, Chen et al. (1997) showed that a significant increase by 34% of the unidirectional rate of CK reaction occurred during stimulation in absence of observable changes of the concentration of HEP in healthy subjects (Figure 3). Changes in the conversion of Cr to PCr have been suggested to influence also the signal intensity at 3.0ppm of the total Cr signal in the proton spectra (Ke et al. 2002) acquired at long echo times.

6. Different Sensitivities of MRI and MRS Methodologies to Neuronal Activation

In vivo MRS methodologies provide complementary insights into neuronal function compared to fMRI approaches. Measurements of intracortical electrical activity and BOLD fMRI in monkeys (Logothetis et al., 2001) demonstrated that the BOLD contrast reflects the input and intracortical processing of a given area (the so-called "synaptic" activity), identified by local field potentials (LFPs), rather than its spiking output identified by multi unit activity (MUA). Indeed, recording sites characterized by strong adaptation showed that, in the absence of any change in the MUA and single spikes, the LFPs were the only regressor that estimated BOLD (Logothetis et al, 2001). A similar conclusion applies also for cerebral blood flow (Lauritzen, 2001). On the other hand, MRS is expected to be sensitive to the global energy requests related to changes in neuronal activity as identified by both synaptic and spiking activity of the region investigated. Several studies conducted in awake animals and under different levels of anesthesia (known to modulate neurotransmission) suggested that energy consumption increases with glutamatergic neurotransmission (Sibson et al., 1998; Choi et al., 2002; Oz et al., 2004). Theoretical work (Attwell and Laughlin, 2001; Lennie, 2003) and experimental evidence (reviewed in Raichle and Mintun, 2006; Sokoloff, 1999) indicate that the majority of energy usage not related to house-keeping work is used to reverse ion movements generated by post-synaptic current and action potentials.

In a study, which combined fMRI/fMRS measurements to investigate neuronal firing suppression in vivo, the time-courses of the BOLD effect and of [Lac] have been measured upon repeated identical 2-min long visual stimuli (Mangia et al., 2007b). While the average amplitude of [Lac] increases was reduced over time, the amplitude of the BOLD effect was persistent during the whole observation period. This observation indicated that the BOLD effect and the [Lac] response may be sensitive to different aspects of neuronal activation and/or metabolic adaptation. Specifically, this finding was ascribed to a differential adaptation of the cortical output that is not reflected at the level of the global excitation-inhibition activity of the cortical canonical circuits. Indeed, the observed persistent BOLD effect during repeated identical stimuli indicated persistent global synaptic activity. In contrast, under the premise that steady-state changes of [Lac] reflect a rise of oxidative metabolism to a new steady state (Mangia et al., 2007a), the progressive reduction of [Lac] changes implied gradual decreases of energy consumption, likely due to adaptation of the cortical output of V1. This is consistent with other findings which suggest that neuronal adaptation reduces firing (e.g. Khon and Movshon, 2003). A decrease of the spiking output concomitant with a persistently elevated synaptic activity during repeated identical visual stimuli can occur based on a shift in the balance between recurrent excitation and inhibition of the cortical canonical circuits (for review, see Douglas and Martin, 2004).

However, many challenging issues are associated with this interpretation, since 1) the cellular mechanisms responsible for neuronal firing suppression are still unclear even in the extensively-investigated visual cortex (e.g. see discussion in Shmuel et al., 2002); 2) it is not possible to quantitatively define the expected metabolic outcomes of neuronal firing suppression, since no energy budget for increased or decreased neuronal activity are available yet; 3) relating changes of metabolite concentrations with energy demands requires further validation. Indeed, it is also possible that reduced [Lac] changes do not reflect reduced oxidative energy consumption upon repeated visual stimuli, but rather they reflect a dynamic interplay of glycolysis compared to TCA cycle rates in the presence of unaffected neural firing. A study that is specifically relevant to this issue is the one conducted by Mintun et al. (2002) with PET. The authors found that oxygen consumption increased 4.7% compared to baseline after one minute of visual high spatial frequency achromatic stimulation; however, after 25 min of stimulation the increase was 15.0%. This slow increase of oxygen consumption was tentatively ascribed to the fact that those stimulations are known to activate the "interblob" neuronal populations (Tootell et al., 1988), which are relatively poor in cytochrome oxidase relative to the neighboring "blob" regions. However, this is an unlikely explanation for the reduced [Lac] observed by Mangia et al. (2007b), since the chromatic stimulus (red/black reversing checkerboard) used in that study is known to activate the "blob" neuronal populations, which have large oxidative capacity.

In conclusion, in spite of the many technical challenges and controversies related to human applications of functional MRS, this approach has proved to be crucial to formulate working hypothesis which can guide future research aiming at notably improving our understanding of the visual cortex, as of the cortex in general.

References

Attwell D, Laughlin SB (2001) An energy budget for signaling in the grey matter of the brain. *J. Cereb. Blood Flow Metab*. 21:1133-45.

Bandettini PA, Wong EC, Hinks RS, Tikofsky RS, Hyde JS (1992) Time course EPI of human brain function during task activation. *Magn. Reson. Med*. 25:390-7.

Baslow MH, Hrabe J, Guilfoyle DN (2007) Dynamic relationship between neurostimulation and N-acetylaspartate metabolism in the human visual cortex: evidence that NAA functions as a molecular water pump during visual stimulation. *J. Mol. Neurosci*. 32:235-45.

Belliveau JW, Kennedy DN, Jr., McKinstry RC, Buchbinder BR, Weisskoff RM, Cohen MS, Vevea JM, Brady TJ, Rosen BR (1991) Functional mapping of the human visual cortex by magnetic resonance imaging. *Science* 254:716-9.

Boucard CC, Mostert JP, Cornelissen FW, De Keyser J, Oudkerk M, Sijens PE (2005) Visual stimulation, 1H MR spectroscopy and fMRI of the human visual pathways. *Eur. Radiol*. 15:47-52.

Chen W, Novotny EJ, Zhu XH, Rothman DL, Shulman RG (1993) Localized 1H NMR measurement of glucose consumption in the human brain during visual stimulation. *Proc. Natl. Acad. Sci. USA* 90:9896-900.

Chen W, Zhu XH, Adriany G, Ugurbil K (1997) Increase of creatine kinase activity in the visual cortex of human brain during visual stimulation: a 31P magnetization transfer study. *Magn. Reson. Med*. 38:551-7.

Chen W, Zhu XH, Gruetter R, Seaquist ER, Adriany G, Ugurbil K (2001) Study of tricarboxylic acid cycle flux changes in human visual cortex during hemifield visual stimulation using (1)H-[(13)C] MRS and fMRI. *Magn. Reson. Med*. 45:349-55.

Chhina N, Kuestermann E, Halliday J, Simpson LJ, Macdonald IA, Bachelard HS, Morris PG (2001) Measurement of human tricarboxylic acid cycle rates during visual activation by (13)C magnetic resonance spectroscopy. *J. Neurosci. Res*. 66:737-46.

Chiappa KH, Hill RA, Huang-Hellinger F, Jenkins BG (1999) Photosensitive epilepsy studied by functional magnetic resonance imaging and magnetic resonance spectroscopy. *Epilepsia* 40 Suppl 4:3-7.

Chih CP, Roberts Jr EL (2003) Energy substrates for neurons during neural activity: a critical review of the astrocyte-neuron lactate shuttle hypothesis. *J. Cereb. Blood Flow Metab*. 23:1263-81.

Choi IY, Lei H, Gruetter R (2002) Effect of deep pentobarbital anesthesia on neurotransmitter metabolism in vivo: on the correlation of total glucose consumption with glutamatergic action. *J. Cereb. Blood Flow Metab.* 22:1343-51.

de Graaf RA, Mason GF, Patel AB, Behar KL, Rothman DL (2003) In vivo 1H-[13C]-NMR spectroscopy of cerebral metabolism. *NMR Biomed.* 16:339-57.

Dienel GA, Cruz NF (2004) Nutrition during brain activation: does cell-to-cell lactate shuttling contribute significantly to sweet and sour food for thought? *Neurochem. Int.* 45:321-51.

Douglas RJ, Martin KA (2004) Neuronal circuits of the neocortex. *Annu. Rev. Neurosci.* 27:419-51

Du F, Zhu XH, Qiao H, Zhang X, Chen W (2007) Efficient in vivo 31P magnetization transfer approach for noninvasively determining multiple kinetic parameters and metabolic fluxes of ATP metabolism in the human brain. *Magn. Reson. Med.* 57:103-14.

Fox PT, Raichle ME (1986) Focal physiological uncoupling of cerebral blood flow and oxidative metabolism during somatosensory stimulation in human subjects. *Proc. Natl. Acad. Sci. USA* 83:1140-4.

Fox PT, Raichle ME, Mintun MA, Dence C (1988) Nonoxidative glucose consumption during focal physiologic neural activity. *Science* 241:462-4.

Frahm J, Kruger G, Merboldt KD, Kleinschmidt A (1996) Dynamic uncoupling and recoupling of perfusion and oxidative metabolism during focal brain activation in man. *Magn. Reson. Med.* 35:143-8.

Giove F, Mangia S, Bianciardi M, Garreffa G, Di Salle F, Morrone R, Maraviglia B (2003) The physiology and metabolism of neuronal activation: in vivo studies by NMR and other methods. *Magn. Reson. Imaging* 21:1283-93.

Gruetter R, Weisdorf SA, Rajanayagan V, Terpstra M, Merkle H, Truwit CL, Garwood M, Nyberg SL, Ugurbil K (1998b) Resolution improvements in in vivo 1H NMR spectra with increased magnetic field strength. *J. Magn. Reson.* 135:260-4.

Henry PG, Adriany G, Deelchand D, Gruetter R, Marjanska M, Oz G, Seaquist ER, Shestov A, Ugurbil K (2006) In vivo 13C NMR spectroscopy and metabolic modeling in the brain: a practical perspective. *Magn. Reson. Imaging* 24:527-39.

Kato T, Murashita J, Shioiri T, Hamakawa H, Inubushi T (1996) Effect of photic stimulation on energy metabolism in the human brain measured by 31P-MR spectroscopy. *J. Neuropsychiatry Clin. Neurosci.* 8:417-22.

Kato T, Murashita J, Shioiri T, Terada M, Inubushi T, Kato N (1998) Photic stimulation-induced alteration of brain energy metabolism measured by 31P-MR spectroscopy in patients with MELAS. *J. Neurol. Sci.* 155:182-5.

Katz-Brull R, Alsop DC, Marquis RP, Lenkinski RE (2006) Limits on activation-induced temperature and metabolic changes in the human primary visual cortex. *Magn. Reson. Med.* 56:348-55.

Ke Y, Cohen BM, Lowen S, Hirashima F, Nassar L, Renshaw PF (2002) Biexponential transverse relaxation (T(2)) of the proton MRS creatine resonance in human brain. *Magn. Reson. Med.* 47:232-8.

Kohn A, Movshon JA (2003) Neuronal adaptation to visual motion in area MT of the macaque. *Neuron.* 39:681–91.

Kuwabara T, Watanabe H, Tanaka K, Tsuji S, Ohkubo M, Ito T, Sakai K, Yuasa T (1994) Mitochondrial encephalomyopathy: elevated visual cortex lactate unresponsive to photic stimulation--a localized 1H-MRS study. *Neurology* 44:557-9.

Kwong KK, Belliveau JW, Chesler DA, Goldberg IE, Weisskoff RM, Poncelet BP, Kennedy DN, Hoppel BE, Cohen MS, Turner R, et al. (1992) Dynamic magnetic resonance imaging of human brain activity during primary sensory stimulation. *Proc. Natl. Acad. Sci. USA* 89:5675-9.

Lauritzen M (2001) Relationship of spikes, synaptic activity, and local changes of cerebral blood flow. *J. Cereb. Blood Flow Metab.* 21:1367-83.

Lei H, Ugurbil K, Chen W (2003a) Measurement of unidirectional Pi to ATP flux in human visual cortex at 7 T by using in vivo 31P magnetic resonance spectroscopy. *Proc. Natl. Acad. Sci. USA* 100:14409-14.

Lei H, Zhu XH, Zhang XL, Ugurbil K, Chen W (2003b) In vivo 31P magnetic resonance spectroscopy of human brain at 7 T: an initial experience. *Magn. Reson. Med.* 49:199-205.

Lennie P (2003) The cost of cortical computation. *Curr. Biol.* 13:493-7.

Logothetis NK, Pauls J, Augath M, Trinath T, Oeltermann A (2001) Neurophysiological investigation of the basis of the fMRI signal. *Nature* 412:150-7.

Maddock RJ, Buonocore MH, Lavoie SP, Copeland LE, Kile SJ, Richards AL, Ryan JM (2006) Brain lactate responses during visual stimulation in fasting and hyperglycemic subjects: a proton magnetic resonance spectroscopy study at 1.5 Tesla. *Psychiatry Res.* 148:47-54.

Mangia S, Garreffa G, Bianciardi M, Giove F, Di Salle F, Maraviglia B (2003) The aerobic brain: lactate decrease at the onset of neural activity. *Neuroscience* 118:7-10.

Mangia S, Tkac I, Gruetter R, Van De Moortele PF, Giove F, Maraviglia B, Ugurbil K (2006) Sensitivity of single-voxel 1H-MRS in investigating the metabolism of the activated human visual cortex at 7 T. *Magn. Reson. Imaging* 24:343-8.

Mangia S, Tkac I, Gruetter R, Van de Moortele PF, Maraviglia B, Ugurbil K (2007a) Sustained neuronal activation raises oxidative metabolism to a new steady-state level: evidence from 1H NMR spectroscopy in the human visual cortex. *J. Cereb. Blood Flow Metab.* 27:1055-63.

Mangia S, Tkac I, Logothetis NK, Gruetter R, Van de Moortele PF, Ugurbil K (2007b) Dynamics of lactate concentration and blood oxygen level-dependent effect in the human visual cortex during repeated identical stimuli. *J. Neurosci. Res.* 85:3340-6.

Merboldt KD, Bruhn H, Hanicke W, Michaelis T, Frahm J (1992) Decrease of glucose in the human visual cortex during photic stimulation. *Magn. Reson. Med.* 25:187-94.

Mintun MA, Vlassenko AG, Shulman GL, Snyder AZ (2002) Time-related increase of oxygen utilization in continuously activated human visual cortex. *Neuroimage* 16:531-7.

Murashita J, Kato T, Shioiri T, Inubushi T, Kato N (1999) Age-dependent alteration of metabolic response to photic stimulation in the human brain measured by 31P MR-spectroscopy. *Brain Res.* 818:72-6.

Murashita J, Kato T, Shioiri T, Inubushi T, Kato N (2000) Altered brain energy metabolism in lithium-resistant bipolar disorder detected by photic stimulated 31P-MR spectroscopy. *Psychol. Med.* 30:107-15.

Ogawa S, Lee TM, Kay AR, Tank DW (1990) Brain magnetic resonance imaging with contrast dependent on blood oxygenation. *Proc. Natl. Acad. Sci. USA* 87:9868-72.

Ogawa S, Tank DW, Menon R, Ellermann JM, Kim SG, Merkle H, Ugurbil K (1992) Intrinsic signal changes accompanying sensory stimulation: functional brain mapping with magnetic resonance imaging. *Proc. Natl. Acad. Sci. USA* 89:5951-5.

Oz G, Berkich DA, Henry PG, Xu Y, LaNoue K, Hutson SM, Gruetter R (2004) Neuroglial metabolism in the awake rat brain: CO2 fixation increases with brain activity. *J. Neurosci.* 24:11273-9.

Oz G, Seaquist ER, Kumar A, Criego AB, Benedict LE, Rao JP, Henry PG, Van De Moortele PF, Gruetter R (2007) Human brain glycogen content and metabolism: implications on its role in brain energy metabolism. *Am. J. Physiol. Endocrinol. Metab.* 292:E946-51.

Pellerin L, Magistretti PJ (1994) Glutamate uptake into astrocytes stimulates aerobic glycolysis: a mechanism coupling neuronal activity to glucose utilization. *Proc. Natl. Acad. Sci. USA* 91:10625-9.

Pellerin L, Magistretti PJ (2004) Neuroenergetics: calling upon astrocytes to satisfy hungry neurons. *Neuroscientist* 10:53-62.

Prichard J, Rothman D, Novotny E, Petroff O, Kuwabara T, Avison M, Howseman A, Hanstock C, Shulman R (1991) Lactate rise detected by 1H NMR in human visual cortex during physiologic stimulation. *Proc. Natl. Acad. Sci. USA* 88:5829-31.

Raichle ME, Mintun MA (2006) Brain work and brain imaging. *Annu. Rev. Neurosci.* 29:449-76.

Rango M, Castelli A, Scarlato G (1997) Energetics of 3.5 s neural activation in humans: a 31P MR spectroscopy study. *Magn. Reson. Med.* 38:878-83.

Sandor PS, Dydak U, Schoenen J, Kollias SS, Hess K, Boesiger P, Agosti RM (2005) MR-spectroscopic imaging during visual stimulation in subgroups of migraine with aura. *Cephalalgia* 25:507-18.

Sappey-Marinier D, Calabrese G, Fein G, Hugg JW, Biggins C, Weiner MW (1992) Effect of photic stimulation on human visual cortex lactate and phosphates using 1H and 31P magnetic resonance spectroscopy. *J. Cereb. Blood Flow Metab.* 12:584-92.

Sarchielli P, Tarducci R, Presciutti O, Gobbi G, Pelliccioli GP, Stipa G, Alberti A, Capocchi G (2005) Functional 1H-MRS findings in migraine patients with and without aura assessed interictally. *Neuroimage* 24:1025-31.

Schurr A (2006) Lactate: the ultimate cerebral oxidative energy substrate? *J. Cereb. Blood Flow Metab.* 26:142-52.

Sibson NR, Dhankhar A, Mason GF, Rothman DL, Behar KL, Shulman RG (1998) Stoichiometric coupling of brain glucose metabolism and glutamatergic neuronal activity. *Proc. Natl. Acad. Sci. USA* 95:316-21.

Siesjö B (1978) *Brain energy metabolism.* New York: John Wiley and Sons.

Sokoloff L (1999) Energetics of functional activation in neural tissues. *Neurochem. Res.* 24:321-9.

Shmuel A, Yacoub E, Pfeuffer J, Van de Moortele PF, Adriany G, Hu X, Ugurbil K (2002) Sustained negative BOLD, blood flow and oxygen consumption response and its coupling to the positive response in the human brain. *Neuron* 36:1195-210.

Shulman R, Hyder F, Rothman D (2001) Lactate efflux and the neuroenergetic basis of brain function. *NMR Biomed.* 14:389-96.

Tkac I, Andersen P, Adriany G, Merkle H, Ugurbil K, Gruetter R (2001) In vivo 1H NMR spectroscopy of the human brain at 7 T. *Magn. Reson. Med.* 46:451-6.

Tkac I, Gruetter R (2005) Methodology of H-1 NMR spectroscopy of the human brain at very high magnetic fields. *Appl. Magn. Reson.* 29:139-57.

Tootell RB, Silverman MS, Hamilton SL, Switkes E, De Valois RL (1988) Functional anatomy of macaque striate cortex. V. Spatial frequency. *J. Neurosci.* 8:1610-24.

Tuunanen PI, Murray IJ, Parry NR, Kauppinen RA (2006) Heterogeneous oxygen extraction in the visual cortex during activation in mild hypoxic hypoxia revealed by quantitative functional magnetic resonance imaging. *J. Cereb. Blood Flow Metab.* 26:263-73.

Urrila AS, Hakkarainen A, Heikkinen S, Huhdankoski O, Kuusi T, Stenberg D, Hakkinen AM, Porkka-Heiskanen T, Lundbom N (2006) Preliminary findings of proton magnetic resonance spectroscopy in occipital cortex during sleep deprivation. *Psychiatry Res.* 147:41-6.

Vaughan JT, Garwood M, Collins CM, Liu W, DelaBarre L, Adriany G, Andersen P, Merkle H, Goebel R, Smith MB, Ugurbil K (2001) 7T vs. 4T: RF power, homogeneity, and signal-to-noise comparison in head images. *Magn. Reson. Med.* 46:24-30.

Zhu XH, Chen W (2001) Observed BOLD effects on cerebral metabolite resonances in human visual cortex during visual stimulation: a functional (1)H MRS study at 4 T. *Magn. Reson. Med.* 46:841-7.

In: Visual Cortex: New Research
Editors: T. A. Portocello and R. B. Velloti

ISBN 978-1-60456-530-0
© 2008 Nova Science Publishers, Inc.

Chapter 7

THE ROLE OF COROLLARY DISCHARGE SIGNALS IN VISUAL PERCEPTION

Christopher C. Pack

Department of Neurology and Neurosurgery, Montreal Neurological Institute,
McGill University, Montreal, QC Canada

Abstract

As your eyes move across this page, the image on your retina shifts from right to left with each eye movement. Yet you do not perceive the world to be moving, despite the evidence presented to your visual system. It appears that our visual systems are equipped with a mechanism for discounting the portion of the sensory input that is due to our own movements.

Such a mechanism is often called a corollary discharge, because it involves neural pathways that duplicate the commands sent to motor structures. These duplicate pathways lead to sensory areas, which combine the sensory input with the impending motor movement to maintain perceptual stability. Thus the neural commands that activate your eye muscles while you are reading also reach your visual system, which effectively ignores the resulting retinal motion.

This chapter will discuss the anatomical, neurophysiological, and behavioral evidence for corollary discharge signals in the primate visual cortex. In particular, I will focus on oculomotor corollary discharge signals that are thought to reach visual areas responsible for measuring visual motion. There is some controversy as to which cortical areas receive a corollary discharge input, what the corollary discharge conveys, and how it influences individual neuronal responses. I will review the existing literature on these subjects, and suggest future research directions that may shed light on the interaction between corollary discharges and sensory processing.

Introduction

The nervous system constantly monitors the consequences of its own actions. This type of feedback serves different purposes in different animals, but a particularly important role is to adjust the ongoing sensory input to compensate for the animal's own motor activity. A few examples illustrate the point nicely:

- Crickets are able to maintain auditory sensitivity while they are chirping, despite the fact that a stridulating male cricket can produce a 100 db song. This sensitivity is maintained because crickets are able to inhibit their own primary auditory neurons during song production, essentially filtering out the sensory effects of their own song production [1].
- Similarly, certain kinds of fish communicate by producing electrical discharges, which their neighbors can detect by means of a dedicated electrosensory lobe in their brains. In order to distinguish the electrical discharges of other fish from those that are self-produced, electric fish have a neural pathway from the organ that produces electrical signals to the part of the brain that detects them [2].
- Bats use mechanisms similar to those of crickets and fish to distinguish between auditory inputs due to their own vocalizations and those due to external objects during echolocation [3].
- Humans are far less sensitive to their own vocal sounds when they are speaking than when they listen to a recording of their own speech [4]. They are also generally unable to tickle themselves [5].

In each of the abovementioned instances, a feedback signal related to a motor action allows the animal to distinguish sensory inputs that correspond to events in the outside world from those that correspond to its own actions.

Such a mechanism is often called a *corollary discharge*, because it involves pathways that transmit duplicates of the motor commands to sensory regions of the brain. For example, as you move your eyes across this page, the oculomotor structures of your brain send corollary discharge signals to visual parts of your cortex, instructing them to ignore the retinal motion that occurs with each eye movement. Without these signals, you would perceive the world around you to be jittering several times per second, as is the case with stroke patients who lack such signals.

The corollary discharge is of fundamental interest to the field of neuroscience, because it is phylogenetically ancient, and there is good reason to believe that it has formed the basis for more abstract, cognitive influences on perception, including attention and expectation. From the clinical perceptive, a recently developed theory links symptoms of mental disease, schizophrenia in particular, to an impairment of corollary discharge function [6]. The hypothesis is that schizophrenic patients lack a high-level corollary discharge that is necessary to distinguish self-generated thoughts from externally-generated ones, leading to delusions of thought insertion and mind control. This review will focus on the relationship between corollary discharge signals and visual perception. More specifically, we will focus on the influence of signals related to eye movements on the visual activity in the primate brain.

Corollary Discharge Signals and Saccadic Eye Movements

In humans and other primates, the retina is marked by a central region of high acuity (called the *fovea*) and a surrounding region of relatively poor acuity. In order to point the high-acuity fovea towards a region of interest, most primates make several eye movements per second. These eye movements are called *saccades*, and they consist of a rapid and highly accurate rotation of the eye towards a particular point in space. Other types of eye movements serve largely the same purpose, and some of them will be discussed in subsequent sections of this review.

Figure 1 shows a subset of the pathways that are involved in the generation of saccades in primates. The blue arrow indicates a pathway that is primarily sensory, involving areas like the middle temporal area (MT) of visual cortex. The green arrow indicates a pathway that is primarily involved in oculomotor control, including the superior colliculus (SC). Neurons along the blue pathway measure the position and velocity of visible objects, and neurons along the green pathway command eye movements towards particular targets. In between, one finds areas such as the frontal eye fields (FEF), which are involved in selecting targets on the basis of sensory information and internal goals. Of course this picture is quite oversimplified, but it captures an intuitive way of thinking about sensorimotor control, both behaviorally and anatomically.

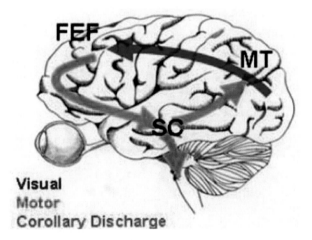

Figure 1. An oculomotor feedback loop in the primate brain. Visual information is analyzed in extrastriate cortical areas including the middle temporal (MT) area. The frontal eye fields (FEF) receive projections from the extrastriate cortex, and are involved in selecting targets for eye movements. Neurons in the FEF project to the superior colliculus (SC), which is involved in the execution of saccades. The red arrow indicates a corollary discharge pathway that relays information about saccades to the visual cortex.

The red pathway relays signals related to saccades to the sensory areas of the visual cortex, including area MT and the lateral intraparietal area (LIP). The function of this pathway is poorly understood, but the following section will describe the circumstantial evidence that it plays a role in regulating sensitivity to visual input during saccadic eye movements.

Perceptual Evidence for a Saccade-Related Corollary Discharge Signal

Corollary discharge signals are not normally perceived consciously in the way that, for example, activity in certain visual areas is causally related to perceptual decisions [7]. However, the effects of corollary discharge signals are readily observable under the right conditions. For example, as you move your eyes around the visual scene, you do not perceive objects to be shifting in space, even though their images on the retina are doing precisely that. By way of comparison, it is instructive to try the following simple experiment, first proposed by Helmholtz [8]: Close one eye and tap gently on the eyelid of the other – in this case the world *does* appear to move, because the corollary discharge normally associated with the eye movement is missing.

Saccade-related corollary discharge signals have been studied quite thoroughly in human psychophysical experiments. Such studies are technically difficult because saccades rotate the eyes very quickly, leading to a high-velocity sweep of the visual scene across the retina. The human visual system is not terribly sensitive to such high velocities, so it is important to distinguish an active suppressive influence (due to a corollary discharge signal) from a general lack of sensitivity that is caused by the visual stimulus itself. Careful experiments by Burr and colleagues [9] successfully demonstrated the existence of an oculomotor corollary discharge signal that suppresses vision during saccades. In particular the suppression targets low spatial frequencies, and overall seems to be useful for decreasing the sensitivity to motion rather than shape or color. This phenomenon is called *saccadic suppression*.

In a typical experiment on saccadic suppression, a human subject is asked to make a saccade, and on some trials a small stimulus is flashed briefly at a random time just before or after the onset of the eye movement (Figure 2, top). The observer's task is to execute the saccade and then to indicate whether or not the target was flashed. For comparison one typically tests observers on fixation trials, in which the eyes remain stationary while the retinal effects of the saccade are simulated by rapidly shifting the visual display. In both cases performance is quantified as the stimulus contrast necessary to yield a criterion level of accuracy on the detection task.

Figure 3 shows the results for two observers in one such experiment[10]. Clearly visual sensitivity to the flashed stimulus decreased around the time of the saccade and recovered only after the saccade was completed (solid triangle symbols in the figure). When the saccade was not executed, sensitivity remained high during the entire stimulus presentation (open squares). This suggests that the eye movement, and hence a corollary discharge signal, was necessary for the suppression to take place. Further evidence in support of this point is the observation that the suppression began before the onset of the saccade.

This nicely eliminates any explanation for the suppression effect that relies on optical factors (e.g., blur) related to the movement of the eye.

Saccadic suppression experiments demonstrate a clear influence of corollary discharge signals on the detection of a visual stimulus. An interesting variation on these experiments involves asking observers to report the position, rather than simply the presence or absence, of a visual stimulus that is flashed around the time of a saccade. In this case one observes a powerful *compression* of visual space about the saccade target [11]. That is, observers report that the flashed stimulus is much closer to the saccade target than it actually is, as if all of visual space were compressed to a small region near the location of the intended eye movement. The relationship between this compression and saccade suppression is not entirely clear, although there is some evidence that they share a common mechanism [12].

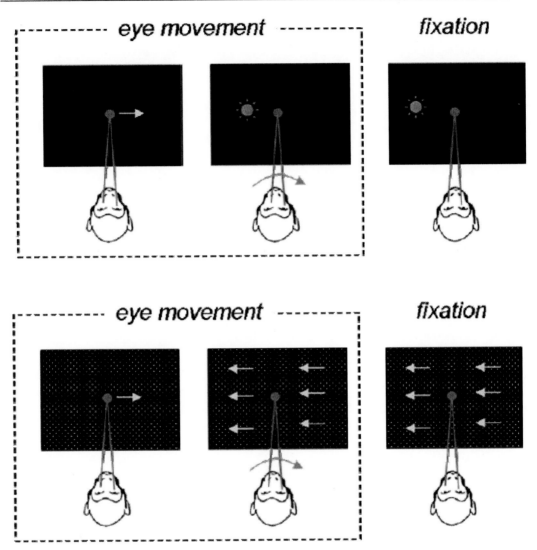

Figure 2. Design of a typical corollary discharge experiment. *Top*: An observer executes a saccade to the right, while a small target is flashed at a random time relative to the eye movement. Identical retinal stimulation can be obtained during steady fixation (right). Corollary discharge is measured by asking the observer to indicate the presence or absence of the target (in human psychophysics) or by recording the neuronal response to the target flash (in neurophysiological experiments). Any differences between the eye movement case and the fixation case can be attributed to corollary discharge influences. *Bottom*: During smooth pursuit the fixation spot moves at a constant velocity, and the animal has to move its eyes to maintain fixation. The motion of the eyes introduces motion of the visual background across the retina. Identical retinal motion can be obtained by keeping the fixation point stationary while moving the background (right panel). Corollary discharge influences can be measured in a manner similar to that used in the saccade experiments.

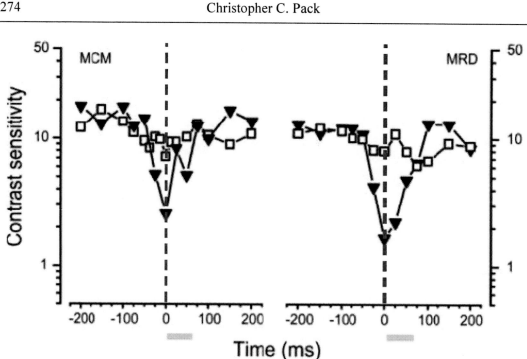

Figure 3. Perceptual suppression of vision during saccadic eye movements. The figure shows data from two observers who were asked to indicate the presence or absence of a visual stimulus that was presented briefly around the time of a saccade. The y-axis plots the threshold stimulus contrast for detection of the stimulus during saccade trials (solid triangles) and fixation trials (open squares). Contrast sensitivity declines sharply around the time of saccade initiation (red vertical lines), and recovers after completion of the saccade. Adapted from Diamond et al. (2000).

In any case it is clear that visual perception changes radically around the time of a saccade, and that these changes are due to a corollary discharge signal related to the eye movement.

Neurophysiological Evidence for a Saccade-Related Corollary Discharge Signal

There is abundant evidence that various brain areas receive corollary discharge signals related to saccades. In particular, recent experiments have revealed an oculomotor corollary discharge that is relayed from the SC through the thalamus to the FEF [13]. The function of this pathway appears to be to maintain an accurate representation of future saccade targets during eye movements. The evidence for this idea has been summarized in several recent reviews [14, 15]. Here I will focus on the evidence for corollary discharge signals in the visual cortex.

The primate visual cortex contains numerous distinct areas devoted to vision. The largest is the primary visual cortex (V1), which projects to a number of *extrastriate* visual areas, each of which contains a complete representation of visual space. Different extrastriate areas have different functional specializations and are integrated to various degrees with signals from other modalities, including signals related to attention, eye movements, vestibular activity, and so forth.

There is scant evidence that neurons in V1 receive a corollary discharge signal related to saccades. Wurtz and Mohler [16] studied the response of neurons in area V1 of the macaque monkey before, during, and after the execution of a saccade. All of the neurons responded to visual stimulation, but neither the strength nor the selectivity of the response was affected in any consistent way by saccades. That is, all neurons responded to a particular set of stimuli (usually oriented bars), and nothing about this response changed if the stimulus was presented just before or just after a saccade.

The negative result in V1 was somewhat surprising, because the same authors had demonstrated a robust corollary discharge influence in the superficial layers of the SC, using the same experimental paradigm [17]. It is natural to think of the cortex as being more sophisticated in terms of sensory processing than the subcortex, but in this instance such an intuition was not confirmed. Many neurons in SC responded more strongly to a stimulus that had been selected as the target of an impending saccade, in essence providing the chosen stimulus with increased saliency. The corollary discharge signal thus had the effect of integrating a purely sensory representation with the animal's motor plan. In contrast neurons in V1 seem to report the presence of a stimulus, irrespective of its role in the animal's behavior.

Later work revealed a second way in which corollary discharge signals influence the visual response of neurons in the superficial layers of the SC. Robinson and colleagues [18, 19] showed that many of these neurons respond well to stimuli that are swept at high velocities through their receptive fields. However the same neurons fail to respond when a saccadic eye movement sweeps the eye across a stationary stimulus at the same velocity. The important point is that the stimulus on the retina is identical in both cases – the only difference is the presence of an oculomotor signal in the case of the saccade. It appears that neurons in the superior colliculus use a corollary discharge of this signal to distinguish between the "real" motion of the stimulus in one case and the self-induced motion that occurs during the saccade. There is a strong similarity between these experiments and the abovementioned ones on saccadic suppression. In both cases the act of executing a saccade leads to a decrease in visual sensitivity relative to identical visual stimulation in the absence of an eye movement.

A follow-up study by Richmond and Wurtz [20] was particularly important because it distinguished between two potential sources for the corollary discharge signals. On the one hand the corollary discharge could be related to the animal's *intention* to move, in which case it would likely (though not necessarily) be of cortical origin. On the other hand, the signal might be a corollary of the movement itself, in which case it would almost certainly originate downstream from the SC, perhaps in the eye muscles themselves. Richmond and Wurtz dissociated these possibilities by means of a retrobulbar block, which temporarily paralyzed the eye muscles. As the animal attempted to execute the saccade, the corollary discharge influence persisted, indicating that it was not related to the metrics of the movement, but rather to the motor command or perhaps even to the decision to move. Further research is needed to distinguish between these remaining possibilities.

The corollary discharge signal discovered by Wurtz and colleagues had two properties that would seem to be useful for visual perception. Prior to a saccade it boosts the saliency of a target that the animal has decided is worthy of fixating, and during the saccade it suppresses the visual responses to stimuli that are swept across the retina during the movement. The latter is similar to the roles for corollary discharge signals listed above in the cricket, electric fish, bat, as well as in numerous other species. While both of these functions have clear implications for visual perception, it is important to point out that humans are not usually consciously aware of visual activity in subcortical areas (although the phenomenon of blindsight suggests that they may be subconsciously aware of it). A more likely role for the corollary discharge signals observed in the SC is as a modulator of ongoing visual activity in the extrastriate cortex.

Of all the extrastriate regions, perhaps the one that would seem most likely to integrate visual and corollary discharge signals would be the middle temporal (MT) area. MT neurons respond selectively to visual motion, and there is very strong evidence for a causal relationship between MT activity and visual perception [7]. Because many MT neurons respond to very high velocities, and because primates make a lot of saccades, one would expect that, in the absence of a corollary discharge input, a substantial portion of MT neurons would be responding almost constantly. These responses would be linked to the rotation of the eyes across the visual background rather than to anything that was actually happening in the outside world, and so they would constitute fairly meaningless chatter from the point of view of any brain region that relied on MT for information about motion.

Circumstantial evidence for a corollary discharge input to motion processing centers like MT came initially from psychophysical experiments (described above) related to the phenomenon of saccadic suppression. Furthermore, anatomical experiments had demonstrated the likely existence of a pathway from the superficial layers of the SC (where Wurtz's group had found cells that were suppressed during saccades) to MT by way of a thalamic nucleus called the pulvinar [21]. Thus the anatomical and perceptual data seemed to converge on the notion of a corollary discharge pathway to MT.

This idea was tested directly by Bair and O'Keefe [22], who measured MT activity during small fixational eye movements. Surprisingly they found that MT neurons seemed to respond to motion on the retina, irrespective of whether it was caused by "real motion" or by eye movements. The fixational eye movements were small in amplitude (less than 1°, and hence called *microsaccades*), but sufficiently high in velocity that one would expect them to disrupt visual perception in some circumstances. Bair et al. concluded that MT was not involved in the suppression of such motion signals.

A different result was obtained by Thiele et al. [23], who performed an experiment similar to those carried out by the Wurtz group in their studies of the SC and V1. Here the animals made 10° saccades across a large, textured background, and the resulting MT activity was compared to the motion of the same pattern during steady fixation. Thiele et al found a large difference in the two cases, with many neurons being silenced during the eye movement condition. This result was similar to that observed by Wurtz and colleagues in the SC. Interestingly, Thiele et al. found that for many cells the corollary discharge modulation was specific to the direction in which the saccade was made. This appears to be an elaboration of the corollary discharge function seen in the SC, where neither the sensory nor the corollary discharge signals appear to be direction-selective.

Thiele et al.'s result has been somewhat controversial, since a subsequent paper [24] failed to replicate their results. However, the latter group used a different stimulus and a different style of analysis, so there need not be a contradiction. Indeed the same group has subsequently found evidence for a corollary discharge input to MT during saccades [25], so it will be important for future research to pin down the nature of the interaction between the corollary discharge signals and the visual stimulus.

Corollary Discharge Signals and Smooth Pursuit Eye Movements

Whereas saccades are used to rotate the fovea to the position of an object of interest, a second kind of eye movement, called *smooth pursuit*, is used to match the velocity of an object of interest. The term "smooth pursuit" captures the behavior quite accurately – one typically rotates the eye smoothly at a velocity that closely matches a visual target. Such movements are necessary in order to navigate through a cluttered environment, particularly if one is interested in tracking or evading other animals.

Many of the visual consequences of smooth pursuit are the same as those related to saccades. During pursuit the object that is being tracked is stationary on the retina (but moving in the world), and the visual background moves across the retina (though it is actually stationary). Thus one might expect that corollary discharge signals would be used to allow the animal to interpret visual information correctly, as appears to be the case for the saccade system.

Perceptual Evidence for a Smooth Pursuit-Related Corollary Discharge Signal

The observation that smooth pursuit induces retinal motion opposite to the direction of tracking suggests a convenient way to test theories about corollary discharge function. To the extent that the observer perceives this motion, one can say that the corollary discharge signal does not contribute much to perception (Figure 2, bottom). Early observations suggested that people do indeed perceive the motion of the background, and this perception was called the Filehne Illusion [26]. However, the perceived speed of the background is usually much slower than when similar motion is presented during steady fixation [27], suggesting that a corollary discharge signal is at play, but that it does not fully suppress the self-induced sensory signals.

The suppression of motion signals due to the visual background is probably useful in several behavioral situations. The most immediate example is in eliminating the optokinetic response that would normally be triggered in response to a large stimulus moving across the retina. Under normal circumstances such a response is involuntary, so that the eyes would rotate in the direction of large-field motion. This would be extremely counterproductive during a smooth pursuit eye movement, the entire purpose of which is to track a small moving target across the visual background. Thus the corollary discharge signal that suppresses the visual motion of the background may actually be essential for accurate pursuit.

A second situation in which it is desirable to suppress background motion is during visual navigation. During navigation the entire visual field is displaced on the retina, and the resulting stimulus is often called *optic flow*. Optic flow is useful for guiding self-motion towards objects and avoiding collisions, but in either case it is helpful to remove the portion of the flow that is due to eye movements. Such eye movements occur frequently when one is navigating through a cluttered environment while fixating an object that is off to the side of the self-motion trajectory (Figure 4). The idea that a corollary discharge signal suppresses the resulting component of the optic flow stimulus was confirmed by Royden et al. [28], who found that observers were better at estimating simulated self-motion trajectories during eye movements than if the same visual stimulus was presented during fixation. In the latter case the visual consequences of the eye movements were simulated and added to the flow field. Thus the retinal stimuli were identical in the two cases, but the presence of an eye movement signal aided observers' perception of their own heading.

An additional piece of evidence for the utility of corollary discharge signals during smooth pursuit came from the case of a patient (R.W.) who had bilateral lesions of the extrastriate cortex as a consequence of stroke [29]. Although the patient's vision was normal, he was unable to use a corollary discharge signal to distinguish "real" motion from retinal motion caused by his own eye movements. In psychophysical testing, he routinely reported the visual background to be moving when he executed smooth pursuit eye movements.

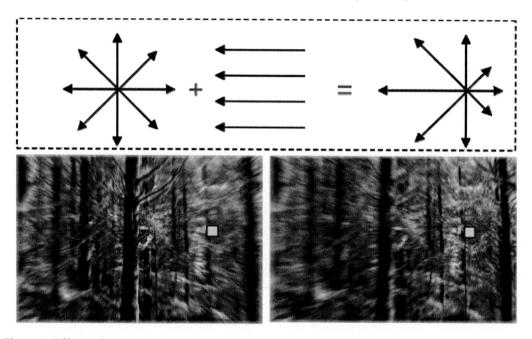

Figure 4. Effects of eye movements on optic flow. The left part of the top panel shows a cartoon of an optic flow field that would be seen by an observer moving forward while looking in the direction of self-motion. The center of the optic flow field corresponds to the direction in which the observer is heading. If the observer makes a rightward eye movement, the resulting optic flow will be in the leftward direction (top, center). When combined with the optic flow caused by forward motion, the complete flow field no longer contains information about the direction of heading (top, right). The bottom panel shows how this would look for a naturalistic flow field. On the left is a depiction of the flow field that is seen by an observer heading towards the center of the image. If the observer makes an eye movement to track the blue square the flow field changes into the one on the right, even though the heading direction is unchanged. Image taken from the Canadian Council of Forest Ministers web page (www.sfncanada.org).

As mentioned above, this Filehne Illusion is present to some degree in most observers, but in patient R. W. it was far stronger, indicating that he had little or no ability to compensate for the consequences of his own eye movements. This naturally leads to the question of which extrastriate areas might be involved in integrating visual and corollary discharge signals.

Neurophysiological Evidence for a Smooth Pursuit-Related Corollary Discharge

Several of the psychophysical paradigms described in the preceding section have been tested on individual neurons in various parts of the extrastriate cortex of the macaque monkey. The early studies by Robinson's group had found evidence for corollary discharge influence for smooth pursuit that was similar to that seen for saccades [18]. That is, many neurons in the superficial SC responded to the retinal motion of a stimulus during fixation but not during pursuit. This suggested that the corollary discharge signal could be used to suppress background motion during pursuit, in a manner similar to that seen in the saccade experiments. Naturally one might expect to find evidence for this signal in the extrastriate cortex.

A series of studies beginning in the 1980s by Galletti and colleagues used a paradigm similar to the used by the Wurtz group [30-32]. Stimuli were moved through the receptive fields of individual neurons during steady fixation, and the resulting neuronal response was compared to the same retinal stimulation that occurred when the stimulus was stationary and the eyes moved. Cells that responded more strongly in the fixation condition were called "real-motion" cells, because they were capable of measuring motion that occurred in the external world, independent of the events that took place on the retina. By this definition, the percentage of cells that receive significant corollary discharge signals was found to increase from around 15% in areas V1 and V2 to nearly 50% in area V3.

A similar study by Erickson and Thier [33] targeted areas V4, MT, and MST. V4 is typically considered part of the ventral processing stream, meaning that it is likely to be more involved in judgments of object shape than of motion. Thus it was not terribly surprising that the authors found little evidence for a corollary discharge input to area V4. More surprising was the finding that neurons in area MT responded in the same way to motion during pursuit and during fixation, suggesting that they also lacked a corollary discharge input. However, the analysis used by Erickson and Thier to characterize corollary discharge modulation was somewhat unusual: They measured the change in direction selectivity during pursuit and fixation. By this metric the corollary discharge input was absent, but their measure would be insensitive to changes in response amplitude, which was the primary criterion used by previous authors. Thus it remains possible that MT neurons receive a corollary discharge input during pursuit that serves a function similar to that observed during saccades. On the other hand, a recent study by Inaba and colleagues [34] has reached a conclusion similar to that of Erickson and Thier, so the issue remains somewhat mysterious.

Area MST (medial superior temporal cortex) receives visual input from area MT, and it appears to be in many ways a more sophisticated processor of sensory information than areas that are lower in the extrastriate hierarchy. Erickson and Thier found that MST neurons did indeed receive a corollary discharge input, and that it rendered the cells less selective for motion direction during pursuit than during fixation. As in V4 and MT, the study did not address the possible modulation of response amplitude by a corollary discharge signal. Nevertheless, the study suggested that MST neurons might be responsible for some of the psychophysical phenomena discussed above.

This possibility was tested more directly by Bradley et al. [35] who recorded MST responses during presentation of a simulated heading stimulus that was quite similar to that used in the psychophysical studies of Royden et al. (1992). As in the psychophysical studies,

MST neurons responded as if the corollary discharge signal were suppressing the portion of the visual input that was due to the smooth pursuit eye movement. The compensation was only partial, so that it was not sufficient to account for the psychophysical performance in the task used by Royden et al. (1992). Subsequent recordings from area VIP in the parietal lobe, which receives input from MST, revealed a near-total compensation [36], indicating that the corollary discharge influence grows stronger as one traces the feedforward progression of visual processing.

Other Types of Corollary Discharge Signals

In this article I have focused on two types of eye movements: saccades and smooth pursuit. There are of course many other kinds of eye movements that can influence vision through corollary discharge mechanisms. Many of these relate to the perception of three-dimensional space: Signals related to eye position allow the observer to localize objects during reaching and navigation, and those for vergence provide a measure of absolute depth that is likewise crucial for interacting with the environment. These issues have been described in recent review papers (eye position:[37]; vergence: [38]). In addition there is very strong evidence for corollary discharge signals that remap the locations of visible objects when a saccade is made. This evidence has been reviewed by several groups [15, 39].

Conclusion

Recent work has found compelling evidence for a corollary discharge pathway that leads from the SC to the FEF in the macaque monkey [13]. This pathway seems to convey information about an impending saccade, and it appears that the FEF uses it to maintain spatial constancy during the eye movement. The pathway was characterized by means of technically challenging experiments in which neurons at each stage along the pathway were recorded simultaneously, allowing the experimenters to record the information that was transferred along the pathway at each stage. The same researchers (Sommer and Wurtz) demonstrated the relevance of the pathway for behavior by blocking the flow of corollary discharge signals, and demonstrating that the animals failed to perform tasks that relied on these signals.

The FEF is involved in target selection, attention, and oculomotor decision-making. To study the influence of corollary discharge signals on visual perception, it will be necessary to perform experiments similar to those performed by Sommer and Wurtz on the pathway leading from the SC to the visual cortex, focusing on areas like MT. As described above, the experiments to date that have been done on this pathway have all tested individual brain areas, using different stimuli, different behavioral paradigms, and different styles of analysis. Consequently, it has been difficult to draw firm conclusions about exactly how corollary discharge signals influence visual cortical areas, and how these signals affect behavior. An obvious direction for future experiments would be to block corollary discharge signals that are known to reach areas like MT, and to observe the effects on the monkeys' visual perception. One would expect that the animals would be more likely to perceive motion during saccades when the corollary discharge signal was absent.

The nature of the corollary discharge signal related to smooth pursuit is even more mysterious. A recent study [40] suggests that the central thalamus may play a role in smooth pursuit that would parallel the role of the thalamus in the corollary discharge pathway studied by Sommer and Wurtz. This makes a certain amount of sense, since both the FEF and the brainstem contain subregions that are dedicated to pursuit, just as the SC and FEF are known to be involved in the control of saccades. Assuming that there are ascending corollary discharge signals for smooth pursuit that are relayed through the central thalamus, it is still not known if these are the same signals that reach the visual cortex. Thus it will be important to perform systematic recordings (ideally with identified neural connections) that use the same stimuli and eye movement behaviors to sort out which signals are relayed through which areas. In this case, as well as in the study of saccades, it will be important for neurophysiologists to make use of the large body of work on psychophysical studies of corollary discharge influences, since in all cases the effects of corollary discharge signals are stimulus-dependent.

References

[1]   Poulet, J.F. and B. Hedwig, A corollary discharge maintains auditory sensitivity during sound production. *Nature,* 2002. 418(6900): p. 872-6.

[2]   Sawtell, N.B., C. Mohr, and C.C. Bell, Recurrent feedback in the mormyrid electrosensory system: cells of the preeminential and lateral toral nuclei. *J. Neurophysiol.,* 2005. 93(4): p. 2090-103.

[3]   Neuweiler, G., Evolutionary aspects of bat echolocation. *J. Comp. Physiol. A Neuroethol. Sens Neural. Behav. Physiol.,* 2003. 189(4): p. 245-56.

[4]   Ford, J.M. and D.H. Mathalon, Corollary discharge dysfunction in schizophrenia: Can it explain auditory hallucinations? *Int. J. Psychophysiol.,* 2005.

[5]   Blakemore, S.J., D. Wolpert, and C. Frith, Why can't you tickle yourself? *Neuroreport,* 2000. 11(11): p. R11-6.

[6]   Feinberg, I. and M. Guazzelli, Schizophrenia--a disorder of the corollary discharge systems that integrate the motor systems of thought with the sensory systems of consciousness. *Br. J. Psychiatry,* 1999. 174: p. 196-204.

[7]   Salzman, C.D., K.H. Britten, and W.T. Newsome, Cortical microstimulation influences perceptual judgements of motion direction. *Nature,* 1990. 346(6280): p. 174-7.

[8]   Helmholtz, H.v., *Helmholtz's Treatise on Physiology Optics,* vol. 3. 1867.

[9]   Burr, D.C., et al., Selective depression of motion sensitivity during saccades. *J. Physiol.,* 1982. 333: p. 1-15.

[10]   Diamond, M.R., J. Ross, and M.C. Morrone, Extraretinal control of saccadic suppression. *J. Neurosci.,* 2000. 20(9): p. 3449-55.

[11]   Morrone, M.C., J. Ross, and D.C. Burr, Apparent position of visual targets during real and simulated saccadic eye movements. *J. Neurosci.,* 1997. 17(20): p. 7941-53.

[12]   Michels, L. and M. Lappe, Contrast dependency of sacadic compression and suppression. *Vision Res.,* 2004. 44(20): p. 2327-36.

[13]   Sommer, M.A. and R.H. Wurtz, A pathway in primate brain for internal monitoring of movements. Science, 2002. 296(5572): p. 1480-2.

[14] Wurtz, R.H. and M.A. Sommer, Identifying corollary discharges for movement in the primate brain. *Prog. Brain Res.*, 2004. 144: p. 47-60.

[15] Wurtz, R.H., M.A. Sommer, and J. Cavanaugh, Drivers from the deep: the contribution of collicular input to thalamocortical processing. *Prog. Brain Res.*, 2005. 149: p. 207-25.

[16] Wurtz, R.H. and C.W. Mohler, Enhancement of visual responses in monkey striate cortex and frontal eye fields. *J. Neurophysiol.*, 1976. 39(4): p. 766-72.

[17] Wurtz, R.H. and C.W. Mohler, Organization of monkey superior colliculus: enhanced visual response of superficial layer cells. *J. Neurophysiol.*, 1976. 39(4): p. 745-65.

[18] Robinson, D.L., et al., Visual responses of pulvinar and collicular neurons during eye movements of awake, trained macaques. *J. Neurophysiol.*, 1991. 66(2): p. 485-96.

[19] Robinson, D.L. and R.H. Wurtz, Use of an extraretinal signal by monkey superior colliculus neurons to distinguish real from self-induced stimulus movement. *J. Neurophysiol.*, 1976. 39(4): p. 852-70.

[20] Richmond, B.J. and R.H. Wurtz, Vision during saccadic eye movements. II. A corollary discharge to monkey superior colliculus. *J. Neurophysiol.*, 1980. 43(4): p. 1156-67.

[21] Maunsell, J.H. and D.C. van Essen, The connections of the middle temporal visual area (MT) and their relationship to a cortical hierarchy in the macaque monkey. *J. Neurosci*, 1983. 3(12): p. 2563-86.

[22] Bair, W. and L.P. O'Keefe, The influence of fixational eye movements on the response of neurons in area MT of the macaque. *Vis. Neurosci.*, 1998. 15(4): p. 779-86.

[23] Thiele, A., et al., Neural mechanisms of saccadic suppression. *Science*, 2002. 295(5564): p. 2460-2.

[24] Price, N.S., et al., Rapid processing of retinal slip during saccades in macaque area MT. *J. Neurophysiol.*, 2005. 94(1): p. 235-46.

[25] Ibbotson, M.R., et al., Enhanced motion sensitivity follows saccadic suppression in the superior temporal sulcus of the macaque cortex. *Cereb. Cortex*, 2007. 17(5): p. 1129-38.

[26] Filehne, W., Über das optische Wahrnehmen von Bewegungen. *Zeitschrift für Sinnesphysiologie*, 1922. 53: p. 134-135.

[27] Wertheim, A., Motion perception during self-motion: The direct versus inferential controversy revisited. *Behav. Brain Sci.*, 1994. 17: p. 293-355.

[28] Royden, C.S., M.S. Banks, and J.A. Crowell, The perception of heading during eye movements. *Nature*, 1992. 360(6404): p. 583-5.

[29] Haarmeier, T., et al., False perception of motion in a patient who cannot compensate for eye movements. *Nature*, 1997. 389(6653): p. 849-52.

[30] Galletti, C., P.P. Battaglini, and G. Aicardi, 'Real-motion' cells in visual area V2 of behaving macaque monkeys. *Exp. Brain Res.*, 1988. 69(2): p. 279-88.

[31] Galletti, C., P.P. Battaglini, and P. Fattori, 'Real-motion' cells in area V3A of macaque visual cortex. *Exp. Brain Res.*, 1990. 82(1): p. 67-76.

[32] Galletti, C., et al., 'Real-motion' cells in the primary visual cortex of macaque monkeys. *Brain Res.*, 1984. 301(1): p. 95-110.

[33] Erickson, R.G. and P. Thier, A neuronal correlate of spatial stability during periods of self-induced visual motion. *Exp. Brain Res.*, 1991. 86(3): p. 608-16.

[34] Inaba, N., et al., MST neurons code for visual motion in space independent of pursuit eye movements. *J. Neurophysiol.*, 2007. 97(5): p. 3473-83.

[35] Bradley, D.C., et al., Mechanisms of heading perception in primate visual cortex. *Science*, 1996. 273(5281): p. 1544-7.

[36] Zhang, T., H.W. Heuer, and K.H. Britten, Parietal area VIP neuronal responses to heading stimuli are encoded in head-centered coordinates. *Neuron.*, 2004. 42(6): p. 993-1001.

[37] Salinas, E. and T.J. Sejnowski, Gain modulation in the central nervous system: where behavior, neurophysiology, and computation meet. *Neuroscientist*, 2001. 7(5): p. 430-40.

[38] Trotter, Y., S. Celebrini, and J.B. Durand, Evidence for implication of primate area V1 in neural 3-D spatial localization processing. *J. Physiol Paris*, 2004. 98(1-3): p. 125-34.

[39] Merriam, E.P. and C.L. Colby, Active vision in parietal and extrastriate cortex. *Neuroscientist*, 2005. 11(5): p. 484-93.

[40] Tanaka, M., Involvement of the central thalamus in the control of smooth pursuit eye movements. *J. Neurosci*, 2005. 25(25): p. 5866-76.

In: Visual Cortex: New Research
Editors: T. A. Portocello and R. B. Velloti

ISBN 978-1-60456-530-0
© 2008 Nova Science Publishers, Inc.

Chapter 8

INFRASLOW POTENTIALS IN THE PRIMARY VISUAL CORTEX: THE NEW APPROACH TO NEUROPHYSIOLOGY OF NEOCORTICAL VISUAL SENSORY INFORMATION PROCESSING

Igor V. Filippov[1]

Department of Physiology and Biophysics,
Yaroslavl State Medical Academy, Yaroslavl, Russia

Abstract

There are many publications dedicated to the studies of the visual cortex and mechanisms of visual information processing. However, it is known that responses of brain visual system sites to adequate stimuli are very different in their properties (including differences in their frequency ranges). It is a matter of fact that some brain electrophysiological phenomena are omitted and sometimes neglected. This happened with infraslow brain potentials (frequencies below 0.5 Hz; periods ranging from several seconds to dozens of minutes). Albeit recently accumulating evidence demonstrated the presence of infraslow activity in the visual cortex, the functional significance and dynamics of this activity remained obscure. The present work is aimed at providing with sufficient evidence our hypothesis that infraslow potentials in the primary visual cortex (V1) are specifically related to some mechanisms of sensory information processing. The experimental subjects were adult rats with chronic stereotaxic electrodes implanted in the V1, lateral geniculate nucleus (LGN), locus coeruleus (LC) and dorsal raphe nucleus (DRN). The recordings of infraslow potentials were performed in these structures during visual stimuli presentation (e.g. darkness, constant illumination and rhythmic flash photostimulation), before and after electrical stimulation of aforementioned subcortical sites of the brain. As a result, specific and significantly different patterns of infraslow potentials appeared in V1 in response to each type of delivered visual stimuli, mainly in the domain of seconds (0.1-0.25 Hz). There were also identified significant spectral changes in the domain of seconds in V1 infraslow activity after LGN electrical stimulation (these alterations were manifested as significant increases in power in the range of 0.1-0.5 Hz). Some responses were detected in V1 multisecond activity (pre- vs. post-stimulus recordings).

---

[1] Corresponding address: Yaroslavl, Revolutsionnaya Street 5, Russia, 150000. Phone: +7(4852)305763; Fax: +7(4852)729142; E-mail: filippov@yma.ac.ru

Finally, it was documented that electrical stimulation of the LC and DRN did not alter significantly V1 activity in the domain of seconds but affected multisecond fluctuation patterns in this structure. The obtained results support the conclusion that different ranges of infraslow activity in the V1 are correlated with different functional mechanisms within this structure: activity in the domain of seconds is related to specific visual information processing, whereas multisecond activity in the V1 is mainly attributed to global transitions and fluctuations of cortical neuronal excitability that are governed both by inputs from visual thalamus and projections from brainstem nuclei (like LC and DRN).

1. Introduction

There are many publications dedicated to the studies of visual cortex neurophysiology and mechanisms of visual information processing in the cortical sites of the brain. Most of these works are generally focused on the studies of bioelectrical activity of visual cortex, and bioelectrical responses of this structure to the different visual stimuli on the different levels of structural and functional organization of this cortical area (e.g., cellular, neuronal populations, systematic, etc.). Such approach is the most popular and essentially productive since it is a generally accepted idea that we can assess internal mechanisms of neuroprocessing in the brain via studies of those electrical phenomena that arise in the pertinent CNS sites in response to presentation of different by their properties stimului. Therefore, the typical investigation in visual sensory neurophysiology involves recording the activity from single neurons or rhythmic field potentials resulting from the activity of many neurons (i.e., EEG). However, it is necessary to reemphasize the necessity to study the entire spectrum of brain activity: from the more slowly changing phenomena to the fastest electrophysiological events [42]. One pitfall is waiting for neurophysiologists here. It is difficult to cover all forms of brain activity in one study due to their significant differences in terms of their amplitude and frequency properties. As a result, most studies are dealing only with middle-range or fast-range events, whereas slower responses are being omitted, neglected or even ignored [5]. This situation leads to accumulation of multiple data in the most popular experimental field, while other important areas remain unexplored without good reason.

This, for example, happened with infraslow brain potential fluctuations (also known as very slow brain potentials or ultraslow potentials). Historically, aforementioned infraslow potentials have been called DC-shifts, DC-potentials, steady potentials, slow potentials, and steady state potentials [1-3,22,31,36]. Existing terminology suggests that from the phenomenological and functional positions it is reasonable to categorize extracellular infraslow brain field potentials into two different classes: specifically, infraslow potential fluctuations and relatively stable potential in the millivolt range [2,3,25,26,11-18]. To standardize terminology, it has been proposed that fluctuations in infraslow brain potentials (ISBP) could be divided into several frequency domains [2,3,25,26,11-18]. These infraslow fluctuations are: (1) fluctuations in the domain of seconds (periodicity of 2 - 10 seconds per cycle, frequencies of 0.1 - 0.5 Hz); (2) multisecond fluctuations (periodicity of 10 - 60 seconds per cycle, frequencies of 0.1 - 0.0167 Hz); (3) activity in the domain of minutes and (4) multiminute fluctuations (periodicity of 1 minute per cycle or greater, frequencies of below of 0.0167 Hz). It has been documented that these different types of infraslow fluctuations have different functional role in sensory information processing in the brain and, obviously, they also have different origin [2,3,25,26,11-18]. Finally, recent works emphasized the necessity to study extracellular infraslow brain potential oscillations more extensively [5] in addition to traditional EEG method (bandwidth of 0.5-30 Hz) and introduced the special term "full-band EEG" for this reinvented methodological approach [47].

On another hand, it is well-documented fact that studies of different by their frequencies brain rhythms and brain oscillatory dynamics are essential for current neurophysiology progress [4,42]. The analysis of various brain oscillatory types leads to the conclusion that in the intact brain, there are no "pure" rhythms, generated in simple circuits, but complex wave sequences (consisting of different, low- and fast-frequency oscillations) that result from synaptic interactions in cortical-cortical, cortical-thalamic and thalamic-cortical neuronal loops under the control of activating systems arising in the brain stem core or forebrain structures [42]. Therefore, we suggest in our laboratory that studies of infraslow brain activity (including infraslow oscillations and fluctuations) are necessary and that this methodology could give to neurophysiologists some principally new data for subsequent analysis, as also these obbservations will provide some new insights into the neurophysiology of visual neocortical area.

Analysis of the literature available on the visual cortex clearly shows that little is known, however, about extracellular infraslow brain potentials fluctuations in this structure and about their neurophysiology or relevance to visual sensory information processing. However, it should be mentioned that several studies have investigated cellular infraslow activity in the cortical regions of the visual system of the brain [41], some works have described extracellular very slow activities of visual cortex [30], and, finally, there is limited number of reports dedicated to slow and infraslow shifts in visual system functions [10,46]. Unfortunately, these publications were singular and they did not induce systematic attention to the problematic mentioned above, also these studies did not answer on some existed question about infraslow bioelectrical activity in the primary visual cortex (V1).

To fill this gap, our work in electrophysiological laboratory (at Department of Physiology and Biophysics of Yaroslavl State Medical Academy) during the past decade has focused on extracellular infraslow brain potentials in both cortical and subcortical sites of sensory systems, including visual system of the brain (V1, LGN, and extra-striate visual sites of the brain, like LC and DRN). Therefore, this chapter should be regarded as an attempt to summarize in one place and discuss our experimental findings concerned visual neocortex to provide by sufficient evidences our previously proposed hypothesis that infraslow potentials in the V1 are specifically related to some mechanisms of visual sensory information processing in the brain [12-17]. To summarize, the specific aims of the present research were three-fold: (1) to study ISBP changes in the V1 during different visual stimulus presentation; (2) to study effects of LGN electrical stimulation on ISBP changes in the V1; (3) to study effects of extra-striate visual brainstem sites (LC and DRN) electrical stimulation on ISBP changes in the V1.

2. General Methodology (Materials and Methods)

In this part only general methodological design will be described; this was identical for all experiments. Other important experimental modifications will be mentioned particularly in the beginning of each subsection of the part 'Results' of this chapter under the rubric

'Methodological Aspects'; technical details of our experiments were described also in our previous publications [11-18].

The subjects were adult male albino rats. All procedures were conducted in strict accordance with humane principles of laboratory animal care (European Communities Council Directive of 24 November 1986, 86/609/EEC).

2.1. Animal Preparations and Surgery

The first step was to prepare animals for chronic intracerebral recordings. Under general anesthesia (sodium pentobarbital, 40 mg/kg i.p.), and in accordance with a rat brain stereotaxic atlas [43], long-term gold electrodes were stereotaxically implanted in the pertinent sites of the brain. Our previous studies and literature review indicated that both bipolar and monopolar electrode commutations are appropriate for ISBP recordings [11-18]. Therefore we used both bipolar and monopolar scheme of electrode commutation for the recordings. Recordings were obtained with high impedance (200 MΩ) differential multi-channel low-noise (internal noise in 0-0.5 Hz band-pass, less than 3 μV), low bias current (less than 10^{-12}A), universal AC/DC-amplifier with graduated DC-offset compensation (model UU-93, IEM, St.-Petersburg, Russia). It is necessary to specially note herein that metal electrodes are adequate for ISBP recordings. Metal electrodes (especially gold) are equal to non-polarizing electrodes for infraslow CNS potential study in the case when they are connected to a high input impedance amplifier [7,11-18,24-26,40,44]; whereas non-polarized electrodes (like silver/silver chloride) are impossible to use as chronic brain implants due to their extremely toxic impact on the tissues [6,19,27,50]. Counter-measures aimed to diminish the chance of possible artifactual origin of ISBP were: (1) All electrodes were absolutely identical by material, construction, and size. (2) Careful individual selection of electrode pairs was used for implantation: all electrodes were tested in physiological saline, and only those pairs were used as implants that had the stable standing inter-electrode potential without any spontaneous transient shifts, fluctuations, noise, etc. (3) Infraslow potentials were recorded in animals after lethal injection of sodium pentobarbital. Dramatically altered ISBP existed in the recordings of comatose paralyzed animals. However, this activity disappeared irreversibly in all recordings (isoelectric line) after confirmed cerebral death. These facts allow the conclusion that observed infraslow activity is from the brain and is not due to artifacts.

2.2. Electrophysiological Recording Technique

A second step was to perform experimental tests in chronic experiments. Experimental sessions and extracellular recordings were started not earlier than 14 days after the implantation procedure mentioned above. This period was necessary to avoid temporary post-traumatic post-operational response of the brain tissue on the injury associated with electrode implantation procedure [11,34]. The rat was placed in double-shielded Faraday's chamber and isolated in the special separate cage with non-transparent walls.

After the end of experimental series, the rats were devitalized using an injection of sodium pentobarbital (100 mg/kg i.p.). Electrode positions were determined histologically, post mortem, using Nissl's staining method for serial brain slices and light microscopy according to commonly accepted technique, which is described in details in the manuals [49].

During recordings the summary bioelectrical signal was artificially separated into 3 frequency domains using corresponding high- and low-pass amplifier filter settings: 0.1-0.5 Hz (activity in the range of seconds), 0.0167-0.1Hz (multisecond activity), and 0.001-0.0167 Hz (fluctuation in the range of minutes and multiminute potentials). It should be reiterated here that this artificial frequency separation was done guiding by three facts. The first one concerns the idea that different ISBP domains contain different kind of neurophysiological information [11-18]. The second one [25,26] is about relative independence and simultaneous presence of aforementioned activities in the recording (when one type of fluctuations superimposed on the others). The third one is explaining by significant amplitude difference between most slow ISBP (i.e. fluctuations in the domain of minutes) and faster ISBP activities (e.g. in the domain of seconds). Therefore, the attempt to plot general fast Fourier transformation (FFT) curve with the same proportional frequency resolution (identical number of point per octave) for the whole spectrum (including the activities in the range of minutes, multisecond activity, and oscillations in the domain of seconds) usually leads to the graph where significant differences in faster but low-amplitude activities will be masked by constant but high-amplitude activities of the slowest ISBP domains. To avoid these pitfalls, we plotted different FFT graphs (although with different frequency resolution) for the different known domains of ISBP [11-18].

Amplified signals were continuously digitized on-line (at a sampling frequency of 1 Hz) by analog-to-digital converter (model KPCI-3101, Keithley Instruments, Inc., Cleveland, Ohio, USA) and stored on computer disk for pre-processing and further off-line analysis.

There were selected the following data sets for subsequent analyses: (a) ISBP in the domain of seconds, 256 data points=256 seconds, (b) multisecond ISBP band, 512 data points=512 seconds, and (c) ISBP in the domain of minutes, 1024 data points=1024 seconds, respectively. Each segment was subjected to the ordinary FFT and power spectral analysis [49], after that those pre-stimulus spectra were compared with stimulus-on spectra or those pre-stimulus spectra were compared with post-stimulus spectra.

2.3. Statistical Procedures

The statistical procedures of this study included averaging of the results of the sessions per animal. After that mean values per animal were obtained, and the statistical procedures were performed over the animals. Obtained pre- and either stimulus-on or post-stimulation spectral differences were analyzed by one-way, repeated-measures ANOVA. An alpha level of $P<0.05$ was adopted for all significance tests. When statistical significance was indicated, post-hoc analysis was performed using multiple-range Duncan's test.

3. Results

In general, both in freely moving animals and in anaesthetized rats under any of experimental conditions the V1 expressed different forms of infraslow extracellular field potentials, these were: oscillations in the range of seconds (dominant frequencies of 0.1-0.35 Hz), multisecond potentials (frequencies of approximately 0.02-0.05 Hz), and irregular single fluctuations in the range of minutes and dozens of minutes (frequencies of below of 0.002 Hz). These types of ISBP dynamics existed in the recordings simultaneously and they were superimposed on each other (when faster types of ISBP activity were modulated by the slower forms of infraslow potentials). Representative original samples of aforementioned ISBP in the V1 extracted by filtering from the summary infraslow bioelectrical signal under different experimental conditions are illustrated in the Figure 1.

Activity in the range of seconds in the primary visual cortex during presentation of different visual stimuli

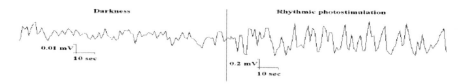

Multisecond activity and potentials in the range of minutes in the primary visual cortex during presentation of different visual stimuli

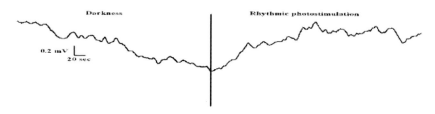

Activity in the range of seconds in the primary visual cortex before and after (not during!) electrical stimulation of the lateral geniculate nucleus

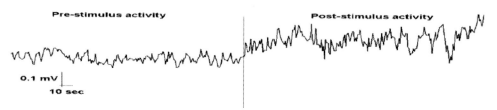

Multisecond activity and potentials in the range of minutes in the primary visual cortex before and after (not during!) electrical stimulation of the lateral geniculate nucleus

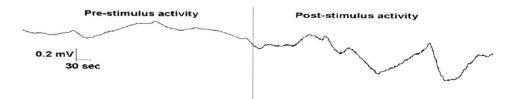

Figure 1. Examples of typical recordings of different types of infraslow activities in the primary visual cortex (V1) of the rat under several experimental conditions are shown here (i.e. during different visual stimuli presentation, like darkness and rhythmic photostimulation; before and after electrical stimulation of the lateral geniculate nucleus).

3.1. Infraslow Brain Potentials in the Primary Visual Cortex during Presentation of Different Visual Stimuli

Methodological Aspects: This part of the work was performed on 30 freely moving rats (n=150 experimental repetitions). Chronic bipolar recordings from V1 region were used in this part of the study. The rats were randomly exposed to three different background illumination changes: darkness (illumination intensity, 0 lx); continuous light (illumination intensity, 2000-2500 lx), and rhythmic flash photostimulation (frequency, 4 Hz; minimal illumination intensity, 0 lx; maximal illumination intensity, 2500 lx).

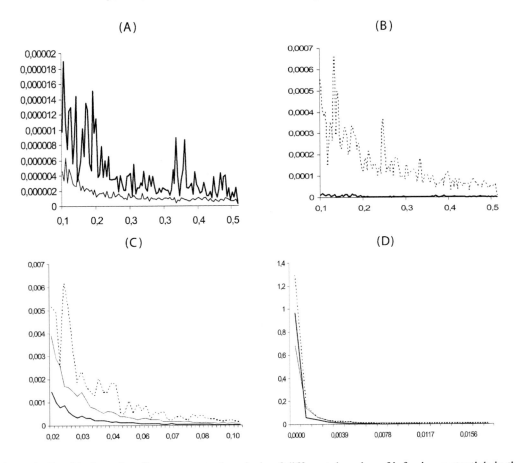

Figure 2. Graphical results of power spectral analysis of different domains of infraslow potentials in the primary visual cortex (V1) during application of different visual stimuli are shown here. Panel (A) shows spectra of oscillations in the range of seconds under condition of darkness (thick line) and under constant illumination (thin line). Panel (B) shows spectra of oscillations in the range of seconds under condition of darkness (thick line) and under rhythmic photostimulation (dashed thin line). Panels (C) and (D) illustrate spectra of multisecond activity and potentials in the domain of minutes, respectively (thick line, under condition of darkness; thin line, under constant illumination; dashed thin line, under rhythmic photostimulation). These summary spectral graphs (A, B, C, and D) were obtained using the following method: first, data were averaged per animal, and than the results were averaged over the animal group. These averaged graphical spectra over the animal group are depicted here. On each of these graphs, on the X-axis is frequency (Hz), and on the Y-axis is amplitude or power spectral density (mV/Hz).

Each of illumination condition was maintained without changes for 1024 seconds. V1 ISBP power spectra within the same frequency domain were compared with each other under different illumination (i.e., darkness vs. light; light vs. photostimulation; and darkness vs. photostimulation). In these experiments the rats were exposed only to visual stimuli and were maximally isolated from other types of accident sensory stimulation by special methodological approach [13-17]; and this allows the conclusion that ISBP changes reported below were associated with visual sensory information processing but not with accidental sensory stimuli or non-specific drifting CNS states.

As a result, it was detected that manipulation on illumination conditions induced significant spectral changes of ISBP in the V1. Specifically, there were dramatic changes in the V1 of infraslow oscillations in the domain of seconds (see Figure 2 A, B).

These changes were manifested as statistically significant depression of spectral powers of ISBP in the domain of second during constant illumination (compared to those in darkness), Figure 2 A; these alterations were statistically significant ($p < 0.05$, in all experiments). In addition, there were revealed prominent increases in powers of oscillations in the domain of seconds during rhythmical photostimulation (compared to those obtained under condition of darkness and constant ambient illumination), Figure 2 B; both of these changes were highly statistically significant (photostimulation vs. darkness and photostimulation vs. light), p value in all experiments in both cases were lower than 0.001.

Analysis of the multisecond activity in the V1 under aforementioned conditions has shown that there were statistically significant changes of this activity only in response to rhythmic photostimulation ($p < 0.05$, in all experiments, darkness vs. photostimulation and light vs. photostimulation), whereas there were no statistically significant spectral changes of multisecond potentials in V1 in response to constant conditions (darkness vs. light), see Figure 2 C.

Finally, there were found no statistical differences in V1 power spectra under any of illumination conditions (e.g. darkness, light, photostimulation) in fluctuations in the domain of minutes (Figure 2 D). Therefore, the details of this analysis will not be discussed here.

3.2. Infraslow Brain Potentials in the Primary Visual Cortex Before and after Electrical Stimulation of the Lateral Geniculate Nucleus

Methodological Aspects: This part of the work was performed on 30 lightly anesthetized by sodium pentobarbital (7 mg/kg, i.p.) rats (n=150 experimental repetitions). Chronic bipolar recordings from V1 region were used in this part of the study. Recordings from V1 were randomly obtained before electrical stimulation of the LGN and after electrical stimulation of this thalamic nucleus (not during stimulation!). Before, during, and after intracerebral stimulation the animal was under constant condition of darkness (illumination intensity, 0 lx). Electrical stimulation parameters were as following: rectangular bipolar pulses, amplitude 80 µA; frequency, 100 Hz; impulse duration 0.4 ms; electrical stimulation duration, 10 seconds). Pre-stimulation ISBP recordings from the V1 were compared with post-stimulus ISBP recordings from this CNS site.

Each recording length (both pre- and post-stimulus) was 1024 seconds. In these experiments, the rats were exposed only to electrical stimulation and were maximally isolated from any types of accident sensory stimulation by special methodological approach [17]. This allows the conclusion that ISBP changes reported below were associated with electrical stimulation of visual thalamus but not with accidental sensory stimuli or non-specific drifting CNS states.

There were detected prominent differences between pre-stimulus and post-stimulus power spectra in the V1, these changes were manifested as an increase in the power in the ISBP in the domain of seconds in the V1 after LGN electrical activation (Figure 3 A). It is necessary to note that accurate evaluation of power changes have demonstrated statistically significant shifts (P<0.01) in the frequencies of 0.1-0.25 Hz, while alterations in other frequencies of this ISBP range (0.25-0.5 Hz) were not statistically significant, p>0.05 (Figure 3 A).

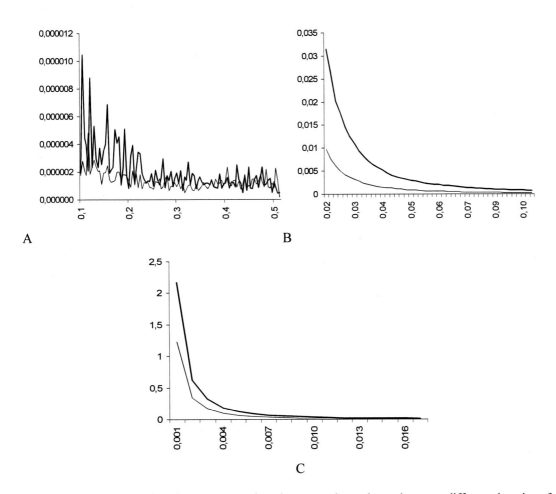

Figure 3. Graphical results of power spectral analyses are shown here, these are different domains of infraslow potentials of the primary visual cortex (V1) before (thin line) and after (thick line) electrical stimulation of the lateral geniculate nucleus (LGN). Panel (A) shows spectra of oscillations in the range of seconds. Panel (B) shows spectra of multisecond activity. Panel (C) illustrates spectra of potentials in the domain of minutes. These summary spectral graphs (A, B, and C) were obtained using the following method: first, data were averaged per animal, and than the results were averaged over the animal group. These averaged graphical spectra over the animal group are depicted here. On each of these graphs, on the X-axis is frequency (Hz), and on the Y-axis is amplitude or power spectral density (mV/Hz).

Last but not least were those changes that have been detected in the V1 in the multisecond activity after electrostimulation of the LGN. These shifts were manifested as a significant (P<0.01) increase of powers in the frequency domain of approximately 0.02-0.05 Hz (Figure 3 B).

Finally, statistically significant changes of the fluctuations in the domain of minutes were absent in the V1 (pre- vs. post-stimulation recordings), Figure 3 C; therefore that data were not subjected for more extensive analysis.

3.3. Infraslow Brain Potentials in the Primary Visual Cortex before and after Electrical Stimulation of the Dorsal Raphe Nucleus and Locus Coeruleus

Methodological Aspects: This part of the work was performed on 30 lightly anesthetized by sodium pentobarbital (7 mg/kg, i.p.) rats (n=150 experimental repetitions). Chronic monopolar recordings from V1 region were used in this part of the study.

Primarily, recordings from the V1 were randomly obtained before electrical stimulation of the dorsal raphe nucleus (DRN) and after electrical stimulation of this brainstem site (not during stimulation!). Secondary, recordings from the V1 were randomly obtained before electrical stimulation of locus coeruleus (LC) and after electrical stimulation of this nucleus (not during stimulation!). Before, during and after intracerebral stimulations the animal was under constant condition of darkness (illumination intensity, 0 lx). Electrical stimulation parameters were as following: rectangular bipolar pulses, amplitude 80 µA; frequency, 100 Hz; impulse duration 0.4 ms; electrical stimulation duration, 10 seconds). Pre-stimulation ISBP recordings from the V1 were compared with post-stimulus ISBP recordings of this area (before and after DRN activation and before and after LC stimulation, respectively).

Each recording length (pre- and post-stimulus) was 1024 seconds. In these experiments the rats were exposed only to electrical stimulation and were maximally isolated from any types of accident sensory stimulation by special methodological approach [15,16]; and this allows the conclusion that ISBP changes reported below were associated with electrical stimulation of brainstem nuclei but not with accidental sensory stimuli or non-specific drifting CNS states.

From this part of the study, it was detected that local electrostimulation of DRN have had no effect on activity of V1 in the domain of seconds (please see the Figure 4 A) since spectral changes presented on this figure were not statistically significant. It was also documented that DRN electrical activation has had no statistically significant effect on the dynamics of fluctuations in the range of minutes in the V1 (Figure 4 C). Nevertheless, DRN activation induced highly significant (P<0.00001) changes of multisecond activity in the V1 (Figure 4 B), in terms of prominent increase of the power of these fluctuations in the frequency domain of approximately 0.02-0.05 Hz in the visual cortex (pre-stimulus vs. post-stimulus spectral graphs).

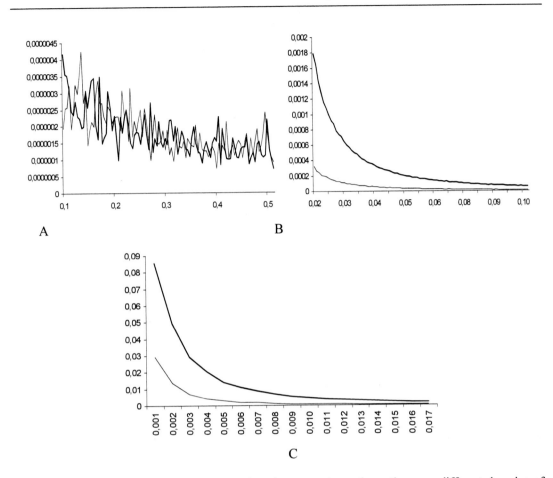

Figure 4. Graphical results of power spectral analyses are shown here, these are different domains of infraslow potentials of the primary visual cortex (V1) before (thin line) and after (thick line) electrical stimulation of the dorsal raphe nucleus (DRN). Panel (A) shows spectra of oscillations in the range of seconds. Panel (B) shows spectra of multisecond activity. Panel (C) illustrates spectra of potentials in the domain of minutes. These summary spectral graphs (A, B, and C) were obtained using the following method: first, data were averaged per animal, and than the results were averaged over the animal group. These averaged graphical spectra over the animal group are depicted here. On each of these graphs, on the X-axis is frequency (Hz), and on the Y-axis is amplitude or power spectral density (mV/Hz).

Another important finding concern effect of LC electrostimulation, LC activation produced statistically insignificant changes in the activity of V1 area in the range of seconds (Figure 5 A). There were found no significant changes in the fluctuations in the domain of minutes in the V1 after LC intracerebral electrostimulation (Figure 5 C). However, LC activation induced significant (P<0.05) decrease in the powers of multisecond fluctuations in the V1 (pre-stimulus vs. post-stimulus spectral graphs), Figure 5 B; albeit this changes were opposite compared to those observed in the V1 after DRN electrical activation.

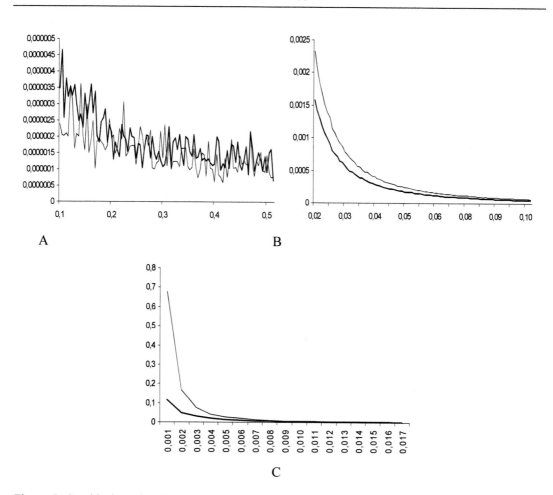

Figure 5. Graphical results of power spectral analyses are shown here, these are different domains of infraslow potentials of the primary visual cortex (V1) before (thin line) and after (thick line) electrical stimulation of the locus coeruleus (LC). Panel (A) shows spectra of oscillations in the range of seconds. Panel (B) shows spectra of multisecond activity. Panel (C) illustrates spectra of potentials in the domain of minutes. These summary spectral graphs (A, B, and C) were obtained using the following method: first, data were averaged per animal, and than the results were averaged over the animal group. These averaged graphical spectra over the animal group are depicted here. On each of these graphs, on the X-axis is frequency (Hz), and on the Y-axis is amplitude or power spectral density (mV/Hz).

4. Conclusion

Based on the results of our experiments described here, together with those findings that were published by us previously [12-18] and on the analysis of the literature, it is possible to make several final general conclusions.

1. Oscillations in the domain of seconds (frequencies of 0.1-0.35 Hz, periods of approximately 10-3 seconds per cycle) are specifically related to the mechanisms of specific visual sensory information processing in the V1. In addition, this activity is

tightly connected with neurophysiological mechanisms of functional interactions within the thalamic-cortical-thalamic axis (LGN-V1-LGN system) during the process of central vision. These results are in line with available literature data about 'up and down' neuronal processing in the cortex that is modulated by intra-cortical and thalamic-cortical-thalamic mechanisms [8,9,20,32,37,45].

2. Multisecond activity in the V1 is mainly attributed to the mechanisms of global neuronal excitability transitions or fluctuations in primary visual neocortical neurons. Such fluctuations are not directly related to the specific process of visual stimulus processing, however, they might affect this neuroprocessing indirectly. These global processes in the V1 are governed both by inputs from the visual thalamus (LGN) and by ascending projections from brainstem nuclei (like the LC and DRN). These findings, on one hand, coincide with the concept that aforementioned brainstem nuclei have visual stimulus sensitive neurons [21,23,28]; and, on the other hand, these data correspond to available notions that structures of the brainstem are responsible for slow EEG modulations [35] and that both DRN and LC are involved in the process of neuronal excitability modulation in the visual cortex [29,33,38,48].

3. Fluctuations in the range of minutes and multiminute potentials in the V1 are not sensitive to visual stimulation that is coming into the visual cortex; these fluctuations are also not correlated with the physiological states that are induced by LGN, DRN or LC electrical activation, since there were no reactions from this type of activity in response to all of these manipulations. Therefore, it is possible to assume that activity in the domain of minutes in the V1 attributes either to basic cyclical neural metabolic processes or to those taking place on the liquor-brain and blood-brain barrier boundary in the visual cortex, and this idea agrees with available literature interpretation of the functional significance of this slowest type of brain activity [2,3,25,26,39].

References

[1] Adey, W.R. (1969). Slow electrical phenomena in the central nervous system. *Neurosci. Res. Program Bull. 7 (2), 75-180.*

[2] Aladjalova, N.A. (1957). Infra-slow rhythmic oscillations of the steady potential of the cerebral cortex. *Nature 179 (4567), 957-959.*

[3] Aladjalova N.A. (1979). *Psychophysiological aspects of brain infra-slow rhythmical activity.* Moscow, Nauka, 214 pp.

[4] Basar, E. (2006). The theory of the whole-brain-work. *Int. J. Psychophysiol. 60 (2), 133-138.*

[5] Bullock T.H. (1999). Slow potentials in the brain: still little understood but gradually getting analytical attention. *Brain Res. Bull., 50, 315-316.*

[6] Cooper, R., Crow, H. J. (1966). Toxic effects of intra-cerebral electrodes. *Journal of Medical and Biological Engineering and Computing, 4(6): 575-581.*

[7] Cooper R., Osselton J.W., Shaw J.C. (1980). Electrodes. In: EEG Technology. Butterworths, London, pp. 15-31.

[8] Cossart, R., Aronov, D., Yuste, R. (2003). Attractor dynamics of network UP states in the neocortex. *Nature., 423(6937), pp. 283-288.*

[9]   Crochet S, Fuentealba P, Cisse Y, Timofeev I, Steriade M. (2006). Synaptic plasticity in local cortical network in vivo and its modulation by the level of neuronal activity. *Cereb. Cortex., 16(5), pp. 618-631.*

[10] Devrim, M., Demiralp, T., Kurt, A., Yucesir, I. (1999). Slow cortical potential shifts modulate sensory threshold in human visual system. *Neurosci. Lett. 270, 17-20.*

[11] Filippov, I.V. (2001). Neocortical very slow electrical activity after the local brain injury: an experimental stereotaxic study in rodents. In: *Abstract Book of the 4-th World Congress on Brain Injury*, 2001, Turin, Italy, p. 313.

[12] Filippov, I.V., Williams, W.C., Gladyshev, A.V. (2002). Role of infraslow (0-0.5 Hz) potential oscillations in the regulation of brain stress response by the locus coeruleus system. *Neurocomputing. 44-46, 795-798.*

[13] Filippov, I.V. (2003). Power spectral analysis of very slow brain potential oscillations in primary visual cortex of freely moving rats during darkness and light. *Neurocomputing. 52-54, 505-510.*

[14] Filippov I.V. (2003) Spectral shifts of very slow brain potentials in lateral geniculate complex and visual cortex of freely moving rats in response to different illumination changes. *Physiol. Res., 52, 4P.*

[15] Filippov, I.V., Williams, W.C., Frolov, V.A. (2004). Very slow potential oscillations in locus coeruleus and dorsal raphe nucleus under different illumination in freely moving rats. *Neurosci Lett. 363, 89-93.*

[16] Filippov, I.V., Frolov, V.A. (2005). Very slow potentials in the lateral geniculate complex and primary visual cortex during different illumination changes in freely moving rats. *Neurosci. Lett. 373, 51-56.*

[17] Filippov, I.V. (2005). Very slow brain potential fluctuations (<0.5 Hz) in visual thalamus and striate cortex after their successive electrical stimulation in lightly anesthetized rats. *Brain Res. 1066, 179-186.*

[18] Filippov, I.V., Williams, W.C., Krebs, A.A., Pugachev, K.S. (2007). Sound-induced changes of infraslow brain potential fluctuations in the medial geniculate nucleus and primary auditory cortex in anesthetized rats. *Brain Res., 1133, pp. 78-86.*

[19] Fisher, G., Sayre, G.P., Bickford, R.G. (1957). Histologic changes in cat's brain after introduction of metallic and coated wire used in electroencephalography. *Proc. of Mayo Clin., 32, pp. 14-21.*

[20] Frohlich, F., Bazhenov, M., Timofeev, I., Steriade, M., Sejnowski, T.J. (2006). Slow state transitions of sustained neural oscillations by activity-dependent modulation of intrinsic excitability. *J Neurosci., 26(23), pp. 6153-6162.*

[21] Gallager D.W., Pert A. (1978). Afferents to brainstem nuclei (brainstem raphe, nucleus reticularis pontis caudalis and nucleus gigantocellularis) in the rat as demonstrated by microiontophoretically applied of horseradish peroxidase. *Brain Res., 144, 257-275.*

[22] Gumnit, R.J. (1960). DC potential changes from auditory cortex of cat. *J. Neurophysiol. 23 (6), 667-675.*

[23] Heym J., Trulson M.E., Jacobs B.L. (1982). Raphe unit activity in freely moving cats: effects of phasic auditory and visual stimuli. *Brain Res., 232, 29-39.*

[24] Ikeda A., Nagamine T., Yarita M., Terada K., Kimura J., Shibasaki H. (1998). Reappraisal of the effect of electrode property on recording slow potentials. *Electroeceph. clin. Neurophysiol., 107, 59-63.*

[25] Iliukhina V.A. (1986). *Neurophysiology of human functional states.* Leningrad, Nauka, 173 pp.

[26] Iliukhina, V.A. (2004). *Human brain in the mechanisms of information and regulation interactions of the organism and environment.* Russian Academy of Sciences, Institute of the human brain. St. Petersburg, 328 pp.

[27] Jackson, W.F., Duling, B.R. (1983). Toxic effects of silver-silver chloride electrodes on vascular smooth muscle. *Circ. Res. 53, 105-108.*

[28] Kratin Yu.G., Zubkova N.A., Lavrov V.V., Sotnichenko T.S., Fyodorova K.P. *Visual pathways and brain activation systems.* Leningrad, Nauka, 1982, 167 pp.

[29] Koh T., Nakazawa M., Kani K., Maeda T. (1991) Significant non-serotonergic raphe projection to the visual cortex of the rat. An immunohistochemical study combined with retrograde tracing. *J. Hirnforsch., 32, 707-714.*

[30] Leopold D.A., Murayama Y., Logothetis N.K. (2003) Very slow activity fluctuations in monkey visual cortex: implications for functional imaging. *Cer. Cortex, 13, 422-433.*

[31] Lickey, M.E. (1966). Localization and habituation of sensory evoked DC responses in cat cortex. *Exp. Neurol. 15, 437-454.*

[32] Llinas, R.R., Steriade, M. (2006). Bursting of thalamic neurons and states of vigilance. *J. Neurophysiol. 95 (6), 3297-3308.*

[33] McLean J., Waterhouse B.D. (1994). Noradrenergic modulation of cat area 17 neuronal responses to moving visual stimuli. *Brain Res. 667, 83-97.*

[34] Maxwell, W.L., Follows, R., Ashhurst, D.E., Berry, M. (1990). The response of cerebral hemisphere of the rat to injury. I. The mature rat. *Phyl. Trans Roy Soc. London B., 328 (1250), pp. 479-500.*

[35] Novak, P., Lepikovska, V. (1992). Slow modulations of EEG. *Neuroreport. 3, 189-192.*

[36] O'Leary, J.L., Goldring, S. (1964). DC-potentials of the brain. *Physiol. Rev. 44, 91-125.*

[37] Saez, J.A.,. Palomares, J.M, Vives, F., Dominguez, I., Villegas, I., Montes, R., Price, D.J., Ferrer, J.M. (1998). Electrophysiological and neurochemical study of the rat geniculo-cortical pathway. Evidence for glutamatergic neurotransmission. *Eur. J. Neurosci. 10, 2790-2801.*

[38] Sato H., Fox K., Daw N.W. (1989) Effect of electrical stimulation of locus coeruleus on the activity of neurons in the cat visual cortex. *J. Neurophysiol., 62, 946-958.*

[39] Shvets-Teneta-Gurii, T.B. (1981). Electrochemical activity at implanted metal electrodes as a response of the brain to injury. *Zh. Vyssh. Nerv. Deiat. Im. I. P. Pavlova., 31(1), 148-157.*

[40] Stensaas, S.S., Stensaas, L.J. (1978). Gold implants and the brain. *Acta Neuropathol. (Berl)., 41(2), 145-155.*

[41] Steriade M., Nunez A., Amzica F. (1993). A novel slow (<1 Hz) oscillation of neocortical neurons in vivo: depolarizing and hyperpolarizing components. *J. Neurosci. 13, 3252-3265.*

[42] Steriade M. (2006). Grouping of brain rhythms in corticothalamic systems. *Neuroscience, 137(4), pp. 1087-1106.*

[43] Swanson L.W. (1998) Brain Maps: Structure of the rat brain. Second Revised Edition. Elsevier, Amsterdam-Tokyo, 1998, 267 pp.

[44] Tallgren, P., Vanhatalo, S., Kaila, K., Voipio, J. (2005). Evaluation of commercially available electrodes and gels for recording of slow EEG potentials. *Clin. Neurophysiol., 116(4), pp. 799-806.*

[45] Timofeev, I., Grenier, F., Steriade, M. (2000). Impact of intrinsic properties and synaptic factors on the activity of neocortical networks in vivo. *J. Physiol. Paris., 94(5-6), pp. 343-55.*

[46] Thoss F., Bartsch B., Stebel J. (1998). Analysis of oscillation of the visual sensitivity. *Vis. Res. 38, 139-142.*

[47] Vanhatalo, S., Voipio, J., Kaila, K. (2005). Full-band EEG (FbEEG): an emerging standard in electroencephalography. *Clin. Neurophysiol. 116, 1-8.*

[48] Watabe K., Nakai K., Kasamatsu T. (1982). Visual afferents to norepinephrine-containing neurons in cat locus coeruleus. *Exp. Brain Res., 48, 66-80.*

[49] Windhorst U., Johansson H. (Eds), (1999). *Modern Techniques in Neuroscience Research.* Springer-Verlag, Berlin, Heidelberg, New-York, 1325 pp.

[50] Yuen, T.G., Agnew, W.F., Bullara, L.A. (1987). Tissue response to potential neuroprosthetic materials implanted subdurally. *Biomaterials., 8(2), 138-141.*

In: Visual Cortex: New Research
Editors: T. A. Portocello and R. B. Velloti

ISBN 978-1-60456-530-0
© 2008 Nova Science Publishers, Inc.

Chapter 9

ORIENTATION AND CONTOUR EXTRACTION MODEL USING UNIT-LINKING PULSE COUPLED NEURAL NETWORK

*Xiaodong Gu**

Department of Electronic Engineering, Fudan University,
Shanghai 200433, P.R. China

Abstract

Visual cortex exists columns detecting orientations, and can extract the contour of the interesting object by binding orientations detected by orientation columns. We proposed a novel orientation and interesting-contour extraction model using Unit-linking Pulse Coupled Neural Network (PCNN). Unit-linking PCNN is the simplified PCNN, which is a kind of spatio-temporal-coding Spiking Neural Network (SNN), and exhibits the phenomena of synchronous pulse bursts in the cat or monkey visual cortex. The orientation and interesting-contour extraction model using Unit-linking PCNN is composed of two layers (the orientation detection layer and the interesting-contour extraction layer). This model mimics orientation detection of the biological visual cortex, and can extract the contour of the interesting object with TOP-DOWN mechanism. The contour of the interesting object periodically oscillates in this model. We use periodical oscillation to extract the contour of the interesting object in this model because synchronous oscillation is the important phenomena in the biological visual cortex. In the interesting-contour extraction layer, when introducing TOP-DOWN mechanism, the chain code of the interesting object contour is used to express the prior knowledge. The input of the orientation detection layer is the edge detection result of the input image by using Unit-linking PCNN edge detection algorithm we proposed. The output of the orientation detection layer is the orientation detection result, which inputs to the interesting-contour extraction layer. In the meantime, the chain code of the interesting-contour inputs to the interesting-contour extraction layer as the prior knowledge. The contour of the interesting object periodically oscillates in the interesting-contour extraction layer. Section 1 is the introduction. In Section 2, Unit-linking PCNN is described. In Section 3 and 4, the orientation detection layer and the interesting-contour extraction layer based on Unit-linking PCNN are introduced respectively, followed by the conclusion in the last Section.

---

* E-mail address: guxiaodong@263.net; xdgu@fudan.edu.cn

1. Introduction

Visual cortex exists orientation columns, and can extract the contour of the interesting object by binding orientations detected by orientation columns. We used Unit-linking PCNN (Pulse Coupled Neural Network), the spatio-temporal-coding artificial neural network, to mimic orientation detection and contour extraction of the interesting object. In recent years SNNs (Spiking Neural Networks), pulse-emitting and spatio-temporal coding models, have attracted the attention of many researches [1-3] because they mimic real neurons better and have more powerful computation performance than traditional AFR (Average-Firing-Rate) neural networks [4]. PCNN (Pulse Coupled Neural Network) is a kind of SNN, which has the biological support. In 1990, Eckhorn introduced the linking field network [5] exhibiting the phenomena of synchronous pulse bursts in the cat or the monkey visual cortex [6-11]. In 1993, Johnson proposed PCNN [12] by introducing the linking strength to the linking model, which can be applied in image processing, object detection, optimization, and so on [13-68]. (Pulse Coupled Neurons) PCNs are very complex. Unit-linking PCN is the simplified model of PCN and retains main characteristics of PCN. We have used the Unit-linking PCNNs composed of Unit-linking PCNs in image processing and other applications, such as image denoising, image segmentation, edge detection, image thinning, image shadow removal, granulometry image authentication, and robot navigation. In this chapter, we introduce how to use Unit-linking PCNN to build the orientation detection and interesting-contour extraction model.

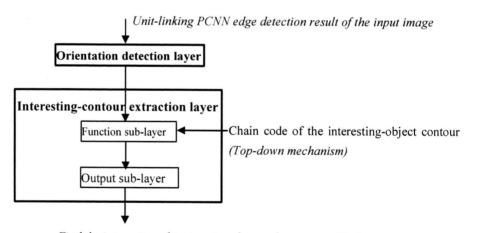

Find the interesting-object contour by synchronous oscillation

Figure 1. Our model of orientation detection and interesting-contour extraction.

See Figure 1, our novel model of orientation detection and interesting-contour extraction model based on Unit-linking PCNN, includes two layers: the orientation detection layer and the interesting-contour extraction layer [69]. The orientation detection layer receives the Unit-linking PCNN edge detection result [19,32]of the input image. The orientation detection layer mimics orientation detection of the biological visual cortex. The interesting-contour extraction layer, consisting of two sub-layers (the function sub-layer and the output sub-layer), extracts the contour of the interesting object. Here the function sub-layer plays the main role at interesting-contour extraction layer. At the interesting-contour extraction layer introducing the TOP-DOWN mechanism, the chain code of the interesting-object contour is used to express the prior knowledge, and the periodical oscillation denotes the contour of the interesting object .In [70], Yu and Zhang used the chain code of the interesting object contour to express the prior knowledge. In our orientation detection and interesting-contour extraction model, introducing the TOP-DOWN mechanism, we also used the chain code of the interesting object contour as the prior knowledge.

In Section 2, Unit-linking PCNN is described. In Sections 3 and 4, the orientation detection layer and the interesting-contour extraction layer based on Unit-linking PCNN are introduced respectively, followed by the conclusion in the last Section.

2. Unit-Linking PCNN

Pulse Coupled Neurons (PCNs) are very complex. The complexities of the structures of PCNs and dynamical behaviors of PCNNs consisting of PCNs limit PCNNs' applications. In the practical application, the simpler neurons are better to implement by hardware. Therefore simplification of PCN with retaining PCN main characteristics is necessary. Unit-linking PCN is the simplified model of PCN and retains main characteristics of PCN. We have used the Unit-linking PCNNs composed of Unit-linking PCNs in many applications. The model in this paper is also composed of Unit-linking PCNs.

A Unit-linking PCN consists of three parts: the receptive field, the modulation field, and the pulse generator. Figure 2 illustrates a Unit-linking PCN j. Equations from (1) to (5) describe the model of Unit-linking PCN j. It has two channels. One channel is feeding input (F_j) called F channel; the other is linking input (L_j) called L channel. $I_j, Y_1, ..., Y_k$ are input signals of neuron j. Y_j is the output pulse of neuron j. I_j, an input signal from the external source, only inputs to the F channel of j (see Eq.(1)).$Y_1, ..., Y_k$, output pulses emitted by neurons connected with j , only input to the L channel of j (see Eq.(1)).In Eq.(2), β_j is the linking strength, and $N(j)$ is the set including the neurons whose output signals input to neuron j. In a Unit-linking PCN, we introduced the concept of Unit-linking, namely as to neuron j, when 1 or more than 1 neurons in $N(j)$ fire, L_j is equal to 1. Compared with conventional PCN, this reduces the number of parameters and makes the linking input of the neuron uniform so that the behaviors of networks consisting of Unit-linking neurons are easy to analyze and control. This is the main difference between Unit-linking PCN and conventional PCN. The uniform L_j is added a constant positive bias firstly. Then it is multiplied by F_j and the bias is taken to be unity (see Eq.(3)). β_j is the linking strength. The total internal activity U_j is the modulation result and it inputs to the pulse generator. If U_j is greater than the threshold θ_j, the neuron output Y_j turns into 1 (namely the neuron j fires, see Eq.(5)). Then Y_j feeds back to make θ_j rises over U_j immediately so that Y_j turns into 0. On the other hand, θ_j drops with time increasing (see Eq.(4)). In Eq.(4), V_j^T and α_j^T are the amplitude gain and the time constant of the threshold adjuster respectively. Unit-linking PCNN consists of neurons depicted in Figure 2.

$$F_j = I_j \tag{1}$$

$$L_j = \text{Step}[\sum_{k \in N(j)} Y_k(t)] = \begin{cases} 1 & if \sum_{k \in N(j)} Y_k(t) > 0 \\ 0, & else \end{cases}$$

(2)

$$U_j = F_j(1 + \beta_j L_j)$$

(3)

$$\frac{d\theta_j(t)}{dt} = -\alpha_j^T + V_j^T Y_j(t), \quad \textit{The lower limit of integration is just before the last firing in solution.}$$

(4)

$$Y_j = \text{Step}(U_j - \theta_j) = \begin{cases} 1, & if \quad U_j > \theta_j \\ 0, & else \end{cases}$$

(5)

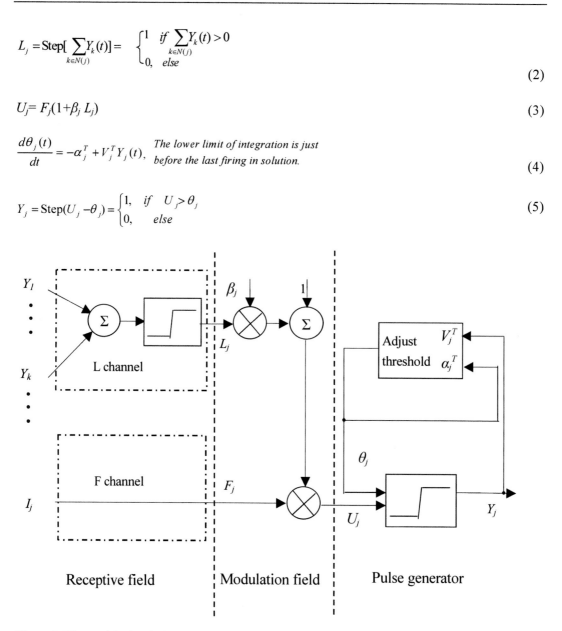

Figure 2. The model of Unit-linking PCN j.

3. Orientation Detection Layer

The input signal of the orientation detection layer is the input image's Unit-linking PCNN edge detection result, which is obtained using Unit-linking PCNN edge detection algorithm we proposed in [19, 27]. In edge detection, Unit-linking PCNN is a single layer two-dimensional array of laterally linked neurons. One-to-one correspondence exists between image pixels and neurons. Each neuron's F channel receives the intensity of the corresponding pixel. Meanwhile, each neuron's L channel receives the pulses emitted by neurons in its neighboring field. In Unit-linking PCNN edge detection algorithm, pulse waves detect edges. For binary images, assume that objects correspond to dark regions and backgrounds correspond to bright regions. First make all neurons corresponding to pixels in the bright regions (namely background) with large intensities fire, and in the mean time make all neurons corresponding to pixels in the dark regions (namely the object) with small intensities not fire. Then pulses emitted by the bright region spread a pixel distance so that neurons corresponding to edges of objects fire. Each neuron may connect with neurons in its 3*3-neighboring field or its 4-neighboring field. In the 3*3-neighboring field connection mode, the edge detection results often are 4-connected. In 4-neighboring field connection mode, according to the shape of the original object, the edge detection results could be 8-connected or 4-connected. Note, in order to be easy to design orientation detection layer, 4-connection edge detection results are necessary, so here in edge detection each neuron connects with neurons in its 3*3-neighboring field. For a 256-level grey image, using Unit-linking PCNN segments the original image into a multi-level image, and at each segmentation level using binary image Unit-linking PCNN edge detection algorithm obtains edges in sequence, and at the end of segmentation the final edge detection result is gotten. More details of Unit-linking PCNN edge detection algorithm are shown in [19, 27].

The orientation detection layer is a two-dimensional array of orientation detection unit and each orientation detection unit consists of 6 neurons. These 6 neurons corresponds to 6 directions $(\phi_0, \phi_1, \phi_2, \phi_3, \phi_4, \phi_5)$:

$$\phi_0 \Leftrightarrow -, \phi_1 \Leftrightarrow |, \phi_2 \Leftrightarrow \ulcorner, \phi_3 \Leftrightarrow \urcorner, \phi_4 \Leftrightarrow \llcorner, \phi_5 \Leftrightarrow \lrcorner.$$

This orientation detection unit roughly mimics the orientation column of the biological visual cortex. We call it Unit-linking PCNN orientation column. The receptive field of each one is 3*3. The overlap area of 2 horizontally or vertically adjacent receptive fields is 2/3 of the area of each receptive field. Figure 3 illustrates the receptive fields of 3 adjacent orientation column $i,j.k$. They cover 15 neurons in the Unit-linking PCNN edge detection layer. All orientation columns are identical.

Each Unit-linking PCNN orientation column in the orientation detection layer receives output signals of 9 edge neurons in the Unit-linking PCNN edge detection layer in its receptive field. When a directional neuron in an orientation column fires, this orientation column chooses the corresponding direction. Sometimes more than one neurons in the same orientation column fire, and in this situation this orientation column chooses more than one directions. Each orientation column bases direction selection on the firing states of 9 edge neurons in its receptive field.

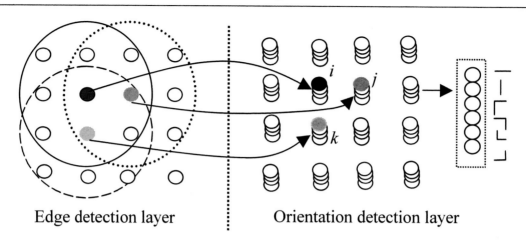

Edge detection layer   Orientation detection layer

Figure 3. Receptive fields of Unit-linking PCNN orientation column i, j, k.

Figure 4 to Figure 9 illustrate how each directional neuron in each Unit-linking PCNN orientation column is connected with the edge neurons in its receptive field. The input signals of L channels of 6 directional neurons in an orientation column are identical and they are the output signal of the center edge neuron in the receptive field of this orientation column. The F channel of each directional neuron in an orientation column receives the output signals of 2 specified non-center edge neurons in the receptive field (see Figure 4 to Figure 9). The unidirectional vertical connection exists from the Unit-linking PCNN edge detection layer to the Unit-linking PCNN orientation detection layer. No horizontal connection exists among orientation columns in the Unit-linking PCNN orientation detection layer.

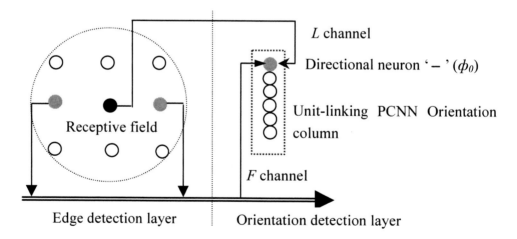

Edge detection layer   Orientation detection layer

Figure 4. The connection mode of the directional neuron ϕ_0

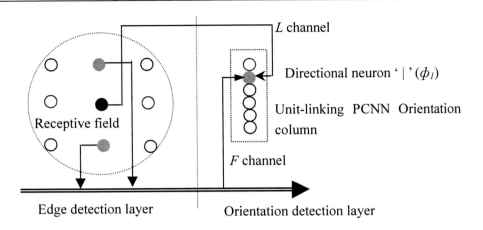

Figure 5. The connection mode of the directional neuron ϕ_1.

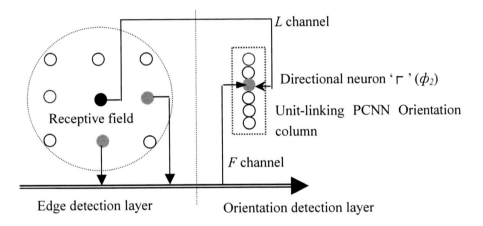

Figure 6. The connection mode of the directional neuron ϕ_2.

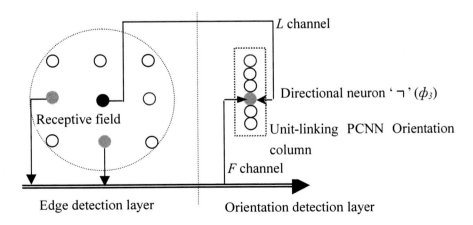

Figure 7. The connection mode of the directional neuron ϕ_3.

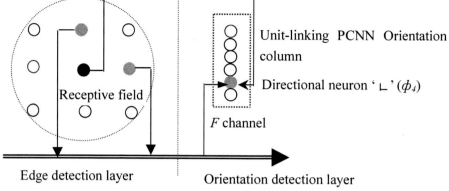

Figure 8. The connection mode of the directional neuron ϕ_4.

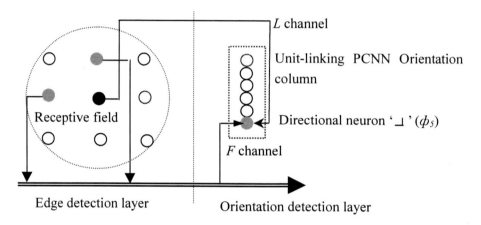

Figure 9. The connection mode of the directional neuron ϕ_5.

All Unit-linking PCNN orientation columns are identical, and the parameters of all directional neurons are equal. In the edge detection layer, when the output value of an edge neuron is '1', the pixel corresponding to it belongs to the edge. When the output value of an edge neuron is '0', the pixel corresponding to it does not belong to the edge. The output signals of edge neurons input to the orientation detection layer. Because the F channel of each directional neuron in an orientation column receives the output signals of 2 specified non-center edge neurons in its receptive field, F_j of each directional neuron in the orientation layer equals to 0,1, or 2. Because the L channel of each directional neuron in an orientation column only receives the output signal of the center edge neuron in its receptive field, F_j of each directional neuron in the orientation layer equals to 0, or 1. Say, the linking strength (β_j) of each directional neuron equals to 1. When a directional neuron j fires, $F_j=2$, $L_j=1$, and $U_j=F_j(1+\beta_j L_j)=4$. In order to detect the orientation, $2\le\theta_j<4$. In the model, θ_j of each directional neuron equals to 3.

An example of Unit-linking PCNN orientation detection is shown in Figure 10. The results of computer simulations show that the Unit-linking PCNN orientation detection approach roughly mimic orientation detection of the biological visual cortex, and can quickly detect the directions of edges with the accuracy. As to 256*256 binary image, it takes 70ms together from edge detection to orientation detection based on PIII 1.7GHz computer. The number of detected directions of each Unit-linking PCNN orientation column can be increased by 1) expanding its receptive field, or 2) integrating the orientation detection results in different small receptive fields together.

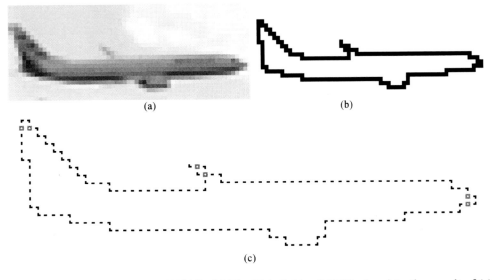

Figure 10. (a) A grey plane image (60*23). (b) The Unit-linking PCNN edge detection result of (a). (c) The Unit-linking PCNN orientation detection result of (b). In (c), '□' denotes that more than one directions are detected in this position.

4. Interesting-Contour Extraction Layer

The interesting-contour extraction layer consists of two sub- layers: the function sub-layer and the output sub-layer. The output signals of Unit-linking PCNN orientation detection layer input to the function sub-layer of the interesting-contour extraction layer. The function sub-layer plays the main role in interesting-contour extraction and consists of arrays of contour extraction columns. Each contour extraction column consists of six neurons. The output sub-layer is used to obtain the final interesting-contour extraction results. At the interesting-contour extraction layer where the TOP-DOWN mechanism is introduced, the chain code of the interesting object contour is used to express the prior knowledge. The chain code of the interesting object inputs to the function sub-layer of the interesting-contour extraction layer repeatedly and its period is its length. The interesting-object contour periodically oscillates at the output sub-layer.

The existing results of cognition science show that human beings use the prior knowledge and TOP-DOWN mechanism in cognition. However, so far we still do not know how to express the prior knowledge in the brain. In [70], Yu and Zhang used the chain code of the interesting-object contour to express the prior knowledge, and hereby introduced the contour matching model including different and very complex neuron models, where many parameters have to choose. In our orientation and interesting-contour extraction model where all neurons are identical, we adopt this idea that using the chain code of the interesting-object contour expresses the prior knowledge.

A. Chain Code of Interesting-Contour

In our model, the elements of chain code of an interesting-object contour correspond to 6 directions of the orientation column at the orientation detection layer. Represent a chain code of a contour with $C = (C[0], C[1], ..., C[k], ..., C[L-1])$, where $C[k] \in \{\phi_n, n = 0,1,...,5\}$. Although the contour of an object is 2-dimensional, its chain code is 1-dimensional and close. In interesting-contour extraction, the 1st code should not equal to the 2nd code in the chain code, namely $C[0] \neq C[1]$. The cause will be given later.

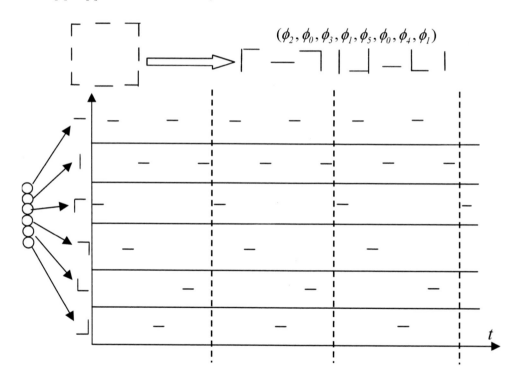

Figure 11. Each contour extraction column receives the chain code of a quadrate contour as the prior knowledge in this example.

Figure 11 illustrates how the prior knowledge, namely the contour chain code of the interesting contour, inputs to each contour extraction column. Making the upper-left point of the quadrate in Figure 11 the initial point obtains clockwise the quadrate contour chain code: $(\phi_2, \phi_0, \phi_3, \phi_1, \phi_5, \phi_0, \phi_4, \phi_1)$. Assume that the interesting contour is this quadrate. The contour chain code periodically inputs to the F channels of corresponding neurons in each contour extraction column at the function sub-layer of the interesting-contour extraction layer. The periodicity is 8, equal to the length of the quadrate contour. Each contour extraction column at the function sub-layer consists of 6 neurons corresponding to the 6 neurons in the orientation column at the orientation detection layer.

B. Function Sub-Layer of Interesting-Contour Extraction Layer

The function sub-layer consists of contour extraction unit that we call Unit-linking PCNN contour extraction column. Each contour extraction column has 6 neurons. One-to-one correspondence exists between contour extraction column and orientation column. One-to-one correspondence also exists between neurons in the contour extraction column and neurons in the corresponding orientation column. In a contour extraction column, the F channel of each neuron has 2 inputs and L channel has 12 inputs. The F channel of each neuron in a contour extraction column receives both the output signal of the corresponding neuron in the corresponding orientation column and the prior contour chain code (see Figure 12).

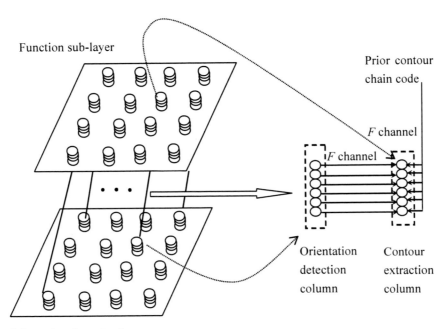

Figure 12. The connection mode of F channels of the neurons in each contour extraction column.

The example in Figure 11 illustrates how each neuron in each contour extraction column receives the prior contour chain code. The response of the F channel of each contour extraction column is decided by output signals of corresponding directional neuron and the prior contour chain code together. The L channel of each neuron in each contour extraction column receives output signals of 12 neurons of two specified non-center contour extraction columns in its 3*3-neighboring field (see Figure 13 to Figure 18).

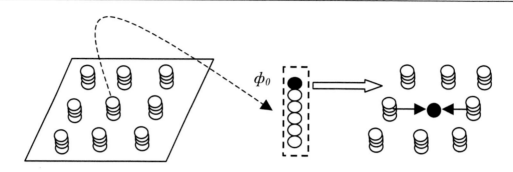

Figure 13. The connection mode of the L channel of neuron ϕ_0 in each contour extraction column.

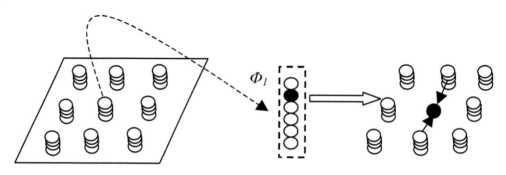

Figure 14. The connection mode of the L channel of neuron ϕ_1 in each contour extraction column.

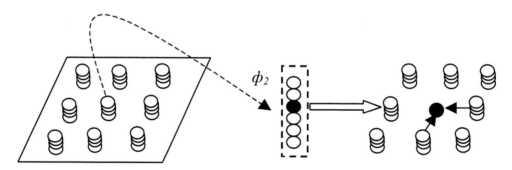

Figure 15. The connection mode of the L channel of neuron ϕ_2 in each contour extraction column.

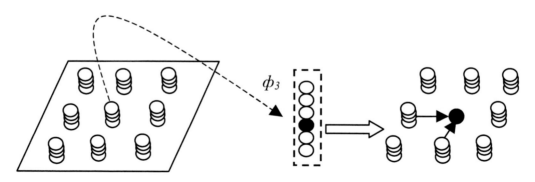

Figure 16. The connection mode of the L channel of neuron ϕ_3 in each contour extraction column.

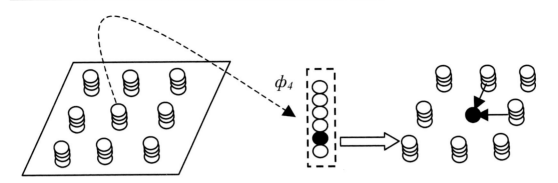

Figure 17. The connection mode of the L channel of neuron ϕ_4 in each contour extraction column.

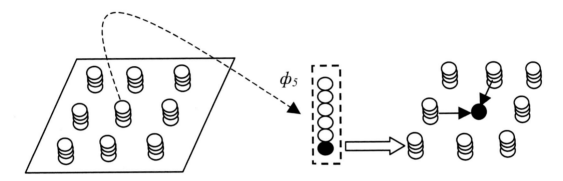

Figure 18. The connection mode of the L channel of neuron ϕ_5 in each contour extraction column.

A contour extraction column fires when a neuron or more than one neurons in this column fire. In general, only one neuron fires in a contour extraction column at a time. In this model, the interesting contour is denoted by the contour periodical oscillation when the chain code of the contour matches with the prior contour chain code. The contour of the interesting object can grow to form a close curve to generate the periodical oscillation. The contour of the non-interesting object cannot grow to form a close curve to generate the periodical oscillation because no complete-matching exists between the contour chain code of the non-interesting object and the prior contour chain code.

We call the firstly firing contour extraction columns the start points, which may correspond to the points in interesting contours or non-interesting contours. There are often more than one start points. Whether a contour extraction column fires at the beginning as the start point, is decided by 1) the output signals of the corresponding orientation columns, and 2) the prior contour chain code.

Whether a contour extraction column fires after start points firing, is decided by 1) the output signals of the corresponding orientation columns, 2) the prior contour chain code, and 3) the output signals of other contour extraction columns in their 3*3-neighboring fields.

Parameters of each neuron in the contour extraction column are identical. Assume the linking strength of each contour neuron equals to 1 ($\beta_j=1$). Initialize the threshold of each contour neuron to 1.5. The threshold-adjusting process is described below.

1) Do the 1st iteration computation. If a contour neuron in a contour extraction column does fire in the 1st iteration computation, its threshold increases to 4.5; else, its threshold increases to 3.

2) Do the 2nd iteration computation. (i).When a contour neuron does fire in the 2nd iteration computation, its threshold adjusts to 4.5. (ii).When a contour neuron does not fire in the 2nd iteration, if its threshold is greater than 4.0, its threshold decreases by 0.3; else, its threshold does not change.

...

k) Do the kth iteration computation. (i).When a contour neuron does fire in the kth iteration computation, its threshold adjusts to 4.5. (ii).When a contour neuron does not fire in the kth iteration, if its threshold is greater than 4.0, its threshold decreases 0.3; else, its threshold does not change.

...

It was mentioned above that in the prior contour chain code, the first code should not equal to the second code, namely $C[0] \neq C[1]$. Why? If $C[0] = C[1]$, the start point P_0 and its succeeding point P_1 in the interesting contour will fire together in the 1st iteration computation. P_1 has fired in the 1st iteration computation so that the high threshold prevents it firing in the 2nd iteration computation. In the 3rd iteration computation, P_2, the succeeding point of P_1, does not fire because it does not receive the pulse emitted by P_1. Contour-growing stops so that contour extraction fails. Therefore, $C[0] \neq C[1]$.

C. Output Sub-Layer of Interesting-Contour Extraction Layer

The output sub-layer is a two-dimensional network. One-to-one correspondence exists between contour extraction columns at the function sub-layer and neurons at the output sub-layer. The F channel of each output neuron at the output sub-layer receives the output signals of the 6 neurons in the corresponding contour extraction column (see Figure 19). All output neurons are identical. The L channel of each output neuron receives nothing. Choosing the suitable threshold value of each output neuron can make the firing state of each neuron at the output sub-layer identical to that of the corresponding contour extraction column at the function sub-layer. The periodical oscillation of the output neurons forms the interesting contour.

Because noise changes the contour chain code, using the chain code of the interesting-contour to express the prior knowledge only can extract interesting-contour in the noise-free situation. An example of Unit-linking PCNN interesting-contour extraction is shown in Figure 20. In Figure 20, the prior contour chain code is obtained from (c) and the upper-left point of the interesting object is used as the initial point of the contour chain code. In (g), ' ■ ' denotes the neurons firing in the 1st iteration computation. In (h), ' ■ ' denotes the neurons firing in the 10th iteration computation, and ' ▩ ' denotes the neurons having fired before the 10th iteration computation. In (i), ' ◖ ' denotes the neurons firing in the 38th iteration computation. In (i), ' ■ ' and ' ◖ ' denote the neurons corresponding to the interesting object contour, and they form the periodical oscillation and the periodicity is 38. In (i), ' ▩ ' denotes the neurons that fire in the 1st periodicity, but do not belong to the interesting contour, and not fire again from the 2nd periodicity (namely after 38 iteration computation).

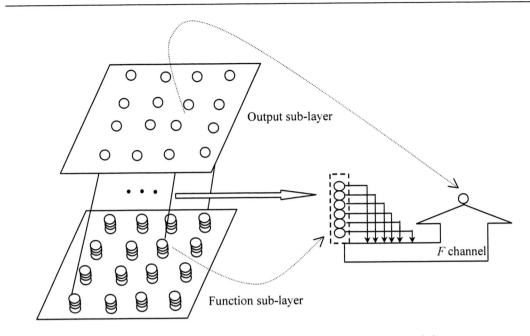

Figure 19. The connection mode of the *F* channel of each neuron at the output sub-layer.

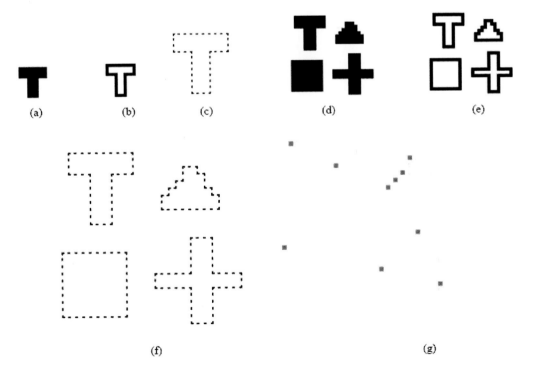

(a)   (b)   (c)   (d)   (e)

(f)   (g)

Figure 20. (Continued).

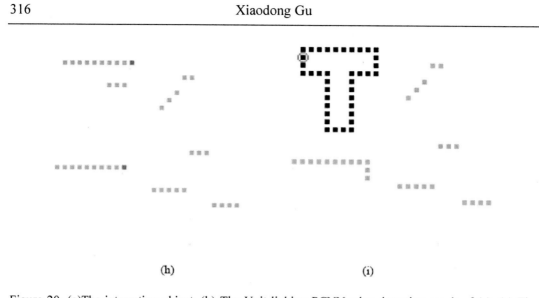

(h)   (i)

Figure 20. (a)The interesting object. (b) The Unit-linking PCNN edge detection result of (a). (c) The Unit-linking PCNN orientation detection result of (b). (d)A binary image including the interesting polygon 'T' in (a) and other non-interesting polygons. (e) The Unit-linking PCNN edge detection result of (d). (f) The Unit-linking PCNN orientation detection result of (e). (g),(h), and (i) are the states of the output sub-layer in the 1st ,10th , 38th iteration times respectively.

5. Conclusion

We proposed a novel orientation and interesting-contour extraction model based on Unit-linking PCNN. This model includes the orientation detection layer and the interesting-contour extraction layer.

The orientation detection layer roughly mimics orientation detection of the biological visual cortex. In our model, the number of detected directions is small (only 6). We can increase the number of detected directions by expanding the receptive field of each Unit-linking PCNN orientation column, or integrating the orientation detection results in different small receptive fields together.

In the interesting-contour extraction layer, the periodical oscillation of the object contour denotes the interesting contour. In this layer, the TOP-DOWN mechanism is introduced by using the chain code of the interesting object contour to express the prior knowledge [70]. However, so far we do not know if this exists in the real biological visual cortex. The research in this paper shows that in bionic aspect, using the chain code of the interesting-contour to express the prior knowledge can extract interesting-contour in the noise-free situation.

Acknowledgements

This work was supported in part by National Natural Science Foundation of China under grant 60671062 and 60571052, and in part by National Basic Research Program of China under grant 2005CB724303.

References

[1]   J.G. Elias, P.M.Northmore, W. Westerman. An analog memory circuit for spiking silicon neurons. *Neural computation*, 1997, 9: 419-440.

[2]   S.H. Kwatra, F.J. Doyle III, I.A. Rybak, J.S. Schwaber. A neuro-mimetic dynamic scheduling algorithm for control: analysis and application. *Neural computation*, 1997, 9: 479-502.

[3]   D.TalandE.L. Schwartz. Computing with the leaky integrate-and fire neuron: logarithmic computation and multiplication. *Neural computation*, 1997, 9: 305-308.

[4]   W. Maass. Fast sigmoid networks via spiking neurons. *Neural computation*, 1997, 9:279-304.

[5]   R. Eckhorn, H.J.Reitboeck, M. Arndt and P. W. Dicke. Feature linking via synchronization among distributed assemblies: Simulation of results from cat cortex. *Neural Computation*, 1990, 2(3): 293-307.

[6]   R. Eckhorn, R. Bauer, R. Jordan, and et al. Coherent oscillations: A mechanism of feature linking in the visual cortex? *Biological Cybernetics,* 1988, 60: 121-130.

[7]   C.M. Gray and W. Singer. Stimulus-specific neuronal oscillations in the orientation columns of cat visual cortex. *Proc. Natl. Acad. Sci., USA*, 1989, 86(5): 1698-1702.

[8]   A.K. Kreiter, W. Singer, Oscillatory neuronal responses in the visual cortex of the awake macaque monkey. *European J. Neurosci.*, 1992, 4: 369-375.

[9]   R. Eckhorn, A. Frien, R. Bauer et al. High frequency oscillations in primary visual cortex of awake monkey. *NeuroRep.*, 1993, 4(3): 243-246.

[10] Frien, R. Eckhorn, R. Bauer, T. Woelbern et al. Stimulus-specific fast oscillations at zero phase between visual areas V1 and V2 of awake monkey. *NeuroRep.*, 1994, 5: 2273-2277.

[11] Frien, R. Eckhorn, R. Bauer, T. Woelbern, Oscillatory group activity reveals sharper orientation tuning than conventional measure in primary visual cortex of awake monkey. *Soc.Neurosci.*,1995, Abstract.

[12] J.L. Johnson, D. Ritter. Observation of periodic waves in a Pulse-coupled neural network. *Opt.Lett.*, 1993, 18: 1253-1255.

[13] G. Kuntimad, H.S. Ranganath. Perfect image segmentation using pulse coupled neural networks. *IEEE Trans. on Neural Networks*, 1999, 10: 591-598.

[14] H.S. Ranganath, M. Banish; J. Karpinsky, et al. Three applications of pulse coupled neural networks. *Proceedings of SPIE-The International Society for Optical Engineering*, 1999, 3728: 375-381.

[15] P.E. Keller; D. McKinnon. Pulse-coupled neural networks for medical image analysis. *Proceedings of SPIE - The International Society for Optical Engineering*, 1999, 3722: 444-451.

[16] P.E. Keller, D. McKinnon. Segmentation of medical imagery with pulse-coupled neural networks. *Proceedings of IJCNN'99-International Joint Conference on Neural Networks*, 1999: 2659-2663.

[17] A.N. Skourikhine; L. Prasad, et al. Neural network for image segmentation. *Proceedings of SPIE - The International Society for Optical Engineering*, 2000, 4120: 28-35.

[18] X.D. Gu, S.D. Guo, D.H. Yu. A new approach for automated image segmentation based on Unit-linking PCNN. Proceedings of ICMLC'02-IEEE International *Conference on Machine learning and Cybernetics*, Beijing, China, 2002, 175-178.

[19] X.D. Gu, D.H. Yu, L.M. Zhang. General design approach to Unit-linking PCNN for image processing, *Proceedings of IJCNN'05-International Joint Conference on Neural Networks,* Montreal, Canada, 2005:1836-1842.

[20] X.D. Gu, D.H. Yu, L.M. Zhang. Image thinning using pulse coupled neural network. *Pattern recognition letters*, 2004, 25: 1075-1084.

[21] X.D. Gu, D.H. Yu, L.M. Zhang. Image shadow removal using pulse coupled neural network. *IEEE Transaction on Neural Networks*, 2005, 16: 692-698.

[22] X.D. Gu, D.H. Yu, L.M. Zhang. *Mathematical morphology granulometry based on PCNN*. China National Conference on Neural Networks (Chinese). 2003: 83-87.

[23] X.D. Gu. *A New Approach to image authentication using local image icon of Unit-linking PCNN*. IJCNN07-International Joint Conference on Neural Networks. 2006: 2015-2020.

[24] X.D. Gu, C.Q. Cheng, D.H. Yu. Noise-reducing of multilevel image using PCNN and fuzzy algorithm. *Journal of Electronics and Information Technology* (Chinese), 2003, 25(12): 1585-1590.

[25] X.D. Gu, S.D. Guo, D.H. Yu. *An image enhancement approach based on rough sets and PCNN*. China National Conference on Neural Networks (Chinese). 2002: 583-588.

[26] X.D. Gu, C.Q. Cheng, D.H. Yu. Image pre-processing based on rough set and PCNN, *Acta Scientiarum Naturalium Universitatis Pekinensis* (Chinese), 2003, 39(5): 703-708.

[27] X.D. Gu. Research on pulse coupled neural network and its applications. *Ph.D. dissertation*, Peking University, 2003

[28] J. Karvonen. A simplified pulse-coupled neural network based sea-ice classifier with graphical interactive training. *Proceedings of IGARSS'00-International Geoscience and Remote Sensing Symposium*, 2000, 2: 681 –684.

[29] J.H. Cooley; T. Cooley. Segmentation and discrimination of structural and spectral information using multi-layered pulse couple neural networks. *Proceedings of IGARSS'99- International Geoscience and Remote Sensing Symposium,* 1999, 1: 80–82.

[30] J. Karvonen; M. Simila. Classification of sea ice types from ScanSAR RADARSAT images using pulse-coupled neural networks. *Proceedings of IGARSS '98-International Geoscience and Remote Sensing Symposium*, 1998, 1: 2505 –2508.

[31] A.Gollamudi, P.Calvin, G.Yuen, et al. Pulse coupled neural network based image classification. *Proceedings of the Thirtieth Southeastern Symposium on System Theory*, 1998: 402-406.

[32] X.D. Gu. Research on pulse coupled neural network and its applications. *Ph.D. dissertation*, Peking University, 2003.

[33] X.D. Gu, S.D. Guo, D.H. Yu. New approach for noise reducing of image based on PCNN. *Journal of Electronics and Information Technology* (Chinese). 2002, 24: 1304-1309.

[34] X.D. Gu, L.M. Zhang. Equivalence relation between PCNN and mathematical morphology in image processing. *Journal of Computer-Aided Design and Computer Graphics* (Chinese), 2004, 16: 1029-1032.

[35] J.M. Kinser. Foveation by a Pulse-Coupled Neural Network. *IEEE Trans. Neural Networks,* 1999, 10: 621-625.

[36] R.P. Broussard, S.K. Rogers, M.E. Oxley et al. Physiologically motivated image fusion for object detection using a Pulse Coupled Neural Network. *IEEE Trans. on Neural Networks*, 1999, 10: 554-563.

[37] M.L. Padgett, J.L. Johnson. Pulse coupled neural networks: biosensors applications, invited paper. Proc.Int.Conf.NN.*IEEE-ICNN'*97, Houston,TX, June 1997: 2507-2512.

[38] M.L. Padgett T.A. Roppel, J.L. Johnson. Pulse coupled neural networks and new approaches to biosensor applications. *Proceedings of SPIE - The International Society for Optical Engineering*, 1998, 3390:79-88.

[39] M.L. Padgett. Pulse coupled neural networks (PCNN), wavelets and radial basis functions: Olfactory sensor applications, *Proceedings of IJCNN'98-International Joint Conference on Neural Networks*, 1998: 1784-1789.

[40] H.S. Ranganath and G. Kuntimad. Object detection using pulse coupled neural networks. *IEEE Trans. on Neural Networks*, 1999, 10: 615-620.

[41] J.L. Johnson, M.P. Schamschula; R. Inguva, et al. Pulse coupled neural network sensor fusion *Proceedings of SPIE - The International Society for Optical Engineering*, 1998, 3376: 219-226.

[42] Th. Lindblad, C.S. Lindsey, M.L. Padgett, et al. Digital x-ray image processing using biologically inspired methods. *Proceedings of IJCNN'98- International Joint Conference on Neural Networks,* 1998, 2: 803-808.

[43] M.L. Padgett, Th.A. Roppel, J.L .Johnson. Pulse coupled neural networks (PCNN), wavelets and radial basis functions: olfactory sensor applications*, Proceedings of IJCNN'98- International Joint Conference on Neural Networks*, 1998, 3: 1784-1789.

[44] S.D.D.V. Rughooputh, R. Somanah, H.C.S. Rughooputh. Classification of optical galaxies using a PCNN*: Proceedings of SPIE - The International Society for Optical Engineering,* 2000, 3962: 138-147.

[45] M.Tanaka, T.Watanabe, Y.Baba, and et al. Autonomous foveating system and integration of the foveated images. *Proceedings of 1999 IEEE International Conference on Systems, Man, and Cybernetics,* 1999: 559-564.

[46] J. Waldemark, V. Becanovic, Th. Lindblad, and et al. Hybrid neural networks for automatic target recognition. *Proceedings of 1997 IEEE International Conference on Systems, Man, and Cybernetics*, 1997, 4: 4016-4021.

[47] F.T. Allen, J.M. Kinser, H.J. Caulfield, Scene evaluation using a pulse-coupled neural network (PCNN). *Proceedings of SPIE - The International Society for Optical Engineering.* 1995, 2565: 20-29.

[48] X.F. Zhang, A.A Minai. Detecting corresponding segments across images using synchronizable pulse-coupled neural networks. *Proceedings of IJCNN'01-International Joint Conference on Neural Networks*, 2001: 820-825.

[49] M.M.I. Chacon; S.A. Zimmerman, A.D. Sanchez. PCNNP: a pulse-coupled neural network processor. *Proceedings of IJCNN '02-International Joint Conference on Neural Networks*, 2002: 1581 -1584.

[50] J.C. Kirsch, B.K. Jones, M. Banish, and et al. Electrical and optical implementations of the PCNN. *Proceedings of SPIE -The International Society for Optical Engineering.* 2001, 4471: 147-158.

[51] M. Banish, H. Ranganath, J.K arpinsky, and et al. Three applications of pulse coupled neural networks and an optoelectronic hardware implementation. *Proceedings of SPIE-The International Society for Optical Engineering.* 1999, 3647: 174-181.

[52] F.T. Allen, J.M. Kinser; H.J. Caulfield. Neural bridge from syntactic to statistical pattern recognition. *Neural Networks*. 1999, 12: 519-526.

[53] Th.Roppel, D.Wilson, K. Dunman, and et al. Design of a low-power, portable sensor system using embedded neural networks and hardware preprocessing. *Proceedings of IJCNN'99-International Joint Conference on Neural Networks*, 1999: 142-145.

[54] Godin; J.D. Muller; M.B. Gordon, and et al. Pattern recognition with spiking neurons: performance enhancement based on a statistical analysis. *Proceedings of IJCNN'99-International Joint Conference on Neural Networks*, 1999: 1876-1880.

[55] E.P. Blasch. Biological information fusion using a PCNN and belief filtering. *Proceedings of IJCNN'99-International Joint Conference on Neural Networks*, 1999: 2792-2795.

[56] S.D. Rughooputh, H.C.S. Rughooputh. Forensic application of a novel hybrid neural network. *Proceedings of IJCNN'99-International Joint Conference on Neural Networks*, 1999: 3143-3146.

[57] S.L. Abrahamson. Pulse coupled neural networks for the segmentation of magnetic resonance brain images. Performer: Air Force Inst. of Tech., Wright-Patterson AFB, OH. School of Engineering. Report: AFIT/GCS/ENG/96D-01, Dec 1996.

[58] Renhorn. Advanced signal processing and smart sensors (avancerad signal behanding och Smarta Sensorer). Performer: Foersvarets Forskningsanstalt, Linkoeping (Sweden). Avdelningen foer Sensorteknik. Report: FOA-R-96-00322-3.1-SE, Nov 1996.

[59] D.E. Hill, Temporal Influence on Awareness .Performer: Air Force Inst. of Tech., Wright-Patterson AFB, OH. School of Engineering. Report: AFIT/GE/ENG/95D-07, Dec 1995.

[60] P. Chandrasekaran; M. Bodruzzaman, G. Yuen, and et al. Speech recognition using pulse coupled neural network. *Proceedings of the Thirtieth Southeastern Symposium on System Theory*, 1998: 515 –519.

[61] R. Varadarajan, G. Yuen, M. Bodruzzaman, M. Malkani. Sensory fusion for intelligent navigation of mobile robot. *Proceedings of the Thirtieth Southeastern Symposium on System Theory*, 1998: 307–311.

[62] J.H. Cooley, T.W. Cooley. Combining structural and spectral information for discrimination using pulse coupled neural networks in multispectral and hyperspectral data. *Proceedings of IGARSS'97-International Geoscience and Remote Sensing Symposium*, 1997: 1666 -1668.

[63] H.J. Caulfield and J.M. Kinser. Finding shortest path in the shortest time using PCNN's. *IEEE Trans. on Neural Networks*, 1999, 10: 604-606.

[64] X.D. Gu, L.M. Zhang, D.H. Yu. Delay PCNN and its application for optimization. *Lecture Notes in Computer Science* 2004, 3173: 413-418.

[65] M.L. Padgett, Th.A. Roppel, J.L. Johnson, Pulse coupled neural networks (PCNN), wavelets and radial basis functions: Olfactory sensor applications, *Proceedings of IEEE International Joint Conference on Neural Networks*, 1998, 3: 1784-1789.

[66] X.D. Gu, L.M. Zhang. Global icons and local icons of images based Unit-linking PCNN and their application to robot navigation. *Lecture Notes in Computer Science* 2005, 3497:836-841.

[67] T.Y. Kim, B.H. Kim, S.O. Kim, H.M. Choi. KLT-based adaptive vector quantization using PCNN. *Proceedings of IEEE International Conference on Systems, Man, and Cybernetics*, 1996: 82 –87.

[68] X.D. Gu. *Research on several theoretical and applied aspects on Unit-linking pulse coupled neural network*. Postdoctoral research report, Fudan University, 2005.

[69] X.D. Gu, L.M. Zhang. *Orientation detection and attention selection based Unit-linking PCNN*. ICNB05-International Conference on Neural Networks and Brain. 2005:1328-1333.

[70] B. Yu, L.M. Zhang. Pulse-coupled neural networks for contour and motion matching," *IEEE Trans. on Neural Networks,* 2004, 15:1186-1201.

Author's Biography

Xiaodong Gu was born in Nantong, Jiangsu Province, China, in 1970. He received the M.S. degree in communication and information system from Soochow (Suzhou) University, Suzhou, China, in 2000 and Ph.D. degree in signal and information processing from Peking (Beijing) University, Beijing, China, in 2003. From 2003 to 2005, he was a Postdoctoral Fellow of Electronic Science and Technology Postdoctoral Research Station, with the Department of Electronic Engineering, Fudan University, Shanghai, China.

Currently he is associate professor, with the Department of Electronic Engineering, Fudan University. He is taking charge of and has taken change of many research projects about neural networks, such as the project supported by China Postdoctoral Science Foundation and the project supported National Natural Science Foundation of China. He has published about 50 papers in journals and conference proceedings. His current research interests include artificial neural networks, image processing, and pattern recognition.

He was the recipient of 2003 Excellent Graduate of Peking University and also was the recipient of 2005 Excellent Dissertation Award of Peking University. He also was the recipient of 2007 Excellent Post-doctoral Fellow Award of Fudan University. He was received Excellent Invited Report Awards in the 12th and the 13th China National Conference on Neural Networks in 2002 and 2003 respectively.

In: Visual Cortex: New Research
Editors: T. A. Portocello and R. B. Velloti

ISBN 978-1-60456-530-0
© 2008 Nova Science Publishers, Inc.

Chapter 10

NEURONAL PLASTICITY IN RETINAL DISEASE

Carlos Gias

Institute of Ophthalmology, University College London, London, UK.

Abstract

Age-related macular degeneration (AMD) and Retinitis Pigmentosa (RP) are degenerative diseases that affect the retina and result in a progressive deterioration of vision leading eventually to photoreceptor death and blindness. There are currently a number of therapeutic approaches attempting to rescue vision by trying to stop or replace the loss of photoreceptors. Does the visual system reorganize as a result of loss of visual input? How does this affect the processing of visual information? The success of those therapies will eventually depend on the ability of the neural pathways to transmit and process the signals generated by the photoreceptors.

Plasticity During Development

During development, there is a period of refinement in the sensory pathways from coarse structural and functional neuronal networks into refined processing systems of sensory information. This plastic capacity is not exclusive of this period. Learning and memory studies have also demonstrated that the adult brain still preserves an ability to change.

Plasticity in the Visual Cortex

Adult plasticity has also been demonstrated as a result of loss in the sensory input. Functional changes in the somatosensory cortex have been described in a number of species as a result of deafferentation (Kaas *et al.*, 1983). Manipulations of the visual input also alter normal function in the visual cortex. Cells in primary visual cortex are differentially driven by input from both eyes. This phenomenon is known as ocular dominance and has been widely used as a model to study the structural and functional changes of neuronal networks and the possible mechanisms underlying those changes as a result of visual deprivation during development

(Wiesel and Hubel, 1963; Hofer et al., 2006a). However, it is not clear to what extent these results can be extrapolated to plastic changes resulting from disease such as those seen in retinal degeneration.

One way of examining experimentally changes in sensory processing is the use of retinal lesions. In normal-sighted subjects, visual space is mapped onto visual cortex with a one-to-one correspondence. By causing retinal lesions, regions of the visual cortex are deprived of an otherwise normal input. Lesions produced on both eyes on corresponding areas of visual space cause a lack of visual response to the projection onto visual cortex (cortical scotoma) followed by reorganization of cortical activity. There are immediate functional changes at the border of the cortical scotoma and extending inside it (Gilbert and Wiesel, 1992). Given enough time to recover, cells located up to several millimetres within the scotoma are again visually responsive (Gilbert, 1998; Kaas, 2002). This functional reorganization is believed to be mediated by long-range horizontal connections (Darian-Smith and Gilbert, 1994; Calford et al., 2003). Despite the large body of evidence accumulated, the existence of any substantial long-term cortical reorganization as a result of binocular retinal lesions in the adult has been recently questioned (Horton and Hocking, 1998; Smirnakis et al., 2005). Therefore, there is still a lack of consensus in the extent and strength of the cortical reorganization as a result of retinal lesions.

In addition to these discrepancies a more fundamental question remains, does the retinal lesion model represent accurately the plastic changes occurring in retinal degeneration? We believe this might not be the case. A recent study using functional magnetic resonance imaging (fMRI) has reported large-scale cortical reorganization in the order of tens of square centimetres in human subjects suffering from macular degeneration (Baker *et al.*, 2005). When a visual stimulus was presented onto the region of macular dystrophy at the retina no response was elicited at V1. However, when stimulating the part of the retina with residual visual function far from the area of dystrophy, activity could be detected not only in its mapped projection onto V1 but also in the cortical area corresponding to the macular dystrophy. This study was carried out in two patients decades after the onset of the disease (late adulthood and late childhood respectively). No previous retinal lesion study in adult animals had reported such massive reorganization. Given that typical horizontal connections in primate V1 extend between 6-8 mm (Gilbert *et al.*, 1996) multiple synapses would be necessary to explain the changes reported. An alternative cortical mechanism that could explain the non-retinotopic V1 activation could be the influence of feedback projections from higher visual areas. Although this has not been observed in normal-sighted subjects the phenomenon could be enhanced in patients with retinal degeneration. This idea is consistent with the activation observed in visual cortex of blind patients when performing a non-visual task (Burton, 2003). However, if this is the main mechanism to induce this massive reorganization, why has this not been detected in previous retinal lesion studies? Does large V1 reorganization only occur after protracted periods of deafferentation or are there any additional structures in the visual system that could also have contributed to this reorganization and have not been identified in retinal lesion studies?

Plasticity Outside the Visual Cortex

There is evidence from the somatosensory system that the thalamus experiences plastic changes following loss of input (Florence *et al.*, 2000) and reorganization has also been observed at the lateral geniculate nucleus in retinal lesion studies (Eysel et al., 1981; Eysel, 1982). Although these changes could not fully explain the size of the receptive field changes observed in visual cortex, they would undoubtedly contribute to them.

Are there any changes occurring also at the retina? Visual information is initially processed at the neural retina before being transmitted to the brain. Is there any evidence of plasticity at this level as a result of degeneration in the sensory part of the retina? The answer is yes. Atrophy of the neural retina as a result of RP in humans has long been recognized (Kolb and Gouras, 1974). These observations have been later confirmed in further RP (Milam *et al.*, 1998) and AMD (Sullivan *et al.*, 2007) studies. The different stages of neural retina plasticity as a result of sensory retina degeneration have been described in detail by using rodent animal models (Jones and Marc, 2005). Even before the death of photoreceptors there are already significant changes in the retina. Many photoreceptors undergo abnormal neurite sprouting followed by retraction and subsequent photoreceptor death. In later stages, all the different neuronal types suffer to some extent from hypertrophy, sprouting, dendrite retraction, translocation, rewiring and death (Marc *et al.*, 2003). Given the extensive amount of structural reorganization it is very likely that the functional responses of the remaining retina will also be altered, especially in those patients at an advanced stage of retinal degeneration. This structural plastic changes will result in functional changes at the retina where visual information is first processed. Unless these functional changes are investigated in detail it will be difficult to infer the functional consequences of plasticity at later visual processing stages. Retinal lesion models result in damage to the neural retina. Therefore, they cannot be used to study neural retina reorganization as a result of the lack of visual input. In addition, there is an expansion in the area of retinal degeneration occurring over a period of time in retinal disease as opposed to retinal lesions that are localized both in space and time. A degenerative loss of input might allow a progressive form of plasticity at the various levels of visual processing. Therefore, the use animal models with a progressive retinal degeneration that mimics the degeneration and reorganization observed in disease.

Animal Models of Retinal Disease

Previous studies have made use of rodents to identify molecular and experience dependent factors influencing the formation of ocular dominance in visual cortex (Hensch *et al.*, 1998; Hofer *et al.*, 2006b). Besides ocular dominance, visual field processing is retinotopically organized in the rodent visual cortex (Schuett et al., 2002; Gias et al., 2005). Therefore, the rodent can be used as a model to study the effects of retinal dystrophies in the formation and distortion of the retinotopic maps. In addition, rodent models of retinal disease such as the royal college of surgeons (RCS) rat or the rd mouse have been used extensively to understand the structural changes in the retina following RPE dysfunction and the retinal functional deficits associated with it by measuring ERG responses (Jiang and Hamasaki, 1994; Li et al., 2001). Some studies have also looked at the spatio-temporal pattern of visual function degeneration by measuring neuronal responses in the superior colliculus in the RCS rat

(Sauve *et al.*, 2002; Sauve *et al.*, 2004) or global changes in the functional responsivity in the visual cortex (Girman et al., 2003; Gias et al., 2007). However, little is known about the reorganization of neuronal structures in these animal models other than the retina, the local or global effects this reorganization might cause on the processing of visual information across the visual system and the molecular mechanisms behind them. Processing of visual information can be studied at various scales using a number of direct measures of electrical activity or indirect measures such as optical or magnetic methods.

Methods to Measure Structural and Functional Plasticity in the Visual System

The advent of fMRI has allowed cortical function to be studied non-invasively at a spatial and temporal resolution previously unobtainable in the human brain. The fMRI signal has been attributed to the local changes in blood oxygenation, blood flow and blood volume as a result of local electrical activity. However, seemingly contradictory results in plasticity studies have been recently presented (Smirnakis *et al.*, 2005). As a result, issues about the spatial resolution and the aspect of neuronal activity that the fMRI signal reflects have been put forward to question the validity of this technique to study plasticity. Instead, higher spatial and temporal resolution can be achieved in animal models by using more invasive methods. Visualization of maps of cortical activity in various species is possible by using optical imaging of intrinsic signals (OIS) due to its high spatial resolution (Grinvald *et al.*, 1986). It has also been used to compare amplitude response differences as a function of various visual parameters (Gias *et al.*, 2007; Heimel *et al.*, 2007) and to study the mechanisms behind ocular dominance plasticity (Hofer et al., 2006a; Heimel et al., 2007). In addition, this technique has been recently adapted to detect local activity in the retina following stimulation (Tsunoda et al., 2004; Nelson et al., 2005). Therefore, we believe OIS will be a basic tool for the study of plasticity at the retina and the cortex. Unfortunately, this technique lacks depth resolution and cortical plasticity has been shown to be layer dependent (Trachtenberg et al., 2000; Oray et al., 2004). Functional optical coherence tomography is a technique currently under development sensitive enough to detect reflectance changes across retinal layers in vitro as a result of stimulation (Bizheva *et al.*, 2006) and expected in the near future to be applicable to in vivo experiments in the retina. A recently developed optical imaging technique based on two-photon calcium imaging has been able to measure local spike patterns in the cortex at the single cell level in vivo (Kerr *et al.*, 2005). This technique is an evolution of two-photon microcopy (Majewska and Sur, 2003) with a spatial resolution high enough to identify spine plasticity in vivo. Traditional measurements of electrical response such single-unit and multiunit recordings and local field potentials can characterize various aspects of neuronal activity offering high temporal resolution from the different cortical layers and are basic for the understanding of information processing. To study neuronal reorganization in detail it will be necessary to examine the changes occurring at different scales in the various parts of the visual system. We believe the combination of the techniques presented here will allow a detailed examination of the structural and functional changes following retinal degeneration.

Functional Benefits of Plasticity

Nowadays, there is an emphasis on implementing retinal therapies aiming at preserving or replacing the sensory retina in patients suffering from retinal degeneration. However, remodelling at the retina influences any rescue strategies since it already begins even before any cells die. Therefore, it will be necessary to understand the reorganization occurring in the visual system to reveal the limits of visual functional recovery expected from therapeutic intervention. Previous studies have shown spontaneous plasticity can be beneficial. This is the case not only during development but also as a result of disease. Structural and biochemical changes are believed to occur in Parkinson's disease patients to compensate for its degenerative effects (Anglade *et al.*, 1995). In AMD patients, the visual system seems to adapt so that the area of retinal scotoma appears complete, although it is not clear what mechanisms are involved to produce this perception (Zur and Ullman, 2003). Even after extensive degeneration at the retina, the remaining neurons are able to form new synaptic contacts and extend their connections. From a visual processing perspective it seems reasonable that the visual system would adapt in order to optimize the response from the remaining visual input. Therefore, it is plausible that spontaneous new connections could provide a functional benefit to patients suffering from retinal degeneration. It remains to be known to what extend this happens and the contribution from the various parts of the visual system.

What if some aspects of plasticity are detrimental for the patient? Could you stop them from happening? Some plastic changes seem to get delayed in some parts of the retina even with a small amount of functional photoreceptors. However, what could you do if all photoreceptors die? One strategy could consist of preserving a normal neuronal structure intact so that when a therapy comes along that replaces the sensory retina the rest of the system will still be able to process those signals normally. An alternative approach could be to guide plasticity so that the system could optimize the visual benefits of the remaining functional units. A more challenging strategy could even be to replace the whole neuronal retina altogether.

Conclusion

Neuronal plasticity is a very complex issue that we are just beginning to understand. However, studying its evolution, mechanisms and functional implications will be crucial to design an appropriate strategy to preserve or improve vision in patients suffering from retinal degeneration diseases. We believe this aim could be achieved by using recently developed high resolution imaging methods to measure the structural and functional changes in various structures in the visual system on appropriate retinal degeneration models.

References

Anglade P, Tsuji S, Javoy-Agid F, Agid Y, Hirsch EC (1995) Plasticity of nerve afferents to nigrostriatal neurons in Parkinson's disease. *Ann. Neurol.* 37:265-272.

Baker CI, Peli E, Knouf N, Kanwisher NG (2005) Reorganization of visual processing in macular degeneration. *J. Neurosci.* 25:614-618.

Bizheva K, Pflug R, Hermann B, Povazay B, Sattmann H, Qiu P, Anger E, Reitsamer H, Popov S, Taylor JR, Unterhuber A, Ahnelt P, Drexler W (2006) Optophysiology: depth-resolved probing of retinal physiology with functional ultrahigh-resolution optical coherence tomography. *Proc. Natl. Acad. Sci. USA* 103:5066-5071.

Burton H (2003) Visual cortex activity in early and late blind people. *J. Neurosci.* 23:4005-4011.

Calford MB, Wright LL, Metha AB, Taglianetti V (2003) Topographic plasticity in primary visual cortex is mediated by local corticocortical connections. *J. Neurosci.* 23:6434-6442.

Darian-Smith C, Gilbert CD (1994) Axonal sprouting accompanies functional reorganization in adult cat striate cortex. *Nature* 368:737-740.

Eysel UT (1982) Functional reconnections without new axonal growth in a partially denervated visual relay nucleus. *Nature* 299:442-444.

Eysel UT, Gonzalez-Aguilar F, Mayer U (1981) Time-dependent decrease in the extent of visual deafferentation in the lateral geniculate nucleus of adult cats with small retinal lesions. *Exp. Brain Res.* 41:256-263.

Florence SL, Hackett TA, Strata F (2000) Thalamic and cortical contributions to neural plasticity after limb amputation. *J. Neurophysiol.* 83:3154-3159.

Gias C, Hewson-Stoate N, Jones M, Johnston D, Mayhew JE, Coffey PJ (2005) Retinotopy within rat primary visual cortex using optical imaging. *Neuroimage* 24:200-206.

Gias C, Jones M, Keegan D, Adamson P, Greenwood J, Lund R, Martindale J, Johnston D, Berwick J, Mayhew J, Coffey P (2007) Preservation of visual cortical function following retinal pigment epithelium transplantation in the RCS rat using optical imaging techniques. *Eur. J. Neurosci.* 25:1940-1948.

Gilbert CD (1998) Adult cortical dynamics. *Physiol. Rev.* 78:467-485.

Gilbert CD, Wiesel TN (1992) Receptive field dynamics in adult primary visual cortex. *Nature* 356:150-152.

Gilbert CD, Das A, Ito M, Kapadia M, Westheimer G (1996) Spatial integration and cortical dynamics. *Proc. Natl. Acad. Sci. USA* 93:615-622.

Girman SV, Wang S, Lund RD (2003) Cortical visual functions can be preserved by subretinal RPE cell grafting in RCS rats. *Vision Res.* 43:1817-1827.

Grinvald A, Lieke E, Frostig RD, Gilbert CD, Wiesel TN (1986) Functional architecture of cortex revealed by optical imaging of intrinsic signals. *Nature* 324:361-364.

Heimel JA, Hartman RJ, Hermans JM, Levelt CN (2007) Screening mouse vision with intrinsic signal optical imaging. *Eur. J. Neurosci.* 25:795-804.

Hensch TK, Fagiolini M, Mataga N, Stryker MP, Baekkeskov S, Kash SF (1998) Local GABA circuit control of experience-dependent plasticity in developing visual cortex. *Science* 282:1504-1508.

Hofer SB, Mrsic-Flogel TD, Bonhoeffer T, Hubener M (2006a) Lifelong learning: ocular dominance plasticity in mouse visual cortex. *Curr. Opin. Neurobiol.* 16:451-459.

Hofer SB, Mrsic-Flogel TD, Bonhoeffer T, Hubener M (2006b) Prior experience enhances plasticity in adult visual cortex. *Nat. Neurosci.* 9:127-132.

Horton JC, Hocking DR (1998) Monocular core zones and binocular border strips in primate striate cortex revealed by the contrasting effects of enucleation, eyelid suture, and retinal laser lesions on cytochrome oxidase activity. *J. Neurosci.* 18:5433-5455.

Jiang LQ, Hamasaki D (1994) Corneal electroretinographic function rescued by normal retinal pigment epithelial grafts in retinal degenerative Royal College of Surgeons rats. *Invest Ophthalmol. Vis. Sci.* 35:4300-4309.

Jones BW, Marc RE (2005) Retinal remodeling during retinal degeneration. *Exp. Eye Res.* 81:123-137.

Kaas JH (2002) Sensory loss and cortical reorganization in mature primates. *Prog. Brain Res.* 138:167-176.

Kaas JH, Merzenich MM, Killackey HP (1983) The reorganization of somatosensory cortex following peripheral nerve damage in adult and developing mammals. *Annu. Rev. Neurosci.* 6:325-356.

Kerr JN, Greenberg D, Helmchen F (2005) Imaging input and output of neocortical networks in vivo. *Proc. Natl. Acad. Sci. USA* 102:14063-14068.

Kolb H, Gouras P (1974) Electron microscopic observations of human retinitis pigmentosa, dominantly inherited. *Invest Ophthalmol.* 13:487-498.

Li Q, Timmers AM, Hunter K, Gonzalez-Pola C, Lewin AS, Reitze DH, Hauswirth WW (2001) Noninvasive imaging by optical coherence tomography to monitor retinal degeneration in the mouse. *Invest Ophthalmol. Vis. Sci.* 42:2981-2989.

Majewska A, Sur M (2003) Motility of dendritic spines in visual cortex in vivo: changes during the critical period and effects of visual deprivation. *Proc. Natl. Acad. Sci. USA* 100:16024-16029.

Marc RE, Jones BW, Watt CB, Strettoi E (2003) Neural remodeling in retinal degeneration. *Prog. Retin. Eye Res.* 22:607-655.

Milam AH, Li ZY, Fariss RN (1998) Histopathology of the human retina in retinitis pigmentosa. *Prog. Retin. Eye Res.* 17:175-205.

Nelson DA, Krupsky S, Pollack A, Aloni E, Belkin M, Vanzetta I, Rosner M, Grinvald A (2005) Special report: Noninvasive multi-parameter functional optical imaging of the eye. *Ophthalmic Surg. Lasers Imaging* 36:57-66.

Oray S, Majewska A, Sur M (2004) Dendritic spine dynamics are regulated by monocular deprivation and extracellular matrix degradation. *Neuron* 44:1021-1030.

Sauve Y, Lu B, Lund RD (2004) The relationship between full field electroretinogram and perimetry-like visual thresholds in RCS rats during photoreceptor degeneration and rescue by cell transplants. *Vision Res.* 44:9-18.

Sauve Y, Girman SV, Wang S, Keegan DJ, Lund RD (2002) Preservation of visual responsiveness in the superior colliculus of RCS rats after retinal pigment epithelium cell transplantation. *Neuroscience* 114:389-401.

Schuett S, Bonhoeffer T, Hubener M (2002) Mapping retinotopic structure in mouse visual cortex with optical imaging. *J. Neurosci.* 22:6549-6559.

Smirnakis SM, Brewer AA, Schmid MC, Tolias AS, Schuz A, Augath M, Inhoffen W, Wandell BA, Logothetis NK (2005) Lack of long-term cortical reorganization after macaque retinal lesions. *Nature* 435:300-307.

Sullivan RK, Woldemussie E, Pow DV (2007) Dendritic and synaptic plasticity of neurons in the human age-related macular degeneration retina. *Invest Ophthalmol. Vis. Sci.* 48:2782-2791.

Trachtenberg JT, Trepel C, Stryker MP (2000) Rapid extragranular plasticity in the absence of thalamocortical plasticity in the developing primary visual cortex. *Science* 287:2029-2032.

Tsunoda K, Oguchi Y, Hanazono G, Tanifuji M (2004) Mapping cone- and rod-induced retinal responsiveness in macaque retina by optical imaging. *Invest Ophthalmol. Vis. Sci.* 45:3820-3826.

Wiesel TN, Hubel DH (1963) Single-Cell Responses in Striate Cortex of Kittens Deprived of Vision in One Eye. *J. Neurophysiol.* 26:1003-1017.

Zur D, Ullman S (2003) Filling-in of retinal scotomas. *Vision Res.* 43:971-982.

In: Visual Cortex: New Research
Editors: T. A. Portocello and R. B. Velloti

ISBN 978-1-60456-530-0
© 2008 Nova Science Publishers, Inc.

Chapter 11

AWARENESS IN PRIMARY VISUAL CORTEX

*Juha Silvanto[1] and Gianluca Campana[*2]*
[1]Beth Israel Deaconess Medical Center and Harvard Medical School, MA, USA
[2]Department of General Psychology, University of Padova, Italy
Reviewed by Giorgio Fuggetta

Abstract

The neural processes that give rise to visual awareness are currently the subject of much debate. One brain region in particular, the primary visual cortex (also known as striate cortex or V1), has been implicated in the neural interactions that give rise to conscious perception. This region, located in and around the calcarine fissure in the occipital lobe, was long regarded merely as a relay station for visual cortical input, with visual awareness believed to arise from the activity of highly specialized visual areas in the parietal and temporal lobes. The perceptual consequences of V1 lesions, however, reveal the indispensable role of this area in conscious perception, and this view is supported by recent neurodisruption and neuroimaging studies carried out in neurologically normal observers. Here we review findings from neuropsychology, cognitive neuroscience, and electrophysiology, and discuss what they reveal about the role of V1 in visual awareness.

V1 and Historical Studies on Visual Perception

In the human brain, the calcarine cortex, and later the whole striate cortex was identified as the "center of vision" or "cortical retina" by Henschen (1893) on the basis of over 160 cases of blindness and hemianopia after cortical lesions. He also found that the upper visual field is represented in the lower bank of the calcarine sulcus and the lower visual field in the upper bank. Point-to-point projection of the retinal image onto the brain had already been proposed by Ibn al-Haytham around the turn of the first century, and this was confirmed by Inoye (1909), who observed a correlation between the visual field defect and the locus of lesion in the striate cortex.

* Corresponding author: Gianluca Campana, Department of General Psychology, University of Padova, Via Venezia, 8. 35131 Padova. Italy. Tel: +39 0498276651. Fax: +39 0498276600. Email: gianluca.campana@unipd.it

The earliest systematic investigations into the effect of posterior occipital lesions concluded that field defects were absolute (Holmes, 1918). Importantly, it was later discovered that in some cases, when assessed through forced choice paradigms, the patient is able to detect stimuli presented in the blind field, despite reporting a complete lack of visual experience. This above-chance level detection performance in the absence of visual experience is known as blindsight. The first report of this phenomenon was by Poeppel et al (1973) whose sample of cortically blind patients was able to localize visual stimuli presented in their blind field at an above chance level with eye movements. Subsequently it was shown that patients with V1 damage can localize unseen stimuli also by pointing (Weiskrantz et al, 1974). The localization performance of the unaware stimuli, assessed through forced-choice paradigms, is more accurate by pointing than by eye movements, implying that the visual processing of targets within the blind field cannot simply be attributed to oculomotor reflex (Weiskranz et al, 1974).

Blindsight and Its Implications on Understanding the Neural Basis of Visual Awareness

The phenomenon of blindsight, namely the manifestation of some visual processing in the absence of V1, has been influential in shaping the current understanding of the neural basis of phenomenal awareness (e.g., Lamme, 2001; Block, 2005). That a stimulus which the subject knew was delivered, and under certain circumstances detected, is not accompanied by a phenomenal visual experience is the hallmark of blindsight that strongly implicates V1 in phenomenal conscious perception (Cowey, 2004).

The remaining ipsilesional extrastriate cortex is believed to be critical for blindsight. Although V1 provides the vast majority of extrastriate feedforward input (see Felleman and Van Essen, 1991), its lesion does not silence the remaining visual cortex altogether; primate electrophysiology (Rodman et al, 1989) as well as neuroimaging studies in human subjects (e.g., Barbur et al, 1993; Goebel et al, 2001) have demonstrated that ipsilesional extrastriate regions do remain responsive to visual stimuli presented in the blind field. This activation is likely to arise through projections from the superior colliculus as well as from a small subpopulation of neurons in the dorsal lateral geniculate nucleus that continue to project to the extrastriate cortex after a V1 lesion (Cowey and Stoerig, 1991; Cowey, 2004). Although likely to underlie the ability to localize and detect stimuli in the blind field (e.g., Barbur et al, 1993), activity in the ipsilesional extrastriate cortex cannot reach awareness; this has been taken to imply that activity in V1 is the neural correlate of phenomenal awareness, and that extrastriate activation needs to be fed back to V1 in order to be consciously perceived (Lamme, 2001; Block, 2005).

Transcranial Magnetic Stimulation Studies on the Role of V1 in Awareness

In recent years, a number of studies have used transcranial magnetic stimulation (TMS) to investigate both blindsight patients as well as neurologically normal observers. In TMS, electric current is used to induce a magnetic field with the objective of altering local electric fields in the brain; the magnetic field passes through the scalp and the skull of the subject inducing current that stimulates the neural tissue. The stimulation induces an electric field both inside and outside the axon (Nagarajan et al, 1993), creating a transmembrane potential, or a nerve depolarization voltage (Rudiak and Marg, 1994). This transmembrane potential can cause membrane depolarization and the initiation of an action potential, which then propagates along a nerve like any other action potential. As TMS can be used to directly activate visual areas that under visual stimulation are dependent on other cortical areas or the thalamus for activation, it allows one to disentangle the information flow that is required to distribute visual information throughout the cortex from the interactions that directly determine whether visual qualia are consciously perceived. This is an important issue with respect to the role of V1 in visual awareness, as it allows one to dissociate any function V1 may play in visual awareness from its important role in providing feedforward input to the extrastriate cortex (cf. Felleman and Van Essen, 1991).

As is the case with direct electrical stimulation, TMS applied over visual cortical areas can induce the perception of flashes of lights, phosphenes. These percepts are a useful tool for studying the neural basis of phenomenal awareness, as they enable one to determine whether the induction of phosphenes by stimulation of one area requires the integrity of another area. This approach was used by Cowey and Walsh (2000), who used TMS to directly stimulate the intact ipsilesional extrastriate visual areas in the blindsight subject GY. This subject suffered from almost total destruction of his left V1, resulting in complete blindness in his right visual field with the exception of some macular sparing (Barbur et al, 1993; Azzopardi and Cowey, 2001). GY was able to perceive phosphenes induced from the contralesional hemisphere, but not when intact extrastriate regions in his ipsilesional hemisphere were stimulated. In contrast, a control subject with blindness due to a subcortical trauma but with an intact V1 was able to perceive phosphenes, demonstrating that it is the lack of V1 rather than the blindness that prevented extrastriate activation from reaching visual awareness.

The importance of V1 in conscious perception of extrastriate activity was subsequently demonstrated also in neurologically normal observers. Pascual-Leone and Walsh (2001) studied the role of V1 in conscious perception of phosphenes induced from V5/MT by applying TMS over V5/MT and V1 in close temporal proximity. When TMS was applied over V5/MT at an intensity sufficient for inducing the perception of a moving phosphene, a subsequent TMS pulse (that was subthreshold for eliciting phosphenes) delivered over V1 degraded or removed the sensation of moving phosphenes. The timing of this effect indicated that the feedback from V5/MT to V1 was critical for conscious perception of the V5/MT phosphene. In a subsequent study, using the same paired-pulse paradigm, it was shown that it is the stimulation intensity over V1 rather than over V5/MT that determines whether V5/MT activation is consciously perceived (Silvanto et al, 2005). This finding is consistent with the evidence that the activation level of early visual cortex is correlated with subjects' conscious percept rather than the physical attributes of the stimulus. Using functional magnetic resonance imaging (fMRI) Ress and Heeger (2003) found that in a contrast detection task, false alarms as well as hits were associated with higher level of activation in V1 than misses and correct rejections. That false alarms evoked more activity than correct rejections shows that the activation level of V1 reflected subjective experience rather than stimulus properties, as the physical stimulus was identical in the two instances.

V5/MT – V1 feedback has been shown to be necessary for conscious perception of not only TMS-induced phosphenes but also of real, visually presented motion stimuli. In a study by Silvanto et al (2005b), TMS was administered over V1 or V5/MT in different time windows during performance of a motion detection task in order to trace the flow of information that gives rise to awareness (Silvanto et al, 2005). The results showed two critical periods of V1 activity, one preceding and another postdating the V5/MT critical period, suggesting that although V5/MT obtains visual information through V1 feedforward activity (reflected in the early V1 critical period predating that of V5/MT), backprojections from V5/MT to V1 remain critical for awareness of motion, as demonstrated by the presence of the late V1 critical period postdating that of V5/MT. This finding demonstrates the importance of backprojections in normal vision (Juan et al, 2004) and shows that the role of V1 extends beyond the feedforward sweep and is consistent with the view that activity in an extrastriate area selective for a particular attribute is insufficient for awareness of that attribute (cf. Zeki and Bartels, 1999). Distinct early and late peaks of V1 activity have also been found for letter detection (Corthout et al, 1999) and figure-ground segregation (Heinen et al, 2005).

Evidence from Electrophysiology

Extrastriate feedback is expressed as modulatory influence from beyond the classical receptive field of V1 neurons (Lamme and Spekreijse, 2000; Albright and Stoner, 2002).

There is indeed ample evidence that extrastriate feedback modulates the tuning of V1 neurons. The most direct evidence comes from the classic studies conducted in Jean Bullier's lab (Hupe et al, 1998, 2001). In these experiments, inactivation of V5/MT lead to a significant decrease in responses of V1 neurons to low salience bars moving against a static background and to a reduction of suppression of a moving background (Hupe et al, 1998; 2001). These findings suggest that backprojections from higher-order areas to V1 potentiate mechanisms of both the excitatory receptive field center (Sandell and Schiller, 1982) and of the inhibitory surround (Bullier, 2001). However, this feedback modulation was reduced when the salience of the moving bars was increased (Hupe et al, 1998), implying that the importance of this feedback on the neural firing in V1 is restricted to specific stimulus conditions. In other words, the finding that extrastriate feedback modulates V1 activity *only* for low contrast stimuli implies that this modulation cannot be critical for *all* phenomenal awareness. Furthermore, this feedback modulation was observed in anesthetized animals, pointing to a general principle of cortical information processing rather than to a critical feature of visual awareness in particular.

There is also evidence of a dissociation between an early and late period of activity in V1, with the latter, presumably in response to feedback from extrastriate cortex, being critical for visual perception. Single-unit work has shown that in response to a textured figure overlying a textured background, at 50 ms after stimulus presentation V1 neurons show selectivity for the local orientation of the line segments that make up the figure. At 80 ms the figure ground boundary selectively evokes a larger response than the rest of the scene, and at 100 ms the elements of the interior of the figure evoke a stronger response than the background elements (Lamme, 1995; Lamme et al, 1996; Zipser et al, 1996). Importantly, it is this late stage of V1 activity that correlates with the monkey's perceptual report (Super et al, 1999), supporting the view that V1 activity in response to extrastriate feedback determines the content of visual awareness. What is not clear, however, whether this finding extends to *all* types of visual experience; figure-ground segregation is a computationally demanding task and it is possible that in such circumstances the importance of extrastriate feedback is amplified. This is an important issue as a V1 lesion abolishes phenomenal awareness of not only complex visual stimuli but also of low-level visual qualia.

In summary, there is plenty of evidence that feedback connections do modulate the responses of V1, and that they are important for accurate encoding of complex visual stimuli. However, this modulation only seems to play a major role for low-contrast, complex visual stimuli. For example, for high contrast stimuli the importance of extrastriate-V1 feedback is diminished (cf. Hupe et al, 1998), yet after a V1 lesion *all* phenomenal vision is lost. Single-cell studies are yet to provide an answer to the question of why a V1 lesion abolishes all phenomenal awareness.

Why Is V1 Necessary for Awareness?

The evidence from neuropsychology, cognitive neuroscience and electrophysiology described above has been taken to imply that activity in V1 is the neural correlate of phenomenal awareness, and that extrastriate activation needs to be fed back to V1 in order to be consciously perceived. Why is this feedback modulation critical for visual awareness? One influential account (Lamme, 2000) proposes a qualitative difference between feedforward and feedback activation in the visual cortex. In this view, unconscious visuo-motor transformations, (as in blindsight), may be executed in an entirely feedforward processing cycle, while visual awareness is critically dependent on feedback connections to the primary visual cortex. This theory however is more of a description of the experimental evidence rather than a neural explanation of visual awareness. It is still unclear why feedback activity in particular (rather than feedforward activity) should be critical for visual awareness.

Is V1 Necessary under All Cirumstances?

Very recent evidence indicates that after a unilateral V1 lesion, the intact hemisphere can enable conscious perception in the blind field. As was discussed above, TMS applied unilaterally over intact extrastriate regions within the damaged hemisphere fails to induce phosphenes in the blindsight subject GY (Cowey and Walsh, 2000). However, when TMS is applied over the extrastriate area V5/MT in both the damaged and intact hemisphere in close temporal proximity, GY perceives two separate phosphenes, one in the good hemifield and the other in the blind hemifield, symmetrical in shape and location (Silvanto et al, 2007). The induction of phosphenes in GY's blind field is likely to result from the stimulation of his ipsilesional V5/MT through callosal connections, increasing and/or modulating the activation level of neurons in V5/MT of the normal hemisphere that have a representation of part of the ipsilateral visual field. The finding that the induction of blind field percepts in GY required bilateral application of TMS is a further demonstration of the inability of GY's ipsilesional hemisphere to support conscious visual perception and thus reinforces the view that V1 is indispensable for phenomenal vision. The main implication of this finding, however, is that a retinotopic representation of the visual field in V1 is not necessary for phenomenal awareness. Even if the contralesional V1 in GY did contribute to the blind field percept, it could not have acted as a "read-out" map for the blind field percept, as V1 does not contain a retinotopic representation of the ipsilateral visual field.

The neural basis of GY's blind field phosphenes is unclear, and combining TMS with neuroimaging techniques such as EEG and fMRI is required to resolve the issue. It needs to be noted however that, as GY sustained his lesion at the age of eight, it is possible that significant reorganization has taken place in his cortex, rendering this finding not directly applicable to the question of how visual awareness arises in the normal brain.

Extrastriate Implications of a V1 Lesion

The phenomenon of blindsight seems to demonstrate that even though extrastriate regions in the damaged hemisphere can be strongly activated, this activation cannot be consciously perceived in the absence of V1. This view is supported by imaging studies that have shown activation in ipsilesional extrastriate areas V5/MT and V4 in response to stimuli presented in the blind field of blindsight subjects (Barbur et al, 1993; Goebel et al, 2001). Furthermore, direct stimulation of the ipsilesional extrastriate cortex using TMS in GY does not induce phosphenes in the blind field when the stimulation is restricted to the damaged hemisphere (Cowey and Walsh, 2000).

However, this view does not take into account the consequences of the V1 lesion on the extrastriate visual cortex. The greatest normal afferent input to extrastriate cortex is from V1 of the same hemisphere (Maunsell and Van Essen, 1983), and the loss of this input must greatly affect the functioning of these regions. This has been shown in single-cell studies. When single moving bars were presented in the presumed field defect resulting from removal of striate cortex, the number of direction-selective neuron was low and their responses were sluggish (Rodman et al, 1989). Furthermore, when random dots moving globally were presented into the field defect, there was no evidence of direction selectivity in V5/MT when the stimulus is restricted into the field defect (Azzopardi et al, 2003). In short, while ipsilesional V5/MT is activated by visual stimuli presented in the field defect, the visually evoked responses are severely impaired. It is therefore possible that V5/MT activation (either by visual stimulation or TMS) in blindsight subjects does not give rise to phenomenal vision because this region is not in the appropriate condition to be properly activated. It is logically possible that blindsight arises because phenomenal vision is computationally more demanding than unconscious visual detection, with the former still possible with a damaged V5/MT. This possibility has not yet been investigated.

Future Directions

Whether the importance of extrastriate – V1 feedback activity extends beyond motion perception is not known. All the evidence so far has come from studies that have looked at the information exchange between V5/MT and V1 in motion perception, and in order to determine whether these findings reflect a general process in which visual information reaches awareness, the cortico-cortical interactions between V1 and other extrastriate areas, particularly within the ventral stream, need to be examined. This can be studied by investigating the role of V1 in a conscious perception of phosphenes induced from various extrastriate areas (Cf. Pascual-Leone and Walsh, 2001), as well as, and in relation to the conscious perception of visually presented shapes and colour. Furthermore, real vision often requires binding of attributes such as colour and motion, and future experiments should investigate how feedback connections from various extrastriate areas into V1 interact in such circumstances.

A more fundamental issue involves whether awareness of basic qualia requires extrastriate-striate backprojections specifically, or whether recurrent activity between any two visual areas is sufficient. Turning visual input into a conscious percept seems to require V1, as is implied by the fact that subject GY does not experience qualia when stimuli are presented to him visually. However, the finding that GY can perceive phosphenes with bilateral application of TMS implies that V1 may not be necessary for phenomenal vision under all circumstances. Further studies are needed to determine the precise role of the contralesional extrastriate cortex in generating blind field phosphenes in GY. It will also be important to determine whether subjects with bilateral V1 damage can perceive phosphenes.

References

Albright T.D. and Stoner G.R. (2002). Contextual influences on visual processing. *Annual Review of Neuroscience*, 25, 339-379.

Azzopardi P. and Cowey A. (2001). Motion discrimination in cortically blind patients. *Brain,* 124, 30-46.

Azzopardi P., Fallah M., Gross C.G. and Rodman H.R. (2003). Response latencies of neurons in visual areas MT and MST of monkeys with striate cortex lesions. *Neuropsychologia,* 41,1738-1756.

Barbur J.L., Watson J.D., Frackowiak R.S. and Zeki S (1993). Conscious visual perception without V1. *Brain,* 116, 1293-1302.

Block N. (2005). Two neural correlates of consciousness. *Trends in Cognitive Science*, 9, 46-52.

Corthout E., Uttl B., Walsh V., Hallett M. and Cowey A. (1999). Timing of activity in early visual cortex as revealed by transcranial magnetic stimulation. *Neuroreport*, 11, 1565-1569.

Cowey A. (2004). The 30th Sir Frederick Bartlett lecture. Fact, artefact, and myth about blindsight. *Quarterly Journal of Experimental Psychology* A. 57, 577-609.

Cowey A and Stoerig P. (1991). The neurobiology of blindsight, *Trends in Neuroscience*, 14, 140-145.

Cowey A. and Walsh, V. (2000). Magnetically induced phosphenes in sighted, blind and blindsighted observers. *Neuroreport* 11, 3269-3273.

Felleman D.J. and Van Essen D.C. (1991). Distributed hierarchical processing in the primate cerebral cortex. Cerebral Cortex, 1, 1-47.

Goebel R., Muckli L., Zanella F.E., Singer W. and Stoerig P. (2001). Sustained extrastriate cortical activation without visual awareness revealed by fMRI studies of hemianopic patients. *Vision Research*, 41, 1459-1474.

Heinen K., Jolij J. and Lamme V.A. (2005). Figure-ground segregation requires two distinct periods of activity in V1: a transcranial magnetic stimulation study. *Neuroreport* 16, 1483-1487.

Henschen S.E. (1893). On the visual path and centre. *Brain*, 16,170-180.

Holmes G. (1918). Disturbances of visual orientation. *The British Journal of Opthalmology*, 2, 449-468.

Juan C.H., Campana G. and Walsh, V. (2004). Cortical interactions in vision and awareness: hierarchies in reverse. *Progress in Brain Research*, 144, 117-130.

Lamme V.A. (2001). Blindsight: the role of feedforward and feedback corticocortical connections. *Acta Psychologica* 107, 209-228.

Lamme V.A. and Spekreijse H. (2000). Modulations of primary visual cortex activity representing attentive and conscious scene perception. *Frontiers in Bioscience*, 5, D232-243.

Nagarajan S.S., Durand D.M. and Warman E.N. (1993). Effects of induced electric fields on finite neural structures: a simulation study. *IEEE Transactions in Biomedical Engineering*, 40, 1175-1178.

Maunsell J.H.R. and Van Essen D.C. (1983). The connections of the middle temporal visual area (MT) and their relationship to a cortical hierarchy in the macaque monkey, *Journal of Neuroscience*, 3, 2563-2586.

Pascual-Leone A. and Walsh V. (2001). Fast backprojections from the motion to the primary visual area necessary for visual awareness. *Science*, 292, 510-512.

Poeppel E., Held R. and Frost D. (1973). Residual function after brain wounds involving the central visual pathways in man. *Nature*, 243, 295-296.

Ress D. and Heeger D.J. (2003). Neuronal correlates of perception in early visual cortex. *Nature Neuroscience*, 6, 414-420.

Rodman H.R., Gross C.G. and Albright T.D. (1989). Afferent basis of visual response properties in areas MT of the macaque. I. Effects of striate cortex removal. *Journal of Neuroscience,* 9, 2033-2050.

Rudiak D. and Marg E. (1994). Finding the depth of magnetic brain stimulation: a re-evaluation. *Electroencphalography and Clinical Neurophysiology*, 93, 358-371.

Silvanto J., Lavie N. and Walsh V. (2005). Double Dissociation of V1 and V5/MT activity in visual awareness. *Cerebral Cortex*, 15, 1736-1741.

Silvanto J., Cowey A., Lavie N. and Walsh V. (2005). Striate cortex (V1) activity gates awareness of motion. *Nature Neuroscience*, 8, 143-144.

Silvanto J., Cowey A., Lavie N. and Walsh, V (2007). Making the blindsighted see. *Neuropsychologia*. 45, 3346-3350.

Zeki S.M. and Bartels A. (1999). Toward a theory of visual consciousness. *Consciousness and Cognition*, 8, 225-259.

Weiskranz L., Warrington E.K., Sanders M. and Marshall J (1974). Visual capacity in the hemianopic field following a restricted cortical ablation. *Brain*, 97, 709-728.

INDEX

Q

R

S

T